BUSINESS-TO-BUSINESS MARKETING

BUSINESS-TO-BUSINESS MARKETING

FOURTH EDITION

Ross Brennan, Louise Canning & Raymond McDowell

Los Angeles | London | New Delhi
Singapore | Washington DC | Melbourne

Los Angeles | London | New Delhi
Singapore | Washington DC | Melbourne

SAGE Publications Ltd
1 Oliver's Yard
55 City Road
London EC1Y 1SP

SAGE Publications Inc.
2455 Teller Road
Thousand Oaks, California 91320

SAGE Publications India Pvt Ltd
B 1/I 1 Mohan Cooperative Industrial Area
Mathura Road
New Delhi 110 044

SAGE Publications Asia-Pacific Pte Ltd
3 Church Street
#10-04 Samsung Hub
Singapore 049483

Editor: Matthew Waters
Assistant editor: Lyndsay Aitken
Production editor: Sarah Cooke
Copyeditor: Martin Noble
Proofreader: Lynda Watson
Indexer: Judith Lavender
Marketing manager: Alison Borg
Cover design: Francis Kenney
Typeset by: C&M Digitals (P) Ltd, Chennai, India
Printed and bound by CPI Group (UK) Ltd,
Croydon, CR0 4YY

Library of Congress Control Number: 2016955262

British Library Cataloguing in Publication data

A catalogue record for this book is available from the British Library

ISBN 978-1-47397-343-5
ISBN 978-1-47397-344-2 (pbk)

At SAGE we take sustainability seriously. Most of our products are printed in the UK using FSC papers and boards. When we print overseas we ensure sustainable papers are used as measured by the PREPS grading system. We undertake an annual audit to monitor our sustainability.

TABLE OF CONTENTS

ABOUT THE AUTHORS

Dr Ross Brennan is the Professor of Industrial Marketing at the University of Hertfordshire. His areas of research interest are relationships and networks in business markets, macromarketing, social marketing and marketing education. Ross's work has been published in journals such as the *Journal of Business Research, Journal of Advertising Research, European Journal of Marketing, Industrial Marketing Management, Journal of Business & Industrial Marketing, Journal of Business-to-Business Marketing, Journal of Macromarketing* and *Journal of Marketing Education.*

Dr Louise Canning is Associate Professor of Marketing at Kedge Business School, France, having previously worked at the University of Birmingham, United Kingdom. Louise's research has primarily been in business-to-business marketing, covering areas such as adaptation, communication and sustainability in inter-firm relationships. More recently Louise has explored the interface between business and consumer markets in relation to disposal, including the handling of end-of life electronic equipment. Her work has been published in journals such as *European Journal of Marketing, Industrial Marketing Management, Journal of Business and Industrial Marketing, Journal of Marketing Management* and *Sociology.*

Ray McDowell is currently Associate Dean for Planning and Resources at Bristol Business School, University of the West of England. His interest in business-to-business marketing, and relationship management in particular, stems from a background leading and managing business-to-business software consortium projects in the private sector. While his current academic leadership role for a large faculty limits recent academically based research contribution, he continues to connect with organizations in a range of sectors, thus perpetuating his enduring interest in business to business relationships and networks.

LIST OF FIGURES

LIST OF TABLES

LIST OF CASE STUDIES AND SNAPSHOTS

Chapter	Type	Organization	Industry	HQ
1	Snapshot 1.1	Air Products and Chemicals Inc.	Agriculture, analytic laboratories, chemical processing, construction, electronics assembly, energy, food/beverage, glass/minerals, industrial/institutional cleaning, leisure/recreation, medical, metals, mining, personal care, pharmaceuticals/biotechnology, rubber/plastics, transport, water and wastewater	Pennsylvania, US
	Snapshot 1.2	LinkedIn	Social media	California, US
	Snapshot 1.3	Hypothetical	House-building	Hypothetical
	Case study 1.1	Rolls-Royce Group plc	Industrial power system company	London, UK
2	Snapshot 2.1	Zara	Retail (clothing and accessories)	Arteixo, Spain
	Snapshot 2.2	Philips	Health technologies	Amsterdam, Netherlands
	Snapshot 2.3	Lucozade Ribena Suntory Ltd	Soft drinks	Osaka, Japan
	Snapshot 2.4	Kimberly-Clark Professional (KCP)	Hygiene solutions	Roswell, US
	Case study 2.1	Compass Group - Medirest	Healthcare support services	Chertsey, UK
		Johnson Controls	Diverse industrial technologies	Milwaukee, US
3	Snapshot 3.1	Marks & Spencer	Retail	London, UK
		William Baird	Clothes manufacturing	London, UK
		Courtaulds	Manufacturing (fabric, clothing, artificial fibres and chemicals)	London, UK
		Coats Viyella (Coats Group)	Clothing	Uxbridge, UK
		Bowyers	Food manufacturing	Trowbridge, UK
	Snapshot 3.2	Nampak Plastics Europe	Plastic packaging manufacturer	UK
	Case study 3.1	Meat retailers and suppliers	Supply of meat to supermarkets	Europe

(Continued)

(Continued)

Chapter	Type	Organization	Industry	HQ
4	Snapshot 4.1	HÅG	Furniture (workplace)	London, UK
	Snapshot 4.2	Texas Instruments	Electronics	Texas, US
	Snapshot 4.3	Air Products and Chemicals Inc.	Agriculture, analytic laboratories, chemical processing, construction, electronics assembly, energy, food/beverage, glass/minerals, industrial/institutional cleaning, leisure/recreation, medical, metals, mining, personal care, pharmaceuticals/biotechnology, rubber/plastics, transport, water and wastewater	Pennsylvania, US
	Case study 4.1	The Carbon Trust	Environmental consultant	London, UK
5	Snapshot 5.1	Small/Medium Enterprises	Social media	Europe
	Snapshot 5.2	XE Travel Expense Calculator and XE Credit Card Charges Calculator	Commerce technology	Newmarket, Canada
	Case study 5.1	Hypothetical	Hypothetical (Liquefied petroleum gas)	Hypothetical
6	Snapshot 6.1	Blue Sheep	Database marketing, campaign managements and data analytics	Cheltenham, UK
	Case study 6.1	Wavin	Manufacturer of plastic pipes	Doncaster, UK
7	Snapshot 7.1	DHL	Logistics	Bonn, Germany
	Snapshot 7.2	Gartner	Technology research and consulting	Stanford, US
	Snapshot 7.3	Michelin	Tyres	Clermont-Ferrand, France
	Snapshot 7.4	Festo	Industrial control and automation systems	Esslingen am Neckar, Germany
	Case study 7.1	Bayer	Healthcare and agriculture	Leverkusen, Germany
8	Snapshot 8.1	General	General	General
	Snapshot 8.2	Wartsila	Marine and energy power solutions	Helsinki, Finland
	Snapshot 8.3	GE Healthcare	Medical technologies and services	Little Chalfont, UK
	Snapshot 8.4	3M	Materials technologies	Minnesota, US
	Case study 8.1	Various	Oil extraction and distribution	Various
9	Case study 9.1	O2	Telecommunications	Slough, UK
10	Snapshot 10.1	National Gummi AB	Rubber and plastics manufacturing	Halmstad, Sweden
	Snapshot 10.2	Airbus	Plane manufacturing	Toulouse, France
	Snapshot 10.3	Honeywell	Conglomerate company	New Jersey, United States
	Scenario 10.1	Astra-Zeneca	Pharmaceuticals	London, UK

LIST OF ABBREVIATIONS

ARA	actor bonds, resource ties and activity links
ARPU	average revenue per user
B2B	business-to-business
B2C	business-to-consumer
BRIC	Brazil, Russia, India, China
CRM	customer relationship management
CRP	continuous replenishment programme
CSR	corporate social responsibility
DMU	decision-making unit
EBIT	earnings before interest and taxes
EDI	electronic data interchange
EPOS	electronic point of sale
ERP	enterprise resource planning
GATT	General Agreement on Tariffs and Trade
GDP	gross domestic product
ICT	information and communications technology
IMP	Industrial Marketing and Purchasing Group
ISIC	International Standard Industrial Classification
JIT	just-in-time
KAM	key account management
MRO	maintenance, repair and operating supplies
NACE	Nomenclature statistique des activités économiques dans la Communauté Européene
NAICS	North American Industrial Classification System
OEM	original equipment manufacturer
PR	public relations
R&D	research and development
RFID	radio frequency identification
RFQ	request for quotations
SBU	strategic business unit

SCM	supply chain management
SIC	standard industrial classification
SWOT	strengths, weaknesses, opportunities, threats
TCO	total cost of ownership
UK SIC	British Standard Industrial Classification
US SIC	United States Standard Industrial Classification
VAR	value-added reseller
WTO	World Trade Organization

PREFACE

The prominent American business-to-business marketing scholar Gary Lilien recently coined the term 'the B2B knowledge gap' (Lilien, 2016). He was primarily using this phrase in connection with the relative amount of effort devoted to research into consumer marketing (of which there is a great deal) and into B2B marketing (of which there is nowhere near as much). However, we are pretty sure that Lilien would agree with us that there is also a B2B knowledge gap when it comes to marketing education. If you are a marketing student who is using this book on a module or course in B2B marketing, then you are taking advantage of an opportunity – to study a specialist module in B2B marketing – that is by no means open to all marketing students. Lilien (2016) tells us that the global economic value of B2B transactions is roughly equal to the global economic value of B2C transactions. There are many, many, great B2B companies out there that are eager to hire marketing talent (you will find quite a few mentioned in the case studies, snapshots, scenarios and examples in this book). Furthermore, while you might think that the value of B2C online business would exceed B2B, you would be entirely and badly wrong; B2B e-commerce is several times larger than B2C e-commerce (Lilien, 2016). So, if your goal is to develop a great career in marketing, the B2B sector is a very good place to look. As we move this book forward into its Fourth Edition, we really hope that it can help you to achieve that goal.

In this edition of the book we have retained the fundamental philosophy that has governed our approach from the outset. That is, we seek to give a balanced treatment that considers B2B marketing both where conventional marketing tools and techniques (such as market segmentation and impersonal marketing communications) are most effective, and where relational approaches (such as relationship portfolio analysis and Key Account Management) are most effective. In fact, we have taken the opportunity in this edition to introduce explicitly the concept of a contingency approach to B2B marketing using George Day's (2000) concept of the relationship spectrum. You can find out more about this in Chapter 4.

Naturally, the Fourth Edition sees continuing evolutionary change in the book in respect of certain important and ever-changing aspects of the business world. Business in general, and B2B marketing in particular, becomes ever more global, relies increasingly on digital media, and faces greater and greater challenges associated with environmental sustainability, corporate social responsibility and business ethics. Our coverage of B2B digital marketing has grown with each new edition, and grows yet further in this edition. Meanwhile, since the publication of the Third Edition in 2014, the world has seen the Paris Climate Conference (December 2015) culminating in a legally binding global climate deal signed by 195 countries. We have striven, in this edition, to keep up-to-date with changes such as these while maintaining a sound grounding in the fundamental theories of B2B marketing.

Perhaps our new 'B2B Scenarios' are the most visible innovation in the present edition. In a subject such as B2B marketing it is essential to provide lots of practical examples of theory in action. In previous editions, for this reason, we have provided the end-of-chapter case studies, in-text examples and 'B2B Snapshots'.

With the addition of 'B2B Scenarios' in each chapter, we are presenting the kind of dilemmas and difficult decisions that B2B marketing managers face in the real world. Each of these scenarios asks you to think about what you would do next.

Many thanks to readers and reviewers who have told us what they think of the previous editions of the book. We are always happy to receive constructive feedback from our readers.

Ross Brennan
Louise Canning
Ray McDowell

COMPANION WEBSITE

Business-to-Business Marketing, Fourth Edition is supported by a free companion website for students and lecturers.

Visit https://study.sagepub.com/brennan4e to take advantage of these extra learning and teaching resources.

For Lecturers

Tutor Guide: A chapter-by-chapter guide to the textbook with additional materials for teaching, including B2B scenario and case study guidance and notes.

PowerPoint Slides: For every chapter for use in lectures in support of the textbook.

Sample Exam Questions: Author-suggested questions to consider setting as students assessments, along with indicative answers.

For Students

Author-Selected Videos: Links to video content which give you interesting insights into important concepts and B2B marketing in practice.

Quiz: An online quiz in addition to the textbook to help students test their knowledge of the subject.

SAGE Journals Online: Free access to full, author-selected SAGE journal articles featured in each chapter to help students engage with the research literature for higher grades.

Weblinks: Links to relevant websites for each chapter to help students make links to practice and industry and find examples.

'This is a very interesting textbook which provides an updated and comprehensive knowledge about B2B Marketing. It offers both in-depth theoretical foundation and accessible, real-world examples, something that is rare to find in textbooks. It will be useful to both students and practitioners alike.'

Dr Nektarios Tzempelikos, Lord Ashcroft International Business School, Anglia Ruskin University, UK

PART I

FUNDAMENTALS OF BUSINESS-TO-BUSINESS MARKETING

1

BUSINESS-TO-BUSINESS MARKETS AND MARKETING

LEARNING OUTCOMES

After reading this chapter you will:

- know what are the defining characteristics of business-to-business markets;
- be able to differentiate between business-to-business markets and consumer markets;
- understand how the characteristics of business-to-business markets affect the practice of marketing management;
- appreciate the changing balance between the agricultural, manufacturing and service sectors in the world's major economies;
- understand the nature and significance of derived demand in business-to-business markets;
- be able to explain the significance of an industry concentration ratio;
- understand the nature and the significance of the accelerator effect in business-to-business markets; and
- be able to apply two complementary classification schemes to the categorization of business products.

INTRODUCTION

Business-to-business marketing is one of those things that lie hidden in full view. Only a little thought is needed to grasp that in order for a consumer transaction to take place, numerous prior business-to-business (B2B) transactions must have success-fully occurred. In other words, lying behind every consumer purchase in a modern economy there is a network of business-to-business transactions. For example, the manicurist on the high street makes the client's nails look perfect using products that were manufactured by a cosmetics company from materials bought from chemi-cal manufacturers; equipment in the nail bar was manufactured by hardware and electrical products manufacturers using components purchased from a range of engineering companies; the client's next appointment is arranged using the salon's wi-fi network, which was designed and installed by a computer systems firm around equipment bought from various IT vendors. Even an apparently simple transaction at the supermarket is only made possible by a web of supporting business-to-business transactions. When you buy a few items of confectionery or some vegetables from your local supermarket, you may give some thought to the supplier of the product itself, but perhaps less to the shop-fitting company that designed and supplied the shelving, the geo-demographic consultancy firm that helped the supermarket decide where to locate its store, the IT systems company that installed the point of sale equipment, and many other businesses that made the simple transaction possible. This book is concerned not with the final consumer transaction – buying the services of a manicurist, or buying some confectionery or vegetables – but with the network of business-to-business transactions, largely invisible to the final consumer, that underlies it.

In this chapter our aims are to clarify just what is meant by *business markets*, to explain why it is considered necessary to distinguish them from consumer markets, and to show how business products and markets can be classified. We begin by discussing the nature of business markets. In order to emphasize the message that business markets involve both goods and services, we spend a little time looking at the industrial structure of modern economies, to see how influential the service sector has become. The subsequent section deals with the core idea of this chapter, namely that business markets can be differentiated from consumer markets along a number of dimensions. Those dimensions can be summarized as market structure differences, buying behaviour differences and marketing practice differences. The chapter then moves on to look at the ways in which business products can be classified. An approach based on the uses to which products are put is contrasted with an approach based on customer perceptions of the risk and the effort (including cost) involved in acquiring a product. The chapter concludes with a case study of Rolls-Royce, no longer the producer of the most famous luxury car in the world (cars bearing the Rolls-Royce name are now made by BMW), but the company that keeps many of the world's aircraft in the air. Yes, Rolls-Royce manufactures aircraft engines. However, as we will see, much of what it does goes far beyond manufacturing. It is the support services that Rolls-Royce provides to aircraft operators as much as the engines themselves that make it still one of the UK's most successful companies. Meanwhile, from Snapshot 1.1 you can get an immediate impression of the scale and breadth of B2B marketing by taking a look at Air Products, a large-scale global business operation that you may never have heard of, but which contributes critically important products and services that have applications in everything from the latest medical scanners to the flat-screen TV in your living room.

B2B SNAPSHOT 1.1   AIR PRODUCTS

The clue is in the name: Air Products (officially, Air Products and Chemicals, Inc.). This is a company that has its origins in the business of producing and manufacturing gases for industrial uses (the company started out as a supplier of oxygen to large-scale users). It is a company that had a turnover of around $10 billion in 2015, employs nearly 20,000 people and operates all over the world. But unless you have a professional interest in this business, then the closest you are likely to come to Air

Products itself is when you order some helium from them for your party balloons – something that you really can do! However, once you go beyond party balloons, Air Products is involved in the manufacture, distribution and marketing of a wide range of gases, equipment and services, and performance materials that play critical roles in many industries that are tremendously important for both human welfare and human pleasure. What sort of industries use Air Products? Adhesives, aerospace, cement, chemicals, electronics, glass, healthcare, metal fabrication, mining, oil extraction, paints, pharmaceuticals, rubber... that's just a brief and very incomplete list. What do these customers get from Air Products? Gases, like argon, helium, hydrogen, nitrogen, oxygen (and others); equipment and services, like cryogenic business applications (that is, ultra-low-temperature technology), heat exchangers and business services; and performance materials, like epoxy resins, polyurethane products, amines, surfactants, and a whole lot else. What does all of this mean for you? Just three examples follow. At the heart of those fabulous MRI (magnetic resonance imaging) scanners in hospitals are extremely powerful magnets that rely on liquid helium: Air Products provides the helium and the specialist low-temperature services (the KeepCOLD® MRI magnet filling and cryo-shielding maintenance services) that keep MRI scanners running. Semi-conductor production relies on the availability of specialist gases provided in extremely high levels of purity: Air Products supplies a wide range of these gases, including Blue Ammonia®, which is 99.99994 per cent pure! Meanwhile, the electronics division of Air Products provides essential products and services to manufacturers in the TFT (thin-film transistor) and photovoltaic markets – meaning that they are heavily involved in the process of making your flat-screen TV or computer monitor, and in facilitating the production of solar panels.

But if all you want is the helium for your party balloons, check out the Air Products party balloons service at http://www.airproducts.co.uk/industries/leisure-recreation.aspx/!

Sources: Datamonitor, 2012a; www.airproducts.com.

THE NATURE OF BUSINESS MARKETS

The key distinguishing feature of a *business-to-business market* is that the customer is an organization rather than an individual consumer. Organizations and consumers often buy the same products. For example, both organizations and individual consumers buy smartphones, laptop and tablet computers, cleaning services, automobile repair services and light fittings. Therefore, one cannot distinguish unambiguously between a business market and a consumer market on the basis of the nature of the product. It is true that there are certain products that are often bought by organizations and never by individual consumers, such as management consultancy services for a corporate merger, or – more prosaically – industrial cranes. On the other hand, it is difficult to think of anything that an individual consumer buys that would not be bought by some organization.

A brief observation on terminology may be helpful at this point. The generally accepted term for the marketing of goods and services to organizations is 'business-to-business marketing'. This gradually superseded the older term *industrial marketing* in the 1980s and 1990s. Industrial marketing is often considered to be a term that is exclusively applied to primary and secondary industries; primary industries include agricultural and the extractive industries such as coal and iron-ore mining, while secondary industries are those that manufacture tangible products such as cars, planes and furniture. In many modern economies the primary and secondary industries account for a relatively small share of economic activity, and it is the tertiary sector of the economy (the service industries) that contributes most to measures of national income (of which gross domestic product (GDP) is probably the best known).

The expression business-to-business marketing is synonymous with 'business marketing'; these will be the two terms that we use throughout this book to refer to our subject matter. However, two other expressions are worth mentioning: 'B2B' and 'organizational marketing'. The term B2B is clearly just a contraction of business-to-business. What makes it important in its own right is that it is the ubiquitous term on the internet for business-to-business marketing and selling, to be contrasted with B2C, which stands for 'business–to-consumer'. The term 'organizational marketing' has been advocated by some authors (Wilson, 1999) as superior to 'business marketing' because it explicitly includes *all* organizations, while 'business marketing' seems to exclude organizations that are not 'businesses'. This may be a legitimate distinction, since charitable organizations, other non-profit organizations and governmental organizations have different fundamental objectives from private enterprise businesses. However, the expression 'organizational marketing' has not yet proved popular, and we will stick to the conventional terms 'business-to-business marketing' and 'business marketing'.

It is important to understand that business-to-business marketing is *not* synonymous with marketing goods and services to the manufacturing industries. Taking the United Kingdom as an example, there has been a prolonged and prominent trend away from manufacturing employment and towards service sector employment. In 1980 there were over 6.5 million people employed in UK manufacturing industries, and by 2013 this had declined to around 2.6 million. Over the same period, service sector employment increased from 15.5 million to around 23 million – service sector employment is now over 80 per cent of total UK employment. The absolute number of jobs created in the service sector considerably exceeded the number of jobs lost in manufacturing, so that total employment in the UK increased over the period (Rhodes, 2015).

In itself this trend is a matter of widespread debate for UK economists and politicians (Hadjimatheou and Sarantis, 1998; Julius and Butler, 1998). In particular, an unresolved debate revolves around the question of whether manufacturing industry is especially important (for example, because it has a high propensity to export and exhibits more rapid productivity growth than the service sector), or whether it is a normal part of the developmental process for an advanced economy to see a shift of activity away from manufacturing and into the service sector. This has important economic policy implications: should the government try to slow down or reverse the decline in manufacturing? However, from the perspective of marketing professionals, the trend away from manufacturing industry and towards the service sector should be seen as an important element of the marketing environment, which suggests that the opportunities to market goods and services to the UK manufacturing sector may decline, and will certainly grow more slowly than opportunities in the service sector of the economy. In passing, it is worth observing that the decline in manufacturing employment in the UK has also been associated with a decline in the manufacturing share of GDP (Hartley and Hooper, 1997); although manufacturing productivity has grown faster than service sector productivity, it has not grown fast enough to compensate for the very substantial decline in manufacturing employment seen over the last few decades.

The trend away from manufacturing and towards the service sector is much more than just a UK phenomenon, as Table 1.1 shows. Over the period from 1990 to 2011 virtually all of the world's major economies saw a decline in employment in agriculture and manufacturing, and an increase in service sector employment. From the marketing point of view it is interesting to observe not only these trends, but also the different structural characteristics of these economies. Despite declines in agricultural employment, this sector remains a large-scale employer in some countries, such as New Zealand. It is important to distinguish between percentages and absolute numbers, however. The UK, with the smallest proportion of the workforce employed in agriculture, nevertheless had more agricultural workers in 2011 than New Zealand. Germany has retained a large, if declining, manufacturing sector. Understanding such trends in the economic environment is a useful foundation for the more complex research and analysis that goes into preparing an international marketing *strategy*.

However, while this analysis of the basic structure of several of the world's major economies probably strikes the reader as both plausible and relevant, it suffers from at least two important deficiencies: first, the analysis is based on the idea that the distinction between manufacturing and service activities is meaningful and, second, we have so far ignored the emerging *BRIC economies* – that is, Brazil, Russia, India and China (sometimes known as BRICS, with the addition of South Africa). In a moment we will turn to the importance of the BRIC economies, but first let's pause to question the validity of the manufacturing/services dichotomy in marketing. Recent years have seen growing prominence for 'service-dominant logic' in marketing (Ballantyne and Varey, 2008; Vargo and Lusch, 2004, 2008). The underlying idea behind service-dominant logic is that whatever it may be that customers buy – tangible goods, intangible services or a combination of the two – in all cases it is services that generate the value that customers desire (the customer's 'value-in-use'). Whether they are buying cranes, computers, cleaning services or consultancy, business buyers are in all cases seeking value-in-use, which in all cases is provided by the services delivered by the various things procured (for example, businesses don't want cranes, they want the ability to move heavy objects around, which is a service delivered by cranes). Hence, according to proponents of service-dominant logic, in the end all marketing concerns services, and the distinction between the marketing of goods and services is artificial, summarized as 'All economies are service economies' by Vargo and Lusch (2008: 7).

Finally, before moving on to the differentiating characteristics of business markets, it is important to emphasize for the reader the importance of the BRIC and other emerging economies to the global economic system. The global financial and economic crisis of 2008/9 clearly affected these emerging economies badly, with lower economic growth than for many years previously and lower inward flows of capital (foreign direct investment). However, even in time of recession, the more robust BRIC economies, namely Brazil, India and China, were still growing, while advanced economies such as the USA, Germany and the UK were experiencing zero or negative growth. (Russia is a slightly different case from the other BRIC economies because it is heavily dependent on oil exports, so that its economic fortunes are strongly

TABLE 1.1 Industry sector employment trends in selected countries, 1990 and 2011. Row values may not total 100% owing to rounding.

	Total civilian employment (thousands)	Agriculture (%)	Industry (%)	Services (%)
Australia				
1990	7,850	5.6	25.4	69.0
2011	12,109	4.0	26.6	69.4
Germany				
1990	27,946	3.4	39.8	56.8
2011	42,240	0.8	28.6	70.6
New Zealand				
1990	1,472	10.6	24.6	64.8
2011	2,380	4.9	23.5	71.6
Sweden				
1990	4,508	3.3	29.1	67.5
2011	5,020	1.8	27.3	70.9
United Kingdom				
1990	26,577	2.1	29.0	68.9
2011	31,632	0.7	21.5	77.8
United States				
1990	117,914	2.8	26.2	70.9
2011	154,947	1.2	19.2	79.6

Sources: CIA, 2012; OECD, 1993, 2003, 2008, 2011.

influenced by oil price fluctuations.) The long-term trend, observed for over two decades now, shows emerging economies, particularly China, India and Brazil, growing much faster than the advanced economies, exporting much of their output to those advanced economies, and rapidly increasing the average income of their populations. While in relative terms these economies can be expected to continue to grow faster than Europe or North America, it is likely that their economic growth rates will be slower than in the peak years at the end of the twentieth century and the beginning of this century. Much marketing attention has focused on the huge consumer market potential in these countries, as incomes grow and consumers demand many of the goods and services that are common in rich countries. For our purposes, however, it is important to appreciate that these economies are fast-growing industrial powerhouses where much of the world's manufactured output is produced, so that their potential as business-to-business markets is virtually limitless. For example, 46.6 per cent of Chinese workers were employed in manufacturing industry in 2011 (CIA, 2012), which is a much larger proportion of a much larger workforce than any of the countries shown in Table 1.1. This is why the BRIC economies generally, and China in particular, have become the focus of a great deal of attention in B2B marketing, with several special issues of major academic journals in the field devoted to them (*Industrial Marketing Management*, vol. 40, issues 1 and 4, and the *Journal of Business & Industrial Marketing*, vol. 22, issue 2 and vol. 27, issue 3). Recent years have seen striking evidence of the growing influence of the BRIC economies in the shape of corporate mergers and acquisitions that would once have been unthinkable; for example, Chinese computer-maker Lenovo acquired the personal computer business of the American firm IBM in 2005, and the Tata Group of India acquired the Anglo-Dutch steel producer Corus (formerly British Steel) in 2006 and British vehicle manufacturer Jaguar Land Rover in 2008. There can be no doubt that the emerging economies, already important to many B2B marketers, will feature ever more prominently in B2B marketing plans in the future.

BUSINESS MARKETS: DEFINING CHARACTERISTICS

Having established that it is not the nature of the product that is bought and sold that differentiates business markets from consumer markets, we move on to examine what are regarded as the defining characteristics of business markets. Many authors have sought to identify the *dimensions* by which business markets can be distinguished from consumer markets, and then the specific *characteristics* of business markets and consumer markets on each of these dimensions. Table 1.2 provides a synthesis of these dimensions and characteristics. The table is organized into three columns. The first column identifies the dimension against which business and consumer markets are thought to differ, the second column provides the characteristic expected of a business market, and the third column provides the characteristic expected of a consumer market.

Table 1.2 is also divided into three major sections, entitled respectively market structure differences, buying behaviour differences and marketing practice differences. In general, it is underlying structural differences between business and consumer markets that bring about important differences in buying behaviour. Marketing practice in business markets differs from that in consumer markets because of the underlying differences in market structure and because of the differences in buying behaviour. For example, it would be wrong to assert that business markets differ from consumer markets because the most frequently used promotional tool in the former is *personal selling*, while in the latter it is advertising. The extensive use of personal selling in business markets can be traced to the market structure and buying behaviour characteristics commonly found in business markets, which are usually not found in consumer markets. Specifically, in many business markets, demand is concentrated in the hands of a few powerful buyers (market structure), who employ teams of purchasing professionals to do their buying (buying behaviour). In most consumer markets demand is dispersed widely throughout the buying public and no single consumer has any real buying power (market structure), and buyers are not trained professionals (buying behaviour). Personal selling makes sense in the first set of circumstances (concentrated demand, powerful buyers, trained professionals), since organizational buyers expect to hear a well-argued case specifically tailored to the needs of their organization, and the costs associated with employing a sales executive are justified by the high potential value of each order. Advertising makes sense in the second set of circumstances (dispersed demand, no powerful buyers), primarily because the relatively low value of a typical transaction only justifies low selling costs. Of course, specifically tailoring the message to the needs of the individual consumer, which was once effectively impossible, is becoming more and more feasible with the deployment of sophisticated IT and customer relationship management (CRM) software (Evans et al., 2004). Indeed, such technologies may bring about a degree of convergence between marketing practices, based around the internet and CRM, between consumer markets and those business markets that have relatively dispersed demand.

You will find that the word 'relationship' is used in Table 1.2, and then widely elsewhere in this book (see the titles of Chapters 3, 8 and 9, for example). Before you go any further it would be a good idea for you to think about what this term means in the context of B2B marketing. To help you think about this, take a look at the dilemma facing new sales and marketing executive Magnus in B2B Scenario 1.1.

B2B SCENARIO 1.1　ADVISE MAGNUS!

Magnus Johanson, only newly arrived as a sales and marketing executive at the engineering consultancy firm ENG Projects, had a problem and was looking for some advice from his boss, Petra Wend. He listened carefully to what Petra had to say: 'Even people who don't know much about business-to-business marketing will often say that "it's all about relationships". This is one of those phrases that is both true and yet can be misleading. First, there's the matter of what "relationship" means. This is not just a dull, academic question. There are relationships between people, and there are relationships between organizations. The two are not the same thing, and shouldn't be confused. Second, the bottom line is that business-to-business marketing is about business (the clue is in the name). So when we talk about relationships between people in B2B we are almost always talking about professional relationships rather than personal relationships. Don't confuse the two. While you may like the people you have professional relationships with, even enjoy their company, the purpose of the relationship is to deliver business results for all parties. Professional relationships have to deliver tangible business results. In this case, Magnus, let's be honest, you have failed to deliver what the client wanted. You have wasted their time and their money. In these circumstances you have to decide on the best strategy to manage the professional relationship. Now, go away and sort this mess out!'

Magnus could not disagree. He had, indeed, wasted the client's time and money, by suggesting that ENG Projects would be able to deliver a technical solution that was beyond the capabilities of this fairly small consulting firm. The client really needed one of the big firms for this kind of project (such as Arup [see arup.com]). Magnus had made a mistake by suggesting that ENG could take the project on, and then another mistake by ignoring the advice of his colleagues and stringing the client along, so that the (organizational) relationship between the two firms was now under some strain. He had already decided that the best thing to do, to soften the blow, was to spend some of his client entertainment budget taking two of the key people from the client firm to watch Arsenal play football at the Emirates stadium, and then to an expensive restaurant for dinner after. Since his future at ENG probably depended on mending fences with this client, he was pretty sure that arranging a great day out was the best way of repairing the damage he had done. And Petra had emphasized the importance of professional relationships. At least that was how he interpreted her words.

Do you agree with Magnus's approach? Has he understood what Petra was saying? What would you do in Magnus's position?

Source: Inspired by Oakley and Bush (2016).

TABLE 1.2 Differences between business and consumer markets

Market structure differences		
Dimension	**Business marketing**	**Consumer marketing**
Nature of demand	Derived	Direct
Demand volatility	Greater volatility	Less volatility
Demand elasticity	Less elastic	More elastic
Reverse elasticity	More common	Less common
Nature of customers	Greater heterogeneity	Greater homogeneity
Market fragmentation	Greater fragmentation	Less fragmentation
Market complexity	More complex	Less complex
Market size	Larger overall value	Smaller overall value
Number of buyers per seller	Few	Many
Number of buyers per segment	Few	Many
Relative size of buyer/seller	Often similar	Seller much larger
Geographic concentration	Often clustered	Usually dispersed
Buying behaviour differences		
Dimension	**Business marketing**	**Consumer marketing**
Buying influences	Many	Few
Purchase cycles	Often long	Usually short
Transaction value	Often high	Usually small
Buying process complexity	Often complex	Usually simple
Buyer/seller interdependence	Often high	Usually low
Purchase professionalism	Often high	Usually low
Importance of relationships	Often important	Usually unimportant
Degree of interactivity	Often high	Usually low
Formal, written rules	Common	Uncommon
Marketing practice differences		
Dimension	**Business marketing**	**Consumer marketing**
Selling process	Systems selling	Product selling
Personal selling	Used extensively	Limited
Use of relationships	Used extensively	Limited
Promotional strategies	Limited, customer-specific	Mass market
Web integration	Greater	Limited
Branding	Limited	Extensive, sophisticated
Market research	Limited	Extensive
Segmentation	Unsophisticated	Sophisticated
Competitor awareness	Lower	Higher
Product complexity	Greater	Lesser

Sources: Chisnall, 1989; Dwyer and Tanner, 2002; Ford et al., 2002; Lilien, 1987; Simkin, 2000; Webster, 1991; Wilson, 1999, 2000; Wilson and Woodside, 2001.

One of the conclusions that academics and professionals interested in B2B marketing draw from the kind of analysis presented in Table 1.2 is that interpersonal networking is a particularly important aspect of business marketing. An important recent development in interpersonal networking is the use of *social media*. B2B Snapshot 1.2 explores LinkedIn, a social media tool specifically designed to facilitate networking between business professionals.

B2B SNAPSHOT 1.2   LINKEDIN

A recent blog aimed at university marketing students argued that LinkedIn might not seem as exciting or accessible as other social media such as Twitter, Facebook and YouTube, but could be of much greater importance for their future careers (http://eye-tea-em.blogspot. co.uk/2012/08/linkedin-and-marketing-student.html). Of course, it would be quite wrong to pretend that LinkedIn is unknown (at the start of 2016 it had over 400 million users and operated in over 200 countries), but equally there can be no doubt that in comparison to the biggest names on the internet it is just a little hidden in the shadows (Facebook has nearly 1.75 billion users). A bit like B2B marketing itself, in fact, compared to its flashier and more extrovert sibling, consumer marketing. And there is more than a superficial parallel between LinkedIn and B2B marketing, because LinkedIn is the social medium for business professionals, a place where they get together to share information about important business and marketing trends, where they look for jobs and hire new staff, and where they engage in B2B marketing activities.

The eye-tea-em blog presented three main arguments for becoming familiar with LinkedIn. 'Firstly, LinkedIn is becoming an increasingly useful tool for generating B2B marketing lists for direct marketing purposes, and this is only going to grow in importance. Secondly, LinkedIn is the location where a lot of specialist marketing forums get together to network and to exchange the latest information about marketing theory and practice. Thirdly ... LinkedIn is increasingly the place where potential employees go to advertise their skills and employers go to find new talent.' More and more marketing professors are insisting that their students must be familiar with the use of social media for marketing purposes before they leave university, and for the prospective B2B marketer there is no doubt that LinkedIn is an essential tool. LinkedIn is becoming the standard mechanism for business-people to maintain their professional network: a sort of super-charged, online substitute for those conventional standbys, the business card and the Rolodex. The beauty of it is that you can gain access to the connections of your connections through a process of recommendation, and you can maintain contact with people with negligible effort, so it makes sense to keep in touch with former university friends and former employers and colleagues. Links that once would have seemed not worth the trouble of maintaining can now be maintained effortlessly. One day they could prove useful!

If you don't have a LinkedIn account it is probably a good idea to get one (www.linkedin.com). If you already have one but don't use it very much, then you should take a look at the ever-expanding list of professional groups to see which might be useful to you professionally. The (official) Harvard Business Review group, the Social Media Marketing group and the B2B Marketing group would be good places to start.

Sources: McCorkle and McCorkle, 2012; Papacharissi, 2009; Skeels and Grudin, 2009; http://eye-tea-em.blogspot.co.uk/2012/08/linkedin-and-marketing-student.html (accessed 22 July 2016); www.linkedin.com.

Market structure differences

Derived demand

> *Bread satisfies man's wants directly: and the demand for it is said to be direct. But a flour mill and an oven satisfy wants only indirectly, by helping to make bread, etc., and the demand for them is said to be indirect. More generally: the demand for raw materials and other means of production is* indirect *and is* derived *from the direct demand for those directly serviceable products which they help to produce. (Marshall, 1920: 316)*

It is the convention in marketing to treat demand by consumers as *direct* and demand from businesses as *derived*. This idea originated with the economist Alfred Marshall (Eatwell et al., 1987). At its simplest, it is supposed that consumers only buy goods and services to satisfy their wants, whereas businesses only buy things to facilitate the production of goods and services. In this case, consumer demand is wholly *direct* while business demand is wholly *derived*. The word derived indicates that the demand for something only exists so long as there is a demand for the goods or services that it helps to produce. Businesses do not 'want' forklift trucks or computerized logistics systems in the same way that consumers want fashion clothing or computer games. The demand for forklift trucks and logistics systems is derived from the demand for the products that they help to deliver. Of course, many industries have no contact at all with final consumers. For example, aero-engine manufacturers (see case study at the end of this chapter) sell their products only to other businesses, aircraft manufacturers; steel manufacturers sell their products and services to a wide range of industries, such as car manufacturing, shipbuilding and the construction sector. So we have a chain of *derived demand*. For example, final consumer demand (*direct demand*) for cars and diesel fuel creates a derived demand for steel (to manufacture cars), ships (to transport crude oil), and many other goods and services besides. The derived demand for ships in turn creates a derived demand for steel, as well as a whole range of other products and services. The derived demand for steel creates many more forms of derived demand, including raw materials, transport services and general business services such as accountancy and management consultancy. The whole chain of derived demand is driven by the direct demand of consumers. The metaphor of a river is often used to describe the chain of derived demand, where 'downstream activities' are those that take place in close proximity to the consumer and 'upstream activities' are those that take place far away from the consumer.

While it is convenient to think of consumer demand as direct and business demand as derived, the stark dichotomy is probably a little misleading (Brennan, 2012; Fern and Brown, 1984; Simkin, 2000). Consumers do not generally buy washing machines because they 'want' a washing machine; rather it is because of the valuable services the machine provides. The consumer may 'want' clean clothes, or to be accepted socially by sending out their children looking smart, or to look good in a clean white shirt for a job interview. The machine is a means to an end, not the end itself, so that arguably the demand for the machine is derived. Equally, one can envisage a manager in a business organization using company funds to buy a particularly attractive painting for the office; while this would no doubt be justified in terms of creating the right ambience for effective working, it is easy to see it as a direct demand based on the intrinsic merits of the painting. Nevertheless, there is little doubt that the great majority of business expenditure represents derived demand. Firms do not buy such things as office buildings, factories, warehouses, raw materials, logistics support, cleaning services, lubricants and backhoe loaders for the pleasure that they give, but for their ability to facilitate the delivery of goods and services to customers.

The accelerator effect

The most straightforward implication of derived demand in business markets is that marketers must be aware of developments, both upstream and downstream, that may affect their marketing strategy. In particular, it is downstream demand that 'drives' the level of derived demand in a specific business market. Of course, this is intuitively obvious – if the demand for new housing increases then clearly, perhaps after a time lag, the (derived) demand for housing materials such as steel and wood will also increase. In due course, and probably after a longer time lag, the (derived) demand for capital equipment used in the construction industry, such as backhoe loaders and cement mixers, may well also rise. However, what is less obvious is that the percentage change in derived demand may be much larger, or much smaller, than the percentage change of original demand. This is a phenomenon that can occur in capital equipment industries, and is known as the *accelerator effect*. The illustration in Snapshot 1.3 shows the basic arithmetic of the accelerator effect.

B2B SNAPSHOT 1.3   AN ILLUSTRATION OF THE ACCELERATOR EFFECT

- Suppose that a house-building firm knows that it needs to own one backhoe loader for every 50 houses that it builds per year. Each backhoe loader is depreciated over five years. The company usually builds around 500 houses per year, and so owns a stock of ten backhoe loaders. This means that it buys two new backhoes each year to replace machines that reach the end of their economic life.

- Now, suppose that because of a house-building boom the firm experiences a growth in demand to 600 houses per year. Let us assume that the managers of the house-building firm expect this increase in production to be permanent. They need to increase their stock of backhoe loaders to 12, as well as replace two worn-out machines. Rather than buying two backhoe loaders, this year they buy four.

- The increase in demand for houses experienced by the building firm was 20 per cent (that is, 100/500), but the increase in purchases of backhoe loaders by the firm was 100 per cent (four instead of the usual two).

- The accelerator effect in this case is five (the 100 per cent increase in demand for capital equipment divided by the 20 per cent increase in demand for houses).

- Notice that if the managers of the house-building firm expect the demand for housing to remain constant from now on, then this will be a one-time-only increase in the demand for backhoe loaders. The long-term demand for backhoe loaders will increase by 20 per cent, exactly in line with the permanent increase in demand for houses. In subsequent years the firm will replace, on average, 2.4 (12/5) machines each year.

- What if the managers of the building firm expect their sales of houses to return to their previous level of 500 per year? The firm would temporarily own two more backhoes than it needed, and for one year only its demand for backhoes would fall to 0.4. The accelerator then works in reverse, and is entirely symmetrical, since sales of houses have declined by 16.7 per cent, and demand for backhoes has declined by 83.3 per cent, giving an accelerator of five (after allowing for rounding error).

The example in Snapshot 1.3 is hypothetical. It illustrates the principle of the accelerator only. A purely hypothetical example is needed because in practice things are never so clear-cut, and the underlying acceleration principle can be difficult to discern. In practice, managers will be cautious about investing in new equipment at the first sign of an increase in demand for their own products, since they cannot be sure that the new demand will be enduring. In the short term managers are very likely to spend a little more on maintaining old equipment (so continuing to use equipment even though it has been fully depreciated on the balance sheet) rather than investing in new equipment, to get a better picture of the trend in demand. Naturally, managers can choose to lease equipment rather than buy it new – although this in itself does not make the accelerator principle incorrect, since the equipment leasing company has to get its equipment from somewhere. For the accelerator principle to work with full effect we have to assume that capital equipment is being worked to full capacity; otherwise the building firm in our illustration could have chosen to work its existing backhoe loaders more intensively rather than buy new machinery.

Despite these various objections, there is considerable evidence that the acceleration principle plays a substantial role in explaining the demand for capital equipment. Almost all macro-economic models of the economy include a version of this principle to explain capital investment, indicating that the principle is valid (Eatwell et al., 1987). The key implication of the principle for business marketers is that, in capital equipment markets, the future trend in demand cannot be predicted straightforwardly from forecasts of demand in downstream markets. Changes in downstream demand can lead to much larger percentage changes in demand for capital equipment. The fact that this is very unlikely to happen with the simple arithmetic precision of our illustration, for the various practical reasons discussed, makes the forecasting job much harder. One task for the business marketer working in such an industry is to understand both the scale of the underlying accelerator principle for the industry, and the moderating influences on the accelerator exerted by conditions in the market and the behaviour of managers in customer organizations.

Market concentration in business-to-business markets

Business-to-business markets in general are characterized by a higher concentration of demand than consumer markets. However, the degree of demand concentration varies from market to market, and it is important to have some means of comparing markets to establish just how highly concentrated they are. The standard measure that is used is the **concentration ratio**. A concentration ratio is defined as the combined market shares of the few largest firms in the market – what is known as the 'oligopoly group' in the market. Quoted concentration ratios are usually based on the top three, four or five firms; that is to say, the concentration ratio is the sum of the market shares held by the top three, four or five firms. For purposes of economic analysis and economic policy, concentration ratios are important because it is supposed that the higher the concentration ratio, the more likely it is that firms in an industry will collude to raise prices above those that would be found in a truly competitive market. Economists also theorize that where concentration ratios are relatively high, industry will be less innovative and production volumes less stable. Empirical economic research has generally shown that prices do tend to be higher, and innovation less dynamic, in highly concentrated industries (Eatwell et al., 1987).

The perspective taken by economists, when studying concentration ratios, is generally that of the *customer* of the industry in question and the *economic efficiency* of the structural conditions of the industry. To the business marketer it is the perspective of the industry *supplier* that is generally most relevant, along with the implications of the industry structure for *sales and marketing strategy*. While economists are generally most concerned about the *monopoly power* that businesses have over their customers because of the concentration of market share, business marketers are usually more interested in the *monopsony power* that businesses have with respect to their suppliers because of the concentration of buying power. The degree of monopsony power in the supply market is symmetrical with the degree of monopoly power in the customer market; those firms that control large shares of the customer market are also the largest customers for suppliers to the industry. So we can use the concentration ratio (concentration of market share) as a proxy for the concentration of buying power within an industry.

Illustrating concentration ratios

The concentration of market power in consumer markets is widely known and understood. For example, anyone who has studied consumer marketing in the UK knows that although there are many *brands* in the laundry detergent market, the market is in fact dominated by just two producers: Procter & Gamble and Unilever. In 2011 the brands owned by Procter & Gamble had a combined share of 52 per cent of the UK market, while Unilever brands had a combined share of 33 per cent (Mintel, 2012). At the company level this market is highly concentrated, since two firms control around 85 per cent of the market, and can be reasonably referred to as a *duopoly*. Clearly, any business wanting to supply products or services to the UK laundry detergent market must take this factor into account when developing a sales and marketing strategy. If your aim is to obtain a substantial share of the business to supply the UK laundry products market, then it is essential to do business with at least one of the industry leaders. To have any chance of achieving this you must become very familiar with the business of those companies and adapt your products and services so that they exactly match their requirements, which may well involve specific investment in new technology or new systems. Throughout this book we will frequently return to the implications of this for the theory and practice of business marketing.

In order to understand business-to-business marketing, it is particularly important to understand the degree of industry concentration that can be found in B2B markets. In some industries market concentration is very high; for example, the global market for heavy electrical equipment is dominated by the GE Company

(31.9 per cent market share), Alstom (19.3 per cent), Siemens AG (12.8 per cent) and Mitsubishi Heavy Industries (12.5 per cent) (Datamonitor, 2011). However, other industries are less concentrated; for example, in the global environmental services and facilities services market the top four firms have relatively small market shares – Waste Management Inc. (5.7 per cent market share), Veolia Environnement (4.6 per cent), Suez Environnement (4.1 per cent) and Republic Services (3.5 per cent) (Datamonitor, 2012b). From these figures we can calculate the four-firm concentration ratio for each sector, which is 17.9 per cent for the environmental and facilities services market and 76.5 per cent for the heavy electrical equipment market (the three-firm concentration ratio is 14.4 per cent in environmental and facilities services and 64.0 per cent in the heavy electrical equipment market). The heavy electrical equipment market is much more concentrated than the environmental and facilities services market. Business marketers aiming to develop a marketing strategy to supply products or services to either of these industries clearly need to be aware of the buying power of the top companies. However, there is also scope to develop sales and marketing strategies based on other segments of these markets, rather than simply focusing on the major players, even in the heavy electrical equipment sector. The estimated value of this market in 2010 was $95.4 billion; this means that firms other than the top four had combined sales of around $22.4 billion.

Other market structure differences

An understanding of derived demand, the accelerator effect and concentration ratios provides a basis for analysing many of the structural differences between typical consumer and business markets. Table 1.2 listed a number of other dimensions, along which lines experts have proposed that there are systematic differences between business and consumer markets. *Demand elasticity* is one of these dimensions. First, it is argued that businesses have less freedom simply to stop buying things than consumers, so that business demand is likely to be less price elastic (that is, less responsive to price changes) than consumer market demand. Second, and for similar reasoning, it has been suggested that there will be more instances of reverse (or 'perverse') price elasticity of demand in business markets than in consumer markets. Both of these hypotheses about demand elasticity arise from the nature of derived demand and assumptions about the availability of substitutes for the inputs to critical business processes. Businesses need critical inputs if they are to continue trading.

For example, if a computer manufacturing firm cannot gain access to the latest generation of microprocessors, then it cannot build machines that will sell, and the very existence of the company is at risk. Should the purchasing professionals at this company see the price of microprocessors rising, then they may take this to mean that there is a shortage of supply (price tends to rise in markets where demand outstrips supply) and may therefore *increase* their orders in the short term in the hope of guaranteeing a sufficient supply of microprocessors to keep the business functioning. In effect this is a case of reverse elasticity, where a rise in price triggers an increase in demand. Even if the purchasing team at the computer firm do not believe that there is likely to be a shortage of microprocessors, price changes are unlikely to affect the volume that they purchase to any great extent. The volume of microprocessors that the company buys is primarily driven by their computer sales forecasts, and not so much by component prices. The expectation is that demand for microprocessors will be inelastic with respect to price.

From Table 1.2 we can see that business markets have been described as more heterogeneous, more fragmented and more complex than consumer markets. All of these characteristics are reflections of the enormous diversity of organizational forms found in business markets. Of course, the point is not that consumers are all alike; consumers are people, and each individual person is unique! Rather, it is that organizations are even more diverse than consumers. For example, most private firms employ fewer than ten people, while global businesses such as those we discussed in the preceding paragraphs – such as Alstom, Siemens, Mitsubishi and Veolia Environnement – employ tens of thousands of people at multiple locations across several continents. A local decorating business employing three or four people has almost nothing in common with, say, a global electrical equipment manufacturer.

Buying behaviour differences and marketing practice differences

In this section we will discuss these aspects of the differences between business markets and consumer markets only briefly. The reason for this is that buying behaviour and marketing practice are the subject matter of the remainder of the book, and we wish to avoid repeating ourselves excessively! In the following chapters you will find detailed discussions of organizational buying behaviour and business-to-business marketing practice.

In essence, organizations tend to have more professionalized buying processes than consumers, often involving formal procedures and explicit decision-making practices, which in many organizations are implemented by managers who are specifically employed as purchasing professionals. Transaction values can be very high. As a result, sellers tend to tailor their product offerings to the needs of the buyer, seeking to offer complete solutions to their business problems rather than just selling them a product. The conventional tools of consumer mass marketing are not very appropriate under these circumstances. Promotional messages must be tailored to the specific needs of the customer. Sales executives (and, for the most important customers, key account managers) are employed to develop and manage the relationship between the buying and selling organization. All of these aspects of buying behaviour and business marketing practice will be explained in much greater detail in subsequent chapters of the book.

As we approach the end of Chapter 1, it is time to check-in again on new B2B sales and marketing executive Magnus, in B2B Scenario 1.2.

B2B SCENARIO 1.2   MAGNUS AND THE ENGINEERS

Despite upsetting an important client (a situation that his boss Petra eventually had to step in and sort out herself), Magnus Johanson still has his job at engineering consultancy firm ENG Projects (see B2B Scenario 1.1). In fact, after a sticky start he has settled in nicely and is definitely starting to make a good impression on the senior team at the firm. As a recent marketing graduate he is familiar with a great many marketing techniques that were previously unheard of at ENG. The company is now leading the way in its sector in the application of social media marketing. Magnus has developed an excellent ENG blog using material sourced from the highly qualified technical staff that the company employs. This blog is generating a lot of traffic and quite a few enquiries from prospective new clients.

Unfortunately, Magnus has hit another problem. He is on the project team to develop a new service designed to audit and improve energy management systems for public sector organizations such as schools, hospitals and local authorities. This is potentially a lucrative business opportunity since governments all across Europe are keen to demonstrate that they are working hard to save energy and contribute to their commitments under international climate change agreements. The problem is that Magnus is having a hard time making his voice heard. Everyone else on the team has an engineering background and when Magnus tries to raise topics like market research, market positioning, market segmentation, and marketing communications, he is very largely ignored. As far as Magnus is concerned, the team seems to spend far too much time discussing unnecessarily complicated technical issues, and strongly resists the idea that the service should be built around a comprehensive understanding of customer needs. Clearly, the engineers think that they are dealing with an engineering problem, and the solution will be an engineering solution. Whereas Magnus sees the design of the new service as a business problem requiring marketing and customer information, the engineers on the team seem to see the service design process as something different. When he talks unguardedly to Petra, Magnus tells her: 'These engineers don't seem to understand that the right solution is the solution that meets the customer's requirements, not some abstract, ideal, perfect engineering solution. They spend ages refining some minor technical point that the customer will simply not be interested in. And they have no idea at all about marketing. They seem to think that marketing is just money down the drain.'

Petra ponders what advice she should give Magnus.

Source: Based on Keaveney (2008).

CLASSIFYING BUSINESS PRODUCTS AND MARKETS

We have emphasized that the key difference between business marketing and consumer marketing is the nature of the customer rather than the nature of the product. In business markets customers are organizations. There are indeed many products that are purchased by organizations that one cannot envisage being bought by consumers, such as management consultancy services and heavy engineering equipment. Equally, there is a vast array of products bought both by organizations and by private consumers, such as tablet computers and health insurance services. This raises the question of whether one can classify business products separately from consumer products, or whether a single classification system will function equally well for both.

The standard approach to classifying business products is to use a classification system that is quite separate from the usual consumer product classifications (Copeland, 1924; Kotler, 1972; Murphy and Enis, 1986). This classification is based on the use to which the products are put, and the extent to which they are incorporated into (or 'enter') the final product. Many things that organizations buy, such as office cleaning services, are not incorporated into the final product at all. Some things, such as the DVD drives that a computer manufacturer buys from an optical drive manufacturer, are incorporated directly and completely into the final product. The distinction between 'entering goods' and other types of purchase is based on the idea that something incorporated into the buying organization's final product contributes directly to the finished product quality and so directly to the customer's business reputation. Other purchases affect the buyer's own customer less directly, and so do not have such an immediate potential influence on the buying organization's business performance. The system of classification is as follows:

- *Installations* are major investment items such as heavy engineering equipment, which are treated as investment items by the customer, so that the costs involved in acquiring them are depreciated over their expected economic life. Customers are expected to plan such investments carefully, perhaps involving the use of extensive financial analysis including discounted cash flow analysis and scenario planning.

- *Accessory equipment* consists of smaller items of equipment such as hand tools. Larger items of accessory equipment may be treated as investment items and depreciated on the financial statements, while smaller items will be treated as expense items. The economic life of accessory equipment is usually shorter than that of installations.

- *Maintenance, repair and operating (MRO) supplies* are individually minor items of expenditure that are essential to the running of the organization. These would include such things as office supplies (for example, stationery), lubricants and abrasives.

- *Raw materials* are unprocessed basic materials such as crude oil, coal and metal ores. These products are often traded on international exchanges (such as the London Metal Exchange, www.lme.co.uk) and are particularly prone to price fluctuations arising from the forces of supply and demand. For example, towards the end of 2015 the spot price per tonne of aluminium was below $1,500 but just over a year earlier at the end of 2014 the price had stood at over $2,000 per tonne. Price fluctuations of this magnitude (in this case a price decline of more than 25 per cent in a year) are not unusual in global commodity markets.

- *Manufactured materials and parts* include raw materials that have been processed (such as finished steel and prepared timber) and component parts (such as computer optical drives and automobile windscreens) that are ready to be incorporated directly into the finished product.

- *Business services* are often subdivided into maintenance and repair services and business advisory services.

From this classification of business products one can easily derive a commonly cited classification of industrial manufacturing organizations into *original equipment manufacturers* (OEMs) and others. OEMs are manufacturing businesses that buy component parts from other firms to incorporate into a finished product that is then sold under their own brand name to other businesses or to consumers. Car manufacturers (such as VW/Audi, Ford and Toyota) and computer manufacturers (such as Dell, Hewlett-Packard and Lenovo) are classic OEM businesses. One can then distinguish between the OEM market (sales of component parts to OEMs for incorporation into the final product when it is first manufactured) and the *after-market* (sales of component parts to the owner of the product *after* it has been sold by the OEM). In the after-market, for example, car owners may need to replace a shattered windscreen, and computer owners may choose to upgrade the RAM capacity of their desktop machine. OEM customers are by definition business customers. They usually buy in large quantities, and are typically large and powerful buying organizations. Customers in the after-market may be either organizations or consumers. Both organizations and consumers buy vehicles and computers, for example, for which they will buy spare parts or upgrades. The OEM market is therefore an exclusively business-to-business market, while the after-market includes both businesses and consumers.

In contrast to the standard classification system for business products that we have cited above, Murphy and Enis (1986) argued that only one classification system was needed for products, and that it could apply equally well to business and consumer products. They proposed a four-fold classification of products based on the buyer's evaluation of the effort involved in acquiring the product and of the risk of making a poor decision. Effort and risk are considered to be the costs incurred by the buyer when making a decision; effort is a variable that includes the amount of money, energy and time that the buyer is willing to expend to acquire a given product.

- *Convenience products* involve very little effort and negligible risk for the buyer. The maintenance, repair and operating supplies described previously would generally be classified as convenience products.

- *Preference products* involve a little more effort than convenience products but substantially more risk. In general, this means that they are a little more expensive than convenience products, but that the buyer perceives a much greater chance of making the wrong decision. Minor items of accessory equipment as described above would generally also be classified as preference products; Murphy and Enis also mentioned business travel as a characteristic preference product.

- *Shopping products* involve a great deal more effort and perceived risk than convenience or preference products. This would include major items of accessory equipment, manufactured materials and parts (that is, products that enter the final product completely), and market research services. Buyers are willing to spend a considerable amount of time and energy on acquiring these products because of their relatively high price and the risk associated with possibly making the wrong decision.

- *Specialty products* are the highest ranked in terms of both buyer risk and effort. Installations (such as major new items of engineering plant) and highly specialized business services (such as the services of a top management consultancy firm) would fall into this category. The main distinction between specialty products and shopping products is effort, rather than risk. Buyers are prepared to invest great amounts of time and energy in seeking to make the right choice about these high-value purchases.

The two principal classification systems described above should be regarded as complementary rather than as alternatives. The first of them concentrates on the nature of the product, the way in which products are used and whether they enter the final product or not. It is a seller-orientated classification scheme. The Murphy and Enis classification is buyer-orientated, classifying products on the basis of dimensions that are considered meaningful to buyers. Although they are logically distinct, there is clearly a degree of consistency between them. For example, 'installations' will almost certainly fall into the category of 'specialty products', and MRO supplies almost certainly into the category of 'convenience products'. The Murphy and Enis classification has the advantage of explicitly treating goods, services and ideas equally. In classifications of business products it is all too easy to relegate services to a single undifferentiated category, with the implication that services are relatively unimportant compared to goods. However, as we saw earlier in the discussion of Table 1.1, the service sector is a much larger employer than the manufacturing sector in the world's major economies, so it is important not to think of the marketing of business services as somehow less important than the marketing of industrial products.

CHAPTER SUMMARY

- Business marketing is concerned with the marketing of goods and services to organizations. The key distinguishing feature of business marketing is the nature of the customer, rather than the nature of the product. Although there are products that are bought only by organizations and not by final consumers, there are many products that are bought by both organizations and consumers.

- Modern economies are becoming increasingly service orientated. The service industries account for close to 80 per cent of employment in countries such as Australia, Canada, the UK and the USA – and the trend is towards even higher levels of service sector employment.

- Business markets can be distinguished from consumer markets along a wide range of dimensions, but those dimensions can be conveniently grouped into market structure, buying behaviour and marketing practice. At the most fundamental level, it is structural differences that tend to drive differences in buying behaviour and in marketing practice. In particular, demand in business markets is derived rather than direct, and levels of demand concentration in business markets are typically much higher than in consumer markets. As a result, buyer power in business markets can be much greater than in consumer markets. In turn, this often means that business marketers prefer relational marketing strategies, developing solutions tailored to individual customers rather than conventional marketing mix strategies.

- A common classification for business products is installations, accessory equipment, MRO supplies, raw materials, manufactured materials and parts, and business services. A key distinction is made between products that are incorporated into the final product (entering goods) and those that are not. Original equipment manufacturers combine components bought from other suppliers into a finished product that is sold to end-users. The after-market comprises sales of parts for repair and upgrade to products that are already owned by an end-user. Business products can also be classified using the customer-orientated categories of convenience, preference, shopping and specialty products. This classification scheme is based on the risk and the effort that buyers perceive in acquiring a given product.

QUESTIONS FOR DISCUSSION

1. Why do we not differentiate between business markets and consumer markets on the basis of the type of product purchased?

2. Draw up an elementary chain of derived demand for the personal computer industry.

3. What is the accelerator effect and why is it important in business-to-business markets?

4. Are business markets fundamentally different from consumer markets?

5. What is a four-firm concentration ratio? What difference does it make to the business marketer whether this ratio is 30 per cent or 70 per cent?

CASE STUDY 1.1   ROLLS-ROYCE GROUP PLC

There are probably still a lot of people around who think that the famous British engineering company Rolls-Royce is a car maker, but that has not been true for many years. Rolls-Royce cars today are manufactured by a division of BMW. There will certainly be many people who believe that Rolls-Royce makes its money by manufacturing and selling aero-engines, and this is true up to a point. The company certainly does produce aero-engines, as well as power units for use in the marine and energy generation sectors. However, if Rolls-Royce's business stopped at the point where it delivers an engine to an aircraft manufacturer (for example, a Trent 1000 delivering over 74,000 lbs of thrust, for use on the Boeing 787 Dreamliner) then the company would be much smaller and less profitable than it is. That is because around 50 per cent of Rolls-Royce revenue is generated from after-market services (Figure 1.1).

In 2015, Rolls-Royce achieved overall revenue of £13.3 billion, split almost exactly 50:50 between original equipment sales and aftermarket services. In Rolls-Royce's largest business unit, the civil aerospace sector (selling and maintaining aero-engines for civil airlines) 53 per cent of the revenue was generated by after-market services.

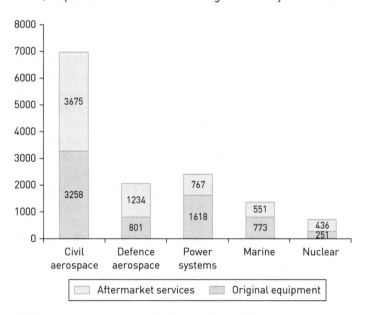

FIGURE 1.1 Rolls-Royce revenue analysis 2015 (£ millions) (based on data from Rolls-Royce, 2015b)

(Continued)

(Continued)

This revenue is created by selling services such as TotalCare® to airlines who specify Rolls-Royce engines on the planes that they buy. The airline pays Rolls-Royce an agreed cost per flying hour, and in return Rolls-Royce delivers a complete engine support service for the lifetime of the engine. As a result the airline knows exactly how much to budget for engine maintenance, transfers many of the risks associated with operating an aero-engine to Rolls-Royce, improves the residual value of the engine (rather like having your premium-brand car serviced regularly by the main dealer), and allows the airline to concentrate on its core business of selling flights and getting passengers and cargo safely to their destination.

Perhaps this rather technical description of the financial and engineering aspects of delivering after-market services is illuminated more entertainingly by a description of what this can all mean to airline operators and their passengers in practice. Imagine a long flight from Asia to America passing high over the Pacific, where the aircraft is struck by lightning. Planes are frequently struck by lightning and usually it does no harm at all, but on this occasion one of the engines loses power briefly. The passengers on the plane hardly notice, but Rolls-Royce engineers in Derby (a city a very long way from the Pacific) start analysing the problem immediately. There is no danger, since the engine is running fine again and the plane could land perfectly well without it anyway. The engineers simply need to work out whether the plane will need a full engine inspection when it touches down in Los Angeles. All of the data the engineers need is silently and automatically sent from the plane to the engineers in Derby, carefully analysed, and conclusions are drawn even before the plane has touched down. Everything is fine, and the plane will not be delayed in its subsequent departure from Los Angeles.

Although there is little publicly available financial information about the relative profitability of selling service contracts on aero-engines compared to the profit margins made on selling the engines themselves, industry analysts believe that Rolls-Royce makes very slim profit margins on engine sales. The real money is made from the long-term partnership with the airline that is created through the sale of a service contract. The emphasis on managing long-term relationships with customers at Rolls-Royce is typical of many business-to-business companies: 'The Group places great importance on working closely in partnership with its customers to understand their operations and align the Group's service capability to meet their needs' (Rolls-Royce, 2009: 22).

So, on what basis has Rolls-Royce built its current success: excellence in engineering and manufacturing, excellence in customer service or excellence in managing customer relationships? Well, the truth is probably a combination of all three. In addition, Rolls-Royce has established a wide geographic base including the Americas, Asia, Australia, Europe, the Middle East and Africa, with manufacturing facilities in 20 countries and customer support facilities in 50 countries. The largest geographic market is the USA, but revenues are geographically diversified. This is a particularly important consideration at a time when the world economy has experienced a slowdown, since growth in the civil aerospace market is closely tied to growth of economic output (or GDP). In particular, Rolls-Royce's strength in Asia looks like a substantial business advantage, as the Asian economies began to emerge from the global economic slowdown much sooner and more strongly than other regions of the world. On the other hand, the substantial exposure of the company to the sluggish economies of North America, the UK and Europe is certainly a matter of concern.

CASE STUDY QUESTIONS

1 How does the concept of service-dominant logic apply in the case of Rolls-Royce?

2 Rolls-Royce has to compete against third-party maintenance operators, who also offer comprehensive service packages to airlines on both Rolls-Royce and other manufacturers' engines. What would you say are Rolls-Royce's key advantages in winning service contracts against such competitors?

Sources: Datamonitor, 2009; Rolls-Royce, 2009, 2012; *The Economist*, 2009; www.rolls-royce.com.

FURTHER READING

Brennan, R. (2012) 'The industrial/consumer dichotomy in marketing: can formal taxonomic thinking help?', *Journal of Customer Behaviour*, 11 (4): 311–24.

This article revisits the arguments discussed by Fern and Brown (1984) in the light of developments in marketing theory over the last three decades.

Fern, E.F. and Brown, J.R. (1984) 'The industrial/consumer marketing dichotomy: a case of insufficient justification', *Journal of Marketing*, 48 (Spring): 68–77.

It may look a little strange to recommend a reading from the 1980s. However, it is worth taking a look at this article to understand the fundamental arguments: on the one hand that 'marketing is marketing' and B2B marketing is simply the application of general marketing principles to a B2B context, and on the other hand that B2B marketing is fundamentally different from consumer marketing. The next reading brings the arguments up to date.

Vargo, S.L. and Lusch, R.F. (2004) 'Evolving to a new dominant logic for marketing', *Journal of Marketing*, 68 (1): 1–17.

While we are on the subject of the fundamental nature of B2B marketing, now is probably a good time to take a look at this highly influential article (arguably the most influential article on marketing in the first decade of the twenty-first century). What does service-dominant logic imply for B2B marketers? Can you see any parallels between the arguments of Fern and Brown (above) and those of Vargo and Lusch? Think about it! If you want to read more about this important topic then take a look at Vargo and Lusch (2011), which addresses the topic from a specifically B2B angle.

For a change from the fairly heavy material found in the three articles suggested above, now would be a good time to become familiar with, and to bookmark, one of the most informative websites about B2B marketing practice, namely www.b2bmarketing.net. Explore the range of information about current hot topics in B2B marketing at this website.

2

BUYER BEHAVIOUR

LEARNING OUTCOMES

After reading this chapter you will:

- know how the nature of a company's activities and its business strategy affect its dealings with supply markets;
- understand differing purchasing orientations and their contribution to a customer's acquisition of supplier resources and capabilities;
- be able to explain the buying process and reasons why this process can vary;
- be able to describe the membership and characteristics of the decision-making unit;
- be able to explain how and why individual needs can sometimes override rational decision-making;
- know about the job of the purchasing professional;
- understand how buying has evolved in the digital era; and
- understand the implications of these factors for the business marketer.

INTRODUCTION

Few customers, private or organizational, are self-sufficient, able to maintain their existence by satisfying their needs without drawing on the capabilities of suppliers, and without purchasing products marketed by those companies. To function and to achieve objectives require that an organization has access to supply markets from which it can obtain products to support its own activities. Behaviour associated with gaining access to necessary supply markets and products is affected by a variety of factors. Some of these are external to an organization, such as general macro-environmental forces, as well as influences that are more peculiar to the sector and market in which the organization operates. In addition to these external dynamics, purchasing is affected by what goes on inside a firm. So consideration has to be given to how organizational characteristics, as well as group and individual factors, affect purchasing behaviour and decisions (Webster and Wind, 1972). The central themes in this chapter lie in understanding what goes on inside a business and how organizational, group and individual forces influence the purchasing behaviour of business customers, and the implications for the business marketer of the way in which organizational customers deal with supply markets as a result of these forces.

ORGANIZATIONAL FACTORS AFFECTING PURCHASING DECISIONS

Organizations are not faceless and monolithic; rather they consist of human beings who repeatedly make decisions and take particular courses of action regarding purchasing. So the organizational factors discussed here inform the purchasing behaviour of managers in customer companies.

The nature of company business

We can think about our customers in terms of the industry sector or market in which they operate and how the dynamics in these industries influence their purchasing behaviour. However, it is possible to operate at a more general level by thinking about the 'technology' associated with our customers' businesses. By this we mean the way that a customer organizes their own activities in order to perform transformation processes that represent the essential components of their value-adding activities (Woodward, 1965). A company can be categorized according to whether its activities are essentially based on unit, mass or process technology.[1] This classification system could be criticized because it is derived from the manufacturing and engineering industries, while in the previous chapter we saw the huge importance of the service sector. Nevertheless the categories can be used – irrespective of whether a customer organization might be viewed as essentially a manufacturing, engineering or service business – to generate some understanding both of the nature of the key product capabilities that customer companies might purchase, and of the expectations that might be placed on suppliers.

Unit production involves the design and supply of products that are tailored to specific customer requirements. The bespoke products are typically associated with major capital investment projects, with a company's production activity being triggered by, and adapted to meet, the requirements of the individual customer. The technological complexity and scale of such projects affect the supply needs and purchasing behaviour of organizations whose business activities essentially revolve around competing for and supplying such major investment projects. A company will have the technical competence and operational capabilities both to design and produce some components/parts that are an essential piece of the final product and to assemble/configure and install the finished product.

However, the company also has to draw heavily on the design and production capabilities of suppliers that provide the materials, components or equipment that are central to the finished project as well. The unit production company typically requires the involvement of such suppliers in its design and production/assembly phases and requires coordination among its various key suppliers to ensure the completion and financing of these major projects. Companies whose business is geared around unit production include organizations such as Mitsubishi Heavy Industries Ltd. The company's Energy Division competes for multi-million dollar projects worldwide to provide power generation installations and distribution systems, requiring it to work with a variety of subcontractors in order to assemble the finished systems. Other

---

[1]The discussion in this section is based on material from Gadde and Håkansson, 2001.

businesses, such as those supplying organizations with bespoke and complex information and communications technology (ICT) systems, again work in a similar way. British Telecommunications plc (BT), for example, installs and manages ICT systems such as that used by the Fiona Stanley Hospital in Perth, Western Australia. The system draws on BT's information communications expertise, but to assemble and operate this bespoke system it has to draw from the technological capabilities of other parties. The complexity, scale and bespoke nature of such products mean that purchasing lies within the remit of the team assembled to oversee the project, with managers that are responsible principally for the technical content of the final product assuming a key role in dealing with suppliers. (Visit www.globalservices. bt.com to learn about other complex, bespoke solutions.)

In contrast to unit production businesses, a *mass production* company is involved in the design and supply of high-volume, standard products. Operational efficiency and a low cost base are central to the ability of mass production companies to compete. This efficiency is in part determined by the equipment used and the integration of the various sections that make up the company's primary production activities. The materials and components used to make up a finished product also contribute to the company's cost base. To maximize the efficient use of its resources, a company's production activities will be characterized by a high degree of inflexibility, requiring that the supply of materials and components used in primary operational activities be precise, regular and consistent. To this end the company would expect key suppliers to adjust logistical and administrative procedures to suit its requirements, to link these procedures with its own operations and to invest in systems such as just-in-time (JIT) delivery and extranets. The importance attached to the stable and secure flow of materials and components to support the buying organization's primary production activities often results in the company seeking to have some influence over the behaviour and activities of businesses that are not immediate suppliers but are nevertheless part of its supply chain.

A mass production company's ability to compete is determined not only by its low cost base but also by the regular introduction of new products into its target market. The company's key material and components suppliers would be expected to contribute to the buying organization's new product development activities. When new products are being developed, a supplier will have regular contact with the buying organization's design and technical managers. However, once a supplier's material or component proposal is accepted and becomes part of the customer's product specification, then the principal point of contact is with the purchasing function. Companies that operate in this way with their supply markets are quite diverse, ranging from high-volume car manufacturers to food processors such as Kraft-Heinz and Nestlé. For food processors, efficient operations are central to the company's ability to remain cost competitive. A key contributor to a food processor's product costs lies not in the food that it provides to consumers but in the packaging that contains and preserves that food. In addition to this, the packaging acts as an important marketing tool for the food company. So the packaging supplier makes a significant contribution to the food processor's finished product, with companies simultaneously trying to reduce packaging costs and develop innovative designs. For example, if you think about olive oil, you might picture it in tin cans or bottles. Oil is particularly vulnerable to light and air, such that the oil's properties quickly deteriorate. So glass bottles are not ideal for olive oil. Packaging supplier Tetra Pak has worked with one of its customers, the Spanish oil producer ArteOliva, to eliminate this problem by developing a carton package for the customer's oil products. Having developed a packaging product that worked, all that remained was to convince retailers and consumers of the added value offered by the new packaging form; that is, an oil with a longer shelf life but one which retains its health-giving properties. (Visit www.tetrapak.com for other case study examples of packaging solutions provided by the company.)

While the ideas of mass production have obvious resonance when we think about companies producing tangible consumer goods, they can be extended to service businesses. If we take the retail sector, for example, and think about large chains such as Aldi, Carrefour, Ikea, Mercadona, Sainsbury and Wal-Mart then these firms operate on the same principles, where the key to business success is the ability to keep costs per square metre to a minimum. Supply continuity is important and retailers will, for example, work with key suppliers to maximize the efficiency of retail operations.

As with mass production, the *process production* company is involved in the manufacture of high-volume products, with low cost, operational efficiency and therefore supply continuity being central to the organization's performance. A key distinction is that the process producing firm does not assemble finished products; rather its business centres on the processing of raw materials for use in other supply chains. The company will typically consume high volumes of necessary materials, with those that have a standard specification being sourced via commodity markets. Others, which may be unique to the buying organization's requirements, will be purchased from specialized suppliers. Consumption volume, the importance of supply continuity and the effect of raw material prices on the processor's business performance mean that although a company might have buyers responsible for purchasing specific commodity materials, corporate management will also have some involvement in purchasing activities. The equipment used as part of the organization's primary processing activities is central to the business's performance. Equipment purchases are infrequent, but they represent complex capital investment projects, with suppliers becoming involved with the buying company's project team at the early stages of an investment project. Businesses involved in process production include steel manufacturers such as Baosteel and utilities companies such as E.ON.

Business strategy

In addition to thinking about a customer's operational 'technology', vendors could also consider the customer's business strategy as this can give some indication of the way in which the customer will deal with supply markets. A firm's generic strategy defines the organization's competitive domain and how it will position itself against competitors. Decisions made at the business level regarding a firm's competitive strategy are guided by and also inform actions and decisions at the functional level, including purchasing. So, for example, a firm that adopts a *product leadership* strategy relentlessly pursues innovation in order to offer customers leading-edge products that consistently enhance the value derived by its customers in their use of the company's products (Treacy and Wiersema, 1993). Product leadership requires that a company has excellent technical and creative abilities and that it is able to use its own experience and learning capability to drive a rapid rate of product innovation and obsolescence. As well as managing its own internal product development processes, the involvement of suppliers in those processes is also key to the firm's ability to pursue a product leadership strategy. Business marketers striving to supply companies such as Intel or Mercedes will need an intimate knowledge of these companies, the ability to offer design and product expertise to contribute to their development activities, and sufficient responsiveness to support Intel and Mercedes' pursuit of innovation.

An alternative strategy is that of *operational excellence*, where a company competes by providing reliable products with minimal inconvenience to customers and at competitive prices (Treacy and Wiersema, 1993). Clearly, businesses adopting this strategy must contain costs to enable them to satisfy customer requirements at the lowest possible cost. A company might rethink the design and implementation of business processes, eliminating activities that are redundant and reconfiguring others, such that the use of resources is more efficient. Business marketers dealing with such companies would expect procurement of products to be organized around keeping costs to a minimum. Cost containment and ways to improve it would be an ongoing and central feature of dealings with suppliers. For example, efficient ground services such as aircraft refuelling and luggage handling are important for any airline. However, these airport services are essential for low-cost companies such as EasyJet and IndiGo to enable fast turnaround and maximize the flying time of aircraft.

Customer intimacy represents the third strategy identified by Treacy and Wiersema (1993), in which a company competes by developing adapted market offerings that are based on a detailed understanding of and ability to predict changes in customer requirements. To satisfy requirements, such that customers value these offerings more than competing alternatives, necessitates that a company has the internal flexibility to respond quickly to shifts in demand and is able to draw from the expertise of suppliers who are equally responsive to changing customer needs.

For an example of how one company's competitive strategy underpins its strong business performance, see B2B Snapshot 2.1.

B2B SNAPSHOT 2.1   CLOTHES MAKETH THE MAN ...

Zara is a leading international fashion company, with stores retailing the 18,000 garments created each year by its Spanish design team. The company responds directly to customers' tastes for specific trends, using information harvested from the shop-floor to adjust design and garment supply. So, for example, if sales figures from store electronic point of sale (EPOS) systems around the world show that a three-quarter sleeve cardigan is selling better than a full-length one, then the most successful is produced in quantity and the information is fed back to the design team who create further variations of this design. Besides trying to be 'in the skin of the customer', Zara's success results from its short supply chain: the company sources items with the broadest and least-transient appeal as finished goods from countries such as Morocco and China, with the majority of its garments being produced in Spain. Although Zara undertakes high-volume activities in-house (dying, cutting, labelling and packaging), labour-intensive finishing is carried out in Spain by a network of 300 small companies, who in return for supply exclusivity receive technological, financial and logistical support from the fashion company. And does it work? Well the system is flexible enough to cope with sudden changes in demand, and in January 2016, Zara's parent company Inditex posted year-end profit growth of 15%.

Source: Adapted from Carter-Morley, 2013; Christopher, 2000.

To realize corporate goals, organizations increasingly seek to undertake activities in a way that might be considered socially responsible, that is, taking account of the social, economic and environmental impact of their actions and considering human rights. Environmental protection and *sustainability* are a central aspect of corporate social responsibility (CSR), not least because of legislative requirements that organizations must satisfy (the nature of which will vary by industry) and its use by some firms as a central part of their business strategy. Its importance relative to an organization's overall strategy guides the behaviour of managers and also affects dealings with suppliers (Giunipero et al., 2012). For example, the business of the small German brewer Neumarkter Lammsbräu is built around the production and marketing of ecological beer. This has required the company to work closely over a number of years with, for example, raw materials suppliers to ensure that supplier production complies with its own ecological policies. The central thing for the business marketer is to understand the nature and priority placed on sustainable purchasing and supply by customers.

Purchasing orientation

A company's approach to acquiring resources and capabilities from external supply markets, its *purchasing orientation*, is guided by the expected contribution of purchasing to that organization's performance. Purchasing orientations will differ between industries and between firms within the same sector. In fact, a single organization will vary its orientation depending on the product to be sourced. Anderson and Katz (1998) identify four different orientations, while Dobler and Burt (1996) propose three. The basic principles that underpin these two different taxonomies are essentially the same. For simplicity and clarity, the discussion that follows uses Dobler and Burt's (1996) classification of purchasing orientations: namely buying, procurement and supply management.

The *buying orientation* uses purchasing practices whose principal purpose is to achieve reductions in the monetary value spent by a company on bought-in goods and services. Decisions are driven by attempts to get the *best deal* for the buying organization and to *maximize power* over suppliers in order to do this. Suppliers are selected based on their ability to meet quality and availability requirements and to offer the *lowest purchase price* or to meet *target prices* set by the purchaser. The buying organization sets target prices for its suppliers by determining the price at which it can sell its own products to its target market. The company then works back from this, calculating what proportion should come from items that it obtains from suppliers and which ones go into its finished product. The supplier is then presented with a maximum price that it cannot exceed if it wants to win the customer's business.

Having and being able to use a powerful negotiating position to broker deals that serve mainly the interests of the customer company is an important factor in the buying orientation. The customer might centralize purchasing decisions, thereby consolidating volume requirements and enhancing its negotiating position. As well as consolidating company supply needs, a customer can enhance their negotiating power by using multiple sources of supply for the same product category and by playing suppliers off against each other. The buying decisions have a short-term focus with orders being awarded to suppliers that offer the best prices, quality and availability. As we will see in our subsequent discussions, web-based search and purchasing activities make it that much easier to identify and transact with sources of lowest cost supply across the globe.

For many companies, the cost of bought-in goods and services can account for up to 70 per cent of net sales. A saving of €10 in purchasing costs has the same effect on company profitability as an increase in sales revenue of €60. The recognition that purchased items and therefore the purchasing function can have such a dramatic effect on an organization's financial performance has led to many firms trying to 'buy better'. The emphasis shifts from getting the 'best deal', to optimizing the purchase resource, to increasing productivity. This is the *procurement orientation* and use of this approach changes the way that purchasing managers deal with suppliers and with other functions inside their own company.

In striving to increase productivity a firm will not select and review suppliers according to specification conformance and lowest-priced offer, but will base the evaluation and decision on *total cost of ownership* (TCO). TCO looks at the true cost of obtaining a product from a given supplier, and involves a company measuring costs that are most significant for that product in terms of its acquisition, possession, use and subsequent disposal. TCO varies depending on the category, value and volume of product purchases. Obvious targets for using a TCO approach are products that are used over an extended time period, such as capital equipment and purchases of raw materials, manufactured parts and MRO items that involve large financial sums and/or ongoing, repetitive buying activities (Ferrin and Plank, 2002). Being able to identify the main cost drivers of different product categories requires that purchasing managers work with and have access to information both from other functions inside the company that handle and use the different products and from product suppliers. For an example of how one company is trying to use TCO in purchase activities, see B2B Scenario 2.1.

B2B SCENARIO 2.1   BROKEN GLASS

If you have ever had the misfortune to be faced with a damaged car windscreen, body glass or rear screen, then the chances are that you will have come across Autoglass, Carglass, O'Brien or Smith-Smith. These are just four names in the family of brands owned by the vehicle glass repair and replacement group, Belron, a substantial international service business which replaces 8.1 million glass pieces in cars around the world each year. Handling annual delivery and stock volumes of 9 million and 3.5 million items respectively in more than 34 countries represents a considerable supply management operation for the company. Of the five continents in which Belron has facilities, Europe is an important region, where the firm operates under the brand name Carglass and it goes without saying that supplies of glass pieces are fundamental to Carglass's business performance.

Automotive glass is supplied as original equipment (OE) spare parts to car manufacturer approved repairers (typically car dealers) or as automotive glass for replacement (ARG) to the independent aftermarket. For a period of time following the launch of new car models, replacement screens can only be sourced as original equipment (OE) from approved car dealers, for which premium prices are charged. However, as soon as possible, producers of replacement pieces (ARG) use reverse engineering to determine windscreen material and pattern specifications for different cars and models, allowing them to supply replacement screens for all vehicles and at reduced prices.

Carglass sources automotive glass for replacement (ARG) from a number of preferred suppliers around the world, with stock being held at any of the firm's seven distribution hubs in Europe and delivered within 24 hours following client orders from its European network of service centres. In terms of physical flow of replacement pieces, Carglass's principal activities include the ordering and receipt of windows, quality checks of delivered items and the shipment of screens to service centres. In cases where suppliers send excess, surplus stock is either retained in Carglass's own warehouse (for future use) or returned to the supplier. Besides excess stock, defective screens are also sent back to suppliers. Although Carglass sources the majority of its screens from its preferred ARG suppliers, this is not always possible. In addition to the introduction of new windows by car manufacturers (for which ARG producers have no copy), poor supplier delivery or quality performance can mean that Carglass has to purchase higher priced OE screens at short notice from approved dealers to satisfy service centre and client order requirements.

For some time, Carglass based purchase decisions on price alone. However, inadequate delivery performance, poor glass quality and subsequent related problems meant that the company was faced with considerable additional costs. Discussions with the board of directors led to Carglass's purchasing team being instructed to extend supplier selection beyond price considerations. Using total cost of ownership as a way of making supply process improvements, deciding on volume allocations and to a lesser extent negotiating price reductions, Carglass's purchasing team called each of its leading ARG suppliers (the two manufacturers who accounted for most of its supply requirements) to meetings to discuss the costs of doing business with them.

Sources: Adapted from Hurkens et al., 2006; www.belron.com; www.carwindshield.info.

By setting a target cost instead of a target price the company gives a supplier considerable scope to determine how this might be realized. Instead of meeting prescribed quality, availability and price specifications, the supplier can look at the customer's acquisition, possession, use and disposal (TCO) of the product that it is being asked to supply, and look at ways in which these might be rethought in order to meet the buyer's cost target. Reducing total ownership costs requires a willingness and a capacity to share information and more closely align activities between supplier and buyer organizations. The purchase-and-supply process and the handling of goods can be improved by the use of e-business tools and JIT delivery systems such that administrative and material flow costs are reduced. The investment and coordination needed to achieve such improvements mean that when dealing with suppliers and making purchase decisions the buyer has to take a longer-term perspective, and negotiations might be informed by efforts to satisfy the needs of both parties rather than just those of the buying organization.

Some firms broaden the scope of their dealings beyond immediate suppliers and customers in the knowledge that their own performance is linked to the activities of other companies in the same value chain. A *supply management orientation* is driven by efforts to *maximize value* along that chain. This typically results in:

- companies assessing core competencies and key capabilities to determine what activities they will perform themselves;
- the outsourcing of activities to which companies do not add value;
- the purchase of 'product systems' that are central to the buying organization's own operations or finished product;
- larger organizations driving change along a supply chain; and
- the restructuring of supply markets such that a company will rely on a small number of direct suppliers and a larger network of second- and third-tier suppliers.

The purchasing function and how it handles a company's supply chain become key strategic contributors to the firm's performance. The firm might be involved with fewer direct suppliers but their contribution will be much more important in terms of product expertise, involvement in the company's development activities, and in the case of systems suppliers, coordination of activities with second- and third-tier suppliers. The purchasing task is obviously more complex with this approach, and those with supply management responsibilities have to work closely with other managers across a variety of functions in their own company and in other firms in the supply chain. The importance of key suppliers means that manager behaviour in dealing with those suppliers is guided by the need to ensure the long-term viability of both parties.

Segmenting purchase categories

All organizations buy a range of products. These products vary in their importance to the company, so the purchasing orientation adopted is likely to vary too. To determine what approach to take in dealing with supply markets, a company might segment its purchases by product category so supply risk can be kept to a minimum and purchasing power can be exploited (Chopra and Sodhi, 2014; Kraljic, 1983). *Profit impact* can

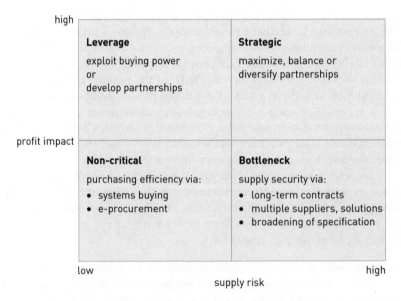

FIGURE 2.1 Segmenting purchase categories (Gelderman and van Weele, 2003)

be explained as the extent to which items add significant value to the organization's output either because they account for a large proportion of that output (for example, hotels for a package holiday company) or because they have a significant impact on quality (for example, packaging used for consumer foods and drinks). *Supply risk* refers to the vulnerability of product availability, either because of scarcity of the item itself or supply chain instability, or because there are simply a limited number of suppliers. Figure 2.1 shows how these criteria result in four purchase categories and possible strategies for the buyer (Gelderman and van Weele, 2003). The interpretation of profit impact and supply risk will of course vary depending on the industry in which a company operates, the firm's own activities, as well as the approach of both supplier and customer companies to exchange relationships. Although the latter is something that we discuss further in Chapters 3 and 9, what needs to be borne in mind is that the buying organization's handling of a supplier can contribute to that organization being attributed preferred customer status by the business marketer (Ellis et al., 2012).

Marketing implications of a customer's purchasing orientation

Knowing the purchasing orientations of customers and the way in which suppliers and their products might be categorized by them can help business market managers decide which customers to target and how to formulate solutions for the supply needs of those customers. If a customer adopts a supply management orientation and a supplier's product is classed as strategically important (high profit impact and high supply risk), then the supplier has the scope to become a key contributor to the customer organization's strategy. Obviously this requires that the supplier has the technical, financial and human resources to operate with the customer in this way.

For less important products such as MRO items, efficiency is the key priority so a customer might adopt a buying orientation. This means that a company supplying such items has little scope to do much other than concentrate on internal efficiency, and deliver according to the buyer's price and contract specification. However, this does not stop some companies from trying and succeeding to add value and changing the way in which the buyer might deal with them. See B2B Snapshot 2.2 to learn how the company, Philips, has successfully done this.

B2B SNAPSHOT 2.2   LET THERE BE LIGHT

The electric light bulb represents the very origin of the global company, Philips. For most of its customers, lighting systems are a necessary part of the buildings and facilities in which they go about their daily activities, but they are not business critical and light bulbs might simply be seen as just one among many MRO items that require regular replacement. However, Philips's focus on innovation and sustainability is allowing the company to change the way in which its customers engage with it as a lighting supplier. Rather than buying lighting systems or replacement components, customers can now purchase 'pay per lux' solutions in which Philips offers 'light as a service' and oversees the network-controlled lighting system. For example, when the

(Continued)

(Continued)

National Union of Students in the UK moved into a new building, key priorities included refurbished offices which both embodied NUS sustainability imperatives and also provided a high-quality working environment for staff. The lighting system designed and installed by Philips consists of 785 light points and an electrical load of just 5.9 w/m2. The light as service agreement means that the NUS pay a flat rate for lighting (with the price fixed for a 15-year period) and Philips monitors consumption online, reporting back to the NUS on an annual basis and if necessary refunding the Union. As the NUS Head of Sustainability explains 'as a registered charity we don't want to own services like lighting: our priority was to ensure the lighting performed as required in terms of light levels and energy consumption'.

Source: www.Philips.com.

THE PURCHASE PROCESS

Decision-making

When a customer buys a product, the purchase is not necessarily a single act or isolated event; rather it consists of a number of linked activities, namely the decision-making process. In business markets, buying consists of the following activities:

- *Need/problem recognition.* Purchases are triggered by two factors. One is the need to solve specific supply 'problems' such as the identification of under-capacity. This would trigger the purchase of extra 'production' capability in the form of operations equipment, temporary staff or the subcontracting of the production activity. Others might relate to ways in which the organization can improve its operational performance or pursue new market opportunities. If the company has to develop new products to realize those opportunities, then it will look to its supply markets for help in doing this. At this stage the organization might explore ways in which 'need/problem' might be addressed by investigating similar solutions, practices or products. E-business systems enable managers to start with online research and engage with other users before contacting potential vendors (Needles, 2010). This could be within their own, related or quite diverse sectors, but the key point is that managers likely to contribute to the purchase process explore possibilities by examining information and engaging in discussion forums within industry sectors or user groups (hosted on, for example, LinkedIn or Facebook), scrutinizing technical content such as that contained in white papers (published online by suppliers), or scanning professional publications. This initial exploration can help the customer company to further refine the precise nature of its requirement.

- Determining *product specification.* Based on the satisfaction of supply need, the company then draws up a specification for the item. The specification could include any or all of the following:

  o   what the product will be required to do (functional);

  o   its physical properties (technical or material);

o how the product should be produced (process); and

o outputs that the customer expects from using the product (performance).

Depending on what is being purchased the specification will obviously vary, as will the range of functional managers from across an organization that contribute to determining the specification parameters. For vendors, this stage in the buying process can be critical. If the company has contact with managers involved in agreeing the specification then it has some scope to influence that specification and potentially lock out competing suppliers.

- *Supplier and product search.* Here the buyer will look for organizations that can meet its product need. This search centres on two basic issues: finding a product that will match the buying firm's specification, and organizations that can satisfy the company's supply requirements. The amount of effort invested in this stage will depend on the cost and importance of the purchase as well as how familiar the buyer already is with the supply market. However, electronic searches, access to product or industry specific directories and the ability to place requests for tender online can accelerate and simplify this search process.

- *Evaluation of proposals and selection of suppliers.* Evaluation of proposals will vary depending on the complexity and risk attached to the purchase decision. The importance attributed to the various choice criteria among members of the decision-making unit will also vary. Evaluation will normally consider the compatibility of a supplier's proposal against the buying company's product specification and an assessment of the supplier organization itself. The weighting attached to and the nature of the assessment of the supplier organization will be determined in part by the customer's purchasing orientation and therefore the expected contribution of suppliers to the buying company's own business. So evaluation can relate to the product specification as well as how a customer wants to engage with potential suppliers. See Table 2.1 for a list of possible criteria and what product and supplier evaluation might look like.

- *Selection of order routine.* Once a supplier has been chosen then the purchasing manager will normally be responsible for negotiating and agreeing processes for order delivery and payment.

- *Performance feedback and evaluation.* This can be a formal process in which user departments regularly complete evaluation sheets designed by the purchasing team. The results will typically feature as an agenda item at meetings between the supplier and customer organizations. Alternatively, evaluation might be more informal, featuring as part of the daily exchanges between the companies.

Variations in the purchase process

The stages in the decision-making process might not be followed sequentially; some of the stages might be omitted altogether; and the time and effort invested in completing the various stages will vary. A key cause of variation in the process is the degree of risk associated with the purchase decision. Risk is an inherent feature of exchange in business markets, where managers have to deal with *uncertainty* and possible *negative consequences* surrounding purchase and supply decisions (Mitchell, 1995). For the business customer the decision-making process can vary depending on the buying organization's familiarity with and experience of the product to be

TABLE 2.1 Supplier selection and evaluation

Criteria	Weighting	Supplier 1 score	Supplier 1 weighted score	Supplier 2 score	Supplier 2 weighted score
Quality	0.25	4	1	5	1.25
Availability	0.25	3	0.75	4	1
Price/Cost	0.25	5	1.25	2	0.5
Operational capability	0.04	3	0.12	5	0.2
Service	0.04	3	.12	5	0.2
Management	0.01	4	0.04	4	0.04
Technology	0.04	4	0.16	5	0.2
Research and Development	0.04	4	0.16	5	0.2
Flexibility	0.01	2	0.02	3	0.03
Reputation	0.01	3	0.03	4	0.04
Relationship	0.01	2	0.02	3	0.03
Risk	0.01	3	0.03	4	0.04
Safety and Environment	0.04	4	0.16	5	0.02
Total rating			*3.86*		*3.93*
1 = Poor, 3 = Average, 5 = Excellent					

Source: adapted from Bevilacqua and Petroni, 2002; Ho et al., 2010.

purchased, such that it is faced with three different buying situations: new task, modified re-buy and straight re-buy (Robinson et al., 1967). These different situations are derived from the 'newness' of the task that the buyer has to deal with, and will affect the extent to which current or alternative suppliers are considered in order to solve the purchasing problem, as well as the amount of information sought and used to guide the decision at hand. Robinson et al.'s (1967) buygrid framework links different buying situations with the use of information and choice of suppliers and is used by managers and researchers alike because of its simplicity and intuitive appeal. The buygrid does, however, consider only one factor likely to affect the buying process (task newness) while ignoring others, such as the importance of purchasing to the organization, and market conditions, such as the range of suppliers from which the company can choose and the purchasing power held by the customer organization relative to its supply market (Bunn, 1993). By extending the range of factors likely to affect the decision process, further variations in it become apparent, such that the customer's *approach* to solving the supply problem can mean that:

- in a new-task buying situation, a judgemental or strategic buying approach might be used;

- a modified re-buy might consist of either a simple or complex buying approach; and
- for straight re-buys, the company might use casual or routine low-priority purchasing approaches. (Bunn, 1993)

New task

In a new-task situation the organization is faced with a purchasing decision that is completely different from previous experiences. This means that the organizational customer needs large amounts of information so that those involved in making the purchase decision can consider alternative ways of solving the supply problem. The uniqueness of the task can also lead to the company considering a number of potential suppliers. Such new-task buying situations can be split into those in which a *judgemental buying approach* is used, while in others a *strategic buying approach* is more likely (Bunn, 1993).

The judgemental buying approach is typically associated with the highest degree of uncertainty. The product might not be of major strategic importance to the firm, but the buying company is in a position where it has difficulty in articulating a precise product or performance specification for its purchasing problem. This difficulty can be the result of the company's lack of prior experience in solving similar supply needs. It can also be because the sought-after solution is technologically complex, with the products available from various suppliers being difficult to evaluate. Such a situation will trigger a moderate degree of search effort both in terms of the breadth and depth of information sought from suppliers as well as the number of suppliers considered to solve the purchasing problem. The fact that the firm has difficulty in clarifying the necessary product/performance specification means that analytical tools normally used to evaluate supplier proposals are not likely to be used, and neither are the formal procedures normally followed for higher-risk purchasing decisions. Instead, the purchase decision will be based on the personal judgement of a small group of managers.

The strategic buying approach, as it suggests, is associated with buying decisions that are strategically important to the business customer. This could be because the purchase represents a key contribution to the customer company's operational activities or to their own products, and/or because the purchase involves significant financial outlay for the company. The potential effect of such purchase decisions on the company's performance means that they can feature as part of corporate planning activities and require a long-term perspective with regard to the management of the business's supply needs. It also means that considerable effort is invested in obtaining and evaluating information regarding suppliers and their proposed solutions, and in negotiating with those suppliers.

Guidelines for the business marketer in new-task buying situations

Suppliers that encounter customers dealing with new-task buying situations can try to build a strong position by becoming involved in the decision-making process at an early stage. This involvement can include obtaining information on the nature of the purchasing problem the customer is seeking to address, identifying specific product/supply requirements and formulating proposals to match those requirements.

Companies that already deal with the buying organization ('in-suppliers') have an advantage over other firms during their dealings with the customer, since they are likely to encounter the new purchasing problems that it is trying to address as a consequence of regular, ongoing exchanges. Alternatively managers from the customer company may approach an in-supplier because of their familiarity with that supplier and its capabilities. The key for the in-supplier is to monitor the changing needs of the customer and to be able to support the company in such new-purchase situations. Although the 'out-supplier' does not have the advantage of dealing direct with an existing customer, digital search and communication technology does nevertheless mean that the business marketer can identify potential opportunities in the early stages of the buying process (which we discuss further in Chapter 7).

Modified re-buy

Situations involving repeat purchases in which the customer deviates in some way from previous purchase decisions to satisfy essentially the same supply need are classed as modified re-buys. Various factors can trigger this deviation, but the principal cause is normally the company's dissatisfaction with its existing supplier. Such repurchase situations can be either simple or complex.

A *simple modified re-buy* involves the purchase of a product and involvement with a supply market with which the customer is already familiar, so the information search can be quite limited. Previous experience and product sourcing also mean that the purchase lends itself to the use of standard buying procedures. The product may be of some strategic importance to the buying organization with only a limited set of choice alternatives open to the company. This results in the sourcing of the product featuring as part of the firm's long-term planning of supply needs and management of relationships with vendors.

A *complex modified re-buy* is characterized by purchase situations in which the customer is faced with little uncertainty and a large choice of possible suppliers, which in turn enhances the negotiating position of the buying organization. This type of purchase situation is the one most likely to exhibit all stages of the decision-making process. A key feature of this is the search for large amounts of information, the use of sophisticated analysis techniques to evaluate proposals, and the adherence to established purchase procedures. A significant proportion of complex modified re-buys involve the purchase of products that originate from previously negotiated contracts. The clarity of the product specification and the choice of possible suppliers mean that the buying organization can readily evaluate costs and prices on a repeated basis. The clarity of the decision is arguably suited to competitive bids, and therefore offers potential scope for the use of online auctions.

Guidelines for the business marketer in modified re-buy situations

A modified re-buy occurs because the customer sees potential benefits from re-scrutinizing alternative supply solutions. An in-supplier's principal objective is to move decision-makers from a modified to a straight re-buy, reducing or eliminating these perceived benefits. To do this the in-supplier should invest significant effort in understanding and satisfying the customer's purchase requirement, and in the event of problems occurring, should act to resolve these immediately. Conversely, the out-supplier has to try to keep the customer in the modified re-buy situation as long as possible to enable the customer to evaluate alternative supply solutions. Having some idea of the factors that led the customer to re-scrutinize alternatives can be helpful, particularly if the out-supplier can offer performance guarantees in relation to these factors.

Straight re-buy

As the term suggests, this type of situation involves purchases in which the customer sources products in order to satisfy a recurring need. Purchases are normally of minor importance and are typically associated with products used to facilitate the customer's operational activities. The company's familiarity with the supply market and required product specification means that little effort is invested in searching for new information or alternative sources of supply. Prior buying experience means that the customer will have clearly developed purchase criteria and might also draw from a narrow range of suppliers to satisfy supply needs. In straight re-buy situations a customer might adopt two different approaches, namely *casual* and *routine low priority*.

A *casual re-buy* can be used for a range of low-value and low-importance items that are purchased incidentally. Little effort is invested in the decision process, with the emphasis being to process the order rather than search for and evaluate information, consider alternative suppliers and reach a purchase decision using formal purchasing procedures.

A *routine, low-priority* re-buy might involve the sourcing of products that are of some importance to the buying organization, and compared to the casual purchase it represents more of a repetitive buying decision. Customers perceive little distinction between the products available from various sources, and for low-value items they are likely to continue using their usual supplier. However, to ensure that technical improvements are not overlooked, a customer may periodically consider alternative supply sources. The automatic and habitual buying procedure adopted lends itself to e-procurement.

Guidelines for the business marketer in straight re-buy situations

In-suppliers have to ensure that there is no reason for the customer to switch to alternative suppliers. Regular contact might be necessary to ensure that the customer has no complaints or to identify and quickly resolve any problem areas. A company could also look at ways of reducing the customer's buying effort, such as automated re-ordering. For the out-supplier, this type of buying situation is particularly challenging. Without any causes of dissatisfaction, the customer will be reluctant to switch. Offering a lower price will not necessarily tempt the buyer. One approach that the supplier could adopt to move the purchase to a re-buy situation is to use TCO and the ways in which it could reduce this cost for the customer company. See Table 2.2 for a summary of how the business marketer might handle these different buying situations.

Obviously, exchanges between suppliers and customers do not always centre around purchase decisions. In some situations, it is a question of parties collaborating to accommodate internal objectives and address external pressures during ongoing contracts or at the point of contract renewal. Take a look at B2B Snapshot 2.3 to see how Ribena works with UK blackcurrant producers on what might be considered a strategic purchase for the juice drink brand.

TABLE 2.2 Buying situations and marketer actions

Marketer actions	Buying situation		
	New task (strategic/ judgemental)	Modified re-buy (complex/simple)	Straight re-buy (routine/casual)
Out-supplier	• track search and communication behaviour • secure purchase and specification information • tailor solutions to specific supply needs	• develop customer insight • create communications messages to present value adding supply alternatives • deliver messages to match customer search behaviour	• examine total cost of ownership • target users, designers, engineers
In-supplier	• anticipate, monitor changing needs • offer consultation in specifying supply need	• try to move to straight re-buy • reduce perceived benefits of supply switch	• reinforce relationship • regular communication • automated ordering

B2B SNAPSHOT 2.3   BUSINESS BUYING: DOING THE RIGHT THING

The UK blackcurrant foundation consists of 45 growers, who between them use ten different fruit varieties to produce almost 15,000 tonnes of blackcurrants each year, 95 per cent of which goes to make the juice drink, Ribena. The relationship is equally important for the fruit farmer and Ribena alike. The world market price for blackcurrants is around £130 a tonne, whereas a UK blackcurrant grower supplying Ribena can achieve up to £600/tonne for their crop. Ribena opted not to source fruit on the world market for a number of reasons. Some of the fruit farmers have been working with the drinks producer for up to four generations, supplying blackcurrant varieties which are unique to the Ribena brand and are grown exclusively in the UK. Sourcing this juice ingredient on the world market might well allow reduced purchase prices, but if, as a consequence, UK fruit growers had to reduce or even abandon supplies to Ribena, then the drinks company's supplies could be at risk. Like many companies, Ribena pays increasing attention to the sourcing and provenance of its ingredients, yet purchasing on the world market would mean having no control over the conditions in which blackcurrants are grown. As it is, the drinks producer can trace the contents of each bottle back to individual farms. What is more, since 2004 Ribena has supported its fruit growers in collaboration with The Wildlife Trusts, so that blackcurrant farms can become wildlife friendly. The outcome of this collaboration was that by 2008, The Wildlife Trusts endorsed the drinks brand, with the trusts' logo being included on Ribena packaging.

Sources: Harvey, 2006; The WildLife Trusts (www.wildlifetrusts.org).

BUYING TEAMS

Few purchase decisions are made by individual managers. The decision-making process involves a range of managers that represent the buying team or *decision-making unit* (DMU). Members of the buying team assume six different roles, as follows:

- initiators, requesting the purchase item and therefore triggering the decision-making process;

- deciders, making the actual purchase decision; these members might not have formal authority but they have sufficient influence such that their decision carries considerable weight within the buying team; the fact that they do not have formal authority can make it difficult for the business marketer to identify such members of the team;

- buyers (purchasing managers), selecting suppliers and managing the buying process such that the necessary products are acquired; a buyer might not select the actual product to be purchased, but can greatly influence the parameters of that decision;

- influencers, contributing to the formulation of product and supply specifications, and recommending which vendors to consider or which products best satisfy the organization's needs; influencers will also contribute to the evaluation of offerings from potential suppliers;

- users, frequently initiating the purchase as well as actually using the product; they may be involved in the specification process prior to purchase and once the product has been supplied will evaluate its performance; and

- gatekeepers, controlling the type and flow of information in to and out of the company and members of the buying team. (Webster and Wind, 1972)

As Figure 2.2 illustrates, members of the DMU can be drawn from a wide variety of departments in the firm. Managers with different functional responsibilities may be involved in the buying process and decisions, and if you take a look at B2B Snapshot 2.4, you will see that this can be a challenge for the business buyer as they try to understand the requirements of different functional areas and to integrate these requirements into specifications which can be communicated to and negotiated with suppliers. A key point is the growing importance of collaboration and communication between functional areas so that an organization's supply needs are secured at minimum cost and enable it to realize its own objectives. Collaboration with other stakeholder groups such as product development, design or engineering has been a priority for purchasing managers for some time but such coordination is extending to other functional areas too. For example, when it comes to buying, efforts of managers with marketing responsibilities might normally be directed at supporting operational issues such as JIT systems, forecasting and inventory management, or alternatively securing external services such as market research, advertising or PR material independently of the purchasing function. Nevertheless, this is changing as purchasing professionals continue to target a firm's indirect costs, including marketing services (Bals et al., 2009; Marshall, 2012), and the continued shift towards demand-driven solutions requires closer internal alignment between an organization's marketing and purchasing teams to ensure delivery of these solutions to its own customers (Sheth et al., 2009).

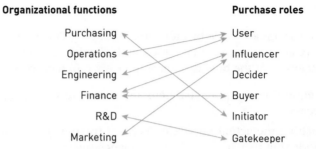

FIGURE 2.2 Decision-making unit (DMU) (buying centre)

To influence purchase decisions successfully the business marketer needs to know who the key members of the DMU are and what their specific concerns or requirements are in relation to the decision at hand. But as B2B Snapshot 2.4. suggests, the marketer's job might, on occasions, be more about helping the buying group reach a consensus, rather than formulating solutions to satisfy individual DMU member needs or reduce specific managers' perceived risk. If the decision involves new purchases or modified re-buys, the marketer has to have contact with members of the DMU at an early stage of the decision process. By doing this the supplier might be able to influence key decisions (such as product specification) that could subsequently determine supplier selection decisions.

Depending on the product to be bought and the buying situation, the DMU will be more or less formal and will draw from the expertise and authority of various functions and levels of responsibility within an organization. Business marketers can use these two factors in order to determine which managers across a range of departments might assume the different roles in the DMU and the type of information likely to be used to guide decisions. Trying to determine influential DMU members can be challenging for the business marketer. As well as assuming that those in senior management positions might exert considerable influence, the business marketer can try to identify employees who:

- work in boundary-spanning roles;
- have close involvement with the buying centre in terms of flow of activities;
- are heavily involved in communication across functional areas in the buying organization; and/or
- have direct links with senior management.

Understanding of the DMU has to be linked to the dynamic nature of the decision-making process and not just the product category and buying situation. We already know that buying is a dynamic process and that, depending on what is being purchased, it can take some time before a product finally satisfies the needs of the buying organization. This affects what happens inside the DMU in terms of composition and behaviour, such that the involvement of managers and their degree of influence in the DMU is unlikely to be continuous throughout the decision-making process. The dynamic nature of the decision-making process and buying team means that the business marketer has to determine:

- what happens to the structure of the DMU during different phases of the buying process;
- the effect that the change in structure will have on the communication and influence patterns inside the unit; and
- the information needs of DMU members at any given point in time. (Ghingold and Wilson, 1998)

B2B SNAPSHOT 2.4   ALL TOGETHER NOW

It is often the case that when it comes to group decisions, reaching an agreement that suits everyone is not easy – and business buying is no exception. We know that the more business critical a purchase is, the more senior executives and different functions will be involved, and with that comes a range of managerial interests and priorities. Research (Schmidt at al., 2015) suggests that agreeing on the solution which they want to source from supply markets is often the most difficult phase in buying, yet when customers finally do arrive at that stage, they will have already completed over one-third of the decision process and when they get round to contacting potential suppliers, they are more than halfway through! Clearly this is a missed opportunity for the business marketer to ease the customer's 'pain' in these early buying stages. Facilitating this process is more about the business marketer enabling the DMU to reach a decision rather than a sales rep promoting their own company's offering. Such facilitation involves helping the customer arrive at a common consensus about the best solution by creating a common language and shared perspective around the problem/solution amongst DMU members. For example when the health and safety products division at Kimberly-Clark Professional (KCP) supports airframe customers seeking maintenance solutions, it offers potential customers the services of its KCP experts who visit facilities and advise on how the customer's maintenance operations might be improved. In doing this, the KCP expert is tapping in to different stakeholder interests and hopefully helping a potential customer reach consensus on solution specification. At least then that company can progress to the supplier search stage and hopefully consider KCP as a possible provider.

Source: Adapted from Schmidt et al., 2015.

The effect of risk on buying teams

Few purchases are likely to be made by a single individual in an organization, and we have already noted growing inter-functional coordination of business buying, although the extent to which procurement is a 'team effort' will vary. In some cases, organizational policy might dictate that purchases must be handled by committees. This is frequently what happens in the public sector when procurement of particular products or those above a certain monetary value must be reviewed and approved by committees before the purchase can go ahead. In many instances, however, the use of buying teams is determined by the complexity and degree of risk attached to the purchase decision. Risk is an inherent feature of business markets, where managers have to deal with *uncertainty* and possible *negative consequences* (Mitchell, 1995) surrounding purchase decisions. The risk that managers may perceive in relation to purchase decisions takes a variety of forms. It could be linked to *financial* or *performance* issues. For example, managers in the buying organization will experience heightened levels of risk if the purchase involves a significant monetary sum or the organization stands to incur costs should the item bought fail to perform as promised. *Social* risk can become an issue if the approval of significant reference groups such as co-workers or immediate superiors is important to the purchasing manager.

Normally perceived risk will be heightened in new-task buying or more complex modified re-buy situations. As the level of risk increases:

- the buying centre composition changes, both in terms of the number of members and the authority of those members;
- the buying team actively searches for information and uses a wide range of sources, including personal contacts (possibly from other companies that have made similar purchases), to guide the decision process;
- members of the buying team invest effort in the process and consider each stage of it more deliberately; and/or
- suppliers with a proven track record tend to be preferred by the buying team.

BUSINESS BUYING AND THE INDIVIDUAL MANAGER

Personal factors

It should be clear from much of the discussion in this chapter that buying activities are performed and decisions are made by people, not the organizations that they represent. As human beings, we have different personalities and learned experiences and we are not necessarily wholly rational or objective in our decisions. The business marketer needs to understand what makes managers tick, to try to influence the behaviour of key players in the buying company.

As we have just discussed, risk can influence business buying and this is indeed an important influence on the various managers that contribute in some way to buying decisions. Experience goes some way to reducing the level of perceived risk in purchase decisions, and some managers who are risk tolerant are more able to deal with the uncertainty of some buying situations. Others, however, are inherently risk averse and will deal with this perceived uncertainty by sticking to known and trusted sources of supply, or by amassing vast quantities of information and involving numerous other people in the purchase decision. As well as being affected by perceived risk and the ability to handle this, an employee's behaviour in purchase situations is influenced by the rewards that they accrue from buying decisions. All employees are rewarded for the roles that they perform in organizations. Some of these rewards are intrinsic, such as feelings of satisfaction and friendship, and others are extrinsic, such as the bonuses and promotions given by organizations. Rewards are not of equal value to individuals, and the importance that a manager attaches to various intrinsic and extrinsic rewards will shape that manager's behaviour with regards to buying activities.

We know that employees involved in buying activities can represent different functions and levels of responsibility in the customer company. They will have varying educational backgrounds, qualifications and employment histories, and their contribution to the organization will differ. These factors will influence both the criteria that a manager holds as important when evaluating products and suppliers, and the mental processes that a manager uses to handle information related to this. By mental processes we mean the type of information that a manager looks for, selects and then recalls when assessing products and suppliers.

The purchasing professional

Many organizations will have a department that is responsible for overseeing the sourcing of the company's supply needs. From what we have discussed in this chapter it should be clear that the scope of the purchasing manager's responsibilities will vary and that organizational factors contribute significantly to this variation. Generally speaking, however, purchasing managers have to be familiar with a firm's specific needs and must be able to use negotiating techniques and pricing methods so that purchase costs can be minimized. They have to try to build good relationships with suppliers while ensuring that a firm gets the best value for its money.

Depending on the size of an organization, the purchasing department might have a senior buyer. Their job would be to oversee the work of individual buyers, direct all purchasing operations, negotiate large contracts and assume ultimate responsibility for the performance of the buying team. Where there are numerous buyers in a company they will typically specialize in dealing with certain product categories. By doing this the managers can get to know the supply market intimately. Whether the buyers are senior or junior managers, whether they work as part of a purchasing team or have sole responsibility for acquiring their organization's supply needs, there are generic tasks that they have to perform and skills that they need to enable them to do this.

Buyer tasks:

- consulting with colleagues in other functional areas;
- determining the necessary parts, materials, services and supplies;
- calculating supply capacity required;
- searching for suppliers and requesting quotations;
- negotiating contracts; and
- monitoring the performance of the organization's various suppliers.

Buyer skills:

- communication and collaboration with suppliers and colleagues;
- negotiating and bargaining;
- managing and supervising people;
- working under pressure;
- selection and use of purchasing metrics and analytics;
- database interrogation; and
- using experience and personal judgement.

As with many functional areas, buyer tasks and skills are increasingly shaped by digital technology, which we touch on below.

BUYING IN A DIGITAL WORLD

Securing supplies incurs significant cost to the buying company, in relation to not only the price paid for those supplies but also the time spent by employees and management in handling the buying process. This includes searching for and selecting potential suppliers, negotiating and agreeing contracts, and raising and processing orders, as well as overseeing the handling and paying for items received. Digital technology assists this process in two critical ways. First of all, as we noted earlier, it facilitates search and information exchange with organizations and individuals outside of the customer company independently of any formal *purchase process*. This means that managers are familiar with and might form views of supply markets, solutions and specific suppliers ahead of the buying process. Second, as part of a company's formal purchasing processes and buying activities, *electronic procurement* enables costs (and therefore reduced employee/management effort) to be greatly reduced by improving communication with external markets and coordination of activities in the buying organization itself, as well as linking specific supply chains with the company's internal systems. Electronic procurement typically consists of connections to electronic marketplaces, the operation of *reverse auctions*, catalogue management, order fulfilment and payment systems. We focus specifically on the first three (marketplaces, auctions and catalogues) and touch on how IT systems enable coordination of buying activities.

Communicating with external markets

Electronic marketplaces represent an important method of transacting, enabling companies to exchange information, do business and collaborate with each other. Buyers and sellers might want simply to find new exchange partners by conducting searches via a web portal, and use the portal in order to be networked with other companies in similar geographic areas or related industries so that the order process between the buyer and seller becomes more efficient.

Electronic marketplaces can be grouped according to their main stakeholders and operators. Many are run by *independent* third parties and can be accessed by buyers and sellers in a particular industry or region. Others operate as *industry consortiums*, in which a limited number of companies either combine their supply capabilities in order to deal with a large customer base and make the sales process more efficient, or combine their product requirements in order to deal with known suppliers and so improve the efficiency of the purchasing process.

Purchase-oriented electronic markets are a popular form of industry consortium in which large companies combine purchase processes and common product requirements, and build a business system to handle these. Electronic markets can be either horizontal or vertical. *Horizontal marketplaces* (such as www.alibaba.com) are used by buyers for items that do not contribute directly to the company's own products; rather they are used indirectly and would normally be classed as MRO items. Companies participate in *vertical marketplaces* in order to buy and sell items that contribute directly to a product chain, so for example, firms that supply and buy components for use in the electronics industry could use www.converge.com, which has a network of over 6,500 trading partners, including companies such as Apple, Cisco, Intel, IBM, Packard Bell and Philips. Such marketplaces typically offer a range of exchange facilities to participants, including auctions, reverse auctions, bulletin boards, exchange, catalogues, catalogues with online ordering, and commodity exchanges. Two of the principal forms of transactions that can be facilitated by electronic marketplaces are auctions and *catalogue purchasing*.

Auctions

Any auction is based on the common principle that it represents a form of exchange in which *competitive bidding* drives a sale or purchase. Auctions have long been a feature of business markets and have normally been used for the sourcing of commodity items by business customers. Auctions conducted via electronic marketplaces operate under the same principles. However, the fact that the bidding process operates in real time (even though buyers and sellers do not need to meet face to face), along with the fact that the auctions can be conducted on a global scale and can offer participants significant reductions in transaction costs, means that use of this market mechanism has become standard practice for most business buyers. The range of specialized auction sites through which buyers and sellers can transact is extensive, with online auctions operating across a wide variety of industries and product categories. Companies operating in the European food industry (as a processor, retailer or restaurant, for example) could participate in fish auctions via www.pefa.com. The consortium connects buyers to 12 different auctions in Denmark, Italy, the Netherlands and Sweden, and buyers can now download Pefa's app onto their tablet or smartphone in order to bid for fish landed at ports all around the world.

In reverse auctions a buying organization hosts the online auction and invites suppliers to bid on announced request for quotations (RFQ). In many ways the reverse auction is simply an electronic form of the competitive tendering process that has long been used to award contracts in numerous business buying situations, although the appeal for some managers is that the reverse auction can free up their time, allowing them to direct more of their effort at strategic issues such as outsourcing decisions, cost management, benchmarking and supplier development (Monzcka et al., 2015). Before bidding starts:

- The buyer must clearly articulate the product specification, quality requirements, delivery lead time, location and transportation needs, order quantity and service issues.
- Communication between the buyer and potential suppliers can be important to ensure that the rules attached to the reverse auction are clear.
- Potential suppliers have to go through a qualification process to ensure that they have the capability to meet the tender conditions should they be awarded the contract.

The buying organization might use an intermediary to manage the entire reverse auction process or it could use the facilities available in vertical marketplaces related to its own industry. For example, companies involved in the aerospace sector might handle reverse auctions via the service available on www.aeroxchange.com. Irrespective of whether a buying organization handles the process itself or delegates this to an intermediary, the fact that reverse auctions require high-value orders for the mechanism to work effectively (by offering suppliers the opportunity to win major contracts) means that purchasing professionals who are experts in the particular supply market and the auction process must control and be closely involved in this purchasing method. The high value of transactions typically conducted via reverse auctions means that they frequently form part of a company's strategic procurement activity. Many large multinational organizations have streamlined purchasing activities across disparate locations and have combined common supply needs across their businesses in order to get the best possible price and cost for items bought. For example, even though the pharmaceuticals giant GlaxoSmithKline has 800 buyers worldwide and an annual budget of $1 billion, using reverse auctions has helped the business realize cost savings on items ranging from hotel rooms to laboratory furniture. This form of trading offers opportunities and risks to both buyers and sellers (see Table 2.3 for a summary of these), but reverse auctions are clearly suited to standard, direct and indirect purchases (e.g. MRO, services etc.) where the principal purpose is to secure price reductions and suppliers can be managed via transactional relationships (Monzcka et al., 2015). However, as professional buyers become increasingly involved in the sourcing of professional services, then the effect of such purchasing tools and practices are beginning to cause a stir in sectors such as the advertising industry. Take a look at B2B Scenario 2.2 and think about how you might respond to Heinz's approach to selecting an ad agency.

B2B SCENARIO 2.2   PITCH-PERFECT?

'Pitching often feels like a blind date. You turn up in your glad rags, with your heart on your sleeve and your soul bared. You attempt to sell your wares for about two hours, with your most intelligent dialogue and wittiest retorts, often to a room of poker faces who promise to call in two weeks. Then you sit expectantly by the phone (they rarely call in two weeks) and if you're lucky, a relationship ensues' (Annie Price, Creative Director, JWT Melbourne, quoted by McDonald, 2015). Organizations do not design and implement communications campaigns in-house, but instead, source this work from specialists in the communications industry, working closely with agencies who have the creative and media expertise to deliver brand objectives. The selection process, out of which a client awards a contract, can be quite fraught for agencies, not least because of the short time scales and size of contracts frequently involved. However, most agencies would consider the pitching and awarding of contracts to be fair where the client's rules of play are clear and consistent from the outset (e.g. deliverables, timings and assessment criteria), and where the pitch process is transparent as well as collaborative, with all contending agencies being treated equally (Steve McArdle, Managing Director, BMF, quoted by McDonald 2015).

Following the merger of Kraft and Heinz (resulting in one of the world's largest food and beverage businesses), the company looked to develop pan-European communication strategies for its brands, and in doing so, to source separately the creative and production elements of agency work. In 2015, Heinz's pan-European team exchanged with various agencies, not only on the separation of creative and production work, but also on longer payment terms expected for future contracts. By the summer of 2015, Heinz's team reached the point of inviting agencies to pitch for the creative contract, and shortlisted three agencies: Bartle Bogle Hegarty (BBH), Leo Burnett and J. Walter Thompson (JWT). However, of these three, Leo Burnett and JWT declined to pitch, with industry sources suggesting that these agencies' decision was in part influenced by Heinz's plan to use e-reverse auction for payment terms (Smith, 2015). CHI & Partners and M&C Saatchi were subsequently added as replacements to pitch alongside BBH for the creative contract.

E-auction software is becoming more prevalent in the advertising world, with software providers such as Ariba and IBM Emptoris adapting their software to make it more suited for services (Bruell, 2012). While Heinz's approach might have ruffled feathers in the advertising world, the company argues that 'an e-auction is used as a mechanism to capture rate information. It is just one part of the process alongside service, creativity and other factors in our decision making. The commercial terms for the agency pitch are clear and if agencies were not comfortable with them they wouldn't be excited about pitching for such an iconic and much loved brand' (Nigel Dickie, European Director of Corporate and Government Affairs, Heinz, quoted by Magee (2015)). Interestingly, Heinz's incumbent agency, AMV BBDO, who had held the contract for seven years, withdrew from exchanges with Heinz before the company got to the shortlisting stage (Smith, 2015).

As one of the agencies shortlisted by Heinz, how would you respond to the requirement that payment terms be determined via e-auction?

Sources: Bruell, 2012; Magee, 2015; McDonald. 2015; Smith, 2015.

As Table 2.3 suggests, this form of trading offers opportunities and risks to both buyers and sellers. For the moment, we will move on from online auctions to discuss other forms of digital business buying. However, in Chapter 12 the theme of online auctions will be discussed further, from the point of view of business-to-business pricing decisions.

TABLE 2.3 Reasons for reverse auctions and the risks involved

Suppliers' reasons	Buyers' reasons
• new business	• reduced purchase price
• market penetration	• lower administrative costs
• cycle time reduction	• shorter contract cycle
• inventory management	• reduced inventory levels
Suppliers' risks	**Buyers' risks**
• low price focus threatens long-term relationships	• undermine relationship trust
• competitive bargaining tool for buyer	• reduced buyer commitment makes supplier less willing to make relationship investments
• offering unrealistic prices	• insufficient suppliers can cause non-competitive auction scenario

Source: adapted from Smeltzer and Carr, 2003: 487.

Catalogue purchasing

The catalogue idea is pretty straightforward – it involves an organization that is effectively acting as an intermediary, collating a wide range of items within a particular product category from a range of suppliers. The catalogue lists the items and provides detailed product specifications as well as current market prices. Buying organizations will normally use catalogue purchasing to handle a wide range of casual and routine re-buys of direct and indirect product/MRO items. For larger organizations that operate online purchasing systems, using electronic catalogues means that the companies can reduce the time (and therefore cost) needed to handle such purchasing and devolve responsibility for initiating the catalogue purchase to users of those items. The purchasing manager retains control of the range of products available from any one catalogue and negotiates the terms and conditions of supply. However, once these have been determined, the routine purchasing activities associated with sourcing catalogue items is transferred to employees. The employee can log on to the company's online procurement system and, depending on their job title and expenditure limits, will be able to browse certain supplier catalogues, view and compare items and prices from those catalogues that have already been negotiated by the purchasing manager, trigger an order, and track the fulfilment/receipt process. For smaller companies, purchasing might be limited to browsing and purchasing items from a range of catalogues available via horizontal or industry-specific electronic marketplaces.

Coordination of buying activities

The range of products bought, the different functional areas that have some purchasing authority, and the geographical dispersion of decision-makers present many large organizations with a major challenge in trying to operate a more efficient purchasing process, in which the business has a clear idea of product and volume requirements and the costs associated with satisfying those needs. In recent years there has been a growth in investments in electronic procurement systems to enable large organizations to coordinate and integrate purchasing across their full spectrum of product requirements. For example, the Latin American hotel operator Grupo Posadas uses Ariba (the procurement solutions business owned by SAP) to enable it to gain insight into spend and spend metrics, as well as to centrally control pricing and consolidate purchasing across the group's 117 hotels in Mexico, Brazil, Argentina and Chile. This has resulted in 18 per cent savings in categories sourced via Ariba's on-demand software, and Grupo Posadas has reduced its supply base from 8,000 down to 3,000 strategic suppliers (www.ariba.com).

Clearly, digital technology provides considerable scope for buying teams to improve the efficiency of their operations both internally and as part of a particular value chain. To enable companies to do this, many procurement teams are increasingly turning to software companies for integrated purchasing systems via B2B managed services or on-demand software (cloud computing).

CHAPTER SUMMARY

- Organizational buying is affected by a number of factors. The successful vendor understands these and tailors its marketing activities accordingly.
- Key areas that have attracted much attention are the buying process and the decision-making unit and how these vary depending on the purchase situation.

- The buygrid (new task, modified re-buy, straight re-buy) is a useful tool for classifying organizational buying decisions, although an important limitation of the buygrid is that it focuses only on the newness of the buying decision.

- The buying process and DMU, while clearly important, have to be placed in the broader context of the company's purchase orientation and overall business strategy. Being familiar with purchase orientation and business strategy allows the vendor to accurately meet the supply expectations of the buying organization.

- What should be clear from this chapter, and is further elaborated in the next, is that the supply expectations of the buying organization do not necessarily centre on product exchange. Rather, depending on the importance of the product and supplier to the company, the buying organization might also have certain relationship expectations of suppliers. This too must be taken into consideration by the vendor when formulating marketing strategies to influence the buying decisions of its customers.

QUESTIONS FOR DISCUSSION

1. How do the buying and procurement orientations differ? How will this affect the way in which an organizational customer might deal with suppliers?

2. How will total cost of ownership affect the way in which a business marketer prices its products?

3. Describe the decision-making process enacted by organizational customers, identifying how and why this process might vary.

4. How has digital technology facilitated the tasks of organizational buying and what are the consequences of this for the B2B marketer?

CASE STUDY 2.1 HEALTHY BUSINESS!

Healthcare systems around the world vary in terms of the mix of public sector and commercial operators and the way in which medical care is structured. This structure and mix will continue to evolve as service providers rethink their systems to achieve cost improvements, implement leaner operational processes and use quality of medical care and patient experience as their point of differentiation. The expectation is that resource intensive, high-capital facilities such as large hospitals will function as centres of excellence concentrated in geographic locations, supported by a network of smaller hospital and clinic facilities operating a mixture of specialist, primary care and ancillary services (KPMG, 2013). Speciality care offers advanced treatment of conditions such as cancer or heart disease; primary care is more general (covering a broad range of physical, psychological and social conditions); while ancillary treatment includes services such as outpatient surgery, diagnostic imaging and physiotherapy.

Whatever the scale and nature of medical provision within a healthcare system, organizations whose central purpose is to provide medical treatment direct their attention at exactly that, i.e. their core expertise, and (as with other sectors)

(Continued)

(Continued)

outsource those activities to which they are unable to add value. In the healthcare sector, outsourced activities can be split into clinical and non-clinical services and may include, for example:

- clinical services: radiology, pathology, dialysis, dentistry, physiotherapy and rehabilitation, pharmacy;
- non-clinical services: cleaning, laundry, catering, patient transport, car-parking, on-site retailing, facilities management, information and communications systems, purchasing. (Guimarães and de Carvalho, 2010)

The scope and value of contracts that a medical facility awards to a specific supplier and the breadth of services that providers might seek to supply to the healthcare sector can be quite varied. So for example, in the UK, healthcare trusts that are part of the NHS might use Medirest (www.medirest.co.uk), a subsidiary of the Compass Group, for onsite retail and catering as well as support services such as logistics, security and cleaning. In providing cleaning services, Medirest needs to comply with NHS contract and performance requirements. This is vital given that patient experience is strongly influenced by the general aspect of a medical facility and that cleanliness is a critical element of that experience and most importantly patient wellbeing. For cleaning purposes, areas within medical facilities are typically grouped according to risk to healthcare users:

- very high: operating theatres, critical care areas, accident and emergency departments;
- high: general wards, sterile supplies, public thoroughfares and toilets;
- significant: pathology, outpatient departments, laboratories, mortuaries;
- low: administrative areas, non-sterile supply areas. (NHS, 2009)

Cleaning contracts specify the levels of cleanliness for these areas, frequency of cleaning and auditing of this, as well as the timeframe within which non-compliance is expected to be rectified. Online systems enable Medirest's performance to be monitored by area in a specific facility, within an entire site, and it could also be assimilated centrally to review Medirest service provision across multiple sites (NHS, 2009).

Meanwhile, companies such as Johnson Controls (www.johnsoncontrols.com) use their expertise in the management of physical buildings and related technologies to target the healthcare sector in North America. The company is present in over 3,500 healthcare facilities and manages more than 12,000 beds – this last figure is important given that building occupancy costs make up more than 6 per cent of annual operating expenses for the average large hospital. Johnson Controls combines facilities management, real estate services, project management and energy efficiency solutions to help hospitals reduce costs by up to 25 per cent. To learn how Johnson Controls has satisfied one American hospital, visit www.johnsoncontrols.com and view the video endorsement of the company by Baptist Memorial Healthcare.

While the Compass Group and Johnson Controls focus on specific non-clinical services, companies such as Sodexo (www.sodexo.com) and Serco (www.serco.com) supply a wider range of integrated solutions to medical centres. For example, Sodexo operates as solutions provider to the specialist medical centre, the German Heart Institute of

Berlin. On a bigger and more complex scale, in 2011 the Department of Health in Western Australia awarded the contract for non-clinical facilities management and support services at the newly commissioned Fiona Stanley Hospital to Serco. The contract consists of 28 different services, including engineering and building maintenance, security, ground maintenance, linen, cleaning, catering, waste services, managed equipment services, transport, procurement, sterilization, reception and clerical services. The Department of Health followed an extensive specification development and procurement process before awarding the contract to Serco, including key performance indicators for each of the services to be supplied. The contract is worth up to $4.3 billion (over 20 years) and is initially for ten years with the option of it being extended for two further five-year periods if the Department of Health in Western Australia decides that Serco is doing a good job. The range of services that Serco is contracted to deliver means that it has to rely quite considerably on subcontractors, of which critical supply partners are:

- BT: deployment of local area network, systems integration services, unified communications, mobility and conferencing technologies;
- Siemens: procurement, installation, maintenance and replacement of medical diagnostic and treatment equipment.

Delivery of the various outsourced services presents Serco with a complex operation to set up and oversee, while for the Department of Health in Western Australia, awarding the contract to a single outsource supplier might be risky, but it means that the new hospital should be able to concentrate on its core business, medical treatment. This might have been the plan, but since its opening in 2014, reportedly waning public confidence in the functioning of the new hospital and an independent review published in 2015 suggests problems with the support services provided by Serco (Australian Commission on Safety and Quality in Health Care, 2015).

CASE STUDY QUESTIONS

1 Choose one of the service examples featured in this case study and:
   - describe what you think should be the decision-making process;
   - outline what evaluation criteria you think might be used for initial selection and ongoing supplier performance;
   - explain how you would classify the buying situation;
   - specify what functional areas and levels of seniority are likely to contribute to the decision process.

2 For your chosen service, assume that you are part of a buying team who are trying to identify a new supplier:
   - visit the website of one of the featured companies who supply the service that your team want to procure;
   - evaluate the usefulness of the company website in providing you with information as part of your initial exploratory search.

Sources: Australian Commission on Safety and Quality in Health Care, 2015; Guimarães and de Carvalho, 2010; KPMG, 2013; NHS, 2009; www.btplc.com; www.johnsoncontrols.com; www. siemens.com.

FURTHER READING

Giunipero, L.C., Hooker, R.E. and Denslow, D. (2012) 'Purchasing and supply management sustainability: drivers and barriers', *Journal of Purchasing and Supply Management*, 18 (4): 258–69.

This article analyses sustainability literature and data from interviews with senior purchasing and supply management executives. The authors conclude that top management initiatives and government legislation drive purchasing and supply management sustainability efforts, while investment costs and economic uncertainty hinder initiatives. The results are consistent with common drivers and barriers identified in previous decades, and might partially explain why environmental purchasing and supply management is not yet extensively developed (in theory and practice). For further insight into this, take a look at other articles that feature in this special issue of the journal.

Makkonen, H., Olkkonen, R. and Halinen, A. (2012) 'Organizational buying as muddling through: a practice-theory approach', *Journal of Business Research*, 65 (6): 773–80.

In this chapter we explained buying as if it were a rational, planned, linear process. Such a representation does not necessarily reflect management activity and human behaviour. This article draws on the concepts of muddling through and disjointed incrementalism to describe one specific buying process. While some of the generic issues associated with buying decisions are evident, the article gives a good insight into what it might be like to live through or experience a complex purchase process.

Wagner, S.M. and Eggert, A. (2016) 'Co-management of purchasing and marketing: why, when and how?' *Industrial Marketing Management*, 52: 27–36.

This paper is a nice follow-up to the arguments made by Sheth et al. (2009) on the integration of these two functions but in doing so, the authors prefer to talk about co-management. The paper offers different approaches to jointly managing these two functions according to resource dependency. As a conceptual piece of work, you might try to think of markets and specific companies in which their alternative co-management approaches might work (or not!).

3

INTER-FIRM RELATIONSHIPS AND NETWORKS

LEARNING OUTCOMES

After reading this chapter you will:

- appreciate that the traditional approach to business marketing based solely upon influencing organizational buying behaviour naively assumes that the marketer is always active while the customer is relatively passive;
- recognize that value creation in business-to-business exchange comes from a clear understanding of the relationship between buyer and seller;
- know what is meant by the relationship concept and what variables affect business-to-business relationships;
- appreciate the range of tasks involved in continually managing a relationship; and
- recognize the impact that the network concept has upon business-to-business marketing and the strategic imperative of network thinking.

INTRODUCTION

Arguably, the greatest change in the marketing discipline in the last 40 years has been the renewed emphasis upon the relationship between marketer and customer as the basis of understanding and sustaining value creation in exchange, something that the *marketing mix approach* under-emphasized. This realignment originated in the business-to-business context; see, for example, the challenges to the prevailing orthodoxy evident in the work of the *IMP Group* of researchers (Ford, 1990, 1997, 2002; Håkansson, 1982; Turnbull and Valla, 1986). However, the refocusing has also extended to the consumer context, driven most notably by the literature on consumer services (Gummesson, 1987), and has been hailed as a paradigm shift (Grönroos, 1997) in marketing theory and practice. This chapter recognizes the central role that relationships play in business markets and discusses how marketing theory and practice have developed in the light of this recognition.

The chapter commences with a reappraisal of the earlier coverage of organizational buying behaviour, identifying the deficiencies both of a marketing approach based solely upon an analysis of buying centres and of attempts by the marketer to influence the buying behaviour of the customer. It then proceeds to re-examine the basis for business marketing, arguing that successful business-to-business marketing comes from an understanding of value-creating exchange. In exploring exchange, a selection of key theoretical perspectives is introduced, along with the key variables that they use, to indicate the contribution they make to our understanding of relationships. Business marketing means constantly appraising relationships in terms of these variables and making changes within relationships cognizant of the effects upon the variables and the relationship at large. These are enduring tasks for the business marketer.

Though the relationship between marketer and customer assumes the greatest importance in the coverage, the chapter goes further than the level of the relationship. It extends the relationship concept to incorporate the network of relationships that surround any single relationship; the strategic understanding of a relationship comes from an understanding of the network within which it is embedded and which affects it directly or indirectly. While managerial action typically takes place at the level of a relationship, strategic thinking also takes place at the network level so that it can be enacted at the level of individual relationships.

INADEQUACIES OF TRADITIONAL APPROACHES TO BUSINESS MARKETING

Traditional approaches to business-to-business marketing, often subsumed under the *4Ps* – product, price, promotion and place – or marketing mix labels, tend to make several assumptions:

- The marketer and customer operate separately and at odds with each other. Marketers market and customers purchase, and as a consequence each has essentially conflicting interests in exchange. Ideally, the marketer wants to obtain the best price possible for the goods, which are preferably standard offerings. Ideally, the purchaser wants to pay the lowest price possible for goods/services that require no further customization. These opposing positions mean that each purchase decision and the associated transaction assume great importance in the dealings between the two.

- The marketer is active while the customer is relatively passive. The traditional approach tends to assume that the marketer is the active party in a business-to-business exchange, bringing offerings to the attention of customers. In this respect, the customers are relatively passive recipients of the offerings created by the active marketer.

- The marketing process typically involves the study of the buying behaviour of business customers, as detailed in Chapter 2, followed by attempts by the marketer to influence that behaviour in their own favour. The marketer establishes the customer need via traditional research activities. It is the marketer who creates an offering that meets this need, and then tries to impact the customer's decision-making to ensure that the evoked set of offerings from which the customer chooses will have this offering at the head of the list.

The traditional marketing approach has been criticized more generally for being overly prescriptive, with the implementation of marketing in practice often lacking a clear conceptual basis because the concept itself has become more of an ideology than a well-supported, clearly elucidated set of principles that benefit the firm (Brownlie and Saren, 1992). However, in the business-to-business context the traditional approach to marketing embodied in the 4Ps has been criticized more specifically for lacking relevance to the way in which business markets actually work (Arndt, 1979; Ford, 1990; Håkansson, 1982). While there is no doubt that success in any market comes from a strong understanding of customers and their needs, in business markets customers are often as active as suppliers, with the process involving substantial *interaction* between the two over time rather than a cool detachment.

Furthermore, there is often a clear understanding that the economic wellbeing of both parties depends substantially upon the relationship. Ford et al. (2002) report that of the top 17 suppliers to vehicle manufacturers, accounting for about 33 per cent of their purchase costs, only two have been supplying for less than five years, while ten have been supplying for more than 15 years. As these figures would indicate, the parties often work together, customers are very active in the exchange, and the process of determining and fulfilling the need is an interactive one.

To all intents and purposes, the neo-classical economic notion of markets involving discontinuous transactions between large numbers of buyers and sellers operating relatively anonymously with lots of choice, and on the basis of full information upon which to make such choices, does not hold. Instead, the situation comes closer to what Arndt (1979) has called 'domesticated markets', where control is established over the exchange by parties cooperating through negotiated ways of working so that choice is foregone, in the expectation that greater value will accrue to the parties through non-market exchange.

The relationships between retailer Marks & Spencer (M&S) and its suppliers in the UK are just one clear example for questioning the assumptions that underlie the traditional approach – see B2B Snapshot 3.1.

B2B SNAPSHOT 3.1 MARKS & SPENCER SUPPLY RELATIONSHIPS: A MANUFACTURER WITHOUT FACTORIES

As a retailer, M&S knows that its ability to add value for its customers comes primarily from the nature of the offerings it can secure from its suppliers, many of whom either produce only for M&S or produce offerings that are unique to M&S. On the food side, it has relationships with suppliers such as Bowyers, a division of Northern Foods, for the supply of prepared cold foods, where it accounts for a large proportion of Bowyers' turnover. On the garment side, there are businesses in the UK that have grown over the last 30 years on the strength of their relationship with M&S. M&S was a major customer of companies such as William Baird for men and women's clothing, Courtaulds for a variety of clothing (leisurewear, swimwear, fitness clothing, knitwear, lingerie and underwear), bed linen and soft furnishings, and Coats Viyella for hosiery. It has even been the sole customer for some companies, including Desmond & Sons for items such as men's and women's trousers, pyjamas and leisurewear.

(Continued)

(Continued)

M&S itself plays a substantial role in the exchange value created with its suppliers. As a customer, it is very active indeed. For instance, in its relationship with Bowyers, its food technologists work with Bowyers to come up with recipes specifically for M&S. It plays equally active roles in the relationships it has with its garment manufacturers. Its close relationship with suppliers such as Courtaulds and Coats Viyella over the years had led to innovations such as the non-iron shirt and machine-washable silk sweaters (Christopher and Peck, 2001). The strong relationship with Coats Viyella meant it could also use electronic data interchange (EDI) technology to pioneer the electronic return of daily garment sale numbers from M&S stores, enabling its supplier to dye semi-finished goods overnight to enable next-day replenishment, thus ensuring that availability at M&S was second to none.

Over time the strong role M&S has played in its relationships with suppliers, and the dedicated production that they have made available, spawned the nickname, 'the manufacturer without factories'. Of late, of course, with the increasing moves to off-shore sourcing, some of its major suppliers have seen their business with M&S contract or disappear completely. However, those suppliers that remain with M&S continue to work very closely with the company, day in, day out.

MATCHING THE UNCERTAINTIES AND ABILITIES OF BOTH PARTIES

Success in business markets comes from the recognition that the customer and marketer together create value in exchange by each providing solutions to the other's problems. Drawing in part on organizational buying behaviour literature, Håkansson et al. (1976) proposed that a business buyer faces particular kinds of uncertainties either concerning the basis of the need itself, or the nature of changes in the marketplace, or the transaction associated with meeting the need, or each of these. Successful business marketing involves cultivating the ability to reduce these uncertainties.

Customers face uncertainties

Need uncertainty relates to the difficulties of knowing exactly what or how much to buy. For example, a customer just may not know how much material is required, perhaps because the level of demand from its own customers is highly uncertain. Alternatively, the customer may not be certain as to which materials technology will be most demanded by customers or integrate best with its own manufacturing processes. The lack of knowledge upon which to make a decision is fundamental here, and thus need uncertainty is typically higher for new-buy tasks. It is also typically higher when the need itself is more important, so the need uncertainty of a critical component will be higher, as will equipment central to the production of the product.

Market uncertainty arises from the degree of choice a buyer perceives in the supply base and the difficulty in knowing which supply choices to make. The degree of difficulty is a function of how different the alternative suppliers are from each other and how dynamic those differences are. Increased knowledge is the route to reducing the difficulty but it comes at a cost: increased time and effort in evaluating the different suppliers before purchase commitments are made. Worse perhaps, when a buyer has made a commitment in a relationship with a supplier, it comes with an opportunity cost since there is always the prospect that a better relationship could be had with another supplier, which is precluded by the commitment to the current relationship.

Transaction uncertainty refers to the degree of exposure that the buyer is faced with once a transaction has been agreed. The integrity of a product may be affected in transit, damaging it irreparably or leading to additional delays in fixing the damage, or delivery may be late. For example, in high street fashions, where the sales window for a season may only be four to six weeks, a delivery delay of two or three days is significant; the retailer literally cannot sell what is not in the store. Delay problems are particularly significant when coordinated production schedules are involved, such as with JIT systems, so transaction uncertainty would be naturally higher here. The extent of transaction uncertainty is also related to how well the buyer and seller know and communicate with each other. If they and their systems communicate well then the degree of uncertainty is reduced. However, different language, *culture* and technological infrastructure raise the uncertainty. Standardization of the transaction process should reduce the scope for transaction uncertainty.

Supplier abilities can reduce customer uncertainties

The *problem-solving abilities* of a supplier in meeting the customer need and/or their ability to transfer the solution create the basis for a successful match as far as the customer is concerned. If a supplier can demonstrate a superior knowledge of the need then it is in the best position it can be. However, this requires a clear customer orientation and a strong recognition that reduced need uncertainty comes from a strong focus on solving the customer's problems, rather than merely a focus on what the supplier's products can do. Further, if a supplier can demonstrate convincingly that it can reduce the customer's market uncertainty then again it is in the best position it can be. This might actually involve recognizing the difficult choice that the supplier faces and attempting to reduce the extent of the customer's exposure. This could be achieved, for example, by limiting contract lengths, or by the use of pilot projects or trials. Not only do arrangements like this limit how exposed the buyer is in the first place, they give the supplier the opportunity to demonstrate its *transfer abilities*, reducing transaction uncertainty at the same time.

Customer abilities can reduce supplier uncertainties

As we have indicated, the primary task for the business marketer is to ascertain the nature and extent of the customer's uncertainties and their own abilities to provide solutions to those uncertainties. While this is already a wider activity than under-standing and influencing organizational buying behaviour, there is another dimension to this task that is truly relationship-based. The happy situation for the customer of having their uncertainties reduced does not necessarily reduce uncertainties for the supplier. Ford et al. (1998) indicate that the specific uncertainties faced by suppliers revolve around the capacity that they must plan for (*capacity uncertainty*) and the sorts of application that the market will demand (*application uncertainty*). In addition, suppliers are subject to *transaction uncertainty* in the same way as buyers. As with the customer, the supplier may be subject to one or more uncertainties, to differing degrees, through time. The relative needs and uncertainties of buyers and sellers are presented in Figure 3.1.

What a customer can bring to resolve the uncertainties faced by the supplier are its demand abilities or transfer skills. Historically in the UK, M&S has demonstrated strong ability to understand the clothing preferences of British women – an important *demand ability* and a substantial strength in its relationships with its suppliers. The capacity and application uncertainties of their suppliers diminished with the strong year-on-year stability of M&S demand ability. However, many of the problems M&S faced at the turn of the century on the UK high street stem from its reduced demand ability. In the competitive womenswear market, it has struggled to demonstrate that it has this differential ability at a time when other stores, most notably Next and international brands such as H&M, Zara and Gap, are showing stronger ability in this respect and with equivalent transfer abilities.

The basic tasks then for the business marketer (in conjunction with the business purchaser) are to establish the respective uncertainties and abilities as a prelude to determining the likelihood of the success of their respective value-creating activities. This undoubtedly incorporates an understanding of the organizational buying behaviour of the customer, but extends beyond that since it means that the business marketer must be as interested in finding customers that reduce its uncertainties as the customers will be in finding suppliers who reduce their uncertainties.

The need to match uncertainties and abilities in order to achieve business marketing success provides a clear indication that relationships matter (Ford et al., 1998). The relationship constitutes the context within which value-creating activities take place, and thus the next level of management activities for both parties involves the relationship. Consequently, anyone interested in business marketing needs to have a clear understanding of relationships – in order to understand individual customer relationships and what drives them, as well as to understand clearly how to manage such relationships successfully. Knowing what relationships to focus upon; what is possible in such relationships; the resource requirements for

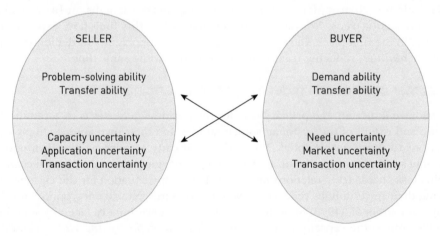

FIGURE 3.1 Matching uncertainties and abilities (from Ford et al., 1998: 18)

With permission from Wiley.

initiating changes in any relationship, and the implications of such changes upon the relationship; the wider portfolio of customer relationships, and beyond – these are just the sort of concerns that a business marketer must have. It is to the bases of relationships that our attention is now turned.

RELATIONSHIP THEORIES AND VARIABLES

Relationships between organizations are complex phenomena. Regardless of the size of the organizations, and the number of people involved, there is a range of variables that can characterize a relationship. A wide variety of variables have been used to study relationships and there is no consensus on the set that is necessary and sufficient to explain a relationship. Despite the lack of consensus, however, relationship-based theories provide us with a set of perspectives that can be drawn upon when trying to understand any relationship, each of which tends to emphasize different relationship aspects.

Some of these perspectives more readily explain discrete exchange transactions while others extend the focus across a series of individual transactions to the relationship more broadly. Some emphasize the political and economic dimensions of relationships, while others focus more upon the social. Table 3.1 lists various perspectives. All have a contribution to make to our understanding of relationships overall. That does not mean that all of them provide prescriptive advice for all situations that a firm faces. Rather, depending upon the particular issues in a relationship at particular times, it is possible to draw lessons from whichever perspective has most to offer on that subject.

Exchange risk and its management

All forms of commercial activity involve risk. It is a fact of life. Previously in this chapter we talked about the uncertainties faced by firms. These are sources of risk, and organizations spend much time trying to eradicate uncertainty or reduce their exposure to it. Perception of risk is a function of the possible negative outcomes and the probability of those outcomes arising. There are many sources of risk.

TABLE 3.1 Key relationship variables

Principal variable(s)	Level of emphasis	Major theoretical source	Theory type(s)	Typical reference sources
Risk and its management	Individual transactions; Agent	Principal–Agent	Political–economic	Arrow, 1985; Bergen et al., 1992
Distribution of transaction costs	Individual transactions	Transaction cost economics	Economic	Williamson, 1979
Dependence; power and its exercise; switching costs	Transactions or Relationship	Resource dependence	Political	Pfeffer and Salancik, 1978
Social embeddedness; trust and commitment	Relationship	Social exchange	Social	Granovetter, 1985
Interaction processes	Individual exchanges and relationship	Interaction	Social/ interactional	IMP Group (Ford, 1990, 1997, 2002; Håkansson, 1982)

For a buying company they might include: late delivery, poor quality, inadequate level of service, unsatisfactory product performance, price increases since order placement, or adverse reaction from one's own management.

In the exchange between two organizations, uncertainties for one party arise from having to rely upon the other to undertake its part in the exchange in a way that delivers the value the first party considers is fair in the exchange. To use a simple example: when a supplier acts to make available the goods that have been negotiated with a customer, it is subject to risk until the goods have been paid for and the money safely transferred. Should a customer default before then, despite the recourse to law, the supplier's business is affected negatively. Similarly, a customer that has negotiated to receive goods of a particular quality, at a particular time, in a particular quantity and at a negotiated price is at risk of any one of these failing to be as expected.

Of course, the parties in relationship exchange may not necessarily react in the same way to the same level of uncertainty because they may have differing attitudes to risk. Indeed, a basic assumption of principal–agent theory is that there is such a difference and that the parties have different goals in the exchange. This assumption stems from the concern with establishing the contractual basis in agency transactions. The perennial difficulty for a company (principal) that is forced to retain an agent to work on its behalf (for instance, in a foreign market) is that there are unknowns and unknowables. These hidden elements are: *hidden characteristics* of the agent, such as their actual abilities; *hidden actions*, such as the way in which they undertake the tasks on the principal's behalf; and *hidden intentions*, such as whether they really have the principal's interests at heart. These constitute risks that have to be managed. Principal–agent theory argues that the *contract* is the basis for the management of the exchange risk because it is through the contract that risk is distributed between the parties. In this respect, it has much to offer the business marketer.

The extent to which the contract is more or less formally stated will depend upon the parties' attitude to risk within the relationship and their propensity to cooperate. A weakly stated contract and a laissez-faire approach to its operation and enforcement may be as much as is required in some relationships. This approach may be more useful in such relationships where perhaps both parties have a similar attitude to risk, where there is substantial uncertainty and where both parties know that they need to work flexibly, sharing information fully, in order to achieve objectives. The relationship itself brings obligations to the parties (Sako, 1992) without the need for a strongly worded contract. Achieving the objectives in this context is not helped by an overly fastidious attention to the details of the contract, and the parties may have sufficient trust that the counterpart will not behave in a way that is obviously self-seeking.

In some relationships it may even be true that the contract is little more than a gentlemen's agreement. In other relationships, however, where there is uncertainty and inadequate information, or power asymmetry, or dissimilar attitudes to risk, then more formally stated contracts that are followed to the letter may be the order of the day. The case of the relationship between M&S and William Baird in the UK paints a salutary lesson in relationship contracts. William Baird took M&S to court in 2000 claiming damages over the latter's decision to stop buying from it after 30 years, in contravention of what it saw as an implied contract. The High Court in the UK ruled that M&S was not liable for damages because the fact that M&S had singularly refrained from introducing a formal contract with William Baird with the express purpose of agreeing future dealing indicated that it had no such intention. This (lack of) action itself indicated that there was no agreement between the two as to the relationship. Thus M&S had broken no contract since what had gone before signified no agreement.

Where greater formality is sought in a relationship then several questions need to be borne in mind when it comes to drafting a contract:

- Can performance as stipulated in the contract be stated more or less behaviourally, as a set of specific activities with descriptions of how they must be undertaken, or does performance equate to specific outcomes of the activities? Here the distinction is between the 'what', i.e. the purpose of the contract, and the 'how', i.e. the way in which the 'what' should be produced. In some exchange situations it is clear what the outcome should be. A physical product such as a component part has clear properties that enable contractual integrity to be established if the component performs to the properties promised in the exchange. In exchanges where the offering is much less tangible, such as in specialist advice or design services, and the outcome itself is not wholly prescribed, there may need to be much greater reliance on behaviour-based contract forms to ensure that contractual integrity is achieved.

- Who controls the contract and thus has greater potential to influence the terms? Essentially, the party with the greater relative power is in the strongest position to specify terms and enforce them. Alongside this question is the related issue of the incentives for the weaker parties to engage in the contract. If the contract is the means by which risk is distributed then attempts to pass greater risk to the weaker party may find that party unwilling to enter an exchange where it feels disadvantaged. Where it does enter the exchange the weaker party is unlikely ever to step outside the confines of the contract; it is more likely to work to the letter of the contract. B2B Scenario 3.1 illustrates the dilemma faced by the weaker party in an exchange characterized by high degrees of power asymmetry. As the scenario indicates, the outcomes are not predetermined or automatic. Nonetheless, dealing with such situations does require a response.

- Even when the basis for the contract is established and the control and engagement issues are dealt with, there are the operational elements to be considered. The nature of the standard operating procedures within the contract may also need to be established. In more formal contracts there needs to be clarity about what is expected from each party, what the specific outcomes are, the relative roles in the contract, and what constitutes acceptable behaviour by the parties. If necessary, there will need to be specific coverage of the procedures for dispute resolution when and if it arises.

Principal–agent theory tends to place the focus upon the contract and the demands of the current transaction. The issues mentioned above tend to be more salient with greater uncertainty and inadequate information. The theory has less to tell us when market forces have a greater role in affecting relationships. When there is great market choice then typically there is less uncertainty and more information so that price-based mechanisms deal with the risk.

Allocating exchange costs

All transactions incur costs. Bruhn (2003) points to costs arising from initiating, handling, controlling, modifying and terminating contracts, as well as opportunity costs. Initiation costs incorporate searching, information access and evaluation as well as the efforts in actually reaching a decision, such as negotiation activities. Control costs include monitoring activities to ensure the counterpart is keeping its part of the bargain, and extend to the actions required to enforce the bargain in order to remedy any perceived inequity. The levels of these transaction costs are directly linked to the nature of market conditions. In perfect economic market conditions, where everyone has equal access to all information needed for a transaction and where the costs for managing the transaction are the same for all, the mechanism for ensuring the most economically efficient transaction is the open market itself. Here price-based competition will ensure efficient transactions. Of course, when markets are not perfect there is unequal access to information, and the costs of managing a transaction are not the same for all possible exchange partners. According to transaction cost theory, the task for companies is to find an exchange partner and a way of working with that partner that creates the most economically efficient transaction possible. That is, the imperative is to establish the sources and nature of transaction costs and to minimize them.

The following three factors affect transaction costs:

1. *Uncertainty* concerns the completeness of information. The level of uncertainty can be affected by many factors and extends from general market structure knowledge right down to the specific details of the transaction and what it involves. Where there are unknowns the level of uncertainty is inevitably greater.

2. Asset *specificity* is the relative amount of assets or resources that need to be committed *specifically* to the transaction. There is a range of asset types, including: site assets, brought about by co-location or geographical consolidation; physical assets, such as special tools or equipment required in the transaction; human assets, where unique skills arise as a consequence of the transaction; and other dedicated assets, where particular investments are made at the behest of a particular exchange partner. For example, a manufacturer may need to invest in tooling for the production of designs for a specific customer. Equally, a customer may have to change its own production processes in order to use the inputs from a specific supplier most efficiently. Both of these constitute transaction-specific investments.

3. The *frequency* of the transaction has implications for costs because the more often it happens the greater the transaction costs.

As the level of these three factors rises, so transaction costs rise (Williamson, 1979). The issue becomes what structure should be adopted by the firm to manage the transaction costs. As transaction costs rise the simple market solution becomes less efficient, and relationships – so-called 'bilateral forms of governance', incorporating cooperation between the exchange parties over the long term – become appropriate. Long-term cooperation should reduce uncertainty levels. Although levels of asset specificity may rise, this will be considered less risky when doing business with a trusted partner.

It is useful to think about transaction costs in the management of business relationships. They help to explain the diversity of relationships that exist, since the combination of different levels of the three factors above leads to a multitude of unique relationships. Transaction cost analysis helps us to understand how relationships change and develop in response to changing levels of uncertainty, asset specificity and transaction frequency. Firms need to give explicit attention to the level of asset specificity in business relationships.

Dealing with relative power dependence

Dependence is inevitable as a consequence of exchange. Requiring access to the resources held by others creates dependence. Of course, there is dependence on both sides of an exchange: buyers are dependent upon suppliers for the goods they provide, while the suppliers are dependent upon the economic value that comes from supplying customers. The issue is the relative extent of dependence since more often than not levels of dependence are asymmetrical. A customer may be relatively more dependent upon a supplier of a critical or scarce resource because the customer's value-adding activities require this *specific* resource or because there are few other suppliers. This puts the supplier in a position of strength with respect to the customer. Of course, it can happen the other way round and it can change over time. Despite having very strong brand positions that often confer substantial political clout in their dealings with retailers, even big brand owners sometimes have to give way to the demands of very important retail customers, particularly in a recession. So, when Wal-Mart, which has done well through the 2008–10 recession, apparently threatens delisting of products from its stores, such as Arm & Hammer Liquid Laundry Detergent (no. 2 in the market next to Purex, owned by Henkel) – unless the brand owners make more funds available for promotion in its stores and provide money in support for 'co-branded' adverts commissioned by Wal-Mart – it is unsurprising that the political reality dictates that the brand owners do just that (WARC, 2006).

From the point of view of either party to an exchange there are several major tasks that must be undertaken:

- Establish the relative levels of dependence and thus the degree of autonomy of the firm.
- Understand the behavioural consequences of that interdependence, including the potential for the exercise of power. For the stronger party this typically concerns the extent to which it needs to exert its power over the weaker party. If the weaker party is compliant then the stronger party may feel no need to exert explicit dominance. For the weaker party the major concern will be the extent to which the stronger party will seek to dominate the exchange and enforce its will.
- Consider the consequences of actions that may change the levels of relative dependence. This typically revolves around switching costs – the costs incurred by leaving the relationship and establishing a relationship with a new partner.

In respect of these tasks, relationship parties don't automatically need to restrict thinking to the narrow confines of the relationship itself. Relationships exist within an economic and social context that partially determines the relative power dependence (rather than just the characteristics of the parties themselves). Consequently, it's wholly understandable over the last four years in the UK that dairy farmers would seek to change the nature of the power dependence that exists in the relationships they have with multiple retailers and dairy processors. At a time when milk prices internationally have been falling, margins at the farm gate have become so low as to drive many dairy farmers out of business (producer numbers in September 2016 indicate 9,517 dairy farms in existence in the UK, 2/3 of the number of 10 years previously (AHDB, 2016)).[1] Farmers' efforts to address the negative impacts of low pricing have led to lobby groups forming, such as Farmers For Action, to increase the collective relative power. As well as organizing large scale marches and demonstrations, it has also led to direct forms of action to raise public awareness of the issues and to target those who appear to have the greatest power in the supply network (the large multiple grocers in the UK). Arranged on social media, there have been blockades of dairy processors as well as some very well publicized direct actions such as the Milk Trolley Challenge in some stores (where farmers enter a store, empty all the shelves of milk, and either pay for them or abandon the trolleys at the checkouts). Recent placatory statements from supermarkets may indicate that the farmers' actions are having some effect. However, the introduction of initiatives such as the 'Farmers Own' dairy sub-brand by Morrisons in the UK, passing the choice to end-consumers of whether to pay an extra premium, could equally be interpreted as using the public to maintain the power balance and negate the basis for the farmers' concerns (by showing that supermarkets are only charging what customers are prepared to pay). It remains to be seen how these power politics unfold.

The social dimensions of relationships

The emphasis thus far in our consideration of relationship variables has been economic. The central role of business relationships is to manage economic exchange. The general assumption is that the parties to an exchange are essentially self-seeking, seeing exchange as a necessity but seeking to control it. While one cannot ignore the self-seeking view, it must also be said that companies do not always behave completely selfishly. They know that the world does not merely operate at the economic level. Relationships also have a social dimension. They are, after all, social constructions, and the parties to an exchange exist embedded within a wider social structure (Granovetter, 1985).

This is not to dismiss the economic dimension, nor is it to underplay the inherently selfish motivations that may surround exchange management. However, exchange parties may recognize that their self-interest is best served by cooperation in exchange. That is, it is best achieved when they behave equitably and in the mutual interests of both. The economic value created within the relationship can only be maximized when the two parties cooperate with each other. The social-exchange view throws relief upon processes that create equitable conditions. Foremost among these are the concepts of trust and commitment:

- *Trust* is seen to be central to a relationship (Moorman et al., 1993; Morgan and Hunt, 1994; Young and Wilkinson, 1989), encapsulating the confidence a party has with the reliability and integrity of a counterpart, and building expectations.

---

[1]Source: //dairy.ahdb.org.uk/market-information/farming-data/producer-numbers/uk-producer-numbers; accessed 10/9/16.

The reliability and integrity comes from displays, in words as well as deeds (Ganesan, 1994), of consistency, competence, honesty, fairness, helpfulness, responsibility and benevolence (Morgan and Hunt, 1994). High levels of trust in a relationship enable the parties to focus on the long-term benefits of the exchange (Ganesan, 1994).

• *Commitment* goes hand-in-hand with trust since it is by a company's behaviour as manifestation of its commitment that trust can be established and maintained. It is essentially a state of organizational mind or intention, where the relationship has significance for a party and where it wishes it to endure. Morgan and Hunt (1994: 23) characterize commitment as 'an exchange partner believing that an ongoing relationship with another is so important as to warrant maximum efforts at maintaining it'. Such efforts involve clear manifestations of the commitment. This could include financial commitments to show willing, or may involve doing something special for a counterpart that is not available to other counterparts such as product or service customization. The larger the scale of commitment, the stronger the signal that is communicated.

Social-exchange theory makes a clear contribution to our understanding of exchange relationships by showing that factors other than the purely economic may apply, and by indicating the role that factors such as trust and commitment play in moderating the impact that power dependency plays in relationships.

B2B SCENARIO 3.1   DEALING WITH POWER ASYMMETRY

Adam Archer[2] was facing a bit of a quandary. His lead architect, Tina, had just informed him that local store representatives from BoxStore had asked that some of the designs for one of the new stores be reworked further. This was on one of the six new-build and refurb projects that Archers Architects currently had with BoxStore and would require another four weeks' work from Tina and two other members of her team. It was also the third time within a month that the client had requested additional work, largely based upon changes being sought at local store level, even though the planned work had been agreed during the contract negotiations with the central estates team at BoxStore HQ. And typically they weren't being channelled through the project manager appointed by BoxStore for each project. The project managers were responsible for working with all the contractors and consultants on each project to ensure the integrity and delivery of the whole project. Adam reckoned they should be approving any adjustments to the scheme.

BoxStore had been an important client for Archers, and it was Adam himself who had won the work on the strength of some well-regarded pilot work he'd done for them. That had been seven years ago and the work with BoxStore had grown strongly since, now accounting for about 35 per cent of income. If only the same could be said of the profit contribution. As a big store group with an international presence and reputation, it had been fantastic

(Continued)

---

[2]Please note that while this scenario is based upon a real case, it has been anonymized for the purposes of publication.

(Continued)

PR value to be associated with their major store expansion in the UK. And it had helped to expand the staff base from seven architects to 27 in six years. But, BoxStore had made it clear from the outset that they could've had their pick of architects and had deliberately chosen just two medium-sized practices for the whole of the UK because they wanted to be important to each of them; the big fish in each of their ponds. And they certainly did expect Archers to jump when they called. They also expected them to develop new ways of working with the CAD systems to produce libraries that would reduce the design costs over successive projects and to share those with BoxStore's other UK practice. All these variations took time and not much of it was billable against the projects themselves. While the negotiated margins on the projects themselves were still just about acceptable, they were low for the sector and there wasn't much scope for each project to go off track before the resulting costs would make that project unprofitable. It would certainly be a major headache for sustaining the current size of the business if most of them didn't make any money.

The business development work Adam and his business partner had been doing with InnovaParks had great promise for the longer term and would certainly be of real design interest to his staff, some of whom weren't that thrilled by the work they were doing for BoxStore (which didn't give much vent to their innate interests as architects to come up with wholly new building concepts; one BoxStore was pretty much the same as the next in design terms). But, remaining in a healthy financial position for the next three years still required meeting the expectations of the contracts with BoxStore and trying to do that without much more margin erosion. Given the relative power asymmetry, how was Adam going to do that?

Business marketing: an interaction perspective

While the previous perspectives provide an understanding of elements of inter-organizational exchange relationship behaviour, they do not focus attention upon the dynamic processes of interaction over time that are the stuff of relationships between companies. Relationships unfold through a whole series of actions and reactions of the parties involved. Managing relationships at the behavioural level necessitates an understanding of these processes of interaction so that the consequences of relationship action can be recognized. The Industrial Marketing and Purchasing Group (IMP) interaction approach (Håkansson, 1982) provides a comprehensive conceptual framework within which to locate a whole host of relationship actions.

- It considers the exchange to embody more than the basic exchange of a market offering for money, extending, as it does, the nature of exchange to cover all forms of interaction between the relationship parties (financial, product, informational and social).

- It adopts a view of exchange that is inherently dyadic, where both parties to the exchange have the potential to act. As Ford et al. (1998) put it, the process of handling company interdependence 'is not simply about cooperation. It involves the manager working *with* other companies, but it also involves working *against* them, *through* them and often *in spite* of them' (1998: 1, italics in original).

- It embodies the politico-economic perspective in respect of the structure of power in an exchange relationship while at the same time focusing upon the processes by which the interaction takes place.

The basic tenet of the interaction approach is that enhanced understanding of business-to-business markets is derived from the recognition that the exchange process between companies is not typically characterized by an active seller and a passive buyer. While this state of affairs frequently exists in mass consumer markets, in business markets the buyer may be as active as, or more active than, the seller. Consequently, the exchange *'process is not one of action and reaction; it is one of interaction'* (Ford, 1997: xi, italics in original). Rather than a large number of individually insignificant customers who are all relatively homogeneous in their needs, customers in business markets come in all sizes with widely differing product/service requirements, 'and marketers seem to talk about them individually so that each seems to be more or less important to the seller' (Ford, 1997: xi). The relative importance leads to distinctive differences in the ways that a business marketer deals with each customer, and therefore relationships can differ substantially.

Some relationships may be complex and long term and bring mutual benefits to the parties, while others may be short term and manifestly dominated by one party. Some may be characterized by trust and cooperation, while others are riddled with conflict and deception. Some may be close while others are more distant. Over time, a single relationship may be characterized in all these ways, sometimes at the same time. The interaction model, proposed by the IMP Group of researchers (Ford, 1990, 1997, 2002; Håkansson, 1982) and based upon their empirical studies (see Figure 3.2), captures the diversity and complexity of the relationships witnessed in business markets. It depicts a relationship in terms of the short-term and long-term interaction process between two organizations and the individuals who represent them. It does this within a wider environmental context and the atmosphere within which the interaction takes place, an atmosphere that affects the interaction on the one hand and is affected by it on the other hand.

The interaction process

The parties in a business-to-business exchange interact with each other. In understanding this interaction over time a distinction can be made between what happens in any individual interaction and what happens at the level of the relationship itself, as an aggregation of and gestalt of these individual interactions (what the IMP Group have termed interaction 'episodes'). The prevailing aspects of the relationship affect, and are affected by, the individual episodes.

The interaction may be of several types:

- *Product/service.* This is often the reason for exchange in the first place; the relationship builds around this central element. The nature of the product/service offering inevitably affects the interaction between two companies. For those situations where there is a relatively simple customer need for a standard offering, the degree of interaction is likely to be low and the type of interaction is likely to be narrow. On the other hand, where there is substantial uncertainty as to the nature of the requirement or the ability of a supplier to provide it, the degree of interaction is likely to be higher and the nature of interaction broader (Håkansson et al., 1976).

- *Financial.* The amount of money involved in the exchange is also likely to affect the interaction. Financial exchange indicates the relative importance of the relationship and thus the imperative for more or less interaction. The interaction may concern anticipated or actual financial exchange.

- *Informational.* It is not always products or money that is exchanged. There is often a large amount of informational contact. For example, technical details may be discussed by research, production or engineering staff from both companies in respect of new product or process initiatives (Cunningham and Homse, 1997). Commercial material such as terms and conditions may be discussed as part of ongoing negotiations between relationship parties. Equally, one party may impart information about planned changes within its organization or its vision for the future of the industry. All of these have no specific reference to money or products/services but are none the less important elements of the interaction process. The content of the information and its width and depth, the number of people involved in the information exchange, the formality of the process, and the use of personal or impersonal communication channels all give an indication of the nature of the relationship between the parties.

- *Social exchange.* This plays an important part in maintaining a relationship between economic transactions and seems particularly important in reducing the uncertainties between parties that arise from cultural or geographical distance (Håkansson and Ostberg, 1975). Over time, social contact between relationship participants creates bonds between the actors that cement the relationship, building the sort of trust that comes from personal experience of interaction (Håkansson and Snehota, 1995a).

Relationships

Interaction episodes over time create a relationship with a history. Each new episode adds to this history such that a relationship assumes an essence that is more than an individual episode. As a result of the elements of interaction above, relationship partners come to know each other better and develop clear expectations of the relative roles and responsibilities of each other. This constitutes a degree of *institutionalization*: they do not really have to think about every step they take with each other. An analysis of the *contact patterns* between the partners that come from the exchange elements above provides an indication of the nature of the relationship: close, distant, cooperative, conflict-ridden, predictable or wildly fluctuating. Furthermore, as a relationship unfolds, one or other party may make *adaptations* in the exchange elements or the process of exchange (Hallén et al., 1991) – adaptations that constitute irretrievable investments unique to that relationship.

The participants in the interaction process

Obviously, a relationship requires parties to the relationship; without the parties there *is* no relationship. The parties are the two organizations and the individuals (at least two people) from those organizations. It is the organizations, or more precisely, the individuals, who interact. Consequently, the process of interaction between two firms and the relationship that ensues will depend upon the characteristics of the firms and the individuals themselves. The *IMP interaction model* posits that the organizational factors include physical characteristics of the firms in terms of *size,*

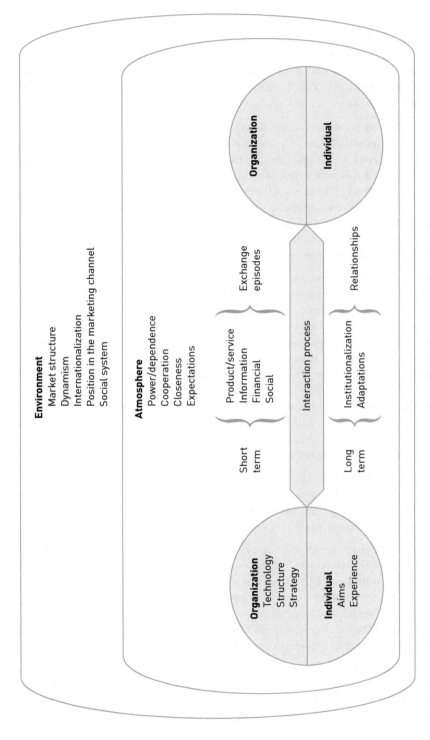

Environment
Market structure
Dynamism
Internationalization
Position in the marketing channel
Social system

Atmosphere
Power/dependence
Cooperation
Closeness
Expectations

Organization
Technology
Structure
Strategy

Individual
Aims
Experience

Short term

Product/service
Information
Financial
Social

Exchange episodes

Interaction process

Long term

Institutionalization
Adaptations

Relationships

Organization

Individual

FIGURE 3.2 The IMP interaction model of business-to-business marketing (reproduced from Håkansson, 1982: 24)

With permission from Wiley.

structure and *technological resource base*. They also include less tangible factors such as *organizational strategy* and the *experience of the firms*. The model also posits that the *personalities, experience* and *motivations of the individuals* working for the firms will very directly affect the interaction between two firms.

Size has a strong bearing upon relative power in a relationship (El-Ansary and Stern, 1972; Stern and Reve, 1980) and, consequently, establishes the pecking order in interaction. The dominant party on the basis of size has greater capacity to call the shots.

The forms of *structure* adopted by the parties and the degree of centralization of authority, formalization and standardization of rules, or levels of specialization of jobs, all affect interaction. They do this to the extent that they allow for more or less interaction of different types between people from different levels and departments within the firms. Where structures are heavily centralized, roles strongly ascribed, staff very specialized and procedures always followed, one might expect the levels of interaction to be low and the substance of the interaction to be narrow. Conversely, where there is little centralized control and less formality there is greater likelihood of wider interaction concerning a wider range of subjects.

Interaction brings together the *technological resource bases* of the two relationship parties and so these bases provide the conditions under which interaction occurs. The technological systems extend beyond equipment-based resources or technology infrastructure. They also include the knowledge bases of the individuals working in the two firms. If the systems match well then the basis for smooth interaction exists. However, if there is a substantial gap between the systems then the basis for smooth interaction is not there. In practice, companies may well get involved in activities to bring their technology systems into closer alignment. For example, a supplier might establish supply capabilities close to a customer's plant or adopt logistics systems (such as more warehousing and extra delivery vehicles) that ensure continuity of supply (Frazier et al., 1988; O'Neal, 1989a, 1989b). It might even go as far as to deploy staff on a customer's premises to facilitate a customer's activities (Wilson, 1996).

In a further example, if the production technology of the seller is geared towards long, continuous runs of the same product, yet a buyer needs varied and relatively small batches of product, then interaction between them may revolve around alternative forms of production. Such is the case in B2B Snapshot 3.2.

What either party seeks to gain overall, and – perhaps more importantly – through its relationships, affects its interaction. If it sees value through exchange, for instance by joint development of products or sharing of expertise, then its interaction will follow suit in terms of willingness to engage and the commitments it may be prepared to make. Where a company perceives that it can attain its goals independently of a counterpart then this is less likely to lead it to make substantial commitments to that relationship, and its interaction will be affected accordingly.

The previous relationship experiences of organizations may affect their propensity to become more or less involved with other relationships. Those who feel that strong commitment to one or several close and deep relationships has left them exposed financially, or subject to perceived negative behaviours from their counterparts, may be less inclined to attain such closeness in future relationships. At the same time, since relationships require a set of skills to manage them, those companies that have managed to build the sorts of relationships that they consider appropriate are likely to feel suitably equipped for other relationships.

Ultimately, it is the interactions between individual participants that create and sustain a relationship. Even when resources such as information or process technology are shared and underpin a relationship, people are still involved in bringing these resources to bear and performing the activities that use the resources. The personalities of these people affect the relationship. Some individuals find it easier to approach new people (a necessary activity for creating the bonds between people that initiate relationships). Further, some individuals are more forthcoming than others, again, a trait that may be appropriate to relationships. This is not to say that relationships only require extrovert personalities. On occasions, the levels of application and single-mindedness that are characteristic of introverts may be more appropriate for a relationship. For instance, these traits are likely to be necessary to overcome obstacles in a relationship such as operational fulfilment problems, or to achieve changes in the basis of exchange such as new process or product development activities. Regardless of the benefit of either set of traits, the point is that individual personality undoubtedly affects relationships. Individual experiences in general and relationships in particular will also affect the way an individual interacts, as will the individual's motivation to interact. These varied personal characteristics alongside the characteristics of the role the individual fills, the functional affiliation he or she has, and the level he or she occupies within the organization all affect the interaction that takes place and thus the relationship that ensues.

B2B SNAPSHOT 3.2   NAMPAK ADAPTS TO DAIRY CREST PRODUCT NEEDS

Among other forms of packaging, Nampak Plastics Europe produces high-density polyethylene (HDPE) bottles for milk and juice using extrusion blow-moulding technology. It has been a major supplier of such bottles for a collection of Dairy Crest locations in the UK. One of Nampak's factories had spent a few happy years providing the local Dairy Crest plant with its needs for 1-, 2- and 4-pint bottles. Its moulds and production-testing equipment were geared to produce these. The Dairy Crest plant sourced its needs for 6-pint bottles from a Nampak sister plant, which involved greater transport distance. The interaction between Nampak and Dairy Crest was heavily affected by the need to source from two separate plants because of the cost implications (for example, greater product mileage and duplication of order processing). The issue was resolved when Nampak added a new moulding machine, new moulds and product-testing equipment. It could then meet the need for all 1-, 2-, 4- and 6-pint bottles from the same location within the vicinity of the Dairy Crest plant, and could respond more quickly and flexibly to the demand for all of these product variants. As a result the local Dairy Crest plant felt happy to source its total requirement from the single Nampak factory, an example of an adaptation involving technological realignment affecting the relationship positively.

The interaction environment

The external environment in which a dyadic relationship unfolds is likely to affect the behaviour of the firms in the relationship (Achrol et al., 1983). These effects can be seen in a variety of ways. *Market structure* affects a relationship in terms of the availability of and scope for switching to alternative relationship partners (Anderson and Narus, 1984). Where there are few alternatives there is a strong tendency for a company to seek close and stable relations with a counterpart buyer or seller. Where firms operate in a dynamic or internationalizing marketplace they may seek to reduce the uncertainty that goes with this *dynamism* through their supplier or customer relationships. This might involve greater interaction in the form of information or social exchanges.

An individual relationship's *position in the manufacturing channel* or the characteristics of the wider *social system* may also be significant, particularly where the strategies of companies elsewhere in the supply chain are able to influence the behaviour of a firm in that dyadic relationship. A relationship's embeddedness in the network that surrounds it (Håkansson and Snehota, 1995a) – or *network embeddedness* – creates constraints upon the freedom to act on the part of the relationship parties – something that has been called the 'burden' of relationships (Håkansson and Snehota, 1995b).

The atmosphere affecting and affected by the interaction

Interaction over time leads to a relationship that is more than the sum of individual episodes. The relationship is dynamic in that it is affected by the individual episodes. However, the passage of time in the relationship brings a degree of stability. This establishes an atmosphere within which relationship participants act. Within the IMP interaction model this atmosphere can be described in terms of the power–dependence relationship between the companies, the degree of cooperation/conflict and the overall closeness/distance in the relationship, as well as in terms of the companies' mutual expectations.

In a relationship the stronger party has great potential to affect the activities of the weaker party. The strength may come from ownership of resources needed by the other party and/or arise where the other party is strongly dependent on its counterpart. With power asymmetry comes the potential for conflict, though this depends upon the stronger party exercising the power that its strength brings. If it does use its power in ways that are considered by the weaker party to affect it negatively then this may give rise to conflict when the weaker party objects. The extent to which the weaker party does object depends on how weak/strong it feels; it may just accept there is nothing it can do about it.

While there will always be moments of conflict in a relationship, there may be greater incentive for companies to cooperate (Anderson and Narus, 1990), the self-interest of each party being best served by mutual action (Heide and John, 1990). Parties might act jointly to develop tools and design products (Drozdowski, 1986); to undertake value analysis or cost targeting (Dowst, 1988); to design quality-control and delivery systems (Treleven, 1987); and to engage in long-term planning (Spekman, 1988). Inevitably, trust also affects the atmosphere of the relationship. With repeated interaction comes the ability of each party to more strongly ascertain the trustworthiness of its counterpart and for trust to affect the atmosphere of the relationship.

The IMP interaction model: criticisms and lessons

While the IMP interaction model has been acknowledged for its contribution to the understanding of inter-firm relationships, there have been some criticisms of it. Theory is often developed from individual examples such that law-like generalizations are not readily derived. This means that there is a lengthy list of concepts (Seyed-Mohamed and Wilson, 1989) and these concepts can lack clarity or overlap (such as with adaptation and adaptation processes (Brennan and Turnbull, 1995)). Criticisms are not generally levelled at the main proposition that the relationship is central to the understanding of business marketing.

The IMP interaction model captures the various elements that may affect the relationship interaction process in the short and long terms as well as clearly showing that the interaction itself may affect the parties to the relationship, either directly or through the atmosphere surrounding the relationship. In this way, organizations adapt to the relationships they have, and as a result may be changed. When it comes to drawing from the model to help with the management of relationships, there are several preliminary points that must be made:

- Relationships are two-way. Even if one party is dominant and can obtain its own way, the fact that it has to use the resources provided by another will mean that there is still an interactive process unfolding, and a relationship is the outcome of the interactions between the two. This means that managers need to consider the aspirations, potential and behaviour of both parties to the exchange if they want to obtain clarity about the way the relationship is and could be.

- Relationships in general are complex and can be described using a multitude of variables, some of which may be of more explanatory use in some relationships than others. In one relationship it might be the power a supplier has over a customer on the basis of its provision of a scarce resource that explains much of the interaction in the relationship. In another, the common history and levels of trust between the partners over time might explain it better. In yet another, despite a history of cooperation, changes in the wider marketing environment may drive impending changes in the relationship. The situational diversity and the range of variables that could explain any individual relationship mean that simple prescriptions for action are not easy to obtain. Rather, managers have to reflect upon the relationship that confronts them, understanding its entirety in its natural setting. Only from that understanding, aided by the analytical tools that this book provides, will sensible development of the relationship result.

- Whether a relationship is long term or short term, at any particular point in time there is a history leading to that moment. The history both makes it what it is and sets the jumping-off point for the future. Understanding the history of a relationship is a prerequisite for establishing what it can be in the future.

IMPACT OF INFORMATION TECHNOLOGY DEVELOPMENTS ON RELATIONSHIP INTERACTION

While the global economy has recently undergone a period of sustained recession, which has affected all local and regional economies to a greater or lesser degree, there is another change in the wider business environment that, irrespective of the recession, has loomed larger for business-to-business enterprises during the last two decades. This change is the convergence of information technology, communications technology and the emergence of the World Wide Web. The impact of the internet has been felt in most areas of life and the same is true of business exchange. While there are examples throughout this book of activities that reflect the capabilities that the web brings, it feels timely to focus specifically upon the role that ICT changes and the web have had upon the substance of business-to-business relationships themselves. The technology changes that can be seen thus far span a range of aspects of relationships, and these are developed below. These effects are neither fixed nor complete; the use of the technology continues to evolve and thus the effects on relationships and relationship building are likely to change further. In the following, we use the relationship content and terminology that has been developed in this chapter to establish how the technology changes relationships and the challenges it poses to relationship managers, as well as the open research questions which remain.

Structural/market changes

As Leek et al. (2003b) indicate, technology changes have facilitated degrees of disintermediation at the level of market structure. This has enabled companies to go direct in ways that were not logistically possible previously at an economically viable level. Along the way, this has enabled even small companies to extend their market definition such that they can now meet the needs of companies on the other side of the globe, something that they perhaps would never even have considered. This is particularly true of information-based companies which are in a position to make their services available around the clock, seven days a week, 365 days a year.

As well as disintermediation, Naudé and Holland (1996) propose that the web revolution has also spawned completely new forms of business-to-business intermediary, often acting as information brokers.

Disintermediation and new forms of intermediation are significant because they are disruptive to forms of institutionalization within relationships that were described earlier as a source of relationship endurance. While micro-level changes within a relationship can affect the extent to which that relationship becomes institutionalized, the prospect of structural changes at the level of a supply chain is perhaps the most drastic challenge to relationship institutionalization. In Taiwan, where the top five customers for information technology manufacturing (HP, Dell, Sony, Apple, IBM) were reported to account for 73 per cent of total sales in this sector in 2005 (Jean et al., 2010), the degree of power asymmetry is such that each manufacturer recognizes that its continued supply to any one of these companies remains uncertain. This is despite substantial tangible and intangible investments on the part of the Taiwanese companies to the requirements of the key customers and without any real manifestation of reciprocal cost commitment from the customers (Kang et al., 2009).

Aspects of exchange that are affected

Using the typology of exchange types presented above (product/service, financial, informational, social), it is possible to see that the digital revolution has affected them all to varying extents (see Table 3.2).

Product/service exchange

Even where the basis of exchange involves a physical product, technology has had considerable impact. Technology for sharing design information and managing review/revise processes has meant that design lead times can be reduced. Furthermore, electronic sharing of information can often lead to design-for-manufacture adaptations that benefit both buyer and seller. Where the product itself is largely information based or has a service component (for example, advice or problem-solving) the technology enables greater speed of response (see the example of the Rolls-Royce engineers in the case study in Chapter 1). Much of the value created here replicates existing people-mediated processes by replacing people with technology. While this replacement reduces the human contribution to relationships, it is seen as largely positive by relationship participants as it improves both the efficiency and effectiveness of the basis of value creation in the exchange – the primary purpose of the exchange in the first place.

Financial exchange

Since much financial exchange in relationships has long been managed by systems, this aspect of exchange has perhaps been less affected by the web revolution. Where further effects may be witnessed is in those situations where people may still occasionally maintain a role in the financial exchange (typically dealing with queries and problem-solving). Increasingly, self-service web-based systems are made available to answer queries. Where stock answers are not already available, web-forms are increasingly used to submit requests, which themselves are typically answered electronically. The overall consequence of further changes in this aspect of exchange is that the level of personal contact declines further.

Informational exchange

Naudé and Holland (1996) foresaw that business-to-business relationships would increasingly be predicated upon information exchange, that relationships would come about as a consequence of the information exchange rather than information exchange just being part of an overall exchange, and largely secondary to product/service preoccupations and the role of personal contact. This does increasingly appear to be the case. As with financial exchange, large amounts of informational exchange can now be mediated via the web. This includes the sorts of hard, technical data that Håkansson (1982) considered suited for impersonal forms of communication, as well as some of the sorts of soft data that Håkansson indicated were more suited to personal forms of communication (such as product usage information, general conditions of agreement, and information about the relationship parties).

Virtually all firms will now have a web presence. Larger firms will often use portals that allow customers' access to substantial amounts of information about their account, current orders and order tracking, specification details, product revisions and new product developments. In some cases, the portal may provide access to market intelligence information or other sectoral insights as well as white papers and case studies. Such portals provide a shop window, but one where fulfilment activities can also be mediated.

However, not all enterprises are yet making use of the emerging technology in such advanced ways. Many businesses are still largely only using a website to present some key company information and to allow emails to be sent to the company.

TABLE 3.2 Personal contact across relationship exchange types in the light of the web revolution

Type of exchange	Net amount of personal contact over time	Relative importance to relationship establishment and maintenance over time
Product/service	Declining further	Similar levels
Financial	Declining a bit further	Similar levels
Informational	Declining noticeably	Increasing noticeably
Social	Declining to a much greater extent than others	Reducing noticeably

The net consequence of the increased provision of information for customers to largely self-serve on a needs basis is that the level of personal contact in individual relationships decreases.

Social exchange

Perhaps the greatest degree of reduction in personal contact has been manifest in respect of social exchange. Turnbull (1990) established empirically the significant role that personal contact has in mediating long-term relationships. As Leek et al. (2003b) describe, such contact appears to have a variety of roles in relationships:

- as the means for soft data information exchange that is often intended to reduce perceived risks through face-to-face contact and free-flowing interactive communication;
- as an aid to partner assessment (either supplier capability or customer viability), proceeding largely on the basis that 'seeing is believing' and that talking face to face leaves less scope for hidden characteristics, hidden actions and hidden intentions;
- to facilitate negotiation and adaptation activities, on the basis that both require interactions to arrive at a position that isn't already predetermined;
- as a form of open channel in the event of crises or problems emerging that cannot be dealt with automatically by the existing relationship decision-making processes/ structures;
- as an outlet for social contact for its own sake;
- as a vehicle for enhancing one's own social and professional status.

This range of contributions shows the important and enduring role of people as actors in relationships and confirms the role that people have in creating trust within them, fundamental to sustaining long-term relationships.

Leek et al. (2003a, 2003b) point out that moving away from face-to-face contact typically leads to communication between participants becoming more psychologically distant, more depersonalized, more task oriented, less spontaneous and less collaborative. The removal of visual and physical presence cues, which accompanies greater reliance upon electronic methods of communication, therefore makes them less compromising and potentially creates barriers to building trust.

These days, buyers and suppliers use new technology to improve the relative ease and efficiency of existing relationship contacts, rather than seeking to replace personal contacts. Consequently, while there has been much more reliance on mobile and email communications technology, face-to-face contact is still present as part of a more mixed communications economy. Despite the loss of visual and physical presence, people do not feel that relationships have become more difficult to manage. Part of the reason for this may be attributable to the less formal and prescribed role that email has, compared to letters and written correspondence. Nonetheless, in the discussion of their survey findings, Leek et al. (2003b) do signal caution to participants about the direction of travel as far as the social dimension of relationships is concerned, particularly in relation to the management of problems and disputes. Without direct social exchange as a means of dealing with difficult situations there is a real danger that a relationship will have little or no capacity to flex so that these situations can be faced and resolved. Given that most relationships have some challenges at some point in their development it is highly likely that there is need for such capacity.

BUSINESS MARKETING AS NETWORK ANALYSIS AND MANAGEMENT

Beyond relationships to the network

Relationships are the primary basis for exchange, and are thus central to business marketing. It is through relationships that companies achieve objectives. However, the decisions taken in relationships and their motivations do not necessarily originate at the level of the relationship (Ford and McDowell, 1999). Often for the business marketing organization there are considerations that extend across the whole portfolio of customer relationships in which it is involved. How the organization behaves within any one relationship will be conditioned by these other relationships. Further, how it behaves in any one relationship will be conditioned not just by its customer relationships at large, but potentially by its own supply relationships: it may be affected by the links that its suppliers have with their suppliers. Beyond that, it may even be affected by its links with other agencies, governments, banks, universities and industry associations. All of these have the potential to affect the single relationship because of 'connectedness' (Cook and Emerson, 1978) – all relationships are connected to the wider network within which they are 'embedded' (Granovetter, 1985). As Ford et al. (2002: 29) argue, 'This network is the arena in which the business marketer must operate. The relationships in the network enable the company to grow and develop, but they are also a constraint on that development and may restrict its activities.'

This points to the fundamental issue for the firm, surrounded as it is by a network of relationships: that its relative value strategically is a function of its position in the network. This requires a different strategic mindset from the traditional one that sees the firm as atomistic, independently deciding upon its own strategic future and having the freedom to pursue that course. The network view means that the firm has to accept that it is interdependent and embedded, and that this limits its ability both to think and to act independently. Thus, the task for the firm, managerially, is to analyse the network in order to establish its network position and engage in relationship behaviour that will enhance that position. This will inevitably involve acting within existing relationships in ways that may achieve this. It might also involve activities aimed at forging new relationships.

Recent research by Manser et al. (2016) points to three distinct modes of network management, where network players try to match the management mode to their own prevailing mental model of relationships as well as to the type of network (e.g. in terms of project innovativeness).

Basically coordinated mode: this mode, necessary for a minimum degree of network management, relies on a combination of communicating for coordination, planning and monitoring but nothing beyond those basics required to ensure all organizations and people in the network know what activities they are contributing towards and the resources it encompasses.

Control-oriented mode: this mode extends the basic situation, to add controlling activities intended primarily to prevent opportunistic behaviour within the network. The activities are controlling in that they rely heavily on social behaviour expectation setting and pressure as well as a focus on sanctions to achieve network compliance. Apart from being a behavioural preference of players in the network, this mode seems to apply most typically where there is little requirement for innovativeness in the network, where it is easier to define tasks and expectations and know when they are being executed as intended.

Reward-oriented mode: in addition to the basic situation, the prevailing focus in this mode is the more positive use of high levels of communication to create an atmosphere of solidarity and to stimulate network actors into continuing their positive contributions to ultimate network goals. This mode seems to apply most readily where the level of innovativeness of the projects being worked upon in the network is high and where there is much ambiguity and need for greater degrees of joint problem-solving.

For any organization within a network context, understanding the prevailing management mode of the network is clearly important. For that organization, however, there is always the enduring selfish need for it to understand how it sits with respect to the network and how it should behave within the confines of what's possible in order to obtain the best network position for itself that is possible. This is the perennial consequence of network embeddedness: to balance selfish needs with the network interdependencies.

Network analysis to establish current position

Given the complexity of individual relationships that we have depicted in the previous section, managers or practitioners would find the application of an analytical framework, such as the interaction model in its entirety, overly cumbersome. In any event, that level of analysis is unnecessary to obtain some knowledge of the relative positioning of firms in a network. Rather, it is possible to employ the sort of shorthand analysis that Håkansson and Snehota (1995a) have used to great effect. This analysis recognizes that there are three important components that networks bring together from all those organizations within the network: what Håkansson and Snehota call the substance of relationships. The three components are the *actors* who engage in relationship behaviour, the *resources* that are created or used in relationships, and the *activities* that are undertaken in relationships. To distinguish the different kinds of interconnection, while at the same time recognizing that they are relational, they are referred to in terms of *actor bonds*, *resource ties* and *activity links* (ARA) – which is why the activity of examining each of these can be called *ARA analysis*.

Actor bonds

It is people within organizations who initiate relationships and typically create and control resources and activities, and it is often easiest to start with an identification of as many companies and people within them that have connections with other actors in the network. The nature of the connections may be economic or social. It is also easiest to start with one's own organization and work out from there.

Activity links

Relationships start operating to achieve their purpose when activities are undertaken that deliver that purpose, whether it is design activity from a supplier or requests for information from a customer. Typically, an activity cycle between two companies would commence with an order and end when it is delivered. However, depending upon the nature of a relationship it may be that other activities are worthy of note in a network diagram, such as a joint research project or combined promotional activity. The consequence of mapping the links between the parties in the network is an indication of the range of activities that are taking place and the relative role that the focal company has in this.

Resource ties

Resources are used by actors, but may also be created as part of the relationship exchange. The resources may be used by actors on their own (such as the use of equipment within their own firms to perform specific tasks) or may be combined with the resources from other parties to create a shared resource. IT makes the sharing of data resources increasingly easy for companies. So, for instance, there may be design inputs from a variety of network actors making use of a shared design system.

By establishing the variety of linkages between the firms in a network in terms of these types of interconnection it becomes possible for a focal company to establish where the critical mass in terms of the ARA components lies. This then enables it to determine where it lies in relation to others in the network in positional terms, whether it has a strong presence and is central to the direction in which things are going, or whether it is relatively weakly joined and on the periphery of network developments.

Initiating changes towards a new network position

On the basis of the analysis of network position, a focal company is better able to consider how it changes its position. This is likely to involve it in attempts to forge stronger relationships with partners that are in stronger network positions, or may lead it to wind down or forsake some of the relationship linkages that it already has. This may seem obvious: getting stronger just involves forging relationships with positionally strong actors, that is, moving from the periphery to a position closer to the centre. However, in examining their own network positions, stronger network parties are unlikely to welcome relationship advances from any party that does not maintain or further enhance their existing positions. Furthermore, stronger network players are likely to be highly sought after. However, in the pharmaceutical or biotechnology sectors, for example, some smaller players can certainly do this if they bring forward a new drug or treatment platform.

Parties to exchange also need to be aware of the costs of attempting to forge lots of relationships. First of all, relationships are not free, and as with any investment decision the firm needs to be sure it will obtain value for the not inconsiderable costs it will incur. At the same time there is also a level beyond which it becomes cognitively difficult to consider the links with counterparts and be clear about what is obtainable from those relationships.

More often network positional change has to be achieved more gradually using existing relationships to forge the sort of actor bonds, activity links and resource ties that will strengthen the parties involved. Moreover, by acting with a relationship partner, or a chain of partners, it becomes possible to exert greater change in position than acting alone. Indeed, an important asset of network thinking is that achieving an improved position may not actually involve specific actions on the part of the focal party. Rather, it may involve encouraging changes in another network party or parties for the benefit of both it and the focal company. For instance, by encouraging a supplier to innovate with new materials technology, it becomes possible that the value-adding activity of the focal company is enhanced with its customers, improving the network positions for both focal company and supplier.

CHAPTER SUMMARY

- As well as an understanding of the behaviour of the buying company, business marketers also have to understand the relationship between the buying company and the selling company.

- Relationships are two-sided: treating customers as passive recipients of the attentions of the marketer is a naive view of business marketing, and inherently flawed.

- Any ability a marketer has to influence the buyer is predicated on the nature of the relationship between the two parties and so must involve a clear understanding of what is possible within the relationship. This means that rather than being solely preoccupied with the buying centre the marketer must analyse the relationship at large.

- A variety of theoretical viewpoints can be drawn upon to understand a relationship. However, it doesn't matter which perspective the marketer draws from, so long as by doing so a clear understanding of what is happening in the relationship is derived. Decisions about the future of a relationship can only come about from such an understanding.

- The business marketer strives for deep understanding of the current state of the relationship, of its likely future development and of the process of value creation within the relationship.

- Success in any individual relationship will depend upon the business marketer's understanding of that relationship within the wider network of relationships in which the company is embedded. Strategic business marketing focuses on a clear understanding of the network and on creating individual relationship strategies that establish the most favourable network position for the company.

- New technology is affecting many aspects of relationship formation and development in business-to-business markets. A key question is whether relationships with more electronic mediation and less face-to-face mediation will become less flexible.

QUESTIONS FOR DISCUSSION

1. Why is an understanding of the buying behaviour of the customer insufficient for successful business marketing?

2. Explain the uncertainties and abilities that buyers and sellers bring to an exchange situation.

3. Explain how principal–agent theory can help our understanding of exchange risk.

4. Identify the three factors that affect the level of transaction costs and how they do so.

5. Why does a stronger exchange partner not always exercise its power?

6. To what extent are parties to exchange only concerned with economic value?

7. What are the four main elements of the IMP interaction model? What has it got to offer that other perspectives may not?

8. Why does a business marketer need to have a network view?

CASE STUDY 3.1   EUROPEAN HORSEMEAT SCANDAL: NETWORK IN DISARRAY

The global headlines said it all: for several months during the first half of 2013 the whole of Europe was rocked with the news that unapproved horsemeat had found its way into the food chain and on to the shelves of the supermarkets. The media coverage was enormous. By July 2013, typing 'horsemeat scandal' into Google produced over 228,000 hits, from news organizations, government agencies, scientific authorities, food industry bodies, and not forgetting the almost obligatory Wikipedia entry.

The scandal broke in Ireland on 14 January 2013, when the Food Safety Authority of Ireland announced the results of analyses of frozen beef burger samples it had tested in November 2012. The results indicated that equine DNA was present in the samples from several major food supermarkets: Tesco, Iceland, Aldi, Dunnes Stores and Lidl. The Tesco beef burgers, supplied by ABP Silvercrest in County Monaghan, revealed as much as 29 per cent horsemeat. Two other factories were cited as providing meat with lower levels of horse DNA: Dalepak in Yorkshire, UK, also owned by ABP, and Liffey Meats in County Cavan, Ireland. It's argued that the scandal knocked almost £300m off Tesco's market value within 48 hours of the news breaking.

Of course, horses are slaughtered for their meat in parts of Europe and horsemeat is readily available for sale in European markets. The issue wasn't horsemeat per se. There was much confusion at first and debates raged about whether it was a food safety issue or a breach of consumer trust or both. Products were recalled, food was taken off the shelves of the supermarkets, and food standards and safety authorities set about trying to establish what had happened.

Ultimately, at issue on this occasion was the fact that the meat in affected burgers and other products was actually intended to be beef and should not have contained

(Continued)

(Continued)

traces of any other animal product. Indeed, analyses of some samples of beef indicated that pig DNA was also identifiable. The concerns became more about consumer trust than food safety. The lack of traceability, for example, meant that people seeking to avoid particular foodstuffs (for example, for religious observance reasons) found it very difficult to know what beef products they could trust.

By the time the full extent of the saga had been played out, 15 European countries had become involved. The European Union, including European agriculture ministers and the European Commissioner for Health and Consumer Policy, were involved in formulating responses at the highest levels. This included a very large programme of DNA testing of 2,250 processed beef samples across the European Union and further plans to bolster food safety legislation within the EU, including more money for food surveillance as well as stronger financial penalties for food operators that commit fraud or fail to comply with food safety laws.

Along the way, a whole collection of household names in food have been affected. Horsemeat traces found their way into consumer food products either manufactured directly by, or sourced by the subcontractors of, Findus, Nestlé and Birds Eye. Own-brand beef products sold by major supermarkets were also affected. In addition to those announced at the time of the initial Irish investigation (Tesco, Aldi, Lidl, Iceland and Dunnes Stores in the UK and Ireland), Asda and the Co-operative Group in the UK, as well as Real in Germany and Ikea across Europe, also withdrew ranges of beef products in the wake of the scandal. Intermediaries such as foodservice companies and catering suppliers were not immune either. Brake Bros, a food service company which supplies the Whitbread Group of companies (which includes Premier Inn hotels, Brewers Fayre pubs, Table Table pubs and Beefeater Grill restaurants) found traces of horsemeat in its beef lasagne and burgers. Catering companies Compass and Sodexo, which supply institutional markets such as schools, hospitals and prisons also found horsemeat present.

There has been subsequent criticism of the extent to which the meat supply trade within Europe has become too complex. One example, relating to how horsemeat found its way into products such as Findus beef lasagne, shows how extended and complex the supply chain can be:

- Comigel, a French company supplying Findus, among others, asks its subsidiary, Tavola in Luxembourg, to manufacture beef products (including Findus beef lasagne).

- Tavola orders the beef from a meat processor, Spanghero, in the south of France, which sub-contracts the supply to a company in Cyprus.

- The Cypriot subcontractor uses Draap Trading Ltd in Belgium to make the order of the meat itself.

- Draap uses two slaughterhouses in Romania (Doly-Com and CarmOlimp) for the supply of the meat, and the meat is sent to Spanghero in France from where it is then sent to Tavola, which makes the products for supply to Findus and retailers across Europe.

Some attribute this longer and more complex chain to the way pricing operates within the meat production industry overall, arguing that prices are squeezed more tightly over time by the powerful supermarkets, which means that animals are sourced from lower cost countries for slaughter, and this creates greater opportunities for fraudulent activity in meat substitution. There seems to have been fraudulent behaviour in knowingly relabelling horsemeat as beef, as well as incompetence in the network in failing to maintain product integrity throughout the whole of the chain.

For companies like Tesco, it brings a salutary warning about relationships and networks. A company is only as good as the relationships it has (and this goes the whole way down the supply chain network). Other major supermarkets, such as Sainsbury and Waitrose in the UK, haven't suffered the same negative consumer responses because their products had no meat substitution. Indeed, they have benefited at the expense of those who were implicated, by arguing that they use local beef from known sources and with supply chains that are much shorter. Relationships bring burdens that mean they will always require attention to what's happening in the network overall. The costs of monitoring relationships and maintaining the quality and integrity of the product have to be borne somewhere in the network. The economic climate may well be a driver for reducing costs overall, but the question becomes one of where the costs are borne since they cannot be eliminated completely. Some of the typically very large companies further downstream relied heavily on the costs being borne upstream, without any real basis for trusting all the actors in the network and/or effective means of identifying and protecting the value chain from fraudulent behaviour. Given what Håkansson and Snehota (1995a) have called the unruliness and stickiness of relationships, where companies don't have total control and are dependent on the associates of associates, in retrospect this appears to have been a risk that came back to bite them. Of course, it was possible for many of the big players to drop key suppliers quite quickly in the light of the scandal as it unfolded. However, adverse consequences did occur, notably, damage to reputation, the likelihood of greater product assurance costs arising from the more stringent requirements of the food standards agencies, and the prospect of having to assume greater relationship costs in the future.

CASE STUDY QUESTIONS

In addition to reading the case material, spend some time on the web trying to get a picture of the complexity of the meat supply network in Europe at the time of this scandal.

1   Using ARA concepts, compare the examples of the networks of companies that were negatively affected by the scandal and those that were less affected.

2   Establish Comigel's relative network position in the light of the scandal and indicate how it may be able to improve it.

3   As a senior executive at Tesco, who has recently read all about business-to-business interaction and networks, what strategic objectives would you set to redress the difficult network position the company now finds itself in?

4   Using the ARA model and relationship management concepts, establish five key relationship management tasks that you feel will help achieve the strategic positioning objectives.

FURTHER READING

Ford, D. (ed.) (2002) *Understanding Business Marketing and Purchasing* (3rd edn). London: Thomson Learning.

This text provides a strong compendium of published output from the IMP Group and captures the fundamental bases of the interaction approach to business-to-business relationships and networks.

Håkansson, H. and Snehota, I. (1995) *Developing Relationships in Business Networks*. London: Routledge.

This book by two of the leading business network thinkers provides the most comprehensive coverage of the substance of relationships and networks. Though out of print, it is available at: www.impgroup.org/uploads/books/0-415-11570-1.pdf (accessed 12 November 2013).

Shelanski, H. and Klein, P. (1995) 'Empirical research in transaction cost economics: a review and assessment', *Journal of Law, Economics, & Organization*, 11(2): 335–61.

This article provides a very comprehensible yet extensive introduction to transaction cost economics and demonstrates the breadth of research interest in the subject.

PART II

BUSINESS-TO-BUSINESS MARKETING ANALYSIS AND STRATEGY

4

RESPONSIBLE BUSINESS-TO-BUSINESS STRATEGY

LEARNING OUTCOMES

After reading this chapter you will:

- understand the significance of corporate social responsibility and sustainability for business-to-business strategic decision-making;

- be able to apply several different ethical frameworks to the analysis of decisions in business marketing;

- know what shareholder value, customer value, supplier value and relationship value are, and what role they play in the formulation of business marketing strategy;

- be able to explain the similarities and differences between the formal, planned approach to strategy and the resource-based view of strategy; and

- understand the role played by the relationships and networks of which the firm is a part in the formulation of business marketing strategy.

INTRODUCTION

Important changes in business thinking have taken place in recent years which place ever greater emphasis on the responsibilities of enterprises towards wider society and the natural environment. More and more business organizations believe it to be necessary to take account of the wider social considerations and environmental effects arising from their activities. Consequently, this chapter addresses the topics of corporate social responsibility and sustainability. The former has been defined in many ways, leading Crane et al. (2008: 5) to call it a 'complex jungle of CSR definitions'. Crane et al. (2008) cite a 2001 European Commission definition of CSR as 'a concept whereby companies integrate social and environmental concerns in their business operations and in their interactions with stakeholders on a voluntary basis', but a more recent European Commission (2011: 6) definition is more succinct: 'the responsibility of enterprises for their impacts on society'. In any case, the topic of CSR is closely related to sustainability, since two of the most fundamental of the 'impacts on society' that must be dealt with are the rapid depletion of non-renewable natural resources and the despoliation of the natural environment. Sustainability can be defined as 'development that meets the needs of the present without compromising the ability of future generations to meet their own needs' (WCED, 1987), which can also be understood as 'consuming resources at a rate which allows them to be replaced, and only producing pollution at a rate that the environment can assimilate' (Peattie, 1995: 33). In this chapter we will also necessarily mention business and marketing ethics, since both CSR and sustainability inevitably involve ethical considerations. This is easily revealed if we ask the simple question 'Why?' That is, why should business consider wider social impacts when designing strategy, and why should we not simply enjoy our preferred lifestyle regardless of the costs in terms of resources and pollution? These 'why?' questions can only be answered using ethical reasoning, so we will give a little thought to how different ethical positions can be constructed. Finally, while all this talk of social responsibility and sustainability is closely aligned with the dominant business discourse of the twenty-first century, we must not forget that businesses must make profits to survive. The way that businesses make profits is by creating value for their customers. Consequently, in addition to the topics of CSR, sustainability and marketing ethics, this chapter also investigates the concept of customer value and how it is created. The central strategic challenge for B2B organizations today is to build a competitive advantage by creating added value for customers while ensuring that the wider social and environmental effects of the enterprise are taken into account, and any negative effects are minimized. B2B Snapshot 4.1 illustrates how HÅG, a Norwegian manufacturer of office chairs, rose to this challenge.

In the later sections of this chapter we examine responsible B2B strategy from the perspective of business ethics, CSR and sustainability, and then explain the importance to B2B marketers of understanding and delivering value to customers. Before addressing these topics, a few words are in order about the fundamental meaning of strategy.

B2B SNAPSHOT 4.1   HÅG – SUSTAINABLE OFFICE CHAIRS

The carbon footprint of a supplier is now frequently used as one of the decision-making criteria for B2B purchasing decisions. In fact, according to the top management of HÅG, a leading manufacturer of office chairs based in Norway, the carbon footprint of the product is a criterion whenever they present a competitive tender in a bidding competition. But HÅG is not a newcomer to the business of sustainability. The story goes that it was in the early 1990s – when one of their employees returned from maternity leave with a raised awareness of the fragility of the earth's environment, and of the need for businesses to take environmentalism seriously – that HÅG became one of the first companies to build sustainability into the essence of what they do.

The HÅG approach takes account of international standards such as ISO 14001 (the criteria for an environmental management system) and ISO 14025 (principles and procedures for environmental labels and declarations), but it pre-dates these international standards and it goes further. The HÅG life-cycle approach to environmental management covers every phase of a product's life, from the initial design criteria all the way through to end-of-life procedures such as recycling and the recovery of raw materials for re-use. Suppliers are extensively involved in this process. They are expected to be accredited to ISO 14001, and they are engaged by HÅG in discussions about how to reduce their impact on the natural environment. For example, can recyclable raw materials replace non-recyclable materials in manufacturing processes? Can an equally high quality office chair be made that is lighter and uses fewer components? Even the third-party logistics company in charge of HÅG's transport contributes: its fleet of modern trucks use biogas fuel and are equipped with low friction tyres, while the drivers are trained in green driving techniques to reduce fuel consumption and maintenance requirements. If you want to become a supplier to HÅG you will have to go through their 'Environmental Requirements towards Suppliers' evaluation process, which considers factors such as the supplier's use of energy, carbon footprint and procedures for waste reduction and management.

According to the top management at HÅG, business sustainability is not a single task, but many simultaneous tasks: managing the design process, managing the production process, managing the procurement process, managing suppliers, and so on. Of course, HÅG employees have to contribute as well; the policy of discouraging business travel and encouraging video-conferencing led to a 34 per cent reduction in HÅG's business travel budget between 2008 and 2010. The CEO of HÅG puts it this way: 'to be an environmentally friendly company one needs to build a system and to document what is being done. This is not a communication activity, but a challenge to the whole supply chain' (Høgevold and Svensson, 2012: 145).

Sources: Høgevold and Svensson, 2012; www.hag-global.com/web/home-global.aspx.

STRATEGY: MEANING AND PROCESS

Strategy is a frequently used word in the business world, but it may often be misused or misunderstood. After brief reflection on the meaning of the word 'strategy' one quickly grasps that it is used in multiple ways. Consequently, Mintzberg et al. (1998) argue that strategy needs five definitions – the five Ps for strategy:

- Strategy as a *plan*: a direction, a guide, a path for getting the organization from where it is now to where it wants to be in the future. This is the organization's *intended* strategy, that is, what it set out to achieve.

- Strategy as a *pattern*: meaning that strategy is a consistency in behaviour over time. This is the organization's *realized* strategy, that is, what it actually achieved. In practice it is likely that the realized strategy will be neither identical to the intended strategy nor completely different from it. As Mintzberg et al. (1998: 11) put it: 'The real world inevitably involves some thinking ahead as well as some adaptation en route.'

- Strategy as a *position*: the locating of particular products in particular markets. Companies seek to establish a position in the market that is both unique and valued by customers.

- Strategy as a *perspective:* a company's fundamental way of doing things. While strategy as position is outward looking, to the external marketplace, strategy as perspective is inward looking, to the overall purpose of the organization. These approaches are complementary. Market positions must be consistent with the fundamental purpose and values of the organization. For example, construction equipment manufacturer Caterpillar aims to be the global leader in customer value in its field, while 'sustaining the quality of the earth'. In positioning Caterpillar products in the marketplace, the company will seek to deliver excellent customer value while taking account of environmental impacts.

- Strategy as a *ploy*: finally, strategy can refer to clever manoeuvres designed to outwit competitors – ploys.

Buzzell and Gale (1987: 18) define strategy as: 'The policies and key decisions adopted by management that have *major* impacts on financial performance. These policies and decisions usually involve significant resource commitments and are not easily reversible.' They make the distinction, which is today widely accepted, between *business unit strategy* and *corporate strategy*. Business unit strategy is concerned with how an individual business competes with its rivals, with what it does and what it could do to stay in business and to beat the competition. Corporate strategy is concerned with decisions made in an organization comprising multiple businesses (often called strategic business units, or simply SBUs). Questions of corporate strategy concern the overall shape of the corporation, in which SBUs should form part of the overall portfolio, and the way in which key resources (such as investment capital) should be divided between them. Strategic marketing management is concerned with business unit strategy, also known as competitive strategy.

The rational planning approach

Conventionally, strategy has been understood as a *process* by which a business systematically: appraises its current position with respect to the immediate competitive environment and the wider macro-environment; establishes its key strengths and weaknesses; identifies opportunities and threats; sets challenging but achievable long-term goals; assesses a range of alternative strategic options; and selects the strategic option or options that best meet the defined goals (Brennan et al., 2008). This is what Henry Mintzberg, in his 5Ps for strategy that we mentioned above, means by strategy as a *plan*. Many companies have formal marketing planning systems that are based on this kind of process, and find formal planning to be a beneficial business activity. However, while any marketing practitioner would acknowledge that a company must have a formal plan, it must not stick slavishly to the plan regardless of what is happening in the real world. In recent years rapid changes in the global business environment – such as the many new marketing opportunities, challenges and technologies associated with the internet, the appearance of competition from emerging economies (Wiersema, 2013), and the economic difficulties faced by European economies – have made it very difficult for businesses to predict the future with sufficient accuracy to write reliable long-term plans. The ability of a business to learn from and adapt to changing circumstances has become a key component of strategic thinking (Leavy, 2004).

Strategy is concerned with big, long-term decisions that will have a substantial effect on the future of the organization. The *rational planning approach* to strategy development is the idea that a formal strategic planning process is the mechanism that is most likely to create a successful strategy. In the marketing field this will usually be known as strategic market planning, or simply marketing planning (McDonald, 1996). The aim of strategic market planning is to create a competitive advantage over rival firms. Michael Porter's (1985) well-known four-fold classification of competitive strategies – differentiation, cost leadership, differentiation focus, cost focus – is one way of classifying competitive advantage. Porter (1980) was also responsible for formalizing the competitive environment into his famous 'five forces' (competitive rivalry, power of buyers, power of suppliers, threat of new entrants and threat from substitutes). In conceptualizing strategic planning as the process of analysing the competitive environment, identifying alternative strategic options open to the firm, and then choosing and implementing the option that best meets the firm's objectives, Porter was continuing an intellectual tradition associated particularly with Igor Ansoff (Ansoff, 1965). This is a prescriptive tradition (meaning that it provides guidance on what *should* be done), which advocates a series of logical, sequential steps through which organizations can arrive at their best strategy. The core components of these logical steps are:

- an 'external audit' examining both the competitive environment and the wider macro-environment to identify key opportunities and threats;
- an 'internal audit' examining the differential strengths and weaknesses of the organization compared to key competitors;
- a summary of the marketing audit in a SWOT (strengths, weaknesses, opportunities, threats) analysis;
- identification of strategic alternatives – different possible strategies;
- evaluation of strategic alternatives – testing the different possible strategies for their efficacy in achieving the organization's goals (which may be as conceptually simple as maximizing long-term shareholder value (Doyle, 2000));
- implementation of the strategy through the budgeting and operational planning systems, and control through a monitoring mechanism.

We refer to this as the rational planning approach because the underlying intellectual framework is an optimization routine employing rational choice theory. Over the last two decades, an alternative approach to strategy formulation based on the resource-based theory of the firm has become increasingly popular, and we turn to this alternative in the next section.

The resource-based view

The *resource-based view* of competitive advantage operates on the assumptions that firms are heterogeneous in terms of their control of important strategic resources and that resources are not perfectly mobile between firms. Firm resources are defined as 'strengths that firms can use to conceive of and implement their strategies' (Barney, 1991: 101). Resources can be classified as physical capital resources, human capital resources and organizational capital resources. Physical capital resources include physical technology, plant and equipment, geographic location and access to raw materials. Human capital resources include the training, experience, judgement, intelligence, relationships and insight of the individual managers and workers of the firm. Organizational capital resources include: the formal reporting structure; the formal and informal planning, controlling and coordinating systems; and the informal relations among groups within a firm, and those between a firm and other agents in the firm's environment.

Jay Barney (1991: 102) has defined a sustained competitive advantage in the following terms:

> a firm is said to have a competitive advantage when it is implementing a value creating strategy not simultaneously being implemented by any current or potential competitors. A firm is said to have a sustained competitive advantage when it is implementing a value creating strategy not simultaneously being implemented by any current or potential competitors and when these other firms are unable to duplicate the benefits of this strategy.

Note that this definition includes potential competitors, not just current competitors – a sustained competitive advantage protects the firm against other firms considering a competitive market entry as well as providing an edge over firms already in the market. Barney makes it very clear that a sustained competitive advantage cannot be defined in terms of a specific period of calendar time; indeed, a sustained competitive advantage is one that cannot be nullified through the efforts of competing firms to duplicate it. A sustained competitive advantage will endure until some structural change takes place in the industry that renders it irrelevant.

In order for a resource to be a potential source of sustained competitive advantage it must be *valuable, rare, inimitable* and *non-substitutable*. These rather daunting-sounding characteristics are readily understood. Firms may have many unique attributes that do not assist them in exploiting opportunities or neutralizing threats. To be a *resource* an attribute must contribute to the firm's ability to deal effectively with the competitive environment – it must be *valuable*. An attribute that is found among most firms cannot be a source of sustained competitive advantage – to be a *resource* it must be *rare*. Even though an attribute may be both valuable and rare, if it is easily imitated by competitors then it will not provide a *sustained* competitive advantage, since current or potential competitors will duplicate it. To be a *resource* it must be *inimitable*, which may arise because of the unique historical circumstances under which it was created, the causally ambiguous link from the resource to enhanced value creation, or the social complexity of the attribute. Unique historical circumstances simply mean that a firm was in the right place at the right time and was therefore endowed with a unique resource (often called *path dependency* in the academic literature on the subject). A causally ambiguous link from the resource to enhanced value creation means that it is not possible to define precisely which resources provide a competitive advantage or why. Every firm comprises a very complex bundle of attributes and it is often not a simple matter – or perhaps not even possible – to identify exactly which characteristics of the firm make it more or less successful. Socially complex attributes, meaning characteristics of the firm that are embedded in its internal and external relationships, are a particularly difficult resource to imitate. This insight is one of the reasons why, in business-to-business markets, so much effort has been devoted to understanding inter-organizational relationships and networks. In turn, this effort has created a related but distinct view of strategy as the management of relationships and networks, which we will discuss in a subsequent section. Finally, to be a *resource* an attribute of the firm must be *non-substitutable*. Even if a characteristic of a firm – for example, the charismatic leadership of its chief executive officer (CEO) – is *inimitable*, it may still be the case that other firms can match its performance by implementing strategies that deliver similar benefits (for example, by having an excellent formal planning system that creates a clear, agreed mission that is shared by all of the employees). The less substitutable a resource is, the more effective it will be in creating a sustained competitive advantage.

Strategy as the management of relationships and networks

While the rational planning approach to strategy and the resource-based view were both developed as generic approaches, equally applicable to businesses operating in consumer markets or business markets, the perspective addressed in this section arose directly out of research into business markets. It may well be the case that businesses marketing consumer goods and services could benefit from adopting a relationships and networks perspective, particularly in relation to the management of their supply chain. However, business-to-business marketing organizations, which interact with identifiable networks of heterogeneous suppliers and customers, certainly have the most to gain from the relationships and networks perspective on strategy.

Many of the important fundamental concepts have been introduced in the preceding chapters, in particular Chapter 3. Business marketing organizations do not deal with vast numbers of relatively homogeneous customers, each wielding relatively little market power. Rather, they deal with relatively small numbers of heterogeneous customers, some of whom wield considerable market power. In practice, suppliers and customers in business markets often do business together for many years, forming dyadic business relationships within which the parties to the relationship often make substantial relationship-specific investments that create structural bonds between the organizations in addition to the social bonds that are often created within business relationships. Each relationship has a unique atmosphere, which is the cumulative outcome of exchange episodes (financial, product/service, information and social) that have taken place. Relationships are connected together in networks that can be characterized in terms of *actors, resources* and *activities*. One cannot hope to understand behaviours at the level of the individual relationship without understanding something of the network context within which it takes place. An action that takes place within a single relationship (for example, if a supplier prefers *not* to deepen its relationship with customer A) may only make sense in the context of other network connections (for example, if the supplier's parent company has decided to focus on developing relationships with customer B, who is a direct rival of customer A).

The relationships and networks approach to strategy has something in common with the resource-based view, in that the current resources of the firm are considered to be the key factor in determining its strategic behaviour. However, while the resource-based view focuses on three principal categories of resource – physical capital, human capital and organizational capital – the relationships and networks approach identifies the firm's *portfolio of relationships* and its *network positional resources* as the key factors in strategy formulation. The relationships and networks approach has very little in common with the rational planning approach to strategy; certainly there is no list of steps to be followed, and no suggestion of an optimization procedure. However, according to Ford and his colleagues (Ford et al., 2003), what clearly distinguishes this approach from both the rational planning approach and the resource-based view is the 'Myth of Independence'. Ford et al. (2003) argue that companies have far less freedom of action than they think, so that independent action (that is, pursuing one's own goals independently of other actors in the network) is a myth. Independence is limited because:

- Companies have a restricted view of the surrounding network.

- Firms have limited freedom to act independently, and the outcomes of their actions will be dependent upon the actions of other firms within the network.

- Strategizing is not simply concerned with competition. Business relationships have to be considered in their entirety, and there is no simple dichotomy between cooperative and competitive relationships. It is frequently the case that two firms will be simultaneously competing and cooperating within the same business relationship – for example, in the automotive industry, where it is quite common for competing automobile manufacturers to collaborate on the development of a new vehicle platform.

Within this perspective, much of the effort involved in developing strategy is concerned with identifying just how much freedom of action the individual firm has within the constraints of the industrial network. Strategy involves dealing with the actions of other network members and achieving the organization's goals by 'working with, through, in spite of, or against them' (Ford et al., 2003: 6). No matter how strategically capable the organization may be, its own performance is inextricably tied up with the performance of other members of the network. According to Håkansson and Snehota (1989: 190):

> The performance and effectiveness of organizations operating in a network, by whatever criteria these are assessed, become dependent not only on how well the organization itself performs in interaction with its direct counterparts, but also on how these counterparts in turn manage their relationships with third parties. An organization's performance is therefore largely dependent on whom it interacts with.

When strategy is conceived as the management of relationship and networks, the primary focus ceases to be the internal allocation and structuring of resources, and becomes the way in which the organization relates its activities and resources to other parties in the network. The activities of strategizing involve far less analysis of a supposedly impersonal external/competitive environment, and far more explicit attention to the nature of the business relationships and the networks of which the organization is a part. Strategic action is concerned with the efforts of actors to influence their positions within networks (Johanson and Mattsson, 1992).

The relationship spectrum

We emphasize throughout this book that business-to-business marketing is *contingent*. That is to say that there is no single right way to do B2B marketing; marketing strategy, tactics and programmes need to be adjusted to take account of the particular circumstances of the markets and the customers the firm is dealing with. Consequently, we would disagree with a proposition such as 'it always makes sense to develop deeper relationships with customers in B2B markets'. Contingency suggests that sometimes it will make sense to develop deeper customer relationships, and sometimes it will not. The particular circumstances of the market and of the customers must be analysed in order to evaluate alternative marketing approaches and decide on the best course of action.

An obvious question that arises is whether there are any simple rules for deciding where particular approaches to marketing strategy, tactics and programmes are more, or less appropriate. The answer is 'probably not', but a number of authors have tried to identify the conditions under which certain general approaches to marketing are more appropriate, or less appropriate. For example, one way in which marketing professionals deal with contingency is by segmenting the market and devising alternative marketing programmes for different market segments; you will find out how this is done in B2B markets in Chapter 6.

Another influential approach to the development of a contingency approach to marketing strategy was created by George Day (2000). He argued that creating and maintaining appropriate customer relationships was at the core of marketing strategy, and proposed the *relationship spectrum* as a tool for analysing whether a deep customer relationship, or a more transactional approach to marketing, was suitable. The relationship spectrum is a simple yet profound tool for developing a preliminary insight into the key contingencies affecting a B2B marketing strategy. It runs from *transactional exchange* to *collaborative exchange*, with *value-adding exchange* lying between these two extremes. Transactional exchange occurs where neither the customer nor the supplier wishes to develop a lasting business relationship; the customer makes a purchase from the supplier, pays for it, and that is the end of the matter. At the other end of the relationship spectrum is collaborative exchange, where the customer and the supplier engage in extensive information sharing, develop close social and process linkages, and become committed to each other because they expect to work together for the long term and generate mutual benefits. Between transactional exchange and collaborative exchange lies value-adding exchange where, without engaging in deep customer relationship building, the strategy of the selling firm moves from a simple selling approach (appropriate for transactional exchange) to a customer retention approach.

The choice of whether to adopt a more, or less, relational marketing strategy can be analysed using the relationship spectrum. In markets for commodity items (which are very hard to differentiate), where it is not necessary to establish complex information linkages to conduct business, and where the buying organization finds the purchase neither complex nor of critical importance to its business (these can be described as 'non-mission-critical' purchases), then it is likely that transactional exchanges will dominate. Under these circumstances marketing organizations should concentrate on having the best deal available to meet the needs of the customer; a strategy of substantial investment in customer relationship development is risky in these circumstances. However, as we move along the relationship spectrum from transactional exchange to value-adding exchange and then collaborative exchange, it becomes appropriate to use more and more relationship-building approaches within the B2B marketing strategy. In markets for specialized, high-technology items (which are easy to differentiate), where it is necessary to establish complex information linkages to conduct business, and where the buying organization considers the purchase to be both complex and critically important to its business ('mission critical' purchases), then collaborative exchanges will dominate. The marketing strategy for this type of exchange involves multi-level contacts between the buyer and the supplier, joint planning, joint problem-solving, and it is to be expected that trust will be developed between the relationship partners. An example of this can be seen in the relationship between the telecommunications firm BT and the financial services firm Standard Life (see the video 'Standard Life working with BT' at www.youtube.com/watch?v=WFlyOqy1lZk).

RESPONSIBLE STRATEGY

Marketing ethics is defined by Laczniak and Murphy (1993: x, italics in original) as '*the systematic study of how moral standards are applied to marketing decisions, behaviors, and institutions*'. A number of authors have claimed that managers generally, and marketing managers specifically, should consider ethical matters in their decision-making. Petrick and Quinn (1997: 25) put forward five reasons why 'managers need to improve ethical decision making', of which four focused on the cost risks associated with unethical conduct, and the fifth on 'the benefits of increased profitability and intrinsically desirable organizational order'. Laczniak and Murphy (1993: 5) claimed that, in the long run, the relationship between good ethics and profitability is 'most likely positive'. Schlegelmilch (1998: 8) also noted that 'some ethicists and practising managers believe that good business ethics is, in the long run, synonymous with good business', although he cited others (Hoffman and Moore, 1990) who disagreed that ethical behaviour would always be in the best economic interests of the firm. Arjoon (2000) concluded that the balance of evidence is that there is a positive relationship between ethical behaviour and long-run profitability.

Four approaches to marketing ethics are generally distinguished: *managerial egoism*, *utilitarianism* (where judgement is based on anticipated consequences), *deontological ethics* (judgement based on the application of rules) and *virtue ethics*.

Egoism is the pursuit of self-interest, and for present purposes we will assume that the interests of the management of the organization are aligned with the interests of the owners, so that the ethical principle underlying managerial egoism is the maximization of shareholder value. One argument used to justify this position is that the economic wellbeing of a society is maximized when individuals make their own choices within a free market (Barry, 2001; Butler, 2007). This accords with Friedman's (1979) proposition that the only responsibility of the manager is to maximize returns for the shareholder, and his observation that 'managers lack the wisdom and ability to resolve complex social problems' (Friedman, 1979: 90). Friedman's position depends upon the existence of a framework of laws that define the 'rules of the game'. Gaski (1999, 2001) has also argued that managers should refrain from moral judgements and concentrate on maximizing returns within the framework of the law, while Doyle (2000) argued that marketing managers, in particular, need to be able to demonstrate the contribution of marketing activities to shareholder value creation. Arguments against the position of managerial egoism revolve around the undue influence that companies may exert over the law-making process (for example, through political donations), the existence of monopoly power in many markets (Schlegelmilch, 1998), and the contention that profits and shareholder value are not an end in themselves but an incentive to encourage firms to provide socially useful goods and services (Koslowski, 2000).

Utilitarianism is the best-known form of consequentialist ethical theory. Consequentialism refers to those ethical theories that judge whether an action is right or wrong on the basis of the consequences of the action. In the case of utilitarianism, the consequences of actions are evaluated in terms of the balance between utility and disutility (or happiness and unhappiness). In choosing between alternative courses of action, someone applying utilitarianism would evaluate the likely net utility resulting from each alternative and select the action with the highest value for net utility (or the lowest value for net disutility). Laczniak and Murphy (1993) argued that utilitarianism was attractive to managers because of its similarity to the analysis of costs and benefits associated with an investment decision and, in principle, the simple decision criterion of 'choose the option with the maximum utility'.

In practice, however, utilitarianism is far from easy to apply (Sandel, 2010). How is one to compare the utilities derived by different people? What is one to do when the outcome of a utilitarian analysis conflicts with what might be regarded as a basic rule of civilized behaviour? For example, suppose that the sales executive for a medium-sized manufacturing company concludes that by lying to a customer he could win a particular order and safeguard the jobs of 25 people for the next year; the customer would be no worse off, and the competitor that would otherwise have won the contract is already operating near full capacity. A utilitarian analysis says 'lie', but most companies and professional associations have codes of conduct that explicitly state that lying is forbidden. This brings us to duty-based or deontological approaches to marketing ethics.

In contrast to the consequentialist approach of utilitarianism, deontological or duty-based approaches to ethics focus on the ethical nature of actions, rather than on the consequences of those actions. Many religious people adopt a deontological approach to ethics, based on the religious faith that they hold. However, deontological ethical systems need not be based on religious teachings. The approach proposed by Immanuel Kant has proved very influential in Western philosophy.

The duty-based approach to ethical decision-making is popular in business and marketing. Professional associations for marketing and sales managers, and large employers, typically have codes of conduct that members or employees are expected to abide by – such that serious contravention of the code of conduct would constitute grounds to be expelled from the professional association, or to be dismissed from employment. B2B Snapshot 4.2 provides illustrations from two professional associations (the American Marketing Association and the Australian Institute of Marketing) and one global IT firm (Texas Instruments).

B2B SNAPSHOT 4.2   CODES OF CONDUCT

AMERICAN MARKETING ASSOCIATION: STATEMENT OF ETHICS (EXTRACT)

As Marketers, we must:

1. Do no harm. This means consciously avoiding harmful actions or omissions by embodying high ethical standards and adhering to all applicable laws and regulations in the choices we make.

2. Foster trust in the marketing system. This means striving for good faith and fair dealing so as to contribute toward the efficacy of the exchange process as well as avoiding deception in product design, pricing, communication, and delivery of distribution.

(Continued)

(Continued)

3. Embrace ethical values. This means building relationships and enhancing consumer confidence in the integrity of marketing by affirming these core values: honesty, responsibility, fairness, respect, transparency and citizenship.

Source: www.ama.org. Reproduced by permission of American Marketing Association, AMA.org.

AUSTRALIAN MARKETING INSTITUTE: CODE OF PROFESSIONAL CONDUCT (EXTRACT)

1. Members shall conduct their professional activities with respect for the public interest.
2. Members shall at all times act with integrity in dealing with clients or employers, past and present, with their fellow members and with the general public.
3. Members shall not intentionally disseminate false and misleading information, whether written, spoken or implied, nor conceal any relevant fact. They have a duty to maintain truth, accuracy and good taste in advertising, sales promotion and all other aspects of marketing.

Source: www.ami.org.au.

TEXAS INSTRUMENTS: CODE OF BUSINESS CONDUCT (EXTRACT)

We respect the rights and property of others, including their intellectual property, and only accept their confidential or trade secret information after we clearly understand our obligations as defined in a nondisclosure agreement or similar document.

We protect and preserve TI assets, including TI business opportunities and intellectual property, for TI's benefit and not for our personal benefit.

We compete fairly without collusion or collaboration with competitors to divide markets, fix prices, restrict production or allocate customers.

We assure that those who seek to do business with TI have fair opportunities to compete for our business.

We actively encourage every TI employee, officer and director to recognize and report any concern about possible illegal or unethical behavior, and we ensure that such reports made in good faith will be acted upon responsibly and without retaliation.

Source: www.ti.com.

In discussing utilitarianism we explained that a utilitarian analysis could, in principle, find that it was ethically correct for a sales or marketing executive to lie to a customer. However, it can be clearly seen from Snapshot 4.2 that such behaviour would certainly break the code of conduct of a professional association to which the executive belonged, and may well also breach the ethical standards set down by an employer. Another example, shown in Snapshot 4.3, is taken from the 'letter to employees' from the CEO to be found right at the start of the *Air Products Code of Conduct*. Air Products, by the way, is a global B2B company that provides industrial gases, electronics and performance materials to an extremely wide range of industry sectors, including aerospace, healthcare, civil engineering, personal care and mining; in 2014 Air Products had sales turnover of more than $10 billion and employed around 20,000 people (you might also remember that we introduced this company in Snapshot 1.1 in Chapter 1). Notice, as you read through Snapshot 4.3, how the CEO emphasizes that employees must, above all, *act with integrity*.

The ethical theories outlined above provide, in principle, criteria that can be used to choose between alternative courses of action. By contrast, virtue ethics stresses the cultivation of virtuous principles and the pursuit of a virtuous life. The foundation of morality is said to lie in the development of good character traits as virtues (Arjoon, 2000). Virtue theory has been criticized on the grounds that it seems to provide no clear-cut rules and principles for use in ethical decision-making. This is because attention is focused on the cultivation of the virtues, from which sound ethical behaviour is expected to flow. If you take another look at Snapshot 4.3 you will see that the CEO of Air Products is advocating a 'virtue ethics' approach in addition to the more deontological 'code of conduct' approach. The CEO's letter emphasizes that employees of Air Products are expected to act with integrity, and that the code of conduct is provided to help them to adhere to this fundamental principle. B2B Scenario 4.1 provides the opportunity for you to reflect on the kind of dilemma that may arise in B2B sales and marketing.

B2B SNAPSHOT 4.3   ETHICAL BEHAVIOUR AT AIR PRODUCTS

(This letter appears at the start of the Air Products corporate Code of Conduct, and is followed by a detailed list of guidelines, which are not reproduced here, but can be found through the Air Products website, www.airproducts.com.)

LETTER FROM CEO JOHN MCGLADE

Air Products has, since its founding, succeeded because of our people. Our people listen, understand and respond to the needs of customers. Our employees' unwavering focus on safety and sustainability maintains our outstanding industry performance. Our shareholders know we will work hard to meet our financial goals. And there's another quality we possess that is a deeply held value and an integral part of our brand. It's integrity.

Upholding our integrity reinforces the trust and respect we've worked so hard to earn in our relationships. Preserved, it strengthens us in powerful ways. If integrity is lost, a priceless asset is not only gone but also very difficult – if not impossible – to earn back.

As a global company, we meet or exceed the laws in the countries where we operate. We must also at all times follow Air Products' policies, practices, standards, and guidelines. We all have an obligation to preserve Air Products' commitment to ethical business and integrous behavior at all times. It's the right way and the only way we

(Continued)

(Continued)

will do business. Consider what's right as you do your daily work, and if a situation is unclear to you, ask for help before you act!

We've highlighted the basics in our Code of Conduct. Read it carefully and consider how the information applies to you. Familiarize yourself with the resources to report violations. Follow your instinct if it tells you to ask questions or express concerns. These are responsibilities we are each accountable to build into our daily work.

You also have rights. It's your right to make a report or ask questions without fear, retaliation, or retribution. Air Products makes a firm promise of non-retaliation.

Winning in the marketplace is our goal. That can be hard work in today's business world. No challenge justifies giving away your integrity. It's a treasure beyond price.

We must all fiercely protect it as we work together to achieve our vision.

Source: Air Products, 2012.

B2B SCENARIO 4.1   A TRIP TO VARISHTA

Jen Forester usually enjoyed her business trips to the historic capital city of Varish in the distant country of Varishta. Even though it meant a lengthy flight and something of a culture shock, since the customs in Varishta were very different from those of her native Denmark, the hospitality was always very good and, more important, there were a lot of good business deals to be done there. Expanding rapidly, Varishta was fast becoming one of the most important sources of commodities such as iron, niobium and copper ore in the world. Consequently, the Varishta government had formed partnerships between its own state-owned businesses and several major mining companies to extract the minerals and export them for processing. The world economy was becoming increasingly reliant on minerals from Varishta to support growth and economic development.

This particular trip was turning out to be a little more difficult than Jen had expected. She had visited Varish several times in her role as sales manager for KPD Construction Equipment, a leading manufacturer of heavy equipment for use in the mining and construction industries. The opportunities in Varishta were more or less endless. On each visit she would meet executives from global mining companies to discuss their orders for mining equipment, and government officials and representatives of local Varishta building firms to discuss their orders for equipment to support the building and infrastructure boom going on in Varishta. Usually everything went smoothly; demand was high and growing and KPD supplied excellent equipment at competitive prices, so her job was not too hard, and she could count on earning good commission on sales from each trip. But this time, for the first time, she had been approached by a senior government official who suggested that, if KPD wanted to enjoy continuing success in Varishta, perhaps Jen should arrange for some substantial gifts for the Minister for Finance and his entourage. As the official said, a few gifts of around $10,000 each, amounting to no more than $50,000 in total, were a trivial amount compared to the profits that KPD were making from their Varishta business. (In fact, as the official did not know, $50,000 was considerably less than Jen expected to earn each year in commission alone from this business.) The official made it clear that if the gifts were not forthcoming then business for KPD in Varishta would become a lot more difficult. After all, although KPD had excellent products, so did several other global construction equipment companies. Without a licence from the Varishta government KPD would no longer be able to operate there.

Jen pondered what she should do. She had heard that bribery was regarded as a normal part of doing business in Varishta, although this was the first time she had encountered it herself. Making a complaint to the local authorities would be pointless; it was a fairly small bribe which was not illegal in Varishta and would probably seem entirely reasonable to local agencies who would wonder why KPD didn't just pay up. However, the KPD code of conduct and EU law were both clear that bribery was not allowed. On the other hand, she could easily get hold of $50,000, and the annual business in Varishta was worth hundreds of millions of dollars. Even though business in Varishta was booming, recession elsewhere in the world meant that the construction and mining industries were struggling, and if KPD lost the Varishta business the company would certainly have to cut back and probably lay people off around the world.

Source: Inspired by Hunt and Vitell (1986).

CSR and sustainability

The foregoing discussion of ethics emphasizes that B2B managers should strive to make correct moral decisions about matters that affect other individuals or companies. However, these ethical principles also provide the justification for sustainable and responsible approaches to B2B strategy. The different ethical standpoints provide rather different guidance. From the perspective of managerial egoism, managers should only pursue sustainability and CSR where they believe that such policies will enhance the economic interests of their company. That is a very limited approach to sustainability and CSR; in many cases it will amount to a window-dressing or 'green-washing' approach. A strict shareholder value maximization approach to sustainability and CSR would insist that the investment in environmental and CSR initiatives must be justified in terms of return on investment.

The other ethical approaches offer richer perspectives. From the utilitarian approach we obtain the idea that the positive and negative effects on all of the affected parties should be considered in ethical decision-making. This leads naturally to the consideration of the interests of the various stakeholders in the organization. Stakeholder theory, originally developed by Freeman (1984), has become an influential approach in the field of strategy generally and in CSR specifically (Crane et al., 2008). In the B2B field, Sharma and Henriques (2005) used stakeholder analysis to investigate the factors affecting the adoption of sustainability practices in the Canadian forest products industry. They explored how stakeholders in forestry products firms had influenced the depth of engagement with sustainability practices, and defined six levels of increasing depth of sustainability practice: pollution control (cleaning up undesirable end-products), eco-efficiency (reducing material and energy use, reducing waste production), recirculation (reducing the ratio of new to recycled material in use), eco-design (redesigning products to reduce environmental impact), ecosystem stewardship (taking responsibility for the environmental and social impact of operations), and business redefinition (moving towards a sustainable business model). Canadian forestry products companies have widely implemented the early phases of sustainability performance (pollution control and eco-efficiency) and are making some progress towards the mid-scale sustainability practices (recirculation, eco-design and ecosystem stewardship), but have barely begun to make fundamental changes to their business models (business redefinition).

The context for sustainability as a managerial issue is the obvious degradation suffered already by the natural environment as a result of human actions, and the emerging scientific consensus that the average global temperature is rising (global warming), that this will have long-term damaging effects on the natural environment with adverse consequences for human beings and many other species, and that human actions are responsible for much of the global temperature increase. Hart (1997) proposed that companies must incorporate sustainability into their strategic thinking, and provided a four-stage model for achieving this. Stage 1 is *pollution prevention*: rather than controlling pollution when it occurs, companies design production systems that actively prevent pollution. Stage 2 is *product stewardship*: designing the entire life-cycle of a product to cause as little damage to the environment as possible. Stage 3 is *clean technology*: this is the process of consciously replacing older, dirtier technologies with newer, cleaner ones. Finally, Stage 4 is the stage at which all of these ideas are pulled together into a coherent whole, the *sustainability vision*, for which Hart (1997: 74) suggested the following question: 'Does our corporate vision direct us toward the solution of social and environmental problems?' Since the publication of Hart's prescient article, many businesses have made sustainability a central part of their corporate vision – B2B Snapshot 4.1 explored how HÅG went about this. Raman (2009) argued that sustainability is now a corporate imperative, without which a company is likely to be shut out of many important markets. Whereas in the past companies tended to launch 'green' products in rich countries, Raman (2009: 137) says that they will now have to 'launch eco-friendly products all around the world at the same time'. For an example of the impact that sustainability has had on a major B2B company, you need look no further than the leading chemical company BASF Group (www.basf.com). 'Sustainability' is one of the main links on the homepage at BASF's corporate website. BASF has four 'strategic guidelines', of which one is 'We drive sustainable solutions', about which they say that 'Sustainable development means for us to combine economic success, social responsibility and environmental protection.'

There is, however, a contrary and more pessimistic view concerning CSR and sustainable business. Indeed, controversially, Fleming and Jones (2013) in their book *The End of Corporate Social Responsibility* argue that despite the many obvious and often expensive initiatives pursued by global corporations (such as BASF Group), '*CSR never really began*' (Fleming and Jones, 2013: 1). This argument is similar to, but goes beyond, the argument that CSR is merely a public relations exercise, and by implication insincere and lacking real substance. Fleming and Jones contend that destructive global trends such as climate change and energy depletion are deeply intertwined with the global capitalist system. CSR, they argue, is an attempt to reconcile two things that are irreconcilable, namely global capitalism with a sustainable and responsible approach to economic development.

CUSTOMER VALUE AND STRATEGY

In recent years, both marketing practitioners and marketing scholars have focused on value as the fundamental determinant affecting satisfaction in exchange relationships. The purpose of marketing exchanges is to create value for all parties to the exchange. This is such a simple idea that it can easily be overlooked. In a straightforward, simple, voluntary exchange of a product for money between two parties, value is created because the buyer values the product at more than the selling price (otherwise they would not buy) and the seller values the product at less than the selling price (otherwise they would not sell). The economic value created through the exchange is the amount that the buyer would have been prepared to pay over and above the selling price (the consumer surplus, in economic jargon) plus the difference between the actual price and the minimum price that the seller would have been prepared to accept (the producer surplus).

Many business-to-business exchanges are as simple as this: for example, when a small shopkeeper goes to the cash-and-carry to stock up on confectionery and snack items, or when a builder buys cement, glass, bricks and other materials from a builders' merchant to build a conservatory for a client. However, it is a particular characteristic of business-to-business exchanges that the process of value creation can become complex, involving several parties and multiple interconnected exchanges (Ulaga, 2001). It is only in a very abstract sense that the value-creation processes involved in developing a major new construction project – such as the development of the Olympic stadium for the 2012 Olympic Games in London – can be analysed as a simple exchange of goods for money. Ultimately the many contractors and subcontractors involved in the project believe that they will derive enhanced economic value from their involvement, and the ultimate clients, such as the London Organising Committee of the Olympic Games, the Olympic Development Authority and the British government, believe that the investment in the project will generate enhanced economic value for them. However, the value created in the project is long term and subject to a considerable degree of uncertainty because of factors internal to the project (such as unexpected delays or cost over-runs) and external to the project (such as the international political relations, the threat of international terrorism and the global economic recession). For this reason, paying explicit attention to the value created through exchange processes is often a matter of particular concern to business marketers.

What is customer value?

In an influential article on customer value, Zeithaml (1988: 14) proposed this definition of customer perceived value: 'Perceived value is the consumer's overall assessment of the utility of a product based on perceptions of what is received and what is given … value represents a tradeoff of the salient give and get components.' She made the point that different consumers will often have different salient give and get components and will weight components differently. Both the give (sacrifice) and the get (benefit) components included a range of different attributes; in particular, the sacrifice components include monetary and non-monetary elements.

Many subsequent authors have used Zeithaml's definition as the essence of their own definitions of customer value. The give–get or tradeoff definition is at the heart of many conceptual and empirical enquiries into customer value (Anderson and Narus,

1999; Blois, 2003; Christopher, 1996; Desarbo et al., 2001; Kothandaraman and Wilson, 2001; Lapierre, 2000; Ravald and Grönroos, 1996; Ulaga, 2001). The definition of customer value by Anderson and Narus (1999) differs from other give–get definitions in a rather more important way, since price is excluded from the definition of value. They define customer value as the benefits that the customer receives minus the costs that the customer incurred *other than the purchase price*. The implications of this are interesting: 'In this concept of value in business markets, raising or lowering the price of an offering does not change the value that offering provides to a customer firm. Rather, it changes the customer's incentive to purchase that offering' (Anderson and Narus, 1999: 7), whereas, of course, in other give–get formulations of customer value, changing the price does change perceived value.

Customer lifetime value

A straightforward use of the term 'customer value' is found in the context of relationship marketing strategies. Such strategies have as their raison d'être the creation of customer loyalty and, consequently, the reduction of customer defections and the retention of customer business. Reichheld (1996) is a particularly strong advocate of the loyalty effect. The essence of this, by now well-known, argument is that customers vary considerably in terms of their profitability, that understanding and managing customer profitability is the key to long-term corporate success (Rust et al., 2000), and that increasing customer loyalty will increase customer profitability. The focus of attention lies on the lifetime net present value to the business arising from doing business with a customer, which is termed *'customer lifetime value'* by McDougall et al. (1997). They define customer lifetime value as the net present value of expected profits over the duration of the customer relationship.

'Customer lifetime value' is quite different from the 'customer perceived value' discussed above. The concept of customer lifetime value measures *the long-term value of the customer to the supplier*, not the value perceived by the customer. This illustrates the dangers of using terminology loosely. Clearly, customer lifetime value is an expression of *supplier value*, not of customer value.

Relationship value

Customer value can be defined more or less broadly. In discussing customer value Desarbo et al. (2001) used a narrower definition than Lapierre (2000); the former defined customer value as the tradeoff between quality and price, the latter as the difference between benefits and sacrifices. Lapierre's conceptual definition of benefits is broader than Desarbo et al.'s definition of 'quality', and this is carried forward into the operational definition. Consequently the two studies, while measuring something similar, are not measuring exactly the same thing. One interpretation is that Desarbo et al. measured the value of the product (or market offering) to the customer, while Lapierre measured the holistic value of the product and the relationship with the supplier to the customer. Of the ten benefit drivers identified by Lapierre, three were relationship related (for example, trust), and of the three cost drivers, two were relationship related (for example, conflict). This opens up the possibility that the customer may derive some value from the characteristics of the relationship with the supplier, rather than simply from the use of the product.

Gassenheimer et al. (1998) used three bases for the analysis of value in relationships between firms: the economic (transaction cost analysis), the social (social exchange theory) and the distributive (distributive justice theory). They argued that most inter-firm exchange relationships required both economic and social value to endure. Their definition of economic value was of a financial give–get nature, while their definition of social value was 'satisfaction with the exchange situation' (1998: 325). Gassenheimer et al. argued that economic value tends to predominate where relational distance is high, and social value tends to predominate where relational distance is low. High relational distance is characterized by factors such as one-time exchange with no future obligation, intolerance of mistakes and asymmetrical dependence. Low relational distance is characterized by factors such as anticipated future exchange, mutual obligation, tolerance of mistakes and interdependence. Similarly, Ravald and Grönroos (1996) argued that in an enduring buyer–seller relationship, the relationship itself could provide some of the benefits and sacrifices perceived by both parties, over and above the value of the money, goods and services exchanged.

Ritter and Geersbro (2015: 19) make an important point very succinctly: 'The creation of value for both the customer and the supplier is the key goal of any customer-supplier relationship.' A consistent line of argument developed by Thomas Ritter, Achim Walter and Hans Georg Gemünden (Ritter and Walter, 2012; Walter et al., 2001) has helpfully clarified and summarized the debate about relationship value. They conclude that relationship value is separate and distinct from product value because relationship value includes additional benefits and sacrifices that go beyond product-related issues. Ritter and Walter (2012: 137) define 'customer-perceived relationship value' as 'the customer's perception of the trade-off between the benefits and sacrifices of a business relationship with a given supplier'. Customer-perceived relationship value is influenced by four 'direct' relationship functions – payment, volume, quality and safeguard – and by four 'indirect' relationship functions – innovation, information, access and motivation (Ritter and Walter, 2012).

The value proposition

Our investigation of the concept of customer value leads naturally to the consideration of the concept of a value proposition. To some extent the idea of a value proposition (or customer value proposition) emerges in a very straightforward way from the idea of customer value. If customer value is considered to be the difference between the customer-perceived benefits and the customer-perceived sacrifices arising from an exchange process, then the (customer) value proposition can be thought of as the supplier's statement of the benefits that the customer can expect to receive in return for the price paid. Here, the notion of 'the price paid' needs to be taken in a broad sense to mean the sacrifices made by the customer to acquire the valued benefits. The immediate purchase price may or may not be a substantial part of the sacrifices; business buyers are well aware of this and are trained to take account of all relevant sacrifices associated with a purchase.

There are reasons to believe that the fairly simple concept of a value proposition outlined in the previous paragraph is insufficiently sophisticated to take account of the wide range of exchange processes that are found in business markets. For example, earlier in the chapter we introduced the idea of a relationship spectrum, running from transactional exchange to collaborative exchange. Towards the transactional exchange end of the relationship spectrum exchange processes are fairly simple, and the idea of a value proposition is easy to understand. However, towards the collaborative exchange end of the relationship spectrum exchange processes are very complex, and the idea that one of the parties to the exchange, the supplier, presents a value proposition for the other party, the customer, to evaluate, is naïve. As David Ballantyne and his colleagues have suggested (Ballantyne et al., 2011), under these circumstances the benefits and the sacrifices to both parties may be uncertain, so that the elementary value proposition concept is inappropriate. Ballantyne and colleagues (2011) propose that under these circumstances reciprocal value propositions emerge through interaction processes between the parties to the exchange process. That is to say that neither party designs a value proposition for the other but, rather, the two (or possibly more) parties co-create a mutually agreeable value proposition through an interaction process.

B2B SCENARIO 4.2   SOLVING THE PROBLEM OF SLOWER GROWTH AT CLEANCO

Business-to-business cleaning services, which range from general office and carpet cleaning to specialized decontamination services for the health sector (such as the cleaning of surgical and dental equipment), represent a substantial industry: around £800 million of sales per year in the UK, involving nearly 3,000 businesses (www.ibisworld.co.uk/market-research/industrial-cleaning-activities.html). In turn, a substantial industry exists to serve the needs of the cleaning firms themselves, supplying them with the equipment, cleaning products, consumable items and services that they need to deliver cleaning services to industrial customers.

Cleanco is a multinational firm that produces and markets professional cleaning products such as chemicals, cleaning systems and consumable goods. Their principal business areas are industrial laundry, office cleaning, hotel cleaning, kitchen hygiene and personal hygiene in the industrial and commercial sector. Cleanco uses both direct distribution channels (to their biggest customers) and distributors. They have a sales team and a customer service team. The sales team initiates, maintains and develops customer relationships. The customer service team processes orders, delivers customer training and advice, delivers product demonstrations, and arranges maintenance and repair service. Market segmentation is along industry sector lines; for example, the healthcare sector, and the dairy products sector.

After enjoying several years of healthy growth, the dilemma facing Cleanco was a slowdown in the growth of sales and profitability. The marketing team had diagnosed the situation and identified three key factors that lay behind the slowdown;

1   the market seemed to be approaching saturation;

2   buyer power was becoming increasingly concentrated; and,

3   the market was becoming increasingly competitive.

In the past, when the market was less competitive and buyer power was less concentrated, it might have been possible to increase sales turnover and, in particular, profit margins, by simply increasing prices. However, this seemed like a much more problematic option now, since powerful buyers would resist price increases, and competitors would no doubt see any Cleanco price increases as an opportunity to make a strong pitch for their customers' business. A key consequence of slower growth was that overhead costs were rising as a proportion of total costs. Overhead costs were not attributed to individual customers, so that it was increasingly difficult to work out which customer accounts were generating profits, which were marginal, and which were unprofitable.

Cleanco formed a team to address this strategic problem.

Source: Based on Van Raaij et al. (2003).

CHAPTER SUMMARY

- Business-to-business organizations are widely striving to incorporate the principles of CSR and sustainability into their business and marketing strategies.

- Business strategists are increasingly convinced that sound business and marketing strategies must be built on sound ethical principles – that long-term economic performance is enhanced by ethical corporate behaviour. In addressing ethical issues in business-to-business marketing, four perspectives may be used: managerial egoism (what is best for the company), utilitarianism (evaluating the costs and benefits to all stakeholders), the deontological approach (abiding by codes of conduct), or virtue ethics (learning and applying sound judgement based on integrity).

- Strategy concerns decisions that have a major effect on the performance of the firm. It can be subdivided into corporate strategy (concerning the overall design of a corporation comprising multiple business units) and business unit strategy (concerning the competitive strategies of individual businesses). Marketing strategies are devised and implemented at the business unit level.

- Three approaches to marketing strategy were discussed in the chapter: the rational planning approach, the resource-based approach and strategy as the management of relationships and networks. The rational planning approach proposes that good strategy results from a systematic, planned approach to strategy development. The resource-based approach focuses on key internal resources of the firm as the source of enduring competitive advantage. The relationships and networks view of strategy contends that network positional resources are the key to success in business markets.

- The overall aim of business strategy in profit-seeking firms is to increase long-term shareholder value. The key contribution that marketing strategy in business-to-business firms should make is to understand, analyse and deliver customer value. Customer value is defined as the tradeoff between what a customer has to give up and what the customer receives in a business transaction or relationship.

QUESTIONS FOR DISCUSSION

1. How can customer value be defined?

2. What are the key differences between the resource-based view of business marketing strategy and the conventional strategic market planning approach?

3. Is the internet completely revolutionizing business-to-business marketing and purchasing?

4. What kind of ethical issues might a business-to-business marketer or salesperson have to take into account when engaged in: (a) a major account sales negotiation; (b) a substantial international market research project; and (c) bidding for a government contract in a foreign country?

5. You are a sales executive for an engineering company. Yesterday one of your clients told you – in confidence – about an important government initiative that could revolutionize their industry. Today you are hoping to close a big deal with a different client in the same industry. It is obvious that they have not heard about this government initiative yet, and if you let them in on the secret they would be impressed and it might help secure the deal. You remember that you learned about several different approaches to ethical decision-making when at business school – how do they help you when deciding whether or not to pass on the information?

CASE STUDY 4.1   THE CARBON TRUST

THE GLOBAL ENVIRONMENTAL CHALLENGE

STRATEGIC APPROACH – MANAGE THE IMPACT OF CLIMATE CHANGE

There is now widespread awareness of the hypothesis that we are in the midst of a gradual, general increase in global temperatures – what is commonly known as 'global warming'. Although gradual in terms of normal human timescales, this increase is rapid in geological terms, and possibly unprecedented. The evidence seems to be consistent with the theory that the current rise in global temperatures has been substantially caused by human activity. In particular, the last two centuries have seen human beings consuming carbon-based energy (particularly coal and oil) in very large quantities. What is undeniable is that human consumption of coal and oil results in the production of large quantities of carbon dioxide. What is more controversial is the hypothesis that the release of all of this carbon dioxide into the Earth's atmosphere has been the principal cause of global warming during the last two centuries.

Nevertheless, the scientific consensus is that humankind bears direct responsibility for a large part of global warming. The implications of this are difficult to predict, and vary from the mildly alarming to the catastrophic. The scientific consensus is also that there is massive inertia in the earth's climatic system, so that whatever we do now will only gradually begin to undo the damage wrought by the last two centuries of burning carbon. Glaciers and possibly polar icecaps will continue to melt, sea levels will continue to rise, low-lying land will be flooded, and the incidence of severe weather events will increase over the next few decades, regardless of what we do now. But if we do nothing, and the burning of carbon fuels continues to increase relentlessly, then the consequences will eventually be far worse.

The most recent international agreement on actions to ameliorate climate change is the 2015 Paris climate change agreement. The Kyoto Protocol of 1997 was a predecessor to the Paris agreement. The British government was a signatory to the United Nations Framework Convention on Climate Change (signed at the Rio Earth Summit in 1992) and agreed to legally binding emission reduction targets by ratifying the Kyoto Protocol. The Carbon Trust is an independent company that was originally set up by the government to help to put into practice Britain's obligations under the Kyoto Protocol. It offers a range of services to businesses and public sector and governmental organizations to assist them to reduce their energy consumption. Those services include advice, carbon footprinting and participation in the development of low-carbon technologies. The Carbon Trust Standard was introduced in 2008 as an independent, verifiable standard to measure progress against carbon reduction goals. Companies that wish to demonstrate their commitment to reducing carbon emissions can seek certification under the Carbon Trust Standard. If they succeed, they are entitled to display the 'Carbon Trust Standard – Reducing CO_2 Year on Year' logo.

KEY FEATURES OF THE GLOBAL CLIMATE CHANGE CHALLENGE

Recent temperatures are warmer than any since direct measurements began. All of the ten warmest years on record have occurred since 1990. Recent years are probably the warmest seen for more than 100,000 years.

- Mountain glaciers are in retreat. The Arctic ice cap is shrinking. The Larsen Ice Shelf in Antarctica is breaking up.
- Many areas of the world have seen fewer long cold spells of weather and more long hot spells.
- Insurance data shows that losses from catastrophic weather events have risen globally by a factor of 10 since the 1950s, after accounting for inflation.
- The most respected estimates suggest that global temperature will rise by 1.5–5.8 degrees Celsius by the end of the century.
- Many species of plants and animals will die out because their ecosystems will be disrupted: possibly as many as a quarter of the world's known species.
- We can expect more intense tropical cyclones, intensified droughts and floods associated with El Niño in the Pacific, and greater variability of the Asian summer monsoon.

THE RESPONSIBILITY OF BUSINESS

Is the responsibility of private businesses solely to maximize the returns they make for their owners, the shareholders, or do they have a wider responsibility to society? Many people – the most prominent in recent years has been the eminent late American economist Milton Friedman – have argued that the sole objective of a private enterprise should be to maximize shareholder value. Others have argued that businesses are an integral part of wider society and must contribute, as responsible corporate citizens, to the wider aims of that society.

One enduring line of argument in this debate is whether there is any contradiction between shareholder value maximization and making a contribution to wider society. Might it not be the case that those businesses that cultivate socially responsible strategies are also the most profitable? There is no simple answer to this question. When a company gets caught out in unethical practice, and sees its brand equity and

(Continued)

(Continued)

share price damaged as a result of public disapproval, it seems obvious that ethical practice is closely related to profitability. But we cannot know how many companies have quietly got away with unethical practices and enhanced their profits as a result. The few high-profile cases of companies that are caught out may represent proof that unethical behaviour (like crime) 'doesn't pay', or they may simply indicate that most unethical companies 'get away with it'.

In the case of reducing human consumption of carbon-based energy, appeals can be made both to profitability/shareholder value and to good corporate citizenship. The case can be made that reducing the use of carbon-based fuels is good business sense. If a company can reduce its use of fuel without any adverse effect at all on its business operations, then this argument is a powerful one. So the simple message of increased energy efficiency (turning off lights and heaters when they are not needed, closing windows to avoid heat loss, and so on) is a good starting point. This is a clear-cut case, since there is little or no expenditure associated with the cost savings. Going beyond this to change business processes in order to increase energy efficiency requires greater justification. For example, improving building insulation or replacing the ageing business vehicle fleet with newer, more fuel-efficient replacements involves an investment in order to reap the energy-saving reward. The Carbon Trust can facilitate the analysis of such decisions, and point to any government initiatives that might provide financial incentives and so sway the decision in favour of energy efficiency, but ultimately this boils down to a private investment decision, which the company must decide is profitable or not. Conventionally, however, a company will only include the *private* costs and benefits of the decision in its investment appraisal. Once a company goes beyond this and includes an allowance for the wider impact of its decision, then it is adopting the message of corporate social responsibility. For example, should the company decide to replace its ageing fleet of vans sooner than expected (and despite an unfavourable investment appraisal) because of the damage that the emissions from their old and unsophisticated engines are doing to the environment, then it is engaging in an act of CSR.

Only when a business forgoes a preferred alternative and consciously chooses an ethical but less profitable alternative can it be said to be pursuing CSR. In the case of carbon emissions, this means taking action to reduce emissions even though an alternative course of action would be more profitable. The job of the Carbon Trust is not only to persuade businesses to do things that they really ought to do anyway in order to improve their profits (like cut energy-running costs and make profitable investments in energy-saving technology) but also to persuade them to go beyond this and make investments for the good of the planet.

CASE STUDY QUESTIONS

This exercise is best done as a debate, with one team being allocated to each side of the argument.

1   Make the case for the proposition that the only legitimate purpose for a commercial business in a free-enterprise system is to maximize the returns to shareholders. What is the role of the Carbon Trust from this point of view?

2   Make the alternative case that all business organizations have a wider social responsibility that goes beyond the pursuit of shareholder value. What is the role of the Carbon Trust from this point of view?

3   On which side of the argument do your sympathies mainly lie? Explain why.

Sources: Carbon Trust, 2004; www.carbontrust.co.uk; Turner, 2003.

FURTHER READING

Kothandaraman, P. and Wilson, D.T. (2001) 'The future of competition: value-creating networks', *Industrial Marketing Management*, 30(4): 379–89.

Here's a quotation from the article to get you interested (p. 382): 'The Ford Motor Company's Rough River Plant, at one time, was perhaps one of the most integrative operations in the world. Iron ore came in one end of the complex and went out as an automobile the other end of the complex. The Ford Motor Company was fully integrated from iron ore to weaving the materials for the seat coverings to assembly and building the total automobile.' Doesn't that sound kind of ... well, kind of neat? So why does nobody do it any more? Why is 'value-creating networks' the new way of doing business?

Lindgreen, A. and Wynstra, F. (2005) 'Value in business markets: what do we know? Where are we going?', *Industrial Marketing Management*, 34(7): 732–48.

There is an emerging consensus that the key to developing effective marketing strategies in B2B markets is to understand customer value. Here is an exhaustive, state-of-the-art review of what B2B value means.

Wiersema, F. (2013) 'The B2B agenda: the current state of B2B marketing and a look ahead', *Industrial Marketing Management*, 42 (4): 470–88.

This is a systematic review of the strategic issues in B2B marketing that are considered to be most important by leading scholars and practitioners in the field.

Visit the Institute of Business Ethics at www.ibe.org.uk/index.html, and in particular read the pages about developing a code of business ethics here: www.ibe.org.uk/ethical-values-and-codes/102/52. This will provide you with a practitioner perspective on the discussion in this chapter about deontological ethics and developing ethical codes.

5

RESEARCHING BUSINESS-TO-BUSINESS MARKETS

LEARNING OUTCOMES

After reading this chapter you will:

- be able to explain why accuracy, timeliness, relevance and uniqueness are valuable characteristics of marketing information;
- understand how the fundamental characteristics of business-to-business markets affect the market research process;
- know how to apply market research sampling techniques in business markets;
- know why survey response rates tend to be low in business-to-business market surveys, and what techniques can be used to improve response rates;
- be able to use a standard industrial classification as a basis for sample selection in business markets; and
- understand how the relationship between a market research agency and a business-to-business client organization can affect the success of a research project.

INTRODUCTION

In the preceding three chapters we have looked at how organizations buy, how inter-firm relationships are becoming ever more important in business markets, and the key aspects of strategy in business markets, in particular how business marketers must deliver superior value to customers. In general terms it is clear that business marketers must be concerned with questions such as:

- What are the buying criteria and buying processes of customers and potential customers?
- How important are inter-firm relationships in their target markets?
- What are the strategic plans, positioning strategies and target markets of those customers with whom they seek to develop partnering relationships?
- How do customers and potential customers define value?

The only way to answer these (and many other) questions for specific markets and specific customers is to undertake market research. In the next chapter of the book we will address market segmentation in business markets, after which, in the succeeding chapters, we will look in more detail at the development of specific marketing plans – planning for integrated marketing communications, for effective distribution and logistics, for competitive pricing, and so on. All of these chapters also raise new research problems that require the application of systematic marketing research. Two examples of the use of systematic marketing research to cast light on important issues in business marketing are provided in B2B Snapshot 5.1; these examples deal with research concerning social media use by small B2B firms, and the size of the buying centre.

B2B SNAPSHOT 5.1   PRACTICAL RESEARCH IN B2B MARKETS

SOCIAL MEDIA

The question of how widely small and medium-sized B2B firms (SMEs) are using social media marketing was investigated by Michaelidou et al. (2011). A mail questionnaire was sent to 1,000 SMEs – firms with no more than 250 employees and less than €50 million turnover – using random sampling from a commercial database (FAME). While 146 questionnaires were returned (14.6 per cent), only 102 were fully completed for a 10.2 per cent effective response rate. Only 27 per cent of respondents were using social media marketing. They used social media to attract new customers, to cultivate relationships, to increase awareness and to communicate the brand online. Although the direct financial costs of implementing a social media marketing strategy are modest, major concerns for the smaller firm are the time involved in managing a social media presence, lack of familiarity with social media and doubts that a social media presence would contribute to their business objectives.

THE BUYING CENTRE

In an American study (McWilliams et al., 1992) 440 questionnaires were sent to purchasing agents in 18 firms; 231 usable questionnaires were returned, for a response rate of 52 per cent. The study concerned the purchasing decision for component parts. The variables measured using the questionnaire were buying centre size, purchase situation (new buy, modified re-buy, straight re-buy) and purchase phase (need identification, establishment of specifications, identification and evaluation of buying alternatives, supplier selection). The study found that the mean size of the buying centre was four people, with a normal range of between three and five. The buying centre tended to be largest for new-buy purchasing situations and smallest for straight re-buys, with modified re-buys lying in between. The buying centre was smallest for the final stage of the buying process (supplier selection), and largest for the identification and evaluation of buying alternatives.

THE VALUE OF MARKETING INFORMATION

It seemed to me that too many people were accepting at face value, uncritically, the idea that information was becoming the most valuable commodity. Information was at the library. Anybody could check it out for nothing.

Didn't that accessibility undermine its value? And information could be wrong, in which case it might have negative value – it might hurt instead of help. Even when the information that bombarded us every day proved to be correct, most of it was irrelevant anyway. And when information was relevant, its value was often ephemeral, decaying with the passage of time or if too many people had it. (Gates, 1996: 22)

Bill Gates, the founder of Microsoft, points out that accuracy, timeliness, relevance and uniqueness are important characteristics of information. In a world in which the internet has made more and more information available ever more easily to businesses and consumers, this is perhaps a useful reminder. Whereas the principal marketing information problem facing B2B marketers was once simply obtaining access to sufficient information, today a key part of the marketing information problem involves sorting the accurate and relevant information out of the vast ocean of information that is available. Information is as important to marketing success today as it was when Baker and Hart (1989) and Hooley and Jobber (1986) showed that the use of market research information is associated with above-average corporate performance. Companies that perform better than average are significantly more likely to gather market research than companies that perform below average; top-performing companies are significantly more likely than other companies to make use of a range of market research techniques. Hooley and Jobber found that industrial firms were less likely to conduct market research than consumer firms (52 per cent of industrial firms, compared to 73 per cent of consumer firms) but that top-performing industrial firms were significantly more likely to conduct research than average-performing firms. They concluded that top-performing business-to-business firms have a strongly proactive approach to planning, put greater emphasis on product differentiation than average performers, and demonstrate a strong commitment to customer orientation through above-average use of formal, objective market research. There is a positive statistical association between business-to-business firm performance and the use of formal, objective market research. This does not prove that greater use of formal market research causes improved business performance, since a statistical association alone cannot prove that one thing causes another. However, it does lend support to the hypothesis that one of the factors driving improved performance for business-to-business organizations is the use of formal market research.

Much attention in marketing research is paid to technical aspects, such as how to design measurement instruments, particularly questionnaires, and techniques for analysing data. These factors are very largely concerned with ensuring that information is accurate, while the other important factors mentioned by Bill Gates – timeliness, uniqueness and, perhaps most important of all, relevance – tend to be neglected. Of these factors, timeliness and relevance, and perhaps uniqueness to a degree, will depend largely on the effective management of the marketing research process. Getting 'accurate' (valid, reliable) data is largely a technical matter. Getting the 'right' (relevant) information, at the 'right time', is a managerial matter. Where marketing research is conducted by a specialist agency on behalf of a client organization, this managerial matter becomes one of managing the relationship between the client and the agency so as to maximize the likelihood of getting the right information, at the right time, and on budget. While B2B businesses have access to ever more data because of the internet and social media, data alone cannot answer the important question of how to make use of market research information in decision-making. As our technologies for gathering and disseminating information grow ever more sophisticated, it is through the effective use of this wealth of information that firms will gain a competitive edge.

In this chapter we will address the issues of accuracy, timeliness, relevance and uniqueness in the context of business-to-business market research. In the next section we return to a theme of Chapter 1 – the differences between consumer and business markets – and assess the implications of these differences for market research. Following this, we address issues affecting information accuracy, by looking at the pros and cons of different approaches to sampling, examining different survey techniques, and investigating the differences between qualitative and quantitative data gathering. We also introduce the concept of the *standard industrial classification* (SIC) as a basic tool for business-to-business market research – subsequently, in Chapter 6, we will see how the standard industrial classification can be used for purposes of market segmentation. Having discussed these fairly technical issues associated primarily with data accuracy, we move on to look at the management of the market research process, and in particular the management of the relationship between the business-to-business client and their market research agency, to see how market research projects can be managed for data timeliness, relevance and uniqueness. In the closing section of the chapter we consider the impact of the internet on business-to-business market research.

MARKET RESEARCH AND THE NATURE OF BUSINESS MARKETS

While there are many similarities between market research in business markets and consumer markets – for example, the statistical principles of sampling and the basics of sound questionnaire design remain the same – the characteristics of business markets introduce some differences. Of particular relevance are the following three aspects of business markets, which were discussed in Chapter 1:

derived demand

accelerator effect

concentration ratios.

You will remember that we define demand in business markets as 'derived demand', because organizations buy goods and services in order to pursue business goals and not for any intrinsic satisfaction to be derived from consumption. The accelerator effect occurs in capital goods industries, where relatively small changes in downstream demand can bring about much larger changes in the demand for investment goods. High concentration ratios are characteristic of business markets – meaning that only a few buying organizations make up a large proportion of the total buying power in an industry.

As a result of derived demand, business marketing organizations cannot simply focus on their immediate customers but may also need to be aware of factors affecting demand further downstream. For example, a manufacturer of plastics that are used in the automobile and aerospace industries will try to keep abreast of developments in business and consumer demand for vehicles and for air travel, rather than simply looking at the immediate pattern of demand from automobile and aircraft manufacturers. This will provide a longer-term view of likely developments in the plastics market. The need to be aware of downstream patterns of demand is even more important where an accelerator effect is present, since a shift in downstream demand will have a multiplied effect on demand for capital goods. For example, the illustration used in Chapter 1 (B2B Snapshot 1.3) showed how a 20 per cent increase in demand for new houses could increase demand for construction equipment used in the house-building industry by 100 per cent in the short term. In general, business-to-business marketing organizations will rely on secondary sources of market research for purposes of keeping up to date with trends in markets that are downstream from their immediate customers. Primary market research would be too time-consuming and expensive. This tends to make secondary market research (that is, the use of existing data sources) particularly important to business marketers.

High concentration ratios affect market research in a different way. First, when conducting a primary market research project in an industry with a high concentration ratio, it is important to include the 'vital few' buying organizations that constitute a high proportion of industry demand. Second, a few key buying personnel in those 'vital few' organizations are likely to receive a lot of requests to provide market research information. This tends to affect adversely the *response rate* to market research surveys, or to requests for market research interviews. As a result – as we will see later in the chapter – response rates to business-to-business market research surveys are often disappointingly low.

RESEARCH FUNDAMENTALS IN BUSINESS-TO-BUSINESS MARKETS

Sampling and sampling frames

The fundamentals of sampling theory are the same no matter what kind of market one is dealing with, and the statistical accuracy of estimates based on sample parameters is the same whether they are business-to-business or consumer markets. However, certain sampling techniques, not commonly used in consumer marketing, are used more frequently in business-to-business markets because of the structure of such markets, in particular because the relevant population is usually fairly small and some members of the population are much more important than others in terms of their buying power.

Table 5.1 shows the sampling techniques available for marketing surveys. A sample is a portion or subset of a larger group called a population. In business-to-business marketing the population might include all business organizations in a particular country (for example, if one was conducting a national survey of business usage of smartphones), but more often would comprise all the organizations in a particular sector of the economy (such as 'all manufacturing industries' or 'all educational establishments'), or only those organizations in a particular industry (for example, providers of commercial cleaning services) or geographical area (all businesses within the boundaries of a specific city, county or province, for example). In general, the aim of sampling is to obtain a representative sample, meaning a sample that reflects the overall population in terms of important characteristics. For example, in taking a sample of 1,000 businesses for a national survey of business use of

TABLE 5.1 Sampling methods

Probability sampling	Non-probability sampling
Simple random sampling	Convenience sampling
Stratified random sampling	Snowball sampling
Systematic sampling	Quota sampling
Cluster/multi-stage sampling	Focus groups

smartphones, the size and industry distributions of firms in the sample should reflect the characteristics of the national economy – if 25 per cent of firms in the economy operate in the manufacturing sector, then around 250 of the firms in the sample should be in manufacturing.

In *probability sampling*, every member of the target population has a known, non-zero probability of being included in the sample. Probability sampling involves the selection of sampling units from a *sampling frame*. The sampling frame is a list of the units (such as firms, managers or industry associations) that are eligible to be included in the survey. Ideally, the sampling frame should be a complete list of all of the members of the relevant population. Good sampling frames, including very nearly all members of the relevant population, are quite easy to find for business markets in developed countries. Commercial information providers, such as Dun & Bradstreet (www.dnb.com) and Reed Business Information (www.reedbusiness.com), make it their business to maintain databases of firms that are as complete and accurate as possible. In *simple random sampling*, every unit within the sampling frame has an equal chance of being selected for the sample. The difficulty with this method is that there is no guarantee that the sample will be representative; the sample may, by chance, contain a higher percentage of one kind of business organization than is found in the sampling frame and in the population. To avoid this problem, *stratified random sampling* is often used, where the population and sampling frame are divided up into meaningful groups or 'strata' and then samples are taken from each of the strata according to their representation in the population. For example, company size and industry sector are typical strata in business-to-business sampling.

Table 5.2 shows how stratified random sampling is applied. A sample of 10,000 firms is to be taken. The sample is stratified using company size and industry sector. The proportions with which those strata are represented in the population are shown in the table. In order to calculate the subsample size in each cell of Table 5.2, it is necessary to multiply the column proportion by the row proportion, and multiply the result by the desired sample size (in this case 10,000). So the desired subsample size for medium-sized firms (10 per cent) from the manufacturing industries (25 per cent) is:

$10\% \times 25\% \times 10,000$

or

$0.1 \times 0.25 \times 10,000$

which equals 250, as shown in the table.

TABLE 5.2 Illustrating stratified random sampling

	Company size categories				
	Proportion in population (%)	1–9 employees (%) 85	10–99 employees (%) 10	100 or more employees (%) 5	Total (%) 100
Primary industries	5	425	50	25	500
Manufacturing industries	25	2,125	250	125	2,500
Service industries	70	5,950	700	350	7,000
Total	100	8,500	1,000	500	10,000

Systematic sampling can also be used as an alternative to simple random sampling. Suppose that we want to take a sample size of 400 from a single industry sector; we have a list of all of the firms in the industry, of which there are 3,600. We need a sample of one-ninth of the firms (400 divided by 3,600). To obtain this we need a random starting number between 1 and 9; let us say that through a random process (even as simple as pulling numbers out of a hat) we get the starting number 2. Our sample will then comprise the firms in the list in places 2, 11, 20, 29, 38, and so on. This method can only be used when we are sure that there is no systematic variation within the sampling frame.

The final approach to probability sampling is cluster sampling. This can be used where there are naturally occurring units in the population. Naturally occurring units include such things as firms, trade associations, factories, schools and departments within firms. For example, if we wish to investigate the use of smartphones by sales executives in the IT industry, we could choose to select a random sample of sales *departments* (rather than a random sample of sales executives) and then conduct a survey with all of the members of the selected departments. The main advantage of this sampling technique over other probability sampling methods is its convenience. It would be difficult to obtain an accurate list of all of the sales executives in a geographical area in order to take a simple random sample; it is easier to get a list of all of the IT companies.

The main distinction when *non-probability sampling* is used is that the units in the population do not have a known, non-zero probability of being selected for the sample. Non-probability sampling may be used either with the aim of consciously building a representative sample, for reasons of convenience, or because in the researcher's judgement some units in the population *must* be included in the sample.

A convenience sample is simply a group of respondents who are ready and available to complete the survey. For example, a building supplies company may ask customers (generally, the owner-managers of small building firms) as they leave the premises to complete a customer satisfaction survey. Such a survey has limited validity.

In *snowball sampling*, the researcher relies on previously identified members of the target population to identify other sample members. Such an approach might be used in researching the organizational buying DMU, for example. Remember, from Chapter 2, that membership of the DMU is not strictly defined and is often not aligned with a particular organizational department or unit. It is quite likely that the only people who really know who was involved in a major buying decision are the members of the DMU. Once you have identified one member of the DMU (such as the purchasing executive who coordinated their efforts) you can ask this person to identify other members, who in turn may point you in the direction of further people who were also involved (remembering, also, that the DMU can extend to people outside of the buying organization).

Quota sampling divides the relevant population into subgroups, such as manufacturing and service firms, and small, medium and large firms. As with stratified random sampling, the proportions of these categories in the population are used to define their proportions in the sample – the sample size for each category is simply the desired overall sample size multiplied by its proportion in the population. The key difference with quota sampling is that the members of each subsample are not selected randomly.

Finally, focus groups represent a form of non-probability sampling that is often used for purposes of exploratory market research. Suppose that the Carbon Trust (www.carbontrust.com), in pursuing its mission to help businesses, governments and the public sector to accelerate the move to a low carbon economy, wants to conduct a large-scale survey of the reasons why firms do not develop and implement energy efficiency plans. Unless similar research has been conducted before, it is difficult to see how one could begin to construct a meaningful questionnaire. There are so many possible reasons why firms may not seek to become more energy efficient (general inertia, energy costs being an insignificant part of the budget, it not being seen as a managerial priority, fear that it would involve high start-up costs, and so on) that one cannot know *a priori* which are genuinely relevant to business attitudes. Focus-group discussions – that is, discussions with small groups (6–10 people) guided by a professional facilitator – with executives who are responsible for energy management are a way of establishing the genuine concerns of the relevant target population. The data (generally qualitative) gathered through focus groups can be very useful in itself. Often, once the key issues have been clarified through the use of focus groups a questionnaire will be developed for administration to a much larger sample in order to generate statistically valid, quantitative results.

Response rates

The purpose and logic of sampling are straightforward. A sample is designed to be representative of the target population, so that results achieved for the sample can be generalized (within known statistical limits) to the whole population. An ideal sample is a miniature version of the population. However, even assuming that the sample is selected sufficiently well that it is indeed representative of the population, there is no guarantee that the effective sample of those who actually respond to the survey will conform to the original sample. The two issues that arise here are, first, what is the response rate from those who are selected for the sample and, second, are those who respond representative of the whole sample (and so of the population)? For example, if we send a questionnaire to 500 firms in the manufacturing industry and receive 113 usable replies, then we have a response rate of 22.6 per cent. How certain can we be that the 113 firms that replied are representative of the 500 firms in the original survey, and hence of the overall population of manufacturing businesses?

B2B SNAPSHOT 5.2   INNOVATIVE USE OF THE INTERNET TO COLLECT VALUABLE B2B INFORMATION

People who travel extensively for business are generally responsible and busy people with a lot on their minds. They are also regularly spending money in different countries and in different currencies, which they then need to claim back in their own currency. Keeping track of overseas business expenses is something these people just have to do, and the more help they can get with this task the better. Enter XE.com (previously Xenon Laboratories): 'the world's favorite provider of online Internet foreign exchange tools and services' (www.xe.com). The XE Travel Expense Calculator (www.xe.com/tec/) provides a simple tool where you can enter details of what you spent, where and when, and have it all converted to your home currency, at the exchange rate that was prevailing on the day when the transaction took place. This means that it is easy to handle different currencies if your trip took in different countries, and the calculator even takes account of the fact that exchange rates fluctuate from day to day. So your claim will be accurate. So far, so good. However, the card issuer will charge you for making purchases in foreign currencies. These charges are built into the effective exchange rate charged on the transaction; so, rather than an explicit cost, the charge appears as a less favourable exchange rate. How much does your card issuer charge you? You can find out quickly and easily by using the XE Credit Card Charges Calculator (www.xe.com/ccc/). That way, you, or perhaps more importantly your financial controller, can work out how much the card issuer is charging and decide how reasonable that is.

What, you might ask, does all this have to do with B2B market research? Well, Andy Lockett and Ian Blackman (2004) provide the answer. XE.com wanted to know how much card issuers charged for foreign exchange credit card transactions, if the charges varied between card issuers, and if the charges varied between currencies. This kind of information would help them advise their corporate clients. As Lockett and Blackman (2004) explain, XE.com *could* have tried intercepting business travellers at the airport and asking them to fill in questionnaires about their business trips and their expenses, but there are a lot of problems to be overcome (for example, obtaining permission from the airport operator, persuading busy business-people to take part, and then obtaining accurate, complex and detailed information from them). What XE.com did instead was to develop the XE Travel Expense Calculator and the XE Credit Card Charges Calculator, providing business-people worldwide with a useful tool which they voluntarily chose to use. By using this tool, those business-people provide XE.com with exactly the information they need (obviously it is only ever used completely anonymously and in aggregate form). Even better, the information is regularly updated and is available more or less in real-time. As Lockett and Blackman (2004: 186) observe: 'The case demonstrates that Xenon, by adopting an innovative methodological approach, has been able to collect data which would have been very costly, time-consuming or simply not available with the use of a more traditional approach to market research.'

Sources: Lockett and Blackman, 2004; www.xe.com.

The first practical consideration associated with non-response in surveys is the effect on important subsamples. Suppose that we wish to investigate differences between large firms and small firms, and between firms from the north and those from the south of the country. With our original sample size of 500, subdividing the sample into four categories (large/north, small/north, large/south, small/south) would result in around 125 firms in each category (assuming for simplicity that there is an equal number of large and small firms, and an equal number of firms in the north and in the south). With our effective sample size of 113, then we would expect to have around 28 firms in each category. If we make statements such as '60 per cent of small manufacturing firms in the north want …', then it is important to remember that the statement is not based on a sample of 113, but on a much smaller subsample. It is important, therefore, to take account of the expected response rate to a survey at the planning stage of a market research survey.

While we hope that everyone we contact will respond to our survey, this is simply not going to happen. A lot of people we send the questionnaire to will simply ignore it (Diamantopoulos and Schlegelmilch, 1996; Faria and Dickinson, 1992; Greer and Lohtia, 1994). Diamantopoulos and Schlegelmilch (1996) argue that low response rates affect the quality of the information obtained, as well as the quantity. The problem of relatively low rates of response to industrial marketing surveys is not a new one; Stacey and Wilson (1969) suggested a typical response rate of 25 per cent to industrial surveys in the 1960s, while Rawnsley (1978) quoted response rates of between 12 per cent and 29 per cent during the 1970s. When new media come along there may well be a short-term boost in response rates because of the novelty factor, but that wears off rather quickly. Sheehan (2001) found that email surveys, when first introduced, had better response rates than postal surveys, but that the average rate of response to email surveys declined sharply as email became a standard business tool. Clearly, business-to-business market researchers must strive to maximize the response rate.

These days, electronic methods of survey delivery are commonly used. A questionnaire can be delivered as an email attachment or through an online survey tool (examples of such tools are BOS – www.onlinesurveys.ac.uk; SurveyWriter – www.surveywriter.net; and SurveyMonkey – www.surveymonkey.com). B2B marketers who need to develop their own complex web surveys can invest the time and money required to master specialist web survey software, such as The Survey System (www.surveysystem.com) or Survey Crafter Professional (www.surveycrafter.com).

In recent years, companies have sought methods of overcoming steadily declining response rates to B2B surveys. Initially, when the internet was a new technology, it was possible to obtain a better response in the virtual world (distributing a questionnaire by email or through an online survey service) than in the real world, but any such advantage of electronic media has long gone. Responses to online B2B surveys are very low. In fact, there may even be some advantage to switching back to old-fashioned 'snail mail' because it is now something of a novelty. However, as B2B Snapshot 5.2 illustrates, the internet does create opportunities for creative approaches that enable B2B companies to obtain the information they need by providing some value added to internet users.

STANDARD INDUSTRIAL CLASSIFICATION

A standard industrial classification is a systematic method of classifying economic activity. In everyday language it is usually sufficient to talk about 'the tourism industry' or 'the banking industry', but for the purposes of marketing research and marketing planning it is important to have clearly agreed definitions of precisely what is included and what is excluded from a definition of an industry. Fortunately governments – for their own purposes – have constructed precise classification systems for economic activity. The original purpose of these standard industrial classifications was to enable governments to gather consistent data about the amount and the growth rate of economic activity in a country. Such information is essential to the conduct of government economic and industrial policies. Governments need to know which industries are growing, which are stagnant and which are declining. Originally, the use of standard industrial classification data for marketing purposes was a by-product of this essential government tool. Today, standard industrial classifications are as useful to industry as they are to governments.

For most everyday purposes it is perfectly acceptable to talk about 'the car industry' or 'the chemical industry'. In a normal conversation we do not normally need to be any more specific than that. However, it is certainly not good enough for market research purposes. If a client asks a researcher to study the growth rate of the car industry, and to profile the key firms in the industry, then the researcher will immediately set about refining the definition of the industry.

> So, when you say the car industry, do you just mean manufacturers of automobiles, or would you include such things as trucks and buses? What about construction equipment like backhoe diggers? Is it only the vehicle manufacturers that are of interest, or are you interested in the suppliers of automotive components as well, like exhaust systems, instrument clusters and tyres? Would you say that car repair firms should be included, or not?

And so might the conversation continue. The answers to these questions will depend upon exactly what it is that the client is trying to find out. If the objective is to establish the potential of the UK original equipment market for fuel injection systems for use in passenger cars, then the car industry will be defined quite narrowly as those very few firms that actually assemble passenger cars in the UK. But fuel injection systems can also be sold to firms supplying engines to car manufacturers and to car repair shops operating in the after-market. So the definition of the industry or industry sector is a matter of fundamental importance to the success of a business-to-business marketing research project. If we do not have a clear and agreed industry definition, then we could end up wasting time and energy researching things that are of no interest. Worse, we could end up *not* researching something that is regarded as central to a targeted marketing strategy.

In order to ensure a common understanding of industry definitions, a rigorous classification of industries, sectors and subsectors is required. Marketing researchers can make use of the standard industrial classification system as used by governments, first, to ensure that industry sectors are defined rigorously, and second, to build lists of similar firms for purposes of primary market research. Although there are many standard industrial classification systems in use throughout the world, there is a fairly high degree of common ground between them.

Details about the British Standard Industrial Classification, or simply UK SIC, can be found at www.ons.gov.uk/methodology/classificationsandstandards/ukstand

ardindustrialclassificationofeconomicactivities/uksic2007. The UK SIC is, for all practical purposes, identical to the equivalent NACE (Nomenclature statistique des activités économiques dans la Communauté) system devised by the EU. Both of these systems are identical to the International Standard Industrial Classification (ISIC) of the United Nations at the two-digit level. In North America, the old United States Standard Industrial Classification (US SIC) was officially replaced some years ago by the North American Industry Classification System (NAICS), which is used throughout the USA, Canada and Mexico.

The principle behind any standard industrial classification system is to put every form of economic activity into a unique numeric (or alpha-numeric) category. A SIC starts with a single letter or digit, which divides an economy into broad industry categories. Each successive digit in the classification then subdivides that industry into smaller and smaller industry sectors and subsectors. Take, for example, the 2012 version of the NAICS (www.census.gov/eos/www/naics/index.html). Categories 31–33 denote manufacturing industries. Category 334 is 'computer and electronic product manufacturing', a subdivision of manufacturing industry, while category 3346 is 'manufacturing and reproducing magnetic and optical media', a further subdivision. The NAICS is a six-digit classification system, so that this process of successively dividing up larger units into their component parts continues until the sixth digit is reached (for example, 334613 indicates 'blank magnetic and optical recording media manufacturing').

For business-to-business marketing researchers, standard industrial classification systems are useful for two key purposes. These purposes are, first, to make an unambiguous definition of an industry or industry sector, and second, as a means of specifying a sampling frame from which a sample will be drawn for purposes of primary data gathering. Commercial information providers, such as Dun & Bradstreet and Reed Information Services, will provide either hard copy or electronic lists of firms within a specified range of SIC codes. Of course, in addition to marketing research, such lists are very commonly used for purposes of business-to-business direct mail campaigns.

USING MARKET RESEARCH AGENCIES

Business-to-business marketing managers collect, analyse and act upon marketing information all of the time. Much of this information comes to them more or less automatically, in the form of internal reports from sales executives, industry association newsletters, the trade press, industry-specific sites on the internet, and so on. Other forms of information necessitate primary information gathering of some sort, through focus groups, mail/email surveys, or one of the other methods discussed earlier in this chapter. In some cases this research might be done in-house, but often primary data gathering is carried out on behalf of the marketing manager by a professional market research agency. The marketing manager will prepare a research brief and then will work with colleagues to select a research agency to undertake the work (this, of course, is a business-to-business purchasing process and the team involved constitutes a DMU or buying centre). Working effectively with a market research agency is one of the skills of a good marketing manager.

The client–agency relationship in business markets

Market research agencies are business-to-business professional services organizations. Logically, therefore, we can analyse the client–agency relationship using the same frameworks that we introduced in Chapter 3. This section may, therefore, serve two purposes: to reinforce and illustrate further the ideas from Chapter 3, and to provide guidance on how to get the most out of a B2B marketing research project when employing a research agency.

Peterson and Kerin (1980: 69) argued that: 'While guidelines have been offered for obtaining and evaluating commercial marketing research proposals ... critical considerations involved in managing the interface between buyers and sellers of marketing research services go virtually uncharted.' There are relatively few studies that focus exclusively on the management of the client–agency relationship in business markets. Peterson and Kerin went some way towards filling the gap that they had identified by soliciting three 'tips' from a sample of market research buyers and users on the best way to manage the relationship between a business-to-business marketing researcher and his or her research suppliers. Content analysis of the responses showed that buyers and suppliers agreed that the three most important tips were:

> have a clear understanding of the problem prior to contacting the research supplier;
>
> get closely involved, at an early stage; and
>
> check past clients of suppliers, and evaluate their prior experience and industry familiarity.

Peterson and Kerin concluded that effective management of the client–agency relationship required the client to 'Open lines of frank and honest communication with the research seller early in the research process and maintain them throughout project implementation. Provide whatever information you have which bears on the problem at hand' (Peterson and Kerin, 1980: 72).

Eborall and Nathan (1989) also focused exclusively on the client–agency relationship in business-to-business marketing research. They argued that:

> *Market research is unique among professional and business services in that the competitive project tender is usually the basis for the client/agency relationship. This means that the contact between the two parties may be sporadic rather than continuous, and that the loyalty, commitment and expertise of the agency will be built more slowly than it would otherwise.*

The competitive tender approach is contrasted with an account-handling approach to supplier relationship management, which allows the incumbent supplier a degree of security and therefore encourages the development of client-specific knowledge and skills. Williamson (1975) has analysed the rationale for the development of transaction-specific assets. In the case of the research agency–client relationship, time spent by the researcher on understanding the client organization and the background to the specific research problem can be regarded as relationship-specific investments – they have very little value outside of the relationship, and can be treated as sunk costs. Where the client insists upon employing a competitive tender approach to relationship management, there is no incentive for the agency to invest in this way (Jackson, 1985a). And yet, it is the absence of such investment that is bemoaned by many researchers as the reason for:

researchers often failing to solve clients' problems;

researchers being unable to participate in the strategic decision-making process;

low perceived value of market research information; and

low status attached to the market research profession.

Deshpande and Zaltman (1987) explored the specific factors affecting the use of marketing research information in industrial marketing organizations. The purpose of the work was to extend the findings from earlier work (Deshpande and Zaltman, 1982, 1984) by extending the analysis from consumer firms to industrial firms. It was expected that differences would emerge between consumer and industrial firms, given the acknowledged differences between the consumer and industrial marketing research processes (Cox and Dominguez, 1979). The factors with the greatest influence on the use of marketing information in industrial firms were:

research conducted for exploratory purposes (this is positively associated with information use in industrial firms, in contrast to a negative association in consumer firms);

the degree of formalization in the organizational structure (again, the positive association for industrial firms contrasts with a negative association for consumer firms); and

the degree of surprise in the research findings (the negative association found for industrial firms was also found for consumer firms, but the negative effect of the surprise variable is lower for industrial firms).

Is it better for businesses commissioning market research to adopt an *'arm's length' contracting* approach towards research agencies, or should they seek to develop closer working relationships with a small number of agencies to whom they give a substantial amount of repeat business? According to Nowak et al. (1997: 488): 'Some clients believe in the benefits of partnering with their marketing research suppliers while others are still skeptical.' However, their research strongly suggested that a partnering approach to managing market research suppliers should be preferred to a transactional approach. Adopting more of a partnership approach towards market research agencies is positively associated with client perceptions of service quality, cost effectiveness, research quality, research timeliness and overall satisfaction. The conclusion is that the positive aspects of engaging in partnerships with research agencies – their better knowledge of your business and understanding of your research requirements – more than offset any negative aspects associated with complacency. A research firm that has developed a close relationship with a client is in a better position to know the client's needs and preferences and to provide more efficient service (Cater and Zabkar, 2009). In their study in Slovenia, Cater and Zabkar (2009) found that the average age of a B2B client–agency relationship was 4.4 years, and recommended that B2B research agencies should actively manage their client relationships in order to increase loyalty.

SECONDARY RESEARCH IN BUSINESS MARKETS

The importance and usefulness of secondary research

Secondary market research is used in all areas of marketing but is particularly important in business-to-business markets. One reason is cost. Secondary research is relatively inexpensive, and marketing budgets are usually less generous in business-to-business marketing than in consumer marketing. Furthermore, since demand in business-to-business markets is derived, it is necessary to study markets beyond the immediate customer market. The marketer must know something about what is happening in the customer's market, and perhaps even in the market of the customer's customer.

This is best explained by example. In marketing instant coffee to consumers, one must try to understand why it is that they buy coffee and how their tastes may change. In marketing component parts to a manufacturer of industrial diggers, one must look beyond the immediate customer (for example, a construction firm) to the customer's customers. These might include the government (for example, with road building), commercial firms (for example, offices and industrial facilities) and private individuals (for example, house building). This makes the marketing research problem much more complicated and means that secondary sources must play a greater part. It would be much too expensive to research all of these downstream markets using primary research.

Another reason for the emphasis on secondary research in business-to-business marketing is the wide availability of excellent information sources at various levels of detail – from the level of an entire economy, down to the level of an industrial sector, a subdivision of an industry, or a single firm. Governments are very interested to gather data on business activity, and much broad information on industry trends can be found in government sources (for example, in the UK the starting point is www.ons.gov.uk, and for European statistics the starting point is http://ec.europa.eu/eurostat). For most industries there is an industry association, to serve the interests of the firms in that industry (see, for example, the listings at the Federation of International Trade Associations, www.fita.org), which collects data on key trends in the industry. At the level of individual firms, commercial information providers such as Reed Information Services and Dun & Bradstreet publish directories containing information on such things as ownership structure, principal lines of business and key personnel (for example, *Key British Enterprises*, *Who Owns Whom*, *Kompass*). Firms are keen to be included in such directories, since their primary purpose is as a source of reference for potential buyers. Marketing researchers benefit from the wide availability of accurate and current information. Directories can provide a quick and accurate method of identifying firms that lie within a target market, together with details of their product range and key management personnel.

Using online sources in business-to-business research

The internet is today, of course, a ubiquitous tool for gathering marketing intelligence. The internet and, in particular, the World Wide Web have made available an unparalleled number of sources of information on a very wide range of topics. Naturally, many of these sources are of potential value to the business-to-business marketer.

We have compiled a list of a few of those sources that we regard as particularly useful and have put links to them at the companion website to this book. However, even with these sources – which are only drawn from credible information providers with well-established reputations – one has to be careful to examine the information critically, to ask how recent it is, how relevant it is to any specific marketing problem, and whether the information may be biased in some way. Where information does not come from such well-known and credible sources, critical examination is of even greater importance. This is why some familiarity with the basic principles of sound research, such as sampling and levels of statistical error, is so important to the business marketing researcher. The internet has provided us with ready access to a plethora of information providers, many of whom are more than happy to give – or sell – us information of dubious quality. Relying on the credibility of a trusted supplier (such as the *Financial Times* or Dun & Bradstreet) is one way to protect yourself from making decisions based on incorrect data, but it can never be a complete substitute for exercising your own critical faculties and asking searching questions about the quality of the original data, the analysis and the interpretation.

B2B SCENARIO 5.1   WHAT SHOULD DAN MCINTOSH DO NEXT?

For a fairly cold country the UK has a surprisingly large and growing air-conditioning market, worth around £1.2 billion and growing at 4 per cent a year. Of course, the great majority of this is for industrial and commercial air-conditioning systems rather than residential air

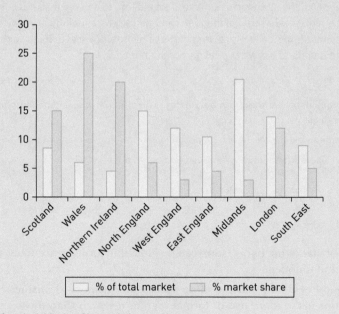

FIGURE 5.1 Airco Ltd, Market Size and Market Share

(Continued)

(Continued)

conditioning. In addition to applications to provide a comfortable environment, such as in office buildings and shopping malls, air conditioning has a wide range of B2B applications including computer data centres, food processing facilities, and hospital operating theatres (to name but a few).

Airco Ltd is a medium-sized player in the UK industrial and commercial air-conditioning sector, operating across the whole of the UK. Having recently bought an industry market research report showing the trends in the UK industrial and commercial air-conditioning market, Dan McIntosh, the Marketing and Sales Director at Airco, is puzzling over some analysis that just landed in his Outlook inbox. His attention is focused on the market size by UK geographical region, and the comparison with Airco's internal market share data (Figure 5.1).

Airco's overall market share is around 10 per cent in the UK, but Dan knows from prior experience, and can now see in the data in front of him, that their market share varies widely across the country from 3 per cent in the Midlands to 25 per cent in Wales. Worryingly, Airco's market share is at its highest in those areas of the country that comprise the smallest regional markets (Scotland, Wales and Northern Ireland), and is much lower in the larger regional markets. While Airco is the clear market leader in some regional markets, in the largest markets it is a long way behind the major competitors. Of course, Dan had some idea of this issue before, but seeing this analysis has impressed upon him the seriousness of the matter. Dan's Sales Manager argues that the sales teams in the low-share regions are struggling against particularly intense competition and receive insufficient support from the marketing team to make headway with the main industrial distributors in those regions. However, the Marketing Manager thinks the main problem is that the sales teams in the low-share regions are poorly motivated and failing to deliver the kind of results that the teams in the high-share regions manage regularly. Before making any kind of decision, Dan appreciates that he needs more information. He opens a fresh document window on his screen, and begins to list what information he needs.

Sources:

www.connectingindustry.com/factoryequipment/uk-ventilation-and-air-conditioning-market-returns-to-growth.aspx

www.bsria.com/news/article/world-air-conditioning-market-grows-thanks-to-hot-spots/

www.amaresearch.co.uk/Ventilation_Air_Conditioning_15.html

CHAPTER SUMMARY

- The value of marketing information can be judged in terms of accuracy, timeliness, relevance and uniqueness.

- There is good evidence that the more successful business-to-business marketing organizations make more use of formal market research than those that are less successful.

- Although many aspects of market research are the same in business and consumer markets – such as sampling theory – there are several practical differences that arise from the basic characteristics of business markets. As well as understanding their direct customers, business marketers need to be aware of developments further downstream in the chain of derived demand, at the level of their customers' customers and perhaps even beyond that.

- Probability sampling methods include simple random, stratified random, systematic and cluster/multi-stage sampling. Non-probability sampling methods include convenience, snowball and quota sampling. Focus groups (non-probability sampling) are often used to identify the factors that are important to a target group (for example, buying criteria considered important by industrial buyers) prior to undertaking a market reseᵃrch survey.

- Response rates to business marketing surveys are often low. Various methods are available to try to increase response rates.

- A standard industrial classification (SIC) is a systematic method of classifying economic activity, originally designed by governments, which is useful for specifying business market research samples from list providers and for defining an industry sector unambiguously.

- Where a market research agency is used to gather data, the management of the client–agency relationship will affect the usefulness of the data collected.

- While the internet has made many more secondary market research sources readily available, it is important to use information from trustworthy sources and to use critical judgement in evaluating secondary research sources.

QUESTIONS FOR DISCUSSION

1. In what ways does the practice of business-to-business marketing research differ from consumer marketing research?

2. Imagine that you are describing the use of the internet/World Wide Web/email/ social media to a business marketing manager who retired in 2000 (and who has had a particularly sheltered life since – let's say, living in a log cabin without electricity or a telephone). To them, this sounds like the perfect marketing tool for gathering primary marketing research, securing secondary market intelligence and communicating with business customers. 'Oh, well,' you say, 'it's not quite as perfect as it sounds.' Why not?

3. While studying for an MBA part time, sponsored by your employer, your boss asks you to ring up a competitive rival, posing as a university student undertaking a course assignment, to try to obtain important commercial information. As your boss says: 'Well, we are paying for the MBA, so we expect a return on the investment, and you are a university student after all, so that bit is true.' What do you do? (You might want to refer back to the material on ethical issues in Chapter 4.)

CASE STUDY 5.1   LIQUI-GAS ENJOYS A LESSON IN SERVICE QUALITY

There was a puzzled look on the face of Jan Smeets, European Marketing Manager for Liqui-Gas Gmbh, who was pondering the latest market research report to arrive from

(Continued)

(Continued)

their research agency. In addition to the regular report on the state of the market – size, growth rate, segment size, competitor market shares and so on – at the urging of the Global Marketing Director, Jan had specially commissioned the agency to do a service quality report for Liqui-Gas. Liqui-Gas concentrates on the industrial market for liquefied petroleum gas (LPG). Jan's major customers were in the manufacturing, construction and agricultural industries. LPG is used in these industries for such things as welding, space heating, fruit and grain drying, and manufacturing aerosols. Jan had never previously given a great deal of thought to whether these customers were concerned about customer service. They were, after all, business-people, and Jan assumed that they would be concerned about the price, the quality and the delivery arrangements for the product, but not much else. Indeed, if they got the right quality of product, at the right price, in the right place and at the right time, Jan had thought that was about all he had to worry about. However, his research agency seemed to think there was more to it than that. Jan continued to read the report.

> The methodology we have applied to understand customers' beliefs about the service quality they are receiving from Liqui-Gas is the SERVQUAL approach. This is the best-established approach to service quality measurement, having originally been developed by American professors Parasuraman, Zeithaml and Berry in the 1980s and successfully applied to the measurement of service quality in a wide range of industries since then. The basic principle of the SERVQUAL approach is to measure service quality as the gap between customer perceptions of a company's actual performance and customer expectations of the company's performance. Simply, service quality is defined as customer perceptions of service minus customer expectations of service. Service quality is usually measured along five dimensions:
>
> 1   Reliability: the ability to deliver a promised service dependably and promptly.
> 2   Assurance: the knowledge and courtesy of employees, and their ability to inspire trust and confidence.
> 3   Tangibles: physical aspects of service delivery, such as equipment and facilities.
> 4   Empathy: providing caring and individual attention to customers.
> 5   Responsiveness: the willingness to help the customer and provide prompt service.
>
> Other dimensions have been suggested, such as 'recovery' (the ability of the organization to rectify problems), but for this study we measured these five only. Each of these dimensions is measured using a number of indicators, all measured using 7-point Likert scales (1 = strongly disagree to 7 = strongly agree). The following tables provide details of the indicators. The same indicators are used for customer perceptions (P) and customer expectations (E); for the former, customers are asked for their 'desired service level' (defined as excellent customer service), and for the latter, customers are asked what they think of Liqui-Gas's actual customer service. For example, 'When firms promise to do something by a certain time, they should do so' is one indicator of service reliability; customers are asked for their desired service level, and then for their perception of Liqui-Gas's service level. Using this approach, we can identify the overall gap between customer perceptions and expectations of service, the gap for particular dimensions of service quality, and the gap for individual indicators within the dimensions.

Although Jan understood most of this, it seemed rather academic and quite far-removed from the day-to-day realities of competing in the European industrial LPG market. Nevertheless, it was important to make sense of the information pretty quickly. The Global Marketing Director was currently visiting the European office and expected Jan to give a presentation based on the latest market research report. The Global Marketing Director would no doubt be particularly interested in the service quality aspects of the report. What Jan had read so far was not much use. The Global

TABLE 5.3 Liqui-Gas customers' desired service levels (expectations)

SERVQUAL dimension	Indicator		Mean score (85 customers)
Reliability	1.	Provide customer service as promised	6.14
	2.	Dependable in handling customer service problems	6.31
	3.	Performing customer service right first time	6.42
	4.	Providing customer service at the promised time	6.11
	5.	Maintaining error-free records	5.80
Responsiveness	6.	Keeping customer informed about when the service will be provided	5.97
	7.	Prompt customer services	5.71
	8.	Willingness to help customers	5.91
	9.	Ability to respond to customer's request	6.21
Assurance	10.	Employees who instil confidence in customers	5.23
	11.	Making customers feel safe in their transactions	5.32
	12.	Employees who are consistently courteous	5.45
	13.	Employees who have the knowledge to answer customers' questions	5.77
Empathy	14.	Giving customers individual attention	5.67
	15.	Employees who deal with customers in a caring fashion	5.33
	16.	Having the customer's best interests at heart	5.66
	17.	Employees who understand the needs of their customers	5.89
	18.	Convenient business hours	5.21
Tangibles	19.	Modern equipment (e.g. delivery trucks)	5.11
	20.	Visually appealing offices	4.56
	21.	Salespeople who have a neat, professional appearance	4.78
	22.	Visually appealing materials associated with service (e.g. order confirmation)	4.97

(Continued)

(Continued)

Marketing Director would expect some hard facts, and was known to believe in the maxim 'If you can't measure it, you can't manage it.' Jan read on, very much hoping to find some hard facts and some concrete measurements.

Using the customer list provided by Liqui-Gas, we obtained 85 complete responses to our SERVQUAL questionnaire. Table 5.3 provides details of customer desired

TABLE 5.4 Liqui-Gas customers' perceived service levels (perceptions)

SERVQUAL dimension	Indicator		Mean score (85 customers)
Reliability	1.	Provide customer service as promised	5.56
	2.	Dependable in handling customer service problems	5.78
	3.	Performing customer service right first time	5.90
	4.	Providing customer service at the promised time	4.55
	5.	Maintaining error-free records	6.12
Responsiveness	6.	Keeping customer informed about when the service will be provided	6.03
	7.	Prompt customer services	5.43
	8.	Willingness to help customers	5.21
	9.	Ability to respond to customer's request	4.89
Assurance	10.	Employees who instil confidence in customers	5.44
	11.	Making customers feel safe in their transactions	5.45
	12.	Employees who are consistently courteous	5.93
	13.	Employees who have the knowledge to answer customers' questions	4.32
Empathy	14.	Giving customers individual attention	5.88
	15.	Employees who deal with customers in a caring fashion	5.11
	16.	Having the customer's best interests at heart	5.45
	17.	Employees who understand the needs of their customers	5.02
	18.	Convenient business hours	5.97
Tangibles	19.	Modern equipment (e.g. delivery trucks)	6.21
	20.	Visually appealing offices	5.65
	21.	Salespeople who have a neat, professional appearance	5.42
	22.	Visually appealing materials associated with service (e.g. order confirmation)	5.88

service levels (customer expectations), and Table 5.4 provides details of customer perceived service levels (customer perceptions).

The overall mean for all expectation items is 5.62 and the overall mean for all perception items is 5.51, so the overall service quality gap is -0.11. We look forward to discussing the implications of these results with you at our meeting in two weeks' time.

Two weeks' time was fair enough, since that was the next scheduled meeting with the research agency. The problem was that Jan had to make a presentation to the Global Marketing Director using this information tomorrow. Jan had already worked out that it was necessary to calculate the difference between the perceptions average score and the expectations average score for each of the indicators, and had quickly

TABLE 5.5 Jan's analysis of the SERVQUAL data

Indicator	Expectations (E)	Perceptions (P)	Gap (P – E)
1	6.14	5.56	−0.58
2	6.31	5.78	−0.53
3	6.42	5.90	−0.52
4	6.11	4.55	−1.56
5	5.80	6.12	0.32
6	5.97	6.03	0.06
7	5.71	5.43	−0.28
8	5.91	5.21	−0.70
9	6.21	4.89	−1.32
10	5.23	5.44	0.21
11	5.32	5.45	0.13
12	5.45	5.93	0.48
13	5.77	4.32	−1.45
14	5.67	5.88	0.21
15	5.33	5.11	−0.22
16	5.66	5.45	−0.21
17	5.89	5.02	−0.87
18	5.21	5.97	0.76
19	5.11	6.21	1.10
20	4.56	5.65	1.09
21	4.78	5.42	0.64
22	4.97	5.88	0.91
MEANS	5.62	5.51	−0.11

(Continued)

(Continued)

done that using a spreadsheet (Table 5.5). A negative difference was presumably not so good (perceptions lower than expectations), and a positive difference was presumably better (perceived service exceeds expectations). But now Jan had to work out what to tell the Global Marketing Director, based on the SERVQUAL results.

CASE STUDY QUESTION

1 Decide what key points Jan should make in the presentation to the Global Marketing Director. As an exercise, it is useful to prepare a set of presentation slides that Jan could use. Remember that the Global Marketing Director likes hard facts, and believes that to manage something you have to be able to measure it. Provide evidence to support proposed actions.

Sources: Datamonitor, 2004; The European LPG Association, www.aegpl.eu/; Wilson et al., 2012.

FURTHER READING

Cater, B. and Zabkar, V. (2009) 'Antecedents and consequences of commitment in marketing research services: the client's perspective', *Industrial Marketing Management*, 38(7): 785–97.

There are several good reasons to take a look at this article. First, it deals with the relationship between market research agencies and their clients, a topic that we discuss towards the end of the chapter. Second, it provides a good overview of much of the research into the concept of commitment in B2B relationships. Third, it provides an interesting example of empirical research among B2B organizations. Finally, this research was undertaken in eastern Europe, which has thus far been an under-researched geographical region in B2B marketing.

If you are planning to undertake your own marketing research project then you should make yourself familiar with one or more of the industry codes of conduct, which provide guidance on both practical and ethical aspects of the conduct of marketing research. It is very worthwhile to become familiar with the ESOMAR (European Society for Opinion and Marketing Research) *International Code on Social and Market Research*, available at www.esomar.org/publications-store/codes-guidelines. php (accessed 13 July 2016), also available in other European languages through www. esomar.org; and the *Market Research Society Code of Conduct*, at www.mrs.org.uk/ standards/code_of_conduct (accessed 13 July 2016).

6

BUSINESS MARKET SEGMENTATION

LEARNING OUTCOMES

After reading this chapter you will:

- know what segmentation is and how the segmentation process unfolds in business markets;
- be able to segment business markets using several segmentation variables;
- know the criteria for successful segmentation;
- understand how segmentation information can be used to aid the process of targeting business prospects; and
- know how segmentation and the identification of target customers influence the establishment of differential positioning for those target markets.

INTRODUCTION

As we saw in Chapters 2 and 3, there is considerable variety in the purchasing behaviour of organizational customers and in the nature of the relationships that may ensue between business-to-business marketers and their customers. These chapters have introduced an important reality for business-to-business marketers: all customers are unique. However, the fact that they are all unique does not mean that for the B2B marketer *all* individual relationships need be managed differently and uniquely. While individual and unique treatment is likely to be necessary for a number of strategically important customers within a B2B customer base (so-called 'segments of one'), it is also the case that there will be a substantial number of customers that do not really require a wholly customized offering. Many customers are happy to purchase a relatively standardized product, and their behaviour to all intents and purposes is the same as that of many other companies that are happy to receive the same offering.

This understanding, that while all customers are different some may share similar needs and behaviours, is at the heart of segmentation. For it is through a process of segmentation that a business-to-business marketer can establish a degree of homogeneity in respect of the different customers in the marketplace. In this way notional groups of like-minded (or like-behaved) customers are created, for whom it becomes possible to talk meaningfully about a range of different market offerings. It enables the marketer to research the needs of specific groups (see Chapter 5), make choices about which groups in the market are worth the investment of marketing effort from the firm, and decide how exactly that effort needs to be managed.

Of course, segmentation for its own sake is of little value; its value comes when it is used to make decisions about target markets and to establish specific competitive positions with respect to those targets that bring value to the firm. Ultimately, it is the success of differential competitive positioning within markets that creates success: doing things differently from competitors to establish advantage (such as more customized offerings or similar offerings at lower costs). In this chapter we deal with the trinity of activities associated with approaching the market in the first place in order to obtain that success – segmentation, targeting and positioning. Consequently, attention is paid first to segmentation. Then the outcome of the segmentation is considered in terms of target market selection. Finally, we move on to consider the establishment of positions within those target markets that are sustainable by the firm.

PRINCIPLES AND VALUE OF SEGMENTATION

As we saw in Chapters 2 and 3, there is great diversity in the needs and behaviours of business customers. At the most basic level, they are all unique. In principle, this would require completely unique market offerings for all customers in order to achieve greatest customer satisfaction. Satisfaction, after all, comes from meeting customer needs and expectations as precisely as possible.

However, in the real world, markets do not conform to the economists' notion of perfect competition; rather they are imperfectly competitive. This means that there is scope to differentiate the products of different suppliers and to identify different market segments, each with slightly different demand characteristics. Apart from anything else there will be many buyers out there that the marketer does not yet supply, or even know about, for whom the basis for individual treatment is not yet even known.

Of course, pushed to its opposite extreme it is entirely possible to produce a standard offering for customers that meets the needs of the maximum number of customers to an acceptable level. Typically, such standardization brings operating efficiencies for the firm. But, since it is designed to meet the needs of the average customer, by definition it does not meet the needs of others particularly well. This is a dangerous position to adopt since others will be only too willing to provide more satisfying offerings to these disaffected customers. It has long been known that single over-generalized offerings to the whole market lead to problems for companies in achieving their objectives: 'cases where failure to recognize the reality of market segments was resulting in loss of market position' (Smith, 1956: 5).

The difficult task of understanding customers and delivering market offerings involves adopting a position somewhere in between the over-generalized and the over-customized. It is in this territory that the value of segmentation to marketers can be seen. The pioneering view of segmentation put forward by Wendell Smith (1956: 6) was that it 'consists of viewing a heterogeneous market … as a number of smaller homogeneous markets in response to differing product preferences among important market segments'. By seeing the market in terms of a set of different customer requirements the marketer can establish clear target markets for the firm. Firms can make clearer choices about those segments that they want to serve, enabling them to more clearly match their own strengths and capabilities with the specific needs of particular segments.

The value of segmentation in aiding company capabilities to design more appropriate marketing programmes has long been understood (Yankelovich, 1964) and accepted (and the benefits of it on the demand side are now also being proposed (Erevelles and Stevenson, 2006). Shapiro and Bonoma (1984) pointed to the value of industrial segmentation in three areas:

facilitating better understanding of the whole marketplace including the behaviour of buyers and why they buy;

enabling better selection of market segments that best fit the company's capabilities; and

enabling improved management of the marketing activity.

A good understanding of the needs of the market in general makes it possible for the successful marketer to identify groups of needs shared by customers. This enables the marketer to deal more effectively with more homogeneously identifiable groups of customers (and by definition the set of groups thus defined are much smaller than the number of individual customers). It makes it possible for the marketer to talk meaningfully about the behaviours of this more manageable number of groups (market segments) so that marketing activity can be undertaken more efficiently than would be the case without segmentation. It also makes it possible for the marketer to determine clearly how the company stands competitively with respect to the market segments, facilitating decisions to leave some segments of the market and pursue others, or to concentrate on meeting the demands of specific segments in ways that confer greater competitive advantage. This strategic use of segmentation means that the marketer can choose which customers to target, which ones to treat similarly and which ones to treat differently, even uniquely. A fundamental skill for superior business-to-business marketing then is knowing just which customers to treat similarly and which to treat differently.

Segmentation process

The process of segmentation involves an iterative (step-by-step) classification of the market in terms of sets of meaningful groupings, with each additional step in the iterative process defining further subdivisions. This means starting with the widest possible definition of the marketplace. Then on the basis of the application of a series of classification criteria, often called segmentation bases, a set of market segments is created. If the process has been done well, these are each clearly defined and the members of each segment share characteristics with respect to their market needs: 'homogeneous with respect to their response to a marketing mix', as Griffith and Pol (1994: 39) put it. It is their behaviour in response to market offerings that makes their association sensible for the purposes of marketing activity.

As far as the process is concerned, the most common difficulties that managers face are knowing the combination of descriptive or explanatory segmentation variables to use, and where to stop with a set of meaningful segments. These issues are addressed directly in the next sections.

SEGMENTATION BASES

The process of segmentation requires the application of criteria that can support the classification activity. Even from the earliest writings on the subject, a range of such criteria has been proposed. For instance, in what appears to be the earliest published consideration of industrial segmentation bases, Frederick (1934) lists five factors that should be taken into account (industry, geographic location, channels of distribution, product use and company buying habits).

Many different variables have been used and we will consider a selection of them in this chapter in greater detail. However, there is agreement that the nature of the process described above means that there are different levels of segmentation. This involves moving from the use of more general or easily observable criteria at initial levels of the process (often using secondary data sources), through to more specific and less observable measures in the later stages. These often require specific knowledge of the personal attitudes or behaviours of customer representatives. The larger-scale analysis is often referred to as *macro-segmentation* while the finer-level analysis is

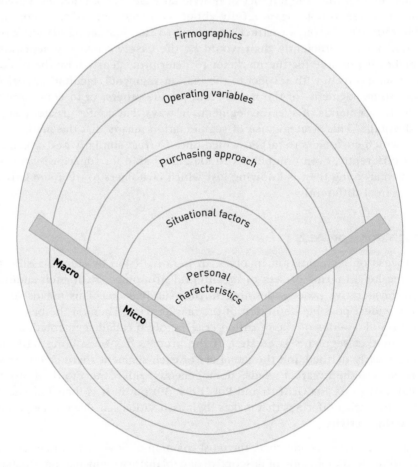

FIGURE 6.1 The segmentation funnel: nested use of segmentation bases (adapted from Shapiro and Bonoma, 1984)

Reprinted with permission from Harvard Business Review.

micro-segmentation (Choffray and Lilien, 1978). Peppers and Rogers (2004) depict the macro/micro split very readily in their two-step segmentation approach. They use externally observable macro-level variables in the first instance to create four broad segments that they label: Most Growables, Most Valuables, Migrators and Below Zeroes. They then use less observable data from attitude surveys and/or subjective judgements from an individual's dress, office décor and demeanour in order to extract more insights from the Most Valuables and Most Growables clusters.

The comprehensive, nested set of segmentation bases proposed by Shapiro and Bonoma (1984) captures this movement from the macro-level to the micro-level, and this is illustrated in Figure 6.1. In order to provide a full range of the segmentation possibilities open to a business-to-business marketer, we will use the nested approach that they pioneered, even though in practice most marketers will choose the best range of macro and micro bases that they feel enables them to adequately understand their markets and put them in the best position to target them with the right offerings. Powers and Sterling (2008) show that it is possible to use a methodology that links macro- and micro-segmentation and obtain the greater discriminating power of the latter in combination with the former for a sample of potential customers in order to establish how the macro variables can be used for other customers without the added cost of analysis at the micro-level of each and every possible prospect. Given the relative cost of getting adequate micro-level information for all customers, their approach has lots to commend it.

Firmographics

While Shapiro and Bonoma (1984) refer to demographics as the most general level of segmentation criteria, Gross et al. (1993) argue that a more fitting term in business-to-business markets is emporographics. Where demography is the study of the characteristics of human populations, such as size, growth, density and distribution, emporographics captures the fact that in the business-to-business context it is the characteristics of the firm that are the focus. However, we prefer the more prosaic term *firmographics*, which is increasingly widely used and makes the link to the firm more directly.

Shapiro and Bonoma (1984) highlight industry and company size as well as customer location as the major macro factors providing a broad classification of customers. These enable a good first pass for many companies in segmenting. The expectation is that companies from the same industry, or of similar sizes or locations, share similar product needs or usage patterns.

Industry

For a company making automatic vision equipment for inspecting surfaces, such as Surface Inspection Ltd – part of the SACMI Group of companies – a sensible first step in segmentation is to consider where such equipment would reasonably be used, now or in the future. To this end, the company has provided solutions in several industries, including checking paint quality in the auto industry and surface quality of ceramic tiles. The tile industry very quickly emerged as a particularly strong fit for the technological capability of Surface Inspection. This is an industry where the inspection process has traditionally been manual, laborious and subject to error, and where the opportunity costs of quality failure are great. For Surface Inspection, any company in this industry constitutes a prospect and thus the use of industry type is a very useful starting position for its segmentation.

Similarly, for any company, knowledge of an industry that may have use for its technology enables it to very quickly identify prospects. Of course, this requires a consistent definition of the activities of companies. Surface Inspection would be interested in all companies that make wall tiles, floor tiles and roof tiles, in a variety of shapes, designs and colours. Looking through a series of phone books for such companies (and it would involve lots of these for an international market) may generate leads, but there would also be lots of wasted time and energy. The name of a company does not immediately give a clear indication of what it does. Likewise, a web search will certainly generate substantial leads but requires that customers have such a web presence in the first place. Many hits in this situation would also be of little relevance to Surface Inspection, as they would bring up distributors of tiles rather than manufacturers.

The use of SIC codes (such as the US-based NAICS codes) aids an industry-based segmentation approach because it provides consistent definitions of the activities of companies as a basis for categorization (see Chapter 5 for a lengthier explanation of SIC codes). Companies are classified according to the nature of their business by government or other agencies.

As Table 6.1 shows, for Surface Inspection Ltd any company with a NAICS code of 327120 would be a suitable prospect. The use of the NAICS code thus helps to define an overall segment of value to the company. The codes can then be used to access databases or compendiums of company information. For example, the Dunn and Bradstreet Million Dollar Database can provide information on 1.6 million US companies with annual sales of more than $1 million and/or more than 20 employees and can be searched using NAICS codes as well as geographic location and sales size. The Orbis product available currently from Bureau van Dijk has information on over 100 million public and private companies across the globe and also enables searches using a range of local and international codes.

Customer location

As well as knowing about the industries that may demand a company's output, it is possible to segment on where those prospects might be. The location of a customer

TABLE 6.1 2012 NAICS codes relevant to ceramic tile manufacturing

Segment	NAICS codes	Category
Sector	31–33	Manufacturing
Subsector	327	Non-metallic mineral product manufacturing
Industry group	3271	Clay product and refractory manufacturing
Industry	32712	Clay building material and refractories manufacturing
US industry	327120	Ceramic wall and floor tile manufacturing

Source: www.census.gov/eos/www/naics.

will often affect the ease with which it can be reached by a company. That is, it may be influential in decisions about where a company makes a presence itself, how it deploys staff, or how it communicates with customers. The value of the ceramic tile manufacturing segment to Surface Inspection was indicated above. In terms of the location of companies engaged in such manufacturing, Spain and Italy assume great significance because of the number of tile manufacturers in those countries, particularly in the areas around Sassuolo in Italy and Castellón in Spain. It is precisely for this reason that Surface Inspection has opened customer support offices in these areas.

While a high degree of prospective customer concentration in a location would seem favourable, this really depends upon the nature of the industry. Companies providing goods or services that are easily transportable, such as maintenance services or specialist advice or design services, are little hampered by geographical distances from customers. Increasingly, many services can even be delivered electronically (for example, translation services or software). For companies in resource-heavy industries (like many manufacturing companies creating bulky products in a few specific locations) there are problems associated with the transportation and delivery of their products over long distances. So, for example, a company like Surface Inspection has to trade off the wish to maintain manufacturing close to its suppliers in the UK with the costs of transporting end products. For customers in Europe the tradeoff favours the maintenance of the whole manufacturing process in the UK. The decision is much more marginal when the transportation involves sea freighting by intermediaries, to the US for instance (particularly when the carriage has led to damage to machines). The decision may swing further away from sole UK manufacture towards a degree of local assembly when the number of business leads starts to increase in the US.

Customer size

The size of customer companies may be a sensible basis for distinguishing one from another. The basis for measuring size differs, depending upon what is being purchased. For a manufacturing company providing blow-moulded plastic bottles, larger companies will typically require greater volumes of product. For a company providing process equipment for inspection of tiles (such as Surface Inspection), larger tile manufacturers will have both the resources to afford enhanced tile inspection as well as the scale of production that will see the greatest value in use of the equipment. Thus, size often matters because of its relationship with the scale of the customer organizations' needs and therefore their demands for volume, or inclination to buy, and their ability to justify specific products or services. Marketers can make decisions about those companies that it is sensible to supply. For example, Surface Inspection typically only targets larger tile manufacturers on the grounds that they are more likely to invest in automatic tile inspection. On the other hand, the company making blow-moulded plastic bottles may decide not to target the largest customers on the grounds that it does not have the capacity to meet their volume needs. It may prefer to supply mid-sized customers that will match its capacity better, so that it manufactures efficiently but without danger of over-stretching and disappointing.

The task of obtaining substantial amounts of firmographic information can of course be eased by purchasing prospect information from organizations specializing in just such insight, as Snapshot 6.1 on Blue Sheep reveals.

B2B SNAPSHOT 6.1   BLUE SHEEP TAKES THE STRAIN OUT OF SEGMENTATION

Companies providing prospect lists have been around for a long time, and the purchase of such lists for outbound mailing purposes has been commonplace. In the increasingly competitive context within which they now exist, it is unsurprising that some companies are aiming to provide more sophisticated services to their customers.

Blue Sheep, a leading UK B2B marketing services provider, is now doing just that by using the information it holds across the marketing databases that it hosts for its major clients. Rather than analysing a single set of buying behaviours, Blue Sheep can analyse the spending patterns of a business across several clients that could be in completely different industries. By employing a view of businesses across several clients, it is able to obtain a more behavioural view of each customer or prospect. Adopting this approach means that customers and prospects can be scored using advanced statistical techniques, such as logistic regression and cluster analysis, to predict their likelihood of responding to marketing campaigns.

Following this analysis both the customer base and prospect list can be segmented using Blue Sheep's customer engagement programme. This segmentation approach consists of three stages: the first stage involves segmenting the entire marketplace in which the business operates using variables that are important to the industry. For example, for a recent segmentation conducted for a large IT retailer, the important variables by which to segment the marketplace were 'potential IT spend' and the 'number of sites' within the organization. The second stage in the segmentation process is to segment the customer base using three factors: industry sector penetration, predicted sector growth and a measure of value (e.g. revenue or margin). Using predicted sector growth allows Blue Sheep to help its clients identify not only which sectors are the most valuable and the easiest for them to penetrate, but also which sectors are likely to be growing or declining over the next 12 months. This segmentation results in eight segments, some of which should be pursued (i.e. high value, easy to acquire and high predicted growth) and some avoided (i.e. low value, difficult to acquire and declining growth).

The final stage in the customer engagement programme is for Blue Sheep to offer advice on how to communicate with the customers and prospects that have fallen into each of the segments that have been created. This would include factors such as media, timing and frequency of communication.

(The contribution of Lee Price, KTP Associate, and Blue Sheep in the writing of this snapshot is gratefully acknowledged.)

Operating variables

The next set of segmentation criteria move from the coarser-grained and most easily observed firmographic variables to those that are more precise descriptions of what customer companies can or could do. They are still relatively easily observed without having to put specific questions to customer representatives because they are visible beyond the firm. They are, however, the first manifestations of how customer companies behave rather than merely the general characteristics of the firms. As with the previous set of criteria, these variables can be applied singly or in combination.

Company technology

As indicated above when discussing customer size, Surface Inspection typically targets large tile firms with its automatic inspection equipment. As well as being a function of size, there is an element of technological readiness involved as well. The bigger tile makers have tended to make the greatest investments in process technology to control the manufacturing process. The technology is also likely to be the most up to date. For Surface Inspection, integrating its inspection machines within such processes is more feasible. Thus, an analysis of the technology of companies may be valuable in segmentation and aiding targeting decisions because it gives a strong indication of a company's buying needs as well as the ease with which the supplying company can meet those needs.

It can also indicate direction of travel in technology terms. Bailey et al. (2009) report that the US-based IT networking company Cisco, which has traditionally segmented by geography and size of company, has more recently started segmenting by technology life-cycle and by purchasing method. With this approach, 'Cisco believes that it is at the beginning of understanding what managers call the customers' "next best move"' (Bailey et al., 2009: 237). The process involves trying to identify the compelling events and triggers that drive technology purchases for companies. These events are grouped into three types:

1. Inherent and known – there are inherent technology demands that a customer faces when starting up or moving office. By obtaining lists of company office moves, Cisco can target those companies at just the right time and with the right offering.

2. Inherent but unknown – there are also inherent demands that may not be as readily known to customers, such as the expiration of a service contract. Again, this offers Cisco the opportunity to target companies at the right time with the right offering.

3. Created and unknown – this category refers essentially to situations where Cisco may be able to draw a customer's attention to a benefit from technology of which it wasn't previously aware.

As well as an example of how segmentation bases can be used strategically in advance to identify targets, Cisco's use of customer insight also shows how this sort of insight information can be used quite tactically and in response to an opportunity that presents itself. For this to happen typically requires a firm to be undertaking regular and frequent customer insight activity as a matter of course, rather than relying upon a less frequent (perhaps annual) activity.

Product and brand-use status

Given that companies segment in order to establish targets for their products, it is only sensible that they would use the behaviour of customers with respect to products or brands to aid their segmentation. Customer reactions to products in terms of readiness to use (for those who are not yet customers) and usage rate (light, medium or heavy, for those who already purchase) are valuable means of distinguishing one from another. Existing customers bring additional knowledge benefits to a supplier: the nature of the need is more clearly understood, as is how they purchase. These customers also know something about the supplier's products and how the supplier has behaved towards them. Retaining heavy users may seem the most obvious use of segmentation on this basis. However, as Chapter 9 (on *relationship portfolio management*) shows, a balanced customer portfolio may come from investing in the growth of lighter users – the heavy users of the future.

While much less may be known about companies that are not yet customers, they may also share similar characteristics in their use of products. A company like 3663 in the UK, a national provider of food and cleaning products to away-from-home organizations (restaurants, bars, hotels, hospitals, care homes and universities), will recognize that all restaurants need washing-up detergent, or that all hotels need housekeeping cleaning products. They will even have a reasonable knowledge, on the basis of room capacity, of what the likely demand for housekeeping products would be by a hotel.

Thomson Financial presents an interesting example of how a switch from a largely coarse-grained sectoral categorization of customers as purchasers (investment banking/ capital markets; brokerage/fund management; corporate clients) to a categorization based on end usage (institutional equity advisers; fixed-income advisers; retail advisers; investment bankers; portfolio risk managers; investment managers; corporate users; back-office users) enabled it to more sensibly establish relative competitive capabilities in the marketplace as a basis for revising product offerings to make them more competitive (Harrington and Tjan, 2008). As a consequence, it could see segments where it had market penetration and opportunities for growth.

Customer capabilities

As we saw in Chapter 3, exchange involves matching the abilities and uncertainties of buyers and sellers. Given this situation, a supplier might genuinely want to establish what customers are capable of doing with either its product or the processes. In the garment industry, a clothes manufacturer that has adopted a modular scheme of production – where work-in-progress is notionally only ever one garment (because the process is geared to working with the pieces of each garment from start to finish within the same work cell) – would be interested in the extent to which customers could use that system. For the scheme to work in its most efficient way, and not require further work, inputs from the customer are needed (such as sales stock tags and fabric care labels). Establishing the extent to which the customer would use the value of the modular scheme is important, not least because meeting the needs of customers who cannot operate in this way will require substantial warehousing for almost-completed garments. While Pilkington, the sheet-glass-making subsidiary of Nippon Sheet Glass, would happily sell float glass to anyone who wants it, it has substantial interest in how the industry changes over time. Merely surrounding glass in extruded uPVC for the domestic double-glazing market does not add any extra value to the glass as a product, though it does constitute volume that may be valuable in itself. For this reason, it may be keen to find customers that work with the glass itself, tempering it, for example, for use in a variety of safety applications. In the past, in recognition of the extra value added to the glass by such customers, Pilkington ran a Key Processor scheme that provided additional services to those customers.

Customer strategic type

Verhallen et al. (1998) demonstrated that the nature of a firm's strategic type is a strong indicator of its industrial buying behaviour for new products. Using Miles and Snow's (1978) four-part typology – prospector (innovative), defender (efficient), analyser (efficient and adaptive) and reactor (no consistent strategy) – they found that it predicted buying behaviour better than firmographic variables like industry type and firm size. Within the nested approach to segmentation one would certainly expect variables that are more nested than others to be more predictive, and Verhallen et al.'s study supports this for the purchase of new products.

Of course, the determination of the strategic type of a company is more difficult to ascertain than its size. It relies for measurement on either self-indication by customer representatives (which is subject to problems of socially acceptable responding), observation (very difficult for outsiders to undertake), or content analysis of company marketing plans (also rarely possible). It is more likely that a strategic type analysis would be further down the segmentation funnel to obtain finer distinctions between customers. It may add greatest value when applied to small numbers of customers, about which there is sufficient knowledge. This may involve input from multiple sources within the marketing company who all have contact with the customer firm (as a means of introducing a degree of triangulation to the evaluation). Such knowledge will not exist for completely new companies and it thus has greatest application for re-buy tasks for customers; it will also have limited value for establishing customer responses to new product launches.

Purchasing approach

It may be stating the obvious to say that the ways that companies choose to buy undoubtedly affect their buying behaviour. But the recognition that this is so has implications for marketing companies. How buying companies are organized to buy and the manifestations of these influences in terms of policies and buying criteria may constitute valuable intelligence to a marketer, as it may enable them to produce an offering that is most valuable to a target segment which is defined in terms of its purchasing approach.

Purchasing function organization

Buying companies differ in how they organize themselves for procurement. In smaller firms there may not necessarily be an identifiable group or department with purchasing responsibility, and there may be attendant uncertainties as to contact points. Where there is an identifiable purchasing function a big issue for the marketer is whether procurement is handled centrally (within a multi-divisional buying company) or whether responsibility is delegated to each division. Indeed, in some companies there may be central purchasing as well as a distributed structure. This was the case at the UK milling company Dalgety, now part of the Kerry Group of companies. It organized its purchasing so that each mill had its own purchasing group. However, in addition there was a corporate purchasing group that also bought grain on the international market. Sometimes local purchasers would have to accept some volumes that had been agreed centrally, even if the local purchasers did not necessarily require those volumes. However, the prices agreed centrally for the volumes purchased made economic sense to the company at large. Understanding how a customer's buying function is organized is invaluable in knowing who to approach, as well as understanding the levels and types of purchasing they control.

Power structures

Following from the previous point about organization, but extending beyond the purchasing activity itself, the relative influence of different departments within the firm may well have an impact upon the nature of the buying process or the criteria that are applied. Ascertaining the priorities of the buying company based on the influence of particular departments will mean that a marketer will have to alter the communication of the strength of its offering to make it most meaningful to this department. For instance, it may be most appropriate to emphasize the technical performance in a situation where the production department strongly affects purchases.

Buyer–seller relationships

As this book emphasizes throughout, the relationship between the buyer and seller will affect how they interact. In respect of segmentation when the purpose is to identify prospects that are not yet customers, some prospective customers might favour the kind of business relationship that the supplier prefers. For instance, customers that have a particular reputation might be preferred, such as those that share similar environmental outlooks. As the earlier example about Pilkington indicates, they have had a strong interest in forging relationships with companies that do more than merely cut float glass.

Freytag and Clarke (2001) point to the value in using customers' intentions towards collaboration with the supplier as a basis for segmentation. If the intention of a firm is to establish longer-term relationships with its customers then that attitudinal intention becomes important. Jackson (1985a) distinguished between customers on the basis of their tendency to behave transactionally or relationally, demonstrating the different needs each has and thus the different supplier behaviour required. Those customers styled *'always-a-share'* do not want relationships. They would rather focus on the current sale and are inclined to switch suppliers on the basis of price. For a supplier, they can always catch these fish; it only requires better bait in the form of better prices to reel them in and take them away from the competition. And how do you spot these sorts of customers? In a similar vein to Jackson's typology for 'always-a-share', Sako (1992) points to the 'arm's length' contracting style adopted by some buying organizations and typified in the auto industry by US/Western purchasing practices. They likewise are only focused on the current sale and their behaviour is directed by price-based market pressures, with no constraint on opportunistic exchange behaviour.

'Lost-for-good' customers are different. They want a relationship. They see value in working longer term with suppliers. This may be due to a more complex exchange situation: a product that is non-standard or customized in some way, or with delivery or fulfilment requirements that necessitate very close working, or where there is a need for flexibility or innovation in supply over time. Whatever the reason for wanting such relationships, 'lost-for-good' customers are prepared to make the commitment to a relationship and expect likewise from suppliers. If a supplier is not prepared to behave that way or behaves opportunistically in the relationship then the customer will act to take their business elsewhere. And better prices will not bring them back; they will be 'lost-for-good'. These customers can also be spotted on the basis of their

procurement behaviour. The buying activity will be characterized by greater interest in total costs of ownership, less focus on the initial sale price, greater concern about service and maintenance activities, and greater willingness to work interactively with suppliers to resolve details of the need and how it can be met.

General purchasing policies

As the last paragraph indicated, the organizational structures and influences and the sorts of relationships preferred ultimately impact on, and are typically embodied in, specific buying policies (and criteria, see below). These will determine the particular practices of the company when purchasing from suppliers. Among other things, this will affect the forms of vendor rating used and forms of accreditation expected, the sorts of pricing and bidding methods used, and the expectations of disclosure of costs. Marketers can use knowledge of policies to determine whether they want (or would be able) to meet the policy needs of a buyer.

Purchasing criteria

A whole range of purchasing criteria could be applied by a buying company. They may be financial, such as purchase price or total life cost, or they may concern more technical performance characteristics of the specified product (for example, weight, speed, power consumption, durability, quality consistency or reliability). Additionally, the quality of the service more generally might be important, including continuity of supply, delivery performance, amount and quality of technical assistance pre- and post-sale, and standards of customer service. Knowing the specific criteria would enable segmentation to be undertaken more precisely. However, buying companies generally do not (and probably cannot) express completely the criteria to be applied or their relative importance. They are more likely to use a set of criteria across the board that suppliers are implicitly expected to meet.

This lack of comprehensive knowledge of exactly what the criteria are and their relative importance poses problems for marketers in segmentation terms. They will want to target those segments where they have the greatest potential and thus will have to make a judgement call as to whether the criteria to be applied are likely to match with their own capabilities. This may mean that a marketer whose products are technically strong, but which are slightly less price competitive, might choose to target those buyers who consistently want that level of product performance, ignoring the price preferences until such time as it becomes clear that price is the order-winning criterion.

Situational factors

Rather than the characteristics of buying companies themselves, how they ordinarily operate and the usual buying behaviour that they manifest, situations arise where companies are instead guided temporarily by the prevailing factors in the business environment. So, rather than defining all companies requiring a product as equivalent and thus putting them in the same segment, it may often be possible to define a segment in terms of the prevailing need. This need may be for urgent order fulfilment, so by considering that such a need may exist, a supplier can arrange to maintain stocks and provide a replenishment service, generally at a price premium.

The important point here is that while the marketer may be providing the same product in each case, there are two separate segments based upon the urgency with which each requires the product.

As well as urgency affecting how companies buy, how they plan to use a product may mean that they will purchase the same product differently at different times. Likewise, companies may change their purchase behaviour depending on the size of the order they are making. There may be some companies that they consider able to supply in volume, while there may be others that they would turn to for smaller order sizes. For the supplier, these constitute opportunities to decide which of these situations they would fit best. As the O$_2$ case study in Chapter 9 indicates, smaller purchasers may well be referred to alternative sources of supply, such as *distributors*.

Personal characteristics of buyers

Ultimately, buying companies are only human. While organizational structures, policies and processes create the framework within which decisions are made, it is the buying staff, perhaps alongside others in a DMU (see Chapter 2), who actually conduct the process. Consequently, marketers can segment in terms of the characteristics of the people themselves, such as what drives their buying behaviour, the extent to which it is believed that they share similar views to the marketer, how fastidious they are in searching for and evaluating suppliers, and their approaches to managing risk. Barry and Weinstein (2009) show the value of insights into a buyer's motives (buyer motivation), risk aversion (buyer risk management behaviour) and relationship style (buyer relationship style) as forms of micro-segmentation which can help determine the buyer's favourable or otherwise predisposition to marketing initiatives. Dawe (2015) points to the necessity of good personal profiles of the decision makers and influencers in purchasing decisions as a pre-requisite for producing better quality email communications to customers that can lead to better open rates and reduced unsubscribe rates.[1]

For a company to use such personal characteristics, clearly it must have some degree of contact with the buying company. The closer the contact, the better the calibre of information obtained and the greater its usefulness for targeting purposes. But, of course, this sort of research and reporting process can get expensive very quickly when there are large numbers of prospective customers in the marketplace. For this reason, the volume of data gathered is likely to be restricted to those prospects that merit it because of sales potential. Information is best obtained by sales personnel from contacts they have had in prospective customers. Sales representatives from a marketing company can often report on how well they get along with the buyer, and how closely the buyer's views seem to favour the marketing company. The addition of such reports from customer contact points to the company marketing information system as a matter of course enables the identification of positively disposed prospects.

SUCCESSFUL SEGMENTATION AND WHERE TO STOP

When it comes to making a success of segmentation, Weinstein (2006: 123) presents nine questions relevant to effectively implementing market definitions and segmentation:

---

[1] For benefits of better segmented business-to-business email use see: www.allbusiness.com/crank-up-roi-email-marketing-campaign-segmentation-17302-1.html

Adequacy of infrastructure to support segmentation:

1. Is management committed to the process?

2. Are lines of communication open throughout the organization?

3. Do you have a management information system (MIS) in place for gathering marketing intelligence?

Adequacy of processes for undertaking the segmentation:

4. Do you have sufficient marketing data and internal consensus for logically grouping market subsets?

5. Does the chosen segmentation scheme fit the organization's mission and strategic planning initiatives?

6. Do you have managerial support to provide appropriate personnel and adequate finances for the segmentation initiative?

Adequacy of basis of response to segmentation operations and implementation:

7. Is communications strategy in place for informing both internal and external constituencies?

8. Are the right people in place and committed to operationalizing the segmentation scheme?

9. Has management shown long-term commitment to segmentation rollout and monitoring?

A company should typically be able to answer in the affirmative to these questions to be able to do justice to the demands of segmentation. If the answer is generally 'no', then the basis for effective segmentation isn't there. Generating poorly defined segments, which aren't adequately communicated and aren't used in earnest as the basis for sensible marketing action, won't facilitate the sort of targeting and positioning which is the point of the exercise in the first place.

Assuming that the answers to Weinstein's (2006) questions are positive, there is still the matter of knowing how far to take it. Given its role in defining market segments about which companies can take clear decisions in respect of targeting, the fundamental issues in segmentation revolve around clarity of the definitions of segments and knowing where to stop. As the previous section has shown, marketers can apply a variety of segmentation bases, using finer-grained bases in combination with coarser-grained ones to derive ever more specific segment definitions. The greater the number of segmentation steps undertaken, and thus the number of differentiating criteria that are applied, the smaller and more fragmented are the segments produced. This fragmentation is, of course, the reason for wanting to segment in the first place. However, when the fragmentation begins to reach the point where further separation does not really lead to meaningful differences with respect to customer purchase behaviour, then it is likely that the process should be curtailed. As indicated earlier in the chapter, by this point there are likely to be a range of segments of differing sizes. So, for example, Palmer and Millier (2004) in undertaking a segmentation exercise with the American fragrance manufacturer, Belmay (acquired in 2013 by the German fragrance and flavourings giant, Symrise Group – www.symrise.com), arrived at five identifiably different segments (see Table 6.2).

TABLE 6.2 Belmay segments and their characteristics (Palmer and Millier, 2004)

Segment name	Segment characteristics
Hippos	High growth potential, low capture of spend, require technical expertise, low price sensitivity, long-term perspective.
Lions	High spend and relatively high capture, independent, price conscious, aggressive style, poor planning leads to high service requirements.
Future milkers	Low growth potential, low service requirements, price conscious but not aware, technically orientated, often family-owned, lifestyle and relationships important.
Sitting ducks	Low growth potential, high service requirements, sole traders or family firms, relationships important, reliable.
Sharks	Low growth potential, very price-conscious, highly transactional, poor facilities and low quality, service hungry, small businesses.

With permission from Elsevier.

In undergoing the process in some sectors, a small number of the segments produced might even be segments of one, each equating to a strategically important customer that requires individual and unique treatment. There may be a collection of segments containing reasonable numbers of potential customers in each (of the order of tens rather than hundreds), with each segment perhaps representing different product categories or applications for the company's products. There may also be a group of segments containing large numbers (thousands) of individual customers. The number of small businesses, many of which are sole proprietorships, means that for some companies there may be segments comprising millions of customers. This is certainly the case for RS Components, leading distributor of a wide range of components and equipment including electrical, electronic, industrial, health and safety, and IT (with headquarters in the UK). It supplies products to 1.5 million engineers across the globe, with an order being placed every ten seconds. In recognition of the many small businesses that could use its products, the company has invested since 1995 in e-commerce technology. Its award-winning Internet Trading Channel (E-Business Strategy of the Year, UK National Business Awards, 2003) brings over 300,000 products to these myriad customers, products which historically would only have been available through a 5,000-page catalogue. This enables it to meet the needs of a range of segments directly, with the UK company alone processing 20,000 orders a day and delivering 25,000 parcels.

Whatever bases are applied there are a series of tests that business marketers can use to establish the quality of the segmentation process and the usefulness of the segments that are proposed.

- Measurable/distinctive. In order to be used successfully, criteria for segmentation must be clearly measurable. For instance, if they are to be used, it must be possible to establish the size of the firm, its capabilities, its purchasing policies and selection criteria, the size of orders it is likely to seek, and its attitude to risk. Without strong measurability it is not possible to define clearly distinctive market segments. Where it is not possible to apply a segmentation variable in a way that is clearly measurable, it is best to avoid its use since the consequences are segments that are insufficiently distinguished. With such segments there is the risk of offerings that are not adequately tailored, and the possibility of being outdone by competitors with more precise segmentation, better targeting and more adequately matching offerings.

- Accessible. For a segment to be targeted usefully it needs to be accessible. If it is not possible to reach customers in the segment then the definition adds little value. 'Reach' includes the physical ease of getting offerings to the customers in the segment, as well as the ability to communicate with them. While technology makes it possible increasingly to communicate directly with prospects around the world, an issue for some companies remains the ability to get goods to far-flung customers, involving as it does logistical and/or channel management issues.

- Substantial/profitable. The size and potential profitability of segments are also important qualities. The segment needs to be big enough, or customers must be prepared to pay enough, to justify the costs of serving the segment. Where this is not the case then it is likely that the segmentation process has been taken too far and that the segments are more fragmented than they need to be. The potential for profitability will certainly influence decisions about which segments to target.

- Actionable. It does not matter how big or accessible a segment is if a company cannot actually bring offerings to bear that will meet the needs of the segment. For this reason another test for a segment is the extent to which the company can put together effective marketing programmes for it. As Hlavacek and Ames (1986: 47) point out: 'One should know what capabilities the company has or needs to develop or acquire to serve the segment profitably.'

Gross et al. (1993) also point to *compatibility* between buyer and seller as important, on the grounds that similar approaches to risk taking, service standards and corporate style will be preferred. However, this compatibility is not really a measure of the quality of the definition of a segment itself, but of the characteristics of the purchasing approach of customers. In this respect, it is encompassed in the variables (presented previously) relating to the purchasing function, and it has strong implications for the ability to forge enduring collaborative relationships between buyer and seller.

SEGMENTATION CHALLENGES IN BUSINESS-TO-BUSINESS MARKETS

In an extensive review, Boejgaard and Ellegaard (2010) highlight the reasons why the process of implementing segmentation is typically more challenging in business markets compared to consumer markets. Chapters 2 and 3 in this book have already identified these as characteristic of business markets.

- Customers are less homogeneous as a matter of course and this is compounded further by their visibility and interaction with suppliers.

- Their interaction with suppliers also complicates stimulus-response approaches by suppliers so that it's less obvious as to when an outcome is the result of a specific approach.

- This interaction can cut both ways; business customers are often very active in communicating their needs to suppliers directly.

- The development of offerings is typically more complex and often developed in conjunction with customers.

- The interactions with customers are often via a variety of different channels.

- As a result of changes in market structure, technology and global competition and product evolution over time, segments themselves often change markedly.

These challenges pose particular difficulties when it comes to executing segmentation plans, and Boejgaard and Ellegaard's (2010) focus on the implementation issues of segmentation in industrial markets highlights how the emphasis on this aspect of the process is changing. Clearly, the benefits of market segmentation strategy cannot be obtained if segmentation plans cannot be implemented. They point out that studies have traditionally adopted an approach to segmentation implementation that is based on an analysis activity of the market in order to generate segments (as we have done above), followed by planning activities in response (what Boejgaard and Ellegaard (2010) call an *analysis-plan* approach). This approach has been subject to criticism for the lack of consideration of how derived segments should be used. Foedermayr and Diamantopoulos's (2008) review of 19 empirical studies indicated that they didn't provide much practical help and guidance to those who want to implement the processes in their companies. In response to the criticisms, recent studies have been more concerned with what Boejgaard and Ellegaard (2010) call a *plan-action* approach that puts the implementation of the plan on a par with the activity of generating segments in the first place and recognizes that they go hand in hand: generating segments may create the basis of the plan but the enacting of the plan will inevitably change the basis of the segments that are defined and how they are used. In this way the process should become a revolving and enduring cycle rather than a series of linear activities undertaken on a periodic basis.

At issue fundamentally is what can be considered the gap between the creation of the segmentation plan and the use of that plan to stimulate customer response. Successful execution of segmentation plans becomes a question of bridging this gap. Given that the execution of the plans is brought about by company representatives, often sales staff, 'acting, interacting, and reacting to and with actors in the customer organization' (Boejgaard and Ellegaard, 2010: 1296) then it is the company's ability to engage these representatives to this task that will enable the gap to be bridged. These are the concerns manifest in the last three of Weinstein's (2006) nine questions for effectively implementing market definitions and segmentation (above).

To enable the engagement, a company needs to adopt appropriate organizational structures that support the segmentation plan and align with it, typically defined around and arranged to meet the needs of identified segments. Further, staff, most typically sales staff, need both to be motivated to make the plans a reality by being resourced and measured on the basis of the extent to which they enact the segmentation plans effectively, and to be given the autonomy to balance the need to maintain a customized on-going interaction with a customer alongside the pressures to conform to the needs of a less customized segmentation approach. For the segments identified in Palmer and Millier (2004), reproduced in Table 6.2, Belway developed different marketing mix variations for each one.

TARGETING

As we have indicated above, segmentation is of little value if it is not then used to make the best-informed choices about what markets to serve and how to serve them. This takes us directly to targeting: making choices about those segments that should be pursued, and devising the most appropriate strategies for pursuing them.

Target segment selection

While the criteria for successful segmentation will establish credible segments, a company will need to consider its possible competitive position in relation to each segment in order to determine whether it merits the company's attention. Abratt (1993) found that a company's competitive position within a market and its ability to reach the buyers were the criteria most often used in practice. The size of the market was also used more often than not. Marketers also cited the extent to which they estimated that the segment was compatible with their own objectives or resources, the extent to which they considered it was profitable, and whether they expected to see growth within that segment. Abratt's criteria correspond to those found in other studies (e.g. Doyle and Saunders, 1985).

Freytag and Clarke (2001) propose a step-wise process for selecting segments which proceeds from the basic evaluation of the relative attractiveness of the segment into the future (see Figure 6.2). They use the following criteria:

- estimates of segment size;
- growth rate;
- customer product/service needs and fit with the company's competence in meeting that need;
- the structure and nature of competition in the segment such that a competitive advantage could be obtained;
- how the activities of important constituencies such as government or the public at large may affect the segment;
- how technology impacts it; and
- how relationships with others affect it or would be affected by it.

This evaluation is followed by an estimation of the demands the segment would make in terms of finance, technology, human resources and use of company assets,

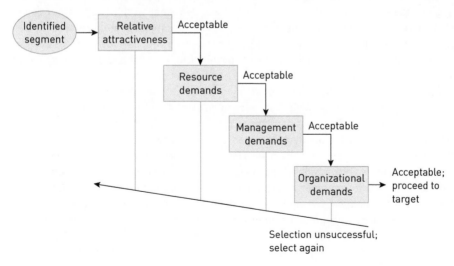

FIGURE 6.2 Step-wise segment selection process (adapted from Freytag and Clarke, 2001)

With permission from Elsevier.

and the extent to which the firm can meet them. Attention then switches to whether the company's management would want to pursue such a segment as part of its strategic development. Having undertaken such a process with a number of segments the firm is now ready to make decisions about how it deals with the range of segments, that is, the sort of targeting strategy it should adopt. These are just the choices that a small but growing business heavily tied to an existing client base faces in B2B Scenario 6.1: to stick with what it knows and what's been tried and tested versus targeting new segments and establishing a new relative position for itself in capability and branding terms.

B2B SCENARIO 6.1   DIGICHERCHE[2] POSITIONING

It was crunch time for digital marketing company, DigiCherche. At a strategy awayday with his senior team in 2015, Guy Digitale broaches the subject of how the company should position itself going forward. Established in 2007, the company began its life by offering digital marketing support to mainstream marketing agencies, acting essentially as their tied digital marketing team. And they had been very successful in this regard; business had quadrupled over an eight-year period and the company had grown from 3 to 15 staff. While the company's reputation had increased with its existing agency client base and with marketing agencies in general, it had necessarily operated as a hidden asset, unknown to end customers and integrated within the agency teams (largely because agencies don't want their clients to feel that they can't meet all their needs on a one-stop shop basis without sub-contracting). This had even meant that there were occasions when campaigns have been predominantly digital and required little contribution from agency researchers, creatives, media planners or buyers, and where largely the work had been powered by DigiCherche almost entirely, with the agency pretty much just managing the client relationship and little else. The increasing demand for digital marketing expertise means that there has been no shortage of orders via this segment of the market, albeit at profit margins that are often subject to erosion as a consequence of the extra demands made by the agencies (through additional reporting and reworking of targeting plans). However, it has also meant that other digital marketing companies who provide services directly to end clients are building brand and reputation while DigiCherche has been slow to do this, preoccupied as it has been with meeting the needs of its agency clients.

That's not to say that DigiCherche has ignored completely the growing demand from organizational customers who would prefer to go straight to digital media specialists for targeted marketing recruitment campaigns rather than employ the services of a broader mainstream agency. Over the last three years the company's customer base has indeed expanded beyond the agencies to such end clients. Network contacts that Guy and his senior team had themselves already developed over many years of recruitment marketing experience has meant that the company has built up a clear sense of the service portfolio in which it has particular technical strengths and experience. And this has enabled them to build direct client relations with, amongst others, membership organizations, universities, banks and insurance companies, all looking for this level of specialized capability. DigiCherche's

---

[2]Please note that while this scenario is based upon a real case, it has been anonymized for the purposes of publication.

forays into the direct channels have not gone unnoticed by their agency clients, one of whom has signalled a concern about DigiCherche wanting to step out from behind its shadow. It has made it clear that it could jeopardize further work with it for DigiCherche.

By the time of the 2015 awayday, the company had evolved to a point where it faced some major choices about where it should head in the future. Should it continue to be a pet provider for the agencies? Should it devote a greater proportion of company resource to building a brand presence that further supports its direct business ambitions? If the latter, what should it do further to build capability and capacity and how should it position itself?

Targeting strategy

In observing how companies target market segments, it is often argued that there are three strategic approaches: undifferentiated, differentiated and niche targeting.

Companies that engage in an *undifferentiated targeting* strategy make essentially the same offer to all segments. While for the most part this strategy is likely to be followed by those companies that do not engage in any segmentation, it is still possible that a company that has engaged in a segmentation of the market might decide to pursue such an approach anyway (on the grounds that its offering will appeal to the market in its entirety because the relationship between the two is such that the market is homogeneous). A standard offering to the whole marketplace has many advantages in respect of operating efficiency and is particularly appealing when large volumes can also produce economies of scale. However, companies operating in this way risk exactly the sort of over-generalized offerings that, as we indicated earlier, expose the company to attack from competitors that might produce a less generalized offering which would meet the needs of one or more segments more effectively. That is not to say that such a strategy has no merit. In new marketplaces (or where there has been a major innovation) a company, recognizing its first-mover advantage, may seek to make as much return as possible before the inevitable arrival of competitors. Philips, the Dutch electronics giant, has often been thought of in these terms.

A *differentiated targeting* strategy involves choosing a variety of different segments and providing offerings that are focused on meeting the needs of those targets more specifically. Such an approach is less subject to the challenges of an over-generalized offering because it should more precisely fit the needs of customers. And there are infinite possibilities to customize what might otherwise be a standard offering. Such customization is possible with respect to all elements of the marketing mix. As Chapter 10 indicates, if one just considers the offering itself, there are possibilities for customizing its physical form as well as the service elements that go along with it.

In competitive markets it is inevitable that some form of differentiated offering will be required. The big difficulty for a marketing company is in knowing whether to produce a different offering for each different segment. This puts the segment selection task into much greater relief. There will always be opinions expressed about new segments that could be targeted and it is always tempting to chase additional sales. However, a company that is acting strategically will temper all the requests with proper analysis of the costs and benefits associated with meeting the needs of a segment, aiming to ensure that over the long haul the benefits outweigh the costs.

Companies can, of course, apply much more *niche targeting* strategies. This concentrates the customer focus to one or a small number of segments. This is often the result of a realization that the company has a particular capability in an area that is particularly desired by these segments. Success in five-year partnership programmes with water utility companies led MJ Gleeson, the UK civil and construction engineering company now owned by Black and Veatch, to take the view that its interests in terms of targeting were best served in managing programmes of this sort rather than bidding for piecemeal engineering projects on a competitive tendering basis in other service sectors. A more *concentrated targeting* approach is more likely to be necessary anyway for smaller companies that lack the resources to meet the needs of a larger number of segments. Niche marketers can often defend those markets very successfully because they know and meet customer needs so well, and because the resources required by larger competitors to overcome this goodness of fit renders such segments relatively less economic for them.

BUSINESS-TO-BUSINESS POSITIONING

Regardless of the segmentation that has been undertaken, the specific target markets that have been selected, and the targeting strategy that has been adopted, when it comes to each individual segment there is a need to consider the position that the marketer occupies in the mind of the buying company. Primarily, the reasons for this are two-fold. First, the offering from a marketer occupies a space in the mind of the buyer. This may be captured in just a few dimensions. For example, Dell has managed to cultivate a position for itself in relation to PCs in the minds of buyers (corporate and individual) as highly customizable but low priced, even though the product itself is quite complex. This position becomes a shorthand that evokes the supplier and establishes it in an idealized position that most closely represents the customer need. UPS and FedEx have managed to establish similar dominant positions when it comes to parcel delivery, while Castrol has achieved the same outcome for industrial lubricants.

Second, in a competitive context, the relative position becomes the basis by which the supplier is compared to others as well as the ideal. It becomes necessary to ensure that the relative position occupied in the buyer's mind is most favourable. It may even be sensible to position against a particular competitor – Ries and Trout (2001) recount how Avis established itself deliberately as the 'no. 2 car rental' company, recognizing that its major competition came from a range of companies other than Hertz, the market leader. By associating themselves implicitly with the market leader rather than trying to compete directly with Hertz, Avis managed to make the no. 2 positioning statement a market reality, catapulting itself well ahead of its primary competition.

In establishing a relative position, the firm has to be clear where its strengths lie. The positioning it adopts also has to be both clear and clearly communicated to buyers. Perhaps the biggest mistake companies make is trying to appear to be all things to all customers. By establishing a clear positioning in target segments on the basis of sound segmentation analysis, the business-to-business marketer is best placed to achieve strong marketing outcomes. Visual means such as *perceptual maps* to capture positioning can often be useful to capture graphically how a company stands relative to key competitors on dimensions that are particularly relevant to customers in a segment. The situation faced by a regional food distributor in

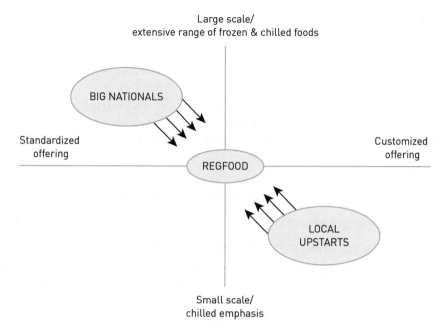

FIGURE 6.3 Relative positioning of a UK regional food service company

the UK provides a strong example. As the perceptual map in Figure 6.3 shows, customers typically see RegFood as being stuck in the middle to some extent: a fairly extensive range of foods but with emphasis more on frozen food and with a relatively limited ability to respond to more customized demands, particularly in terms of delivery schedules. The 'big national' companies occupy the territory of 'large-scale and extensive range', with quite a standard treatment of customers. The 'local upstarts' are especially strong at providing specialist requests, particularly for chilled foods, in highly responsive ways but at a reduced scale. Occupying the space in the middle may not have been problematic in the past but the rise of the upstarts (who are growing in size and ambition) and the big nationals' attempts to become more regionally responsive mean that RegFood is being squeezed from both sides. A consideration of this relative positioning by RegFood has led the company to try to reposition itself in the minds of customers by extending its range of foods into the chilled area, introducing more responsive delivery schedules, and changing its livery and branding to communicate its new positioning.

CHAPTER SUMMARY

- This chapter has introduced important processes for the business marketing company that enable it to make strategically important decisions about where it stands in relation to the market in general.

- Segmentation provides the marketer with the basis to achieve efficient as well as effective solutions to customer problems by establishing degrees of homogeneity in what would otherwise be a heterogeneous marketplace.

- The homogeneous groups that result from a process of segmentation enable the marketer to decide what parts of the market to target with its solutions, in the expectation that it can solve customer problems more effectively and profitably than competitors.

- Segmentation enables the best match between the problem-solving abilities and uncertainties of both buyer and seller so that sustainable relationships can be created.

- In deciding what segments of the market to target, the marketer can establish more clearly their particular competence with these segments and how they can position themselves most effectively against competitors.

QUESTIONS FOR DISCUSSION

1. What are the benefits of segmentation? What are the drawbacks?

2. List four macro-segmentation variables and explain their value in business markets.

3. List four micro-segmentation variables and explain their value in business markets.

4. How might a company making and distributing kitchen equipment segment the marketplace? Compare this with a company making kilns for the manufacturing process in the ceramics industry?

5. What criteria are used to select target markets?

CASE STUDY 6.1   SEGMENTING THE MARKET FOR WAVIN

Wavin Group provides plastic pipe systems (the name derives from a contraction of the words WAter and VINyl chloride). Its products are used in the building industry for all aspects of water management, plumbing, heating and drainage. Headquartered in Zwolle in the Netherlands (where it was founded in 1955) it is the leading global supplier of these systems and solutions in Europe, with a presence in 25 European countries and 40 manufacturing sites. Outside Europe, it has a global network of agents, licensees and distributors. It employs about 880 people and reported an operating profit of £7.9 million from sales of over £181 million in 2014. Since the middle of 2012, Wavin has been owned by Mexichem, the leader in plastic pipe systems and in the chemical and petrochemical industry in Latin America, together creating the global market leader in plastic pipe systems.

As its UK website (www.wavin.co.uk) reveals, Wavin's products span a range of well-known brand names (WAVIN, OSMA, Hep$_2$O, Hepworth) with a very extensive range of products and systems, designed and produced for a wide range of applications including gas, water, sewer systems, building, land drainage and irrigation, and cable ducting. It holds over 300 patents on products and processes and has a strong commitment to innovation as part of its 2015 Strategy; the group aims to achieve 20 per cent of its income from products less than five years old. There have also been recent environmental initiatives in the company, including the introduction of technologies to ensure that its plastic pipes contain over 50 per cent recycled materials. It is ISO 9001 qualified and its products meet the requirements of BS EN ISO 140-1 and BS EN 1329-1 for non-pressure underground drainage pipes, and soil and waste discharge pipes, respectively.

Wavin provides complete solutions for customers, backed by a dedicated sales force with full marketing, technical, sales and operational infrastructure. And there is a very extensive range of different end-users for Wavin products, including:

- the jobbing builder replacing a set of gutters, fitting a new kitchen, building a new bathroom or repairing cracked drains below ground;
- the small building contractor refurbishing a whole house or building from scratch;
- large building contractors engaged in a whole residential housing development;
- engineering companies engaged in pipelining repairs or laying public access cable networks; and
- large civil and mechanical engineering companies building infrastructure projects such as whole water treatment plants.

However, end-users typically aren't able to buy products from Wavin directly. Rather, products are purchased through a range of merchants. This makes relationships with the distributors very important for the company (and some of these companies are very large in their own right, e.g. Saint-Gobain, Wolseley, Travis Perkins). Of course, this does not mean that the company has no contact with many end-users. For example, Wavin's strength in specification appeals to national house builders (such as Persimmon and Taylor Wimpey). At the same time, while the company is interested in demand for its products in the round, with its sales team it recognizes that it may need to talk to clients and their designers about a whole solution, involving an entire range of products configured in the most appropriate way to solve a customer problem.

As well as contractors and distributors (and others such as clients, developers, trade jobbers and utility providers) in the marketplace, there are specifier markets that affect whether or not Wavin products are used. Professionals such as architects and structural and mechanical engineers have substantial reference power. Furthermore, high-profile reference projects have substantial value in showcasing Wavin product solutions – the more publicly known and impressive the better. The installation of a new soil and waste plumbing system for La Scala Opera House in Milan that was efficient and reliable was only the starting point. Demonstrating that they were best able to meet the requirements for range completeness and performance in terms of low noise levels swung it for Wavin. Wavin has also provided the bespoke underfloor heating for 'The Core' education centre at the Eden Project in Cornwall, sitting along-side the large biomes featured at the attraction, as well as a new five-star Hilton hotel in Bournemouth, UK. As well as these high-visibility projects, the company has been involved in reference projects for residential development companies like Persimmon in upmarket housing at Newcastle Great Park, where the customer was looking for ease of installation, flexibility and cost effectiveness when choosing the plumbing system for the development.

The company segmentation strategy continues to develop in order to adapt to the changes in the marketplace. Unsurprisingly then, the company engages in category management activities with important customers. After all, when you're one of the biggest manufacturers in the world of industrial plastic pipe systems and other industrial plastics products, then you undoubtedly know much more than many of your customers.

(Continued)

(Continued)

CASE STUDY QUESTIONS

1   Identify some of the bases that Wavin can use to segment the market.

2   How would you characterize Wavin's overall targeting strategy?

3   Compare Wavin's possible market positioning with respect to the following, and describe how it might target each segment: small, jobbing builders; large, typically national, house builders; specifiers.

4   Using Wavin's websites (www.wavin.com and wavin.co.uk) to help provide greater knowledge of its products and technologies, identify additional segments for it, stating the segmentation bases that you use. Use the criteria for successful segmentation to evaluate the usefulness of these proposed segments.

Sources: www.wavin.co.uk; www.mexichem.com.

FURTHER READING

Ries, A. and Trout, J. (2001) *Positioning: The Battle for Your Mind*. New York: McGraw-Hill.

This is the standard and most comprehensive text on the subject of positioning, from the people who pioneered the concept and its use in marketing communications.

Shapiro, B. and Bonoma, T. (1984) 'How to segment industrial markets', *Harvard Business Review*, 62 (3): 104–10.

This remains the most widely used source on business-to-business segmentation. Later sources still refer extensively to this article and its consideration of segmentation in terms of the iterative refinement of a series of nested bases.

PART III

COMMUNICATING AND INTERACTING WITH CUSTOMERS

7

MARKET COMMUNICATION

LEARNING OUTCOMES

After reading this chapter you will:

- understand the nature and role of brands in business markets and the impact of communication on business brands;
- be able to explain the meaning and importance of integrated marketing communications;
- understand the factors affecting the composition of the communications mix in business markets;
- be able to explain the budgeting methods used for communications programmes;
- be able to explain the role of company websites, content and search marketing, advertising, public relations, and sales promotion in the business communications mix; and
- be able to explain strategic and tactical decisions made by managers in relation to advertising and trade shows.

INTRODUCTION

Organizations interact with other parties; they send signals, communicate messages and engage in dialogue. The business marketer is concerned with formulating a communications strategy that sends a consistent message to target audiences, one that is of interest to and also engages those audiences so that the organization is able to achieve whatever objectives were set for its communications activities. This chapter and the next are concerned with marketing communications in business-to-business markets. We start this chapter with a discussion of business brands, given their role in communicating information to customers. The signals and messages communicated or dialogue engaged in by a company will shape a customer's view of an organization's brand as well as the company itself. It is important therefore that the actions undertaken by a company are consistent with its core values and customer expectations so that its brand and corporate image are enhanced. From this discussion of business brands, we go on to introduce what can be classed as generic aspects of communication, because whatever the context (whether business or consumer market) these issues are essentially the same. They include the components and nature of *integrated communications strategy*, the formulation of the *communications mix* and budgeting for communications activities. We then focus on what we call 'market' communication, discussing in more detail the use and design of communications tools such as advertising, sales promotion, public relations and *trade shows*. These tools are used to engage whole markets (albeit specific segments and target audiences) rather than specific individuals. A central focus in our discussion of these is the way in which digital technology contributes to their use and shapes the behaviour of marketers and customers alike. The next chapter centres on 'relationship' communication, where the tools that are used involve some form of direct contact (whether tactical/transactional or strategic/ongoing) with known representatives in specific customer companies. 'Market' communication and 'relationship' communication are sometimes referred to, respectively, as 'impersonal' and 'personal' communication. However, we prefer the terms market and relationship communication since they emphasize the scope of the communication (broadly to a market or narrowly to a known individual) without in any way constraining the communications medium that may be used. Both market and relationship communication contribute to an organization's representation of its brands and to customers' perception and experience of them.

BUSINESS BRANDS

Meaning and relevance in business markets

The importance of brands has gained currency in business-to-business markets in recent years with the recognition that a powerful brand can be a critical success factor in increasingly competitive markets (Kotler and Pfoertsch, 2007). That brands are central to B2B marketers is certainly reflected in Interbrand's annual assessment of the best global brands – companies such as GE (General Electric) and IBM consistently feature in the consultancy's top ten. Try visiting www.interbrand.com to learn more about why these two brands are rated so highly and to find out where other B2B brands sit. In most instances, brands in business-to-business markets are at the corporate level so we can in fact explain a brand as comprising the expression and stakeholder images of an organization's identity (Abratt and Kleyn, 2012). Identity relates to the characteristics by which something is recognized, and as marketers our interest lies particularly in the expressions directed at and images held by one critical stakeholder, namely the customer.

Brand expression

Keeping with the notion that brands in business markets are more often than not at the corporate level, then a business's expression of its identity to the marketplace is guided by organizational choices regarding mission, vision, strategic intent, values and culture (Abratt and Kleyn, 2012; Coleman et al., 2015; Simões and Mason, 2012). These frame a business's representation of its brand characteristics and are signalled through various means including:

> *visual identity*: the corporate name, logotype and/or symbol, typography and colour used on all mediums (e.g. vehicles, buildings, clothing, communications materials), which allow enhanced stakeholder recognition and association;
>
> *brand purpose*: the articulation of an organization's definitive position on what it believes in and what difference it can make;

brand personality: the human traits with which an organization might be associated and which, according to Keller and Richey (2006), can be expressed in terms of feelings (passion, compassion), thoughts (creativity, discipline) and actions (agility, collaboration);

brand communication: deliberate, integrated forms of communication (internal and external) that provide the basis for constructive relationships with key stakeholders and which for us centre on customers (but equally employees; after all, employees are central to the projection of many B2B brands).

See B2B Snapshot 7.1 for an example of ways in which one company signals its brand identity.

B2B SNAPSHOT 7.1   AIN'T NO MOUNTAIN HIGH ENOUGH

In 2009 DHL laid out its vision to become 'the Logistics Company for the World' through respect, simplifying customers' lives and making a positive contribution to the world. Come 2015, and DHL is still set on its ambition to become *the* logistics company. This intent is reflected in its association with leading and internationally recognized organizations in sectors for which it provides logistics solutions and also sponsorship deals – for example Formula 1, Fashion Week, Cirque du Soleil, the Gewandhaus Orchestra, as well as soccer teams such as Bayern Munich. Red and yellow are the two colours used by DHL to create its visual identity and building on this it uses the 'Speed of Yellow' concept in marketing communications to show how the company makes key events possible. Besides this signature yellow beam of light, the company also uses a remixed version of the classic 'Ain't No Mountain High Enough' in its commercials – a song which has been the brand's anthem for over 20 years.

Source: www.dhl.com.

Solo or co-brand expression?

Although many B2B companies focus their efforts solely on the communication of their own corporate identity, for some organizations, association with other brands can be particularly helpful. Co-branding operates whereby two or more companies cooperate to associate any of their brand identifiers either with one another or with a specific product. This can operate in a number of ways; for example, companies might allow their respective brands to be allied to others because of the underlying exchange relationship. For the B2B marketer, an important form of alliance lies in their ability to associate their own brand with those of their customers. This requires close alignment of supplier and customer corporate brands (Campbell et al., 2010) and willingness on the part of the customer to feature in the marketer's expression of its own brand identity. A related aspect of co-branding is ingredient branding where two or more independent brands feature on the same product. In doing this the intention is that the firms strengthen their competitive advantage by increasing the attractiveness of the combined offering to customers further down the supply chain. For example, Covestro has co-branding agreements with the sports equipment company Uvex, whose products contain and carry the logo of Covestro's branded polycarbonate, Makrolon®. While ingredient branding is normally associated with tangible products, it can also be used for services. For instance, Anderson Consulting joined forces with Fasturn e-business solutions to offer web-enabled solutions to retailers. Whatever the type of product, engaging in ingredient branding can provide firms with relationship, competitive, cost and advertising benefits (Erevelles et al., 2008; Helm and Özergin, 2015).

Brand image

Alongside expression, stakeholder images of a brand – i.e. the way in which those parties describe, remember and relate to an organization – are the other critical aspect of brand identity. Once again, considering specifically the customer as our principal stakeholder, brand image will likely result from:

brand experience: customer affective, cognitive and behavioural responses to supplier brand-related stimuli such as visual identity, brand purpose and communication; the key point with regards brand experience is that it provides a means through which customer memories can be strengthened and associations deepened in relation to a particular brand (Brakus et al., 2009);

brand relationships: in a B2B context employees in any boundary-spanning role play a critical role in shaping a customer's perception of the organizational brand; this means that consistency between the communication and delivery of brand promises by employees is critical, as is trust in building relationships (Power et al., 2008) between individuals who represent the supplier brand and managers from customer companies;

brand communities: these groups essentially comprise self-selected individuals who share positive beliefs in relation to a specific brand; the communities can provide a means through which information is shared between, or help is provided to, members, and the culture of the brand can be maintained (Abratt and Kleyn, 2012). Web-based brand communities can be particularly important in B2B markets. This is perhaps unsurprising given that professional users typically have a strong and long-standing interest in exchanging product-related information (Andersen, 2005), and the community can serve as a platform through which members are able to connect, interact and share with one another (Bruhn et al., 2014), rather than engaging in brand worship that might feature in consumer brand communities.

If brand image can be explained as the way in which people describe, remember and relate to an organization via experience, relationships and communities, then this results from stakeholders' judgements of that organization's actions and achievements, that is, its brand reputation (Abratt and Kleyn, 2012).

So the corporate brand, the level prevalent in most B2B markets, is the expressions and images of an organization's identity. The key point is that the more consistent those expressions and the greater the number of people that share common images of the organization, the more powerful the corporate brand becomes (Kapferer, 2008). Figure 7.1 shows the elements that contribute to the corporate brand, and therefore, as far as we are concerned, the business brand.

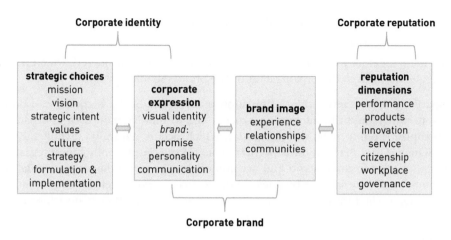

FIGURE 7.1 Corporate brand (adapted from Abratt and Kleyn, 2012)

With permission from Emerald Publishing.

INTEGRATED COMMUNICATIONS STRATEGY

Communications strategy involves planning, implementing and controlling an organization's communication with target audiences, the purpose being to achieve specified objectives in relation to each audience. Companies use a variety of tools to do this, including advertising, public relations, sales promotion, *direct marketing* and personal selling. The digitization of much communication means that there has been a seismic shift in marketer practices and user engagement (Wiersema, 2013) in relation to these tools. This shift has included a switch from offline to online media for market communication and a growing use of search, content and social media marketing to support reach, conversion and retention activities (Kantrowitz, 2014). Whatever the mix of tools and media used by a company, these are combined into a communications programme with the purpose of engaging buyers, but equally other stakeholders, that can influence or have an interest in an organization's activities. Responsibility for the management of the various communications tools may be split between departments. Strategies for advertising, public relations, sales promotion and direct marketing are normally separated from personal selling. Equally companies might also operate with separate teams responsible for website design and operation or digital communication and even within this, others who focus on specific elements such as social media. This division of responsibilities may carry risks of poor assimilation among communications tools, yet the integration of marketing communications is vital (Schultz, 2006) to coherent and consistent brand expression as well as to customer experience via multiple and repeated touchpoints throughout their decision journey.

So it is important that companies formulate communications strategies that are integrative, to ensure that consistent messages are conveyed through the different tools and that links between them are seamless, enabling the customer to move with minimum effort between them. An organization does, however, have to bear in mind that members of a target audience will aggregate a marketer's communication material whether the organization does this or not – integration occurs at the audience rather than organizational level. Members of that audience will assimilate the information encountered in some way and it may be that they:

- arrange the messages as the marketer intended;
- ignore the messages and materials; or
- put them together in a way that the marketer never even considered, which could even be harmful to the organization or the brand (Schultz, 1996).

Companies cannot control this assimilation process; the best a marketer can do is to 'try to understand the integration process and to modify their own approaches to maximize the return on the integration which occurs naturally' (Schultz, 1996: 140). Whether an organization concentrates its efforts on presenting an integrative message or tries to understand and accommodate a target audience's assimilation of promotional material, the business marketer has to put together a communications strategy. The formulation of this strategy requires a number of decisions to be made, including:

- setting communications objectives;
- deciding on the role of each component to be used in the communications mix;
- determining the communications budget; and
- selecting specific strategies for each component of the communications mix.

These are inevitably guided by an organization's choice of target market (including customer preference for different communications tools and online vs offline behaviour) and positioning strategy, which determine the role that communication will play relative to the product, distribution and pricing in a firm's overall marketing strategy.

Communications objectives

Communications objectives help with deciding how the various communications tools will be used in a marketing programme. Essentially, the objectives might normally be related to how the target audience uses (or what the firm would like that audience to do with) the information transmitted via an organization's communications tools and, with this in mind, many objectives are associated with 'buyer readiness states' or the hierarchy-of-effects model. This model describes the stages through which a buyer progresses when engaging with communications material. The stages in the model can be linked to the process enacted by a company for acquiring and retaining customers and to the communications tools that might be used at the various stages of these processes. Figure 7.2 illustrates this progression. A significant adjustment resulting from the established importance of digital communication, particularly in the early stages of the model, is the shift from push to pull marketing communications, from *outbound* to *inbound communications* activities, and to potential customers who are well informed on alternative solutions and suppliers prior to contacting companies (Kantrowitz, 2014; Trailer and Dickie, 2006; Wiersema, 2013).

Awareness is developed when potential customers become familiar with a product or brand. At this stage a company is trying to generate *leads* by directing its communications campaign to all potential customers within a particular target market segment. The marketer has to maximize *reach* to ensure that as many potential customers as possible might be exposed to the company's message, so the company is likely to use tools such as advertising (including pay-per-click and banner), search and *content marketing* and public relations.

Communications objectives	Potential customers Target segments	Communications tools
awareness	**leads**	advertising PR content and search marketing
interest	**enquiries**	website content marketing webinars trade shows
evaluation	**prospects**	online screening telemarketing field sales visits
trial	**new customers**	telemarketing field sales visits email and mobile marketing social media marketing
purchase	**established customers**	transactional and relationship sales teams social media marketing

FIGURE 7.2 Communications mix and customer acquisition process (adapted from Anderson and Narus, 2004; Chaffey, 2014; Järvinen and Taiminen, 2016)

Interest is the next step, reflecting a potential buyer's desire to learn more about what (e.g. product, brand, company) is being presented. Essentially, a company is trying to *acquire* potential customers by triggering a response from a target audience – if members of that audience seek out more information or make enquiries then the marketer has entered into the early stages of the customer decision process. Where advertising, PR, content and search marketing catch the eye of potential buyers, then those interested parties would typically be directed to the marketer's website – the company's main page or alternatively content- or campaign-specific landing pages. The website acts as the crucial focal point through which potential and existing customers can be directed, interest and contact details noted, and information needs satisfied via, for example, downloads, webinars, brochure requests, call requests and posting of questions (Chaffey, 2014; Järvinen and Taiminen, 2016).

Desire is the recognition by the buyer that when a supply need arises, a particular product or brand is the preferred option. To reach this point, target customers will *evaluate* the product, brand and company information available from alternative suppliers. The number of *prospective* customers within a particular target for whom a company becomes a potential supplier falls, as those interested customers evaluate and eliminate some companies as potential sources of supply. Although trade shows, personal selling and direct marketing assume more importance at this stage, online screening via company websites can also be useful here.

To progress from the evaluation stage and to *convert* prospects into actual customers, the business marketer uses communications tools to elicit specific courses of *action*, which might be the placing of *trial* orders by its target audience. Prospects who place trial orders and who become *new customers* will obviously need to enter into dialogue with the supplier. At this stage personal selling (possibly including field sales representatives and inside sales teams) becomes the important communications tool.

Critical for the business marketer, is the need to ensure that the different tools serve the potential customer with relevant communication content and a compelling brand experience. Combined with this is the need to make best use of the limited resources available, as well as provide the sales team with leads and prospects which can be acted upon. In describing the customer acquisition process, we noted the role which can be played by a company's website, and while not ordinarily being used for commercial transactions, automation can enhance its contribution to early stages in customer acquisition by:

- generating mailing lists using landing pages that offer content which fits subscriber profiles;
- welcoming prospects with relevant email messages and creating personalized messages on the website;
- reviewing interaction with messages and content, segmenting purchase intention based on lead scoring;
- following-up with additional prospect nurturing messages (which help qualify purchase intention);
- passing qualified leads to sales;
- encouraging customer loyalty and social media advocacy through ongoing personlized messaging to deliver engaging promotions and content.

(Chaffey, 2014)

Take a look at Figure 7.3 to see how these activities might contribute to early stages of customer acquisition.

The various stages of the state of buyer readiness that we describe represent a progression that is assumed to be essentially rational and over which the marketer has control (Schultz, 1996). In principle, the marketer sends messages via communications tools to affect the attitudes and behaviour of target audiences and is able to isolate the use and impact of each selected tool on members of those audiences. In reality this is not necessarily feasible (although the use of digital communication tools and related software does enable the tracking of behaviour). Customers (prospective and actual) are not passive recipients of messages; rather they play an active part in the communications process, searching for, accessing and requesting information as needed (from multiple sources – not just the marketer), sharing information within communities and approaching rather than simply responding to messages from marketers. This has always been the case in business markets but digital media and mediums allow customers to understand and determine their engagement with supply markets much more easily. The key for suppliers is to identify the type of information and messages preferred by customers and the format in which these are required. This does not negate the use of certain communications tools or online (in preference to offline) media; rather there has to be a balance between the interests of supplier and customer companies in the communications process.

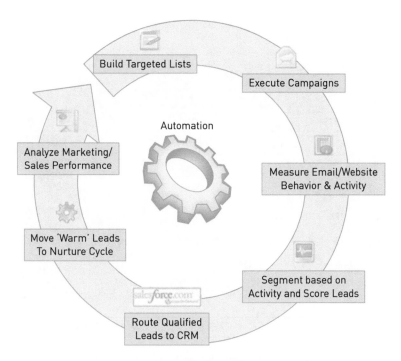

FIGURE 7.3 Communication automation for customer acquisition (Chaffey, 2014)

Communications mix

The promotional tools at the business marketer's disposal are not interchangeable and their effects at the different stages of the purchase process are not the same. So a company has to select the tools and their relative importance in the communications mix to reflect marketing communications objectives and the way in which potential buyers prefer to access and use information. The transition to digital media for some communications tools has enhanced marketer capacity to reach, engage and acquire customers, as well as enabling greater precision and evaluation of tools used for these (Järvinen and Karjaluoto, 2015). More important, perhaps, is the shift from outbound to inbound communications driven by increasing buyer preference for researching supply markets and engaging with suppliers online at different stages in the decision process. Digital media allow potential and existing customers to stay informed, and while not undermining the role of personal selling in the final stages of the decision process or in ongoing relationship exchanges, they can replace the sales force as an information conduit (Wiersema, 2013), enabling sales teams to focus on more value-adding activities. See Figure 7.4 for an indication of how buyers rate information obtained from different sources – note this does not include personal selling. Interestingly according to this survey, information obtained via a supplier's website is ranked third in terms of usefulness (after colleague/friend recommendations and industry-specific intermediaries) but dominates, nevertheless, in terms of buyer data gathering practice. The customer's use of such information channels for purchasing decisions should guide the design of a business marketer's promotional mix, and the design of this mix, will vary depending on the product category. Clearly,

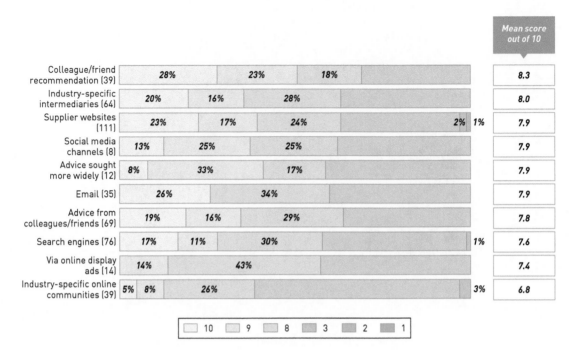

FIGURE 7.4 Influence of information from different sources (Buyersphere, 2015)

© 2015 Base One (part of the Gravytrain Group) and B2B Marketing in association with McCallum Layton and Research Now.

the importance attached to the various communications tools and their capacity to *engage* customers will be reflected in the business marketer's allocation of funds to support the use of those components.

Budgeting

A number of factors contribute to a company's sales performance. Some of these are determined by the organization itself, such as the design of the various elements of its marketing mix programme (including, of course, promotional activities), while others, such as competitor behaviour, government policy decisions or economic conditions, are beyond a firm's control. This means that setting a communications budget in relation to sales targets is difficult, with companies typically specifying improvements in the effectiveness of promotional activities and using practical methods to set budgets. These approaches include the following.

Objective and task

In using this approach, managers decide on the communications objectives, the tasks to be performed by the various promotional tools, and the associated costs involved in achieving these objectives. Adopting this method allows managers to set the communications mix that is most appropriate for the tasks that are to be performed. This is by no means easy, since estimating the level of effort (and therefore cost) to achieve certain tasks is particularly difficult.

Percentage of sales

This is more widely used and involves managers calculating the communications budget by multiplying a company's past sales by a standard percentage (for example, if last year's sales turnover was £1.5 million and the company aims to spend 4 per cent of turnover on communications, the budget will be £60,000). The calculation can be adjusted to take account of planned sales growth or decline; it reflects what an organization normally spends on communications activities; and it may also take account of average spending levels in the industry. The problem with this approach is that it ignores the fact that sales are a consequence of promotional activities rather than the other way round. During a buoyant sales period, promotional expenditure may be wasted unnecessarily. By the same token, declining sales could trigger a downward spiral for a firm, where, rather than investing more to try and boost revenue, the communications budget as a percentage of those poor sales figures is reduced accordingly.

Competitive parity

Companies that use this method base their budget decisions on the amount invested by competitors, and try to match it. Obviously it pays to have some idea of competitor expenditure levels (and many companies will engage in competitive tracking) but a firm cannot make budgeting decisions based solely on this approach. Competing organizations are likely to have different marketing strategies and so the communications strategies to help achieve these will also differ. The funds needed to support promotional activities should therefore be expected to differ also.

All that can be afforded

This approach bases expenditure on what a business can afford, with senior management determining how much can be spent on promotional activities. Budget limits are a fact of life in most organizations, so the majority of decisions, whatever overall method is taken, will often include an element of affordability. Problems can occur when affordability is the only means for setting the budget, as it ignores a firm's marketing strategy and opportunities that might be open to a company to build sales and profitability via suitable investment in promotion.

These various approaches might typically be used to determine investment levels for advertising, sales promotion and public relations. Planned expenditure on advertising and sales promotion may be combined into one budget allocation, with firms having further budgets for website, public relations activities and personal selling respectively. Even if a firm does have separate accounts for these, at some point an overview of the various activities and associated resource needs/costs has to be taken to avoid fragmentation of an organization's promotion strategy.

Website

A key purpose of communication is to present a compelling value proposition to the marketplace, to present messages of such quality and substance via integrated tools that customers engage with those messages, share them and seek to learn more.

So at a time when digital technology has resulted in a radical overhaul of market communication, a company's website is critical to ensuring that the B2B marketer makes a good first impression and to supporting the customer in their decision journey (particularly given our earlier observations regarding customer use of supplier websites). For most B2B companies, their websites are not designed to support transactional or commercial activities; rather they act as a key and possibly initial point of contact to which potential customers are directed (via various communications tools), and visitors judge the extent to which an organization is a credible supplier. Ways in which a potential supplier's credibility can be enhanced through visitors' web experiences include:

- presenting website information that is easily verifiable;
- clearly expressing the identity of the organization that 'lies behind' the website, e.g. visual identity, organizational purpose, explanation of divisions and multiple site operations, corporate brand personality, as well as key people and their roles;
- highlighting expert content and services offered that are relevant to customer needs;
- signalling honesty and integrity via tone of voice throughout the site but including *About us, Our philosophy* and *FAQs* pages;
- making it easy for site visitors to contact the organization on every page;
- ensuring that the site reflects the way that the company does business (thus mirroring the brand personality) so that the customer experience is consistent both online and offline;
- accessibility and ease of navigation;
- using frequently updated, relevant and useful content that requires customers to part with personal data in order to receive it;
- avoiding errors! (Power and Chaffey, 2012)

Public relations and content marketing

Public relations is one means through which an organization can express its identity in the marketplace, the aim being to achieve a close alignment between the communication of identity and customer perception of an organization. PR activities include the use of lobbying and charitable donations, press releases, corporate advertising, articles in publications and seminars. All of these uses and activities are relevant to organizations operating in business markets, but staging events such as conferences and seminars can be particularly valuable in enhancing a company's reputation and signalling expertise. See B2B Snapshot 7.2 for an example of this.

In addition to such 'staged' events, the business-to-business marketer can place PR content online in various forms to reinforce an organization's standing and demonstrate its capabilities to potential or existing customers. For example:

Company blogs: text content used to present in-house expertise, comment on industry-specific issues or announce new products. In sharing information via a blog, the B2B marketer must decide where in the company website to feature the blog, who should contribute to it and frequency of postings. Given that blogs, like other communications activity, are intended to engage audiences, they require compelling titles and content that are both relevant and informative for the potential reader.

Podcasts: audio recordings that the listener can access via for example RSS feeds or Tweets, download and listen to at any time. Effective podcasts provide a mix of topical news and information that appeals to listeners and might focus on industry-specific issues rather than promoting the business marketer's products, for example. Current podcasts would normally feature in a specific section of a company website, with past episodes also available for downloading.

B2B SNAPSHOT 7.2   SPREADING THE WORD

Gartner is an international organization that provides research and analysis about the global information technology industry. Key elements of this company's business activities are:

- engagement in consultancy work, where it guides major enterprises in their formulation and implementation of technology-based strategies; and

- organization of events in different geographic locations, including its Technology Summits and Symposium IT/xpos.

The Technology Summits are organized around the world, including events in North and South America, Europe, Japan and Australia. These conferences focus on particular topics such as security, wireless technology and outsourcing, and are made up of presentations by Gartner analysts as well as contributions from leading experts in the IT industry. As these are fee-paying events Gartner has to convince its target audience of its expertise, and ensure that the company is automatically associated with selected IT topics by its audience. The events that it organizes itself may go some way to achieving this, but equally important is the regular appearance of the views, expertise and work of its analysts in readily accessible publications. Its analysts will frequently comment on industry trends in IT-related publications and feature in professional and management publications.

Besides such summits, Gartner operates a series of regular webinars (online seminars) on selected issues hosted by Gartner analysts (visit www.gartner.com to learn more about the company's expos and seminars).

Webcasts: recorded video content streamed to a computer or internet device and watched as it is downloaded. Successful video content can be informational (providing, for example, in-depth company, product and/or solution insight), educational (showing the viewer how to do something) and entertaining (albeit with an underlying serious message). Whatever the approach, brevity is key as viewers are unlikely to watch content lasting more than 1–2 minutes and many may switch off after less than 30 seconds. While words contained in blogs and podcasts can be isolated, this is not possible with video content, so webcasts posted on a company's YouTube, Vimeo or DailyMotion page need to be supported by a textual description that includes key words and a URL that directs viewers to a topic or video-specific landing page.

Whitepapers: long-form documents used by a marketer to, for example, present a solution to a particular business or industry problem or alternatively to outline the technical or business benefits of the supplier's offering. Whitepapers have been used for some time by business marketers but are now more readily accessible via online distribution.

The above are just some of the content forms that the business marketer might create in order to share information and ideas with current and prospective customers – others include the provision of presentation material and images via social media sites such as SlideShare and Flickr. For an example of how one company uses content as part of its communications strategy, visit www.deloitte.com, or for a content-specific illustration, view Siemens' SlideShare (www.slideshare.net/Siemens). Business marketers have used content to engage customers for some time (John Deere launched its publication *The Furrow* in 1902, advising farmers how to improve profitability) but digital technology has made the creation of content easier, expanding the possible formats, and it is certainly much more accessible via the internet. While this might have led to considerable investment in digital content by companies, to be of use, content:

- must be attractive to potential or existing customers by offering information that is of value and relevance and which can be readily absorbed by an audience; in an increasingly information-rich marketplace managers expect key messages to be transmitted in 'bite-size' pieces – overly long or complex content risks disengaging the audience;
- needs to be current: the nature of some content is such that it can quickly date so the business marketer must ensure that material is regularly reviewed and where appropriate purged;
- should be readily accessible: content is redundant if it cannot be found – which we go on to discuss in relation to search.

Search engine marketing

If a website is key to the way in which a company presents itself as a credible organization, and content provides a means through which the business marketer signals its expertise and problem-solving ability, then search engines are essential in ensuring that a company is found by a customer and remains visible. As individuals, we typically use search engines such as Google as information sources, and business customers are no different – web searches are an important means of identifying potential suppliers (take a look at Figure 7.4). Given that search engines drive so much traffic to company websites, it stands to reason that the business marketer wants to make sure that their organization sits as close as possible to the top of search results lists. There are two critical points that a manager needs to understand and account for:

Words used by customers when undertaking searches. The marketer must ensure that words contained on the company website (the home page as well as specific content pages), online advertising and marketing content not only reflect the identity that it wishes to express but also match those used by customers in product and supplier searches.

Operation of search engines. Search engines are intended to provide the best answers, the closest matches to a user's query. A search engine identifies keywords (words or phrases entered as part of a query) that feature on webpages, in marketing content and in HTML tags, determining their importance according to prominence on a page – both in terms of position and frequency. So the nearer the top of a page and the more frequently a word appears, the more important it is ranked by the search engine. This means that the marketer has to give thought to creating copy that is both engaging and search engine friendly. Being search engine friendly involves using words (not pictures), including keywords in the copy, repeating these words and phrases naturally, and ensuring that important content (concepts and keywords) is prominent.

The business marketer might look to optimize performance in horizontal search engines such as Google, but equally important can be general B2B engines such as www.business.com and vertical engines such as www.globalspec.com which serves engineering, manufacturing and related sectors. Vertical engines allow searchers to locate more specific and focused information, and for the marketer it enables a more precisely targeted message as well as providing more valuable sales leads given that vertical searches are typically conducted later in the buying process.

Advertising

From our earlier discussion of brands, it should be apparent that advertising represents an important means through which an organization can express its visual identity, purpose and personality to stakeholder groups such as government bodies, financial markets, local communities, pressure groups and of course customers. Presenting the brand via advertising campaigns might be undertaken with the intention of raising awareness, changing perceptions or reinforcing existing beliefs among these groups, and for which messages would have to be adjusted to reflect the interests of these groups. Take a look at B2B Scenario 7.1 to see how HP has been trying to foster engagement with its brand.

B2B SCENARIO 7.1   MAKE IT MATTER

HP is a provider of imaging and printing solutions to individual and business customers. Faced with declining market performance for the best part of a decade (Bandler and Burke, 2012), the appointment of new CEO, Meg Whitman in 2011, was followed by communication campaigns to raise awareness and create brand engagement amongst IT decision makers. Under the theme 'make it matter', the company invested $15m and $10m in the US and UK respectively in 10-week communication campaigns to show how the company helps businesses embrace information technology challenges of the twenty-first century. Centred around solutions related to enterprise mobility, cloud computing, big data and information security, the campaigns included advertisements screened on TV (in the UK from ITV to Sky Sports), in cinemas as well as magazines and newspapers. These advertisements were supplemented with significant outdoor campaigns in high impact digital and static format, which in the UK, were across the country at bus stops and roadside hoardings, as well as at locations such as Heathrow Airport and London Underground tube stations. This campaign was supported by different content streams on YouTube, Twitter, Facebook and

(Continued)

(Continued)

LinkedIn with the #makeitmatter hashtag. Key to the overall campaign was the intention to reach the different individuals involved in purchasing, whether IT decision makers, financial or procurement managers. In using the various media channels, HP recognized that those individuals would likely consume media in different ways. For example, in the UK, some might read the *Financial Times*, some might watch *The X-Factor*, while others might spend all of their time on their phone or tablet. On LinkedIn, HP used display and follower ad campaigns to highlight the overall 'make it matter' campaign, using LinkedIn to target its professional audience both during and post campaign with custom design and content options. The scale and coverage of the campaign was pretty impressive, but important to HP was the intention to move away from the traditionally rational approach to IT marketing communication and instead address business decision makers with content that created a strong emotional connection, built confidence and ultimately resonated. By sharing human narratives, HP hoped to encourage organizations to rethink their approach to technology. However it is not just about emotion and storytelling. After all, the product, price point and deliverables have to be right to make sales. Clearly short-term promotions might be expected to have some immediate impact, but equally important is the longer-term effect of the 'make-it-matter' campaign on purchase decisions that often have a six to nine month cycle. Working with its internal communications team, as well as agency partners, HP's global brand and communications manager has to agree what those short and longer term metrics might be to determine the effectiveness of this campaign.

Sources: Bandler and Burke, 2012; McGreal, 2014; www.communicus.com

Besides being part of broad corporate brand communications activities, advertising is important in positioning an organization in the marketplace and in engaging representatives of target customer companies. It can serve a variety of purposes and in doing so can spread the marketer's message to a far greater audience compared to other tools. As far as the hierarchy-of-effects model is concerned, advertising supports the business marketer's investment in its principal communications tool, personal selling, and is typically used to create awareness among target customers, provide information and identify potential leads.

Advertising strategy

A firm must make a number of decisions that result in the articulation of its advertising strategy, consisting principally of:

- setting advertising objectives;
- formulating the creative plan;
- media selection; and
- evaluation of advertising effectiveness.

Throughout the process of strategy development and implementation, what must be borne in mind is that advertising is only one component of a firm's overall communications mix and it must be integrated with other elements in order to realize strategic marketing goals.

Setting advertising objectives

Advertising objectives normally consist of *performance goals* (what should it accomplish?) and also the *target audience* (who does the organization wish to engage?). Clear articulation of objectives is crucial as they give direction to those involved in the formulation and implementation of an advertising programme. The goals are the principal means by which campaigns are evaluated, and as such should both reflect the functions that advertising can realistically perform and also take account of the fact that immediate changes in sales which may result from campaigns are difficult to observe. So the objectives must be unambiguous but also realistic and expressed in such a way that the effect of an advertising programme can be measured. Where objectives are underpinned by the hierarchy-of-effects model, they are normally expressed in terms of communication goals such as level of brand awareness, recognition and buyer attitudes, or audience interest and engagement in terms of level of traffic directed to corporate website or campaign-specific landing pages.

One of the principal purposes of advertising is to attract members of a customer organization who influence that company's purchasing activities. Clearly these will not necessarily be restricted to employees with purchasing responsibilities; rather they could include managers from a variety of functions. As we have already noted in previous chapters, managers' choice criteria and interest in product attributes and the relative importance attached to them are in part determined by their functional responsibilities. Advertising objectives for a particular target audience must also reflect the choice criteria that are important to members of that audience.

Formulating the creative plan

The creative plan builds on the objectives set for an advertising campaign and essentially centres on the *development of a message* that will engage the specified target audience. The advertiser uses language, format and style in a campaign in order to present this message. Decisions in message presentation are informed by the creative philosophy of the advertiser and target audience choice criteria, but equally should reflect the words, phrases and images with which an organization wishes to be associated and that are relevant and meaningful to customers. So consistent expression in all forms of brand communication is important but this has to be allied with messages for specific advertising campaigns so that it results in audience engagement.

In consumer markets it is often believed that messages which appeal to the emotions (notably humour) are particularly effective, with brand identity, resonance or anomaly (West and Ford, 2001) driving message creation and presentation. While this approach might be successful in consumer markets, is there room for emotion in business-to-business advertising? This may seem unlikely given the nature of the purchase process, the fact that buyers are accountable for purchases made, and that products are not for personal consumption and are bought using non-personal funds. However, this ignores the contribution that emotion can have in shaping brand attitudes in business markets (Gilliland and Johnston, 1997) and the fact that emotional headlines are indeed prevalent in advertising copy (Cutler and Javalgi, 1994). At a strategic level a business brand might be presented using a rational approach but the tactical execution can, nevertheless, include emotion (West and Ford, 2001) and as Lohtia et al. (1995) suggest:

B2B SNAPSHOT 7.3   GET INTO THE GROOVE

Look around and you will find Michelin tyres on all types of vehicles that have wheels – bikes, cars, lorries and planes. The haulage industry represents a key part of Michelin's business, for which it has over 16 per cent of the global market by value, and the company wants to maintain its position – but to do this it plans to sell fewer tyres and instead develop its regrooving service. Although regrooving delivers 10 per cent fuel savings and extends the life of tyres by 25 per cent, 70 per cent of hauliers in the United Kingdom do not return tyres for regrooving because this type of 'reconditioned' tyre is considered unsafe. So the challenge for Michelin and its agency IAS (now merged with US based agency Stein to become SteinIAS) was to create positive awareness by educating the market about regrooving benefits and dispelling safety concerns. The central creative aspect of the communications campaign involved using Bibendum, Michelin's iconic figure, and associating it with groove, groovy, grooving ... the result was a 1970s-style Bibendum getting down on the dancefloor. The combination of advertising, PR and direct marketing campaign resulted in increased regroove rates and 69 per cent ad recall. If you want to see Bibendum grooving, find him on Flickr (www.flickr.com/photos/iasb2b/3532556291/).

- information on performance and product quality should be included;
- this should be presented in a logical manner; and
- symbolism and metaphors can be useful in delineating the value proposition.

Read B2B Snapshot 7.3 for an example of how humour featured in one company's advertising campaign.

Media selection

Getting the message right is obviously crucial to gaining the target audience's attention and in ensuring that the signals conveyed in it are interpreted in the way intended by the advertiser. But for this to happen the audience has to have access to the advertisement in the first place, so media have to be chosen that will ensure that the audience is reached. Decisions about media selection are determined by the capacity of the selected medium to adequately convey the advertising message, the degree to which the medium can provide access to the target audience, and cost.

Outbound communications (where the marketer drives the communication directed at target audiences) can be effective in raising awareness and is normally associated with broadcast and print media. Forms of *broadcast media* that a business marketer may choose from include television and radio. Although these feature to a lesser extent in business-to-business than in business-to-consumer markets, TV advertising can play an important role in raising the profile of an organization, contributing to corporate identity or positioning. The benefit of using TV for advertising lies in the speed with which it can raise awareness and its capacity as a platform through which reach and coverage are enabled while other tools serve functions in terms of specific calls to action. As part of its 'make it matter' campaign, TV advertising was a key medium through which HP sought to make an emotional connection with as wide an audience as possible. *Print media* continues to play an important role in business-to-business advertising for outbound communication where the principal purpose is to raise brand awareness and build reputation. Nevertheless this 'broadcasting' approach inevitably incurs waste because of the need to maximize exposure in order to reach the intended target audience. In contrast, the 'narrowcasting' of digital media means that adverts can be much more targeted and directed at specific audience profiles within an online publication or website.

The idea behind online and offline advertising is essentially the same, i.e. displaying adverts in publications or on a website, and the more prominent an ad placement, the more expensive it is. However, while part of print advertising costs is driven by exposure (in addition to placement), the dominant cost model for online advertising is pay-per-click whereby the advertiser incurs cost when a viewer responds by clicking on the ad itself. To be able to click on the advertisement, the viewer needs to be exposed to it in the first place and this is where keywords come into play once more. Associating an advertisement with keywords means that it is likely to feature on sites with similar content or on search-results pages when someone conducts a search. Pay-per-click advertising is context sensitive – ads will only appear on websites for which the advertiser has purchased keywords, so identifying and paying for the right to use keywords that best reflect customer behaviour and marketer's offering is critical. When it comes to search engines, however, note that the frequency and prominence depends on how much an advertiser is willing to pay for keywords, and online users tend to trust organic searchers over paid placements.

Leaving aside the mechanics of exposure and costing, online ads do provide the marketer with more dynamic and interactive means of attracting and engaging with target audiences. For example, online ad display can be enriched with assets such as videos, podcasts, technical briefings and case studies – essentially content which is able to validate an offer or present a clear benefit statement to a prospective buyer. As with other communication, it has to be of relevance and value to the target audience to ensure click-through and to maximize ad effectiveness; managers who do respond should be directed to landing pages that display content that relates to the advertisement itself. To determine whether members of a desired target audience are being reached and whether the level/nature of engagement among website visitors is being achieved, the business marketer can use a variety of measures including click-through rates from different traffic sources to website landing pages, the depth/range of digital content viewed from landing pages, conversions from browser to customer, as well as attrition rates (Järvinen and Karjaluoto, 2015). Whichever metrics are used will of course depend on the objectives set for the online advertising.

Sales promotion

The use of sales promotion in business markets can be classified according to whether it is designed to trigger a response from members of a company's sales force, channel partners or organizational customers. For *sales personnel* promotional tools are used principally to motivate staff or to support them in their selling roles. Where a company is trying to hit short-term targets, staff are offered *incentives* such as prizes and cash rewards or may be awarded 'salesperson of the month' status in an organization's recognition programme. Such tools work well in one-off, transactional selling situations. However, they can have a detrimental effect when a company is trying to build long-term relationships with key clients, because such incentives encourage sales personnel to pursue short-term results.

To perform their various tasks sales staff may draw heavily from *informational material* provided by an organization. This material includes brochures, catalogues and selling aids such as presentation kits which might be used to explain the features and benefits of new or existing products. Online access to a lot of this material and the use of portable multimedia presentations can ensure consistency in overall message content while allowing interactivity via access to complete product information systems and the customization of proposals to clients.

Sales promotion is also an important tool for organizations that rely on *intermediaries* in order to reach customers. Financial mechanisms (*incentives* and *promotional pricing*) are typically used as part of a company's push strategy (that is, trying to 'push' sales through distribution channels) and might be used to gain acceptance of new products by middlemen or to hit short-term sales targets. Given the fact that intermediaries assume a selling function on behalf of principals, the provision of *informational material* to support a distributor's sales efforts can also be important.

Trade missions and trade shows/exhibitions

Trade missions and trade shows bring supplier and customer companies together in one location. Organizations operating in business markets will normally participate in these promotional events because marketers are able to showcase their product expertise to a fairly well-qualified target audience, and customers can examine a large number of potential new suppliers and products/technologies with relative ease. Whether this is a government-sponsored promotional event or an industry-specific trade show, the basic idea remains the same: the events take place in specific locations and consist of multiple booths where suppliers display their products for anything from two days to two weeks. In many industries where firms are involved in or wish to develop overseas markets, trade missions and trade shows represent a key component of a firm's international communications activities.

Trade missions

A trade mission is a government-sponsored promotional activity. The purpose of a trade mission is to facilitate the economic growth of a particular region or country, typically via international trade in overseas markets. To achieve this, trade missions can involve:

• the representation of particular regions or countries at major international trade fairs;

• major export drives where a government designates an overseas market as a priority for business development and then arranges, leads and partly funds promotional events in that target country; and/or

• major drives where a host government tries to encourage overseas companies to invest in its country. This type of activity is important for the economic development of countries and is a key method for those countries to acquire skills, technology and know-how.

In Britain, the government body UK Trade & Investment provides financial support to allow companies to participate in selected industry exhibitions, for example, in the Paris Airshow in France, the Asian Oil, Gas and Petrochemical Exhibition in Kuala Lumpur, Malaysia, and the Bio US 2017, in San Diego. The support is designed to help firms gain initial exposure in new markets. Trade missions can be particularly useful where firms are trying to develop export markets, especially if a company has limited international marketing experience in general, or with a specific country. Trade missions enable participants to acquire information fairly quickly about overseas markets as well as knowledge about the process of exporting to those countries (Seringhaus and Rosson, 1998).

Trade shows and exhibitions

Trade shows are a bit like temporary versions of the shopping centres or retail parks that are such a prominent feature in consumer markets. Potential buyers visit prospective sellers, with most of the visitors having specific plans to buy a product or influence the eventual purchase decision for a particular product (Gopalakrishna and Lilien, 1995). Key differences include *representation* and *permanence*. In consumer markets, intermediaries such as retailers are the principal means through which producers are able to present their products to target customers. In business markets, distributors will represent producers at some industrial trade shows (typically at regional or smaller national exhibitions) but in many instances suppliers will participate directly in shows that are key events within their industry.

Shopping centres and the retailers found within them are permanent, unless of course a retailer closes down its store. The location sites of most industrial trade shows are also fixed and can be quite substantial in terms of size. See Table 7.1 for details of the largest exhibition sites in various countries.

The events that take place within them, however, are not permanent; rather, they are temporary. Throughout any given year, a site will play host to numerous trade shows from a variety of industries. For example, Frankfurt, the second largest convention site in the world, plays host to some of the biggest trade fairs. See Table 7.2 for details of the world's largest fairs.

Functions performed by trade shows

Tasks that can be performed by trade-show participation are typically divided between those which are sales related and others that are not linked to the selling process. *Non-selling functions* include building or maintaining company image, gathering competitor information, product testing/evaluation, and maintaining company morale (Bonoma, 1983). Non-sales tasks are cited by companies as reasons for participating in trade shows, but sales-related functions are nevertheless the principal motivation for investment in these promotional events (Blythe, 1997). The key *sales-related functions* that can be performed by trade-show participation include: the identification of prospects; gaining access to key decision-makers in current and potential customer companies; disseminating facts about vendor products, services and personnel; actually selling products/winning orders; and servicing current accounts' problems via contacts made (Bonoma, 1983).

TABLE **7.1** Key exhibition and convention centres around the world

	2015	2014	2013
Reed Exhibitions (GB)	1,183.0	1,104.0	1,017.0
UBM plc (GB)	855.5	561.1	546.0
Messe Frankfurt (D)	647.8	554.2	544.8
GL events (F)	456.0	409.8	397.7
MCH Group (CH)	384.5	373.6	385.5
Informa (GB)	356.1	248.7	196.0
Fiera Milano (I)	337.3	245.5	245.1
Deutsche Messe (D)	329.3	280.6	312.0
Koelnmesse (D)	321.2	231.2	280.6
Messe Düsseldorf (D)	302.0	411.5	322.9
VIPARIS (F)	283.0	303.8	297.4
Emerald Expositions (USA)	281.0	225.4	132.9
Messe München (D)	277.4	309.4	353.0
Messe Berlin (D)	242.0	269.4	187.6
HKTDC (HK)	223.1	172.8	163.4
Coex (ROK)	217.0	163.1	139.0
i2i Events Group (GB)	204.0	177.3	145.3
NürnbergMesse (D)	203.7	228.7	192.8
ITE Group (GB)	183.1	223.7	229.4
Tokyo Big Sight (JP)	n/a	159.5	140.8
Fira Barcelona (E)	148.0	152.6	117.8
Jaarbeurs Utrecht (NL)	133.3	131.6	140.9
Svenska Mässan Göteborg (S)	128.9	97.4	88.0
dmg :: events (GB)	128.1	128.0	103.8
Amsterdam RAI (NL)	126.2	119.7	116.6
BolognaFiere (I)	119.0	120.0	109.9
Tarsus Group (GB)	117.9	77.4	90.9
SNIEC Shanghai (CN)	115.7	139.0	116.6
Landesmesse Stuttgart (D)	115.0	137.0	98.8
Comexposium (F)	108.5	129.3	117.5
Artexis Group (B)	107.0	92.8	94.0

Source: AUMA, 2013. AUMA: With permission from AUMA.

TABLE **7.2** The largest trade fairs worldwide (based on exhibitor numbers for 2012)

Location	Hall	Location	Hall
Hannover Exhibition Center	463,165	Georgia World Congress Center Atlanta	130,112
National Exhib. and Convention Center (NECC) Shanghai	400,000	BVV Veletrhy Brno	121,314
Frankfurt/Main Exhibition Center	366,637	NRG Park (formerly Reliant Park Houston)	120,402
Fiera Milano	345,000	Fiera del Levante Bari	120,000
China Import & Export Fair Complex Guangzhou	340,000	Yiwu International Expo Center	120,000
Cologne Exhibition Center	284,000	Kentucky Expo Center	120,000
Düsseldorf Exhibition Center	261,817	Tüyap Istanbul Fair	120,000
Paris-Nord Villepinte	242,082	Fiera Roma	118,910
McCormick Place Chicago	241,549	Fira Barcelona – Montjuic	115,211
Fira Barcelona – Gran Vía	240,000	Brussels Expo	114,445
Feria Valencia	230,837	EUREXPO Lyon	114,275
Crocus Expo IEC Moskau	226,399	Leipzig Exhibition Center	111,300
Paris Porte de Versailles	219,759	Essen Exhibition Center	110,000
Chongqing International Expo Centre	204,000	New Int. Conv. & Exp. Center, Chengdu Century City	110,000
The NEC Birmingham	201,634	Rimini Fiera	109,000
BolognaFiere	200,000	KINTEX Goyang/Seoul	108,483
IFEMA Feria de Madrid	200,000	BEC Bilbao Exhibition Centre	108,000
SNIEC Shanghai	200,000	Palexpo Genf	108,000
Orange County Convention Center Orlando	190,875	Poznan International Fair	107,654
Las Vegas Convention Center	184,456	New China Int. Exhibition Center (NCIEC) Beijing	106,800
Munich Exhibition Center	180,000	Messe Stuttgart	105,200
Nurimberg Exhibition Center	170,000	Shenzhen Convention & Exhibition Center (SZCEC)	105,000
Berlin ExpoCenter City	170,000	Ernest N. Morial Convention Center New Orleans	102,230
Veronafiere	151,536	Singapore Expo	101,624
Wuhan International Expo Center	150,000	ExCeL London	100,000
Messe Basel	141,000	Fiere di Parma	100,000
IMPACT Muang Thong Thani Bangkok	140,000	Royal Dutch Jaarbeurs Exh. & Conv. Centre Utrecht	100,000
VV Moskau	132,720		

Source: AUMA, 2013. AUMA: With permission from AUMA.

Money well spent?

As can be seen from Figure 7.5, trade shows are useful in the early stages of the purchase decision process and in identifying and qualifying prospective new customers. However, as customers progress to evaluating potential suppliers and reaching final purchase decisions, and the sales process moves to presenting the sales message, closing a sale and even servicing an established account, then the trade show is less valuable compared to personal selling.

As a communications tool, trade shows are important to companies operating in business markets not only in terms of the potential to contribute to a firm's communication activities but also because of the money invested in these events. Leaving personal selling aside, trade shows are one of the most significant expenditure items for many firms, accounting for up to 20 per cent of advertising spend in 2014 (Kantrowitz, 2014). And that is without taking account of the time taken up by involving sales teams and senior management in the events. There has been growing scrutiny in recent years of the return on monies invested in trade shows, yet this promotional tool continues to play a major role in communications activities, and perhaps with good reason. Even if funds allocated to trade shows and exhibitions are considerable, it has long been argued that, compared to personal selling, these promotional events offer significant savings. For example, the cost of the entire sales-cycle can be reduced four-fold if the transaction is triggered by a supplier's participation in a trade show (Browning and Adams, 1988; Hart, 1988).

New customer/prospect buying phase	Key seller communications objective and tasks		Relative communication effectiveness
	Communications objectives	Task	Low High
need recognition	generate awareness	prospecting	
developing product specifications	feature comprehension	opening relationship qualifying prospect	
search and qualification of suppliers	lead generation	qualifying prospect	
evaluation	performance comprehension	presenting sales message	
supplier selection	negotiation of terms/offer customization	closing sale	
purchase feedback	reassurance	account service	Advertising Trade Personal shows selling

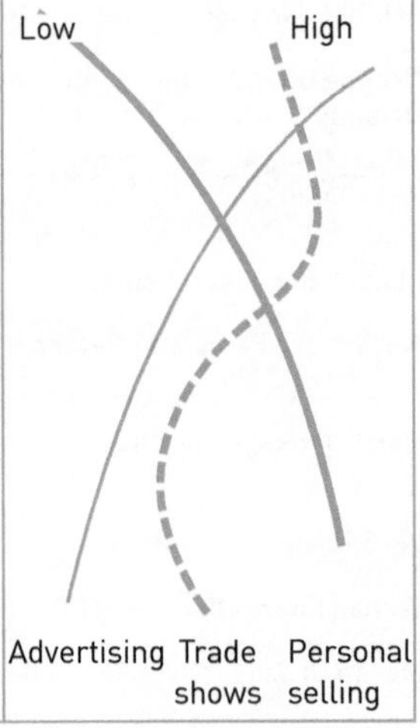

FIGURE 7.5 Relative effectiveness of business communications tools (Gopalakrishna and Lilien, 1995)

With permission from INFORMS.

Audience attention and quality

If one of the reasons for communication is to engage a target audience and one of the challenges lies in attracting that audience's attention, then trade-show participation can certainly facilitate this. Visitors to trade shows will select the events that they choose to attend purposefully, and will go with specific objectives in mind (see Table 7.3). Trade shows therefore provide the business marketer with a means of influencing purchase behaviour, but more critically, access to DMU members other than the buyer. Audience quality at trade shows is much broader than simply consisting of managers with specific purchasing roles, who might be the business marketer's usual point of contact. Indeed, a large number of visitors have no role in purchasing and are instead involved in the areas of sales and marketing, general administration, design, engineering, and research and development (R&D) (Blythe, 2002). Managers with these functional responsibilities can influence different stages of the decision-making process and it is known that these stages can be affected by information obtained at trade shows (Moriarty and Spekman, 1984). The variety of managers and their motivations for attending mean that a marketer needs to give some thought to the staff present, communication behaviour and type of information available at an exhibition, and it should not necessarily be sales driven.

One of the problems with a trade show is that it lasts for only a short period of time, with the result that interested parties might overlook some stands or not be able to attend. Meanwhile exhibitors might fail to reach key members of their target audience. One way that is increasingly being used to deal with this and to provide ongoing access to trade-show information and exhibitors is the use of *virtual trade shows* (Axelson, 2001; Geigenmüller, 2010). For example, InnoTrans offers a virtual marketplace – which is an electronic variation of the way in which a trade show normally operates (www.virtualmarket.innotrans.de). Attendees are able to visit virtual halls and booths online and to talk to booth staff or visitors, via chat rooms or video conferences and forums, as well as post messages in online diaries or blogs (Geigenmüller, 2010).

TABLE 7.3 Visitor reasons for trade-show attendance, by job role

Reasons	Sales and marketing	General administration	Design	Engineering	R&D
See new products/developments	19.1	16.6	6.66	7.5	4.16
Obtain product/technical information	0.83	4.16	3.33	7.5	5.0
Try new products/demonstrations	2.5	4.16	3.33	7.5	5.0
See new companies	2.5	4.16	1.66	0.83	1.66
See a specific company/product	3.33	0.83	0.0	0.0	0.83
Discuss specific problems	0.0	0.83	1.66	4.16	1.66
Compare products	0.83	1.66	0.83	0.0	3.33

Source: Blythe, 2002.

Planning trade shows

Although a trade-show event lasts for a relatively short period of time, planning for it can take much longer, particularly when preparation prior to and evaluation after an event are taken into account. The planning process normally includes the following stages.

Setting trade-show objectives As we discussed previously, trade-show participation can serve a variety of selling and non-selling purposes. A company might select any number of these as its principal reasons for investing in a particular trade show, focusing on short-term objectives such as performing product and sales presentations (selling functions), gathering competitor intelligence information or making new contacts (non-selling functions). Longer-term objectives could include launching new products, generating new leads (selling functions) and building customer relationships or company image (non-selling functions) (Shipley and Wong, 1993). However, to have any meaning, objectives have to go beyond the functions that can be served by trade-show participation and, as with any objectives, must be articulated in such a way that they are measurable, can be achieved (given a firm's resources) and are realistic. For example, by performing product presentations, what exactly is a firm hoping to achieve, what types of leads is a firm trying to generate (and how many would it expect to accumulate over the exhibition period), and what systems will be used to monitor the number and types of leads generated?

Trade-show selection   From setting objectives, a key decision for a company is to decide on the shows in which it should participate. Large, prestigious international shows will attract massive visitor numbers and will therefore have an obvious appeal to a company when it selects events. However, this does not guarantee that the larger the show, the more people will visit a company's stand. In fact, the reverse can be the case: the larger the event, the more there is to choose from and therefore the greater the likelihood that a company's booth will not be visited. It is not only the size of events and multitude of competing participants that can make it difficult to attract visitor attention. Most visitors do not attend for the full duration of a show; rather they are likely to be present for a few days at the most and therefore the number of booths at which a visitor can spend a significant amount of time is quite small, no matter how big the event itself. This means that trade-show tactics can be critical in ensuring that a company's involvement in a show is known and that visitors are motivated to seek out and/or stop at the firm's stand. See B2B Snapshot 7.4 to learn how one company tries to attract attention.

B2B SNAPSHOT 7.4   IS IT A BIRD ...?

Festo, an engineering firm headquartered in Germany, supplies pneumatic and electrical automation technology to customers around the world. For the firm, participation at Hannover Messe is a major event in the company's communication calendar but like many organizations, the challenge for Festo is to think of ways in which it can showcase its technical and innovation capabilities at the show. To this end the company assigns project teams the task of developing creative and dynamic ways in which it can help exhibition visitors appreciate its technological development and application expertise. The project teams work in secret – other Festo employees don't find out about the exhibition feature until the unveiling at the Hannover Messe. In recent years these have included a remotely controlled bird, jellyfish and dragonfly – all of which are designed to look and move like the real thing using Festo's automation expertise. And does it work? Well there's always a buzz around the company's stand, and being visited by Angela Merkel probably helps too. To learn more, visit the company's website (www.festo.com) and view the 'unreal' creatures on YouTube (www.youtube.com/user/FestoHQ accessed 18 July 2016).

Tactics Crucial to the success of trade-show participation are the tactics surrounding involvement in a specific event. Decisions that can affect a company's degree of success include:

Promotional activities to support participation: if a company is going to take part in a trade show, then prospective visitors to the event need to know about it! Pre-show promotion can include posting of forthcoming exhibition participation on the company website, advertising and direct mail including invitations to potential visitors to call at the company's stand. Listings can be developed using a show organizer's advance registration list as well as the firm's own customer/prospects database.

The design and location of a firm's stand: this can be a key factor in determining the number of visitors to a company's stand. Given that a large number of exhibition visitors want to see or try new products, obtain technical or product information or meet with company representatives, the stand needs to be sufficiently eye-catching to make someone want to enter a company's display area rather than just pass by. Sample products, models, demonstrations and informational material must be readily visible and the message conveyed by these display items clearly articulated. In fact, considering and designing the stand based on the way in which it might be experienced by a visitor much in the same that marketers typically consider retail settings from an experiential point of view can have a positive impact on exhibitor performance (Gilliam, 2015; Rinallo et al., 2010). Besides booth design, a company has to try to ensure footfall either by selecting a prime location or by directing targets to the stand via mobile communication.

The selection and behaviour of staff on the stand: the composition and behaviour of stand personnel can be critical to successful trade-show involvement. Unless an organization is trying to generate leads or is using an exhibition for relationship building, sales personnel or account managers are not the obvious choice given that a large proportion of trade-show audiences do not have purchasing responsibilities and will typically use events for information-gathering. So involvement of staff other than those with primary boundary-spanning roles can be important for communication purposes and signalling of organizational identity.

Post-exhibition follow-up: to make best use of opportunities that arise during a trade show a firm must pursue leads quickly after the event, before interest from those contacts starts to decline. The nature of the leads will vary so the urgency and the business marketer's response and responsibility for pursuing them should also vary. For example, details of the various leads that have been logged can be handled according to three characteristics:

1. Are visitors mainly interested in company rather than product information? In such instances communications material can simply be posted (electronically) and any particular queries handled in an accompanying communication. Processing of such leads can be handled by a company's internal sales team.

2. Are visitors interested in the company's products and likely to make a purchase decision at some point in the future? Again, a firm's internal telemarketing team can qualify the prospect and handle the contact's queries.

3. Is a purchase decision imminent? These leads should be registered with sales representatives during the trade show so that the potential customer can be contacted on their return from the event.

Post-show evaluation: assessment of the effectiveness of trade-show participation requires, as already discussed, objectives that are measurable and realistic. In addition to this, there has to be a means of recording activities in relation to these specific objectives during the show, and conducting research once the event is over might also be necessary.

CHAPTER SUMMARY

- Brands are a critical point of differentiation and source of competitive advantage for firms and are frequently associated with company names in business markets. Communication provides a means of signalling a firm's value proposition and requires consistency across all tools to ensure consistency in customer expectations and brand experience.

- Communication is central to positioning strategy and, as such, companies must ensure that communication is integrated so that consistent messages are conveyed to target audiences.

- By understanding and accommodating customer information needs and ways in which information contained in the various communications tools is processed, there is a greater likelihood that the audience's assimilation of the marketer's messages will be unified.

- The communications tools available to an organization can serve a number of purposes, and their importance (in terms of the resources allocated to fund them) will vary, reflecting the objectives for the overall communications programme as well as each of the communications tools, and accounting for market conditions and customer information needs.

- The capacity for customers to undertake extensive market and supplier search and evaluation prior to contact with sales personnel means that inbound communication – driven by content and search marketing and directing customers to company websites or material on content and social media sites – is assuming increasing importance.

- Leaving personal selling aside, advertising represents the largest share of an organization's communications budget and is typically used to create awareness, develop leads and generate enquiries. The formulation of an advertising strategy requires decisions on the role of advertising in the overall communications mix, objectives, creative strategy and the media to be used.

- Trade shows are a key element in the business marketer's communications mix, performing a variety of selling and non-selling functions. Trade-show participation requires the business marketer to determine objectives, to choose specific shows at which to exhibit, and to make tactical decisions in relation to pre-show promotion, stand design and location, staff involvement and behaviour, and post-exhibition follow-up and evaluation.

QUESTIONS FOR DISCUSSION

1. Explain what is meant by brand identity and the importance of this to the business marketer.

2. To what extent is the business marketer able to present an integrated communications message to target audiences?

3. Explain the role of a company website in shaping a customer's experience of a business brand.

4. The facility to place marketing content online in a variety of forms and on numerous sites means that potential and existing customers have a wealth of sources and material with which to inform themselves about markets and suppliers. Is this a good or a bad thing?

5. Describe how a business marketer might use search engines to guarantee being found and recalled by potential customers.

6. Trade shows can be prohibitively expensive for some companies to participate in, as well as being time-consuming for visitors. What alternative ways can participants and visitors access the benefits normally associated with being physically present at a trade show?

CASE STUDY 7.1   BREAK-AWAY BRAND

The global firm Bayer has been in operation for over 150 years, with the growth of its business in that time driven by the development of 'new molecules for use in innovative products and solutions to improve the health of humans, animals and plants' (Bayer, 2016). Historically, the company's operations were built around healthcare, agriculture and high-tech polymer activities, these latter functioning for some years as a cash machine for the Bayer group. Its expertise in high-tech polymer activities enabled the Bayer's material sciences division to offer products and material solutions to sectors as diverse as automotive, construction, electronics, medical, cosmetics and textiles. Sometimes the division's materials are visible, but more often than not, they work 'behind the scenes', whether as insulation for houses or the refrigerators inside them, in mattresses, automobile headlights and stadium roofs, as protective coatings or extremely thin films.

(Continued)

(Continued)

While the material sciences division had been an important part of the group's activities, by 2014, Bayer decided to realign its interests in order to concentrate on its core life science business. This was perhaps to be expected, given that by 2013, life sciences represented 71 per cent of company revenue and 88 per cent of adjusted earnings. Added to this was the fact that Bayer could not fund expansion for both divisions and its fast-growing position in healthcare would require considerable capital as well as research and development investment to maintain that position. Announcing its move away from materials in 2013, Bayer's intention was to create a legally and financially independent materials science unit which could be floated on the stock market. Such a move would require the support of financial markets, customers and employees so that the new entity represented a credible business proposition as an investment, a solutions provider and an employer.

As one of the biggest corporate launches in 2015, the task of creating the corporate identity to support that credible business proposition fell to the agency Landnor (www.landnor.com), part of the global communications agency, WPP. According to Kirsten Foster, executive director of strategy at Landnor, while communication with clients and investors was important, most critical were employees. In a B2B space, employees are particularly involved in the delivery of the brand promise, which means that it is important that they remain engaged – the brand has to speak as much internally as externally. Internal engagement in Bayer's materials science division was challenging as employees had a particularly strong relationship with their employer. Working for Bayer was like a badge of honour so that when the materials division was separated from Bayer, members of staff lost the Bayer brand name and associations with it such as name, its reputation and brand values of leadership, integrity, flexibility and efficiency.

Working with the company's employees, the Landnor team determined descriptors for the new company: courageous, curious and colourful (or diverse) – quite a statement for what is essentially a chemicals business. Important in this process was the identification and surfacing of values which were already present, rather than trying to impose new ones. While the values might have already existed, what did have to be created was the name and visual elements of the new corporate brand. Unveiled in 2015, the name Covestro is made from a combination of words that is intended to reflect the identity of the new company. For example, the letters C and O are meant to be associated with the word collaboration, while VEST is aimed at signalling that the company is well invested in state-of-the-art manufacturing facilities. And the final letters, STRO, were chosen to show that the company is strong in terms of innovation, market position and its workforce. Alongside the name, Covestro's identity is signalled visually through its name in lower case surrounded by a multi-coloured open ring (perhaps echoing the Bayer logo?) on a black background.

Sources:

- Andrews, E. (2015) 'Break away brands', *Transform Magazine*, 30 November. Available from www.transformmagazine.net/articles/2015/breakaway-brands/. Accessed 13 July 2016.
- Bayer (2015), Bayer Materials Science to be called Covestro. 1 June Available from www.press.bayer.com/baynews/baynews.nsf/id/Bayer-MaterialScience-to-be-called-Covestro. Accessed 12 July 2016.

- Bayer (2015) Hello Covestro. 6 October. Available from www.bayer.com/en/covestro. aspx. Accessed 12 July 2016.

- Covestro, 2016, Company Overview. Available at http://covestro.com/en. Accessed 12 July 2016.

CASE STUDY QUESTIONS

With reference to the case study and Covestro's website (www.covestro.com)

1 What do you consider to be Covestro's core competencies?

2 Based on information contained on the website, how do you think the company positions itself within the materials sciences industry?

3 Assess the coherence of the new corporate identity chosen for Bayer's independent spin-off materials science division based on the online presentation of this new business.

4 In what way are the traits courageous, curious and colourful signalled via Covestro's brand identity?

FURTHER READING

Abratt, R. and Kleyn, N. (2012) 'Corporate identity, corporate branding and corporate reputations: reconciliation and integration', *European Journal of Marketing,* 46 (7/8): 1048–63.

The article's focus on corporate brand is particularly pertinent in business markets, where brand is mainly at the organizational level. As a review of corporate branding literature, the authors examine corporate identity, corporate brand and corporate reputation, providing a useful synthesis of material in these areas, examining the range of terms and phrases in relation to these. The resulting framework offers a valuable structure with which to understand and explore business-to-business brand and reputation building.

Gilliam, D.A. (2015) 'Trade show boothscapes', *Journal of Marketing Management,* 31, 17/18: 1878–98.

This article provides an interesting approach to the design of trade show stands, suggesting that the B2B marketer might do well to draw from what is already understood around retail atmospherics and servicescapes. Combining this with prior tradeshow studies and observational research, the author suggests how different design elements can both meet exhibitor objectives and accommodate the different visitor roles.

Järvinen, J.J. and Karjaluoto, H. (2015) 'The use of web analytics for digital marketing performance measurement', *Industrial Marketing Management,* 50: 117–27.

So having managed to direct potential customers to their website, how does the business marketer ensure that visitors stay interested and encourage them to progress along the

(Continued)

(Continued)

purchase process? The authors combine understanding of performance metric systems with an empirical examination of the analytics used by B2B companies to evaluate digital communications activities. The investigation determines that aside from the metrics themselves, equally important to the effective use of data obtained are internal factors such as company resources, IT infrastructure as well as organizational commitment, leadership and culture. Using analytics to convert leads to prospects and beyond is staple business for B2B agencies such as Lead Forensics. Take a look at this article and visit Lead Forensics' website (www.leadforensics.com) to learn how this agency helps companies deal with the challenges of getting best use from web analytics for sales conversions.

8

RELATIONSHIP COMMUNICATION

LEARNING OUTCOMES

After reading this chapter you will:

- understand the nature and role of direct marketing (social media, mail, telemarketing) and personal selling in relationship communication;
- be able to describe how direct marketing and personal selling can be used to acquire new customers and secure business;
- be able to describe the customer and order acquisition process;
- understand the importance of culture in the relationship communication process;
- understand the issues and decisions related to the coordination of relationship communication between firms and within the vendor company; and
- be able to describe the control systems that a firm can use to direct the behaviour of employees who communicate with customers.

INTRODUCTION

In the previous chapter we considered the overall process of communications, the components and nature of integrated communications strategy, the formulation of the communications mix and budgeting for communications activities. We also distinguished between tools that are impersonal, allowing little scope for dialogue, and others that involve some form of direct contact and interaction between the business marketer and known individuals in customer companies. The latter, which we term relationship communication and consider in this chapter, consists of direct marketing (within which we include social media) and personal selling. To start with we look at general features of these communications tools before going on to discuss how they are used in the processes of gaining new customers and building relationships. An important point which we made in the previous chapter, and which needs to be borne in mind here is the shift from outbound to inbound communication, such that relationship communication might result from potential customers initiating contact and managers signalling interest in or willingness to engage with the business marketer. From this use of communication tools for customer and relationship 'nurturing', we then consider the coordination of relationship communication activities, both between supplier and customer companies as well as within the vendor organization itself.

DIRECT MARKETING

Direct marketing involves interaction between individual customers and the vendor organization. It centres on the acquisition, retention and development of customers through which the needs of both customers and the organizations serving them, are met. Direct marketing does this by providing a framework for three activities: analysis of individual customer information (e.g. communication and transaction behaviour), strategy formation, and implementation such that customers engage directly with the vendor through a variety of on and offline channels and media (Tapp et al., 2014). Key features of direct marketing include:

- the absence of face-to-face contact;
- the use of on- and offline media for direct, one-to-one communication and transactions;
- the facility to monitor and measure communication and transaction behaviour.

Our discussion of direct marketing includes social media as well as more established forms such as mail and telemarketing, on the basis that they all offer scope for direct interaction, although communication via social media marketing is more suited to a 'soft-sell' approach while mail and telemarketing might be more appropriate for sales-specific campaigns.

Social media

In Chapter 7 we discussed the development of a company's market presence, how this should contribute to signalling an organization's expertise and credibility, and ways in which a company might be found and remain visible to interested parties. Exposure to advertising campaigns or viewing marketing content generated from online searches might increase awareness and inform or educate an audience, but key to building positive associations with a business brand or supplier is customer engagement. Social media can contribute to this through the combined use of information sharing sites such as YouTube, SlideShare, Flickr and Instagram and social networking sites on which community members can express or share an opinion (Schroeder, 2013). These include broad-reaching sites such as Facebook, Google+, LinkedIn and micro-blogging sites such as Twitter, and while some business marketers direct their attention at LinkedIn (because it operates as a networking site for professional users) others use generic sites such as Facebook; see for example, Ingersoll Rand's Facebook page. Other organizations find such sites too generic and prefer to direct community building efforts at more specialist sites (Power and Chaffey, 2012) – for example, the French publisher SpecialChem created Omnexus (www.omnexus.specialchem. com) for those interested in plastics and elastomers. With regard to social networking, whether a company creates its own page on Facebook, engages in or sponsors an issue-based community on LinkedIn, or locates its conversations on its corporate blog or on Twitter, the business marketer must bear in mind a number of key factors:

> *Integration*: content, commentary and conversations accessible via social media need to be part of a firm's communications strategy and combined with other material so that, as we noted in Chapter 7, the customer's experience of the business brand is one of seamless integration – a Twitter feed, for example, might direct followers (via tags) to content specific landing pages on the company website. Take a look at the German chemicals company BASF's explanation of its use

of social media and integration with other online communications tools: www.
slideshare.net/basf/basf-social-media-2011.

Consistency: the identity expressed through, for example, pages created on
LinkedIn, content shared on Flickr and the ideas articulated by company representatives via blogs or Twitter accounts must be consistent with that communicated
via other media. Care needs to be taken to ensure that the tone of voice used by
employees in blogs or when posting tweets reflects the desired brand identity or
is consistent with a particular communications campaign, for example, when the
business marketer might opt for an informative, authoritative, helpful, controversial or fun tone of voice (Morley-Fletcher, 2011).

Control: Brennan and Croft's (2012) examination of social media use in the IT sector notes variation in the extent to which companies exert control over the content,
commentary and conversations linked to them; so for example, while Cisco's social
media activity appears highly structured and closely controlled, Oracle's appears
less so. Perhaps an important point to note is that communities are not necessarily
designed to serve the marketing and commercial aims of the B2B marketer –
rather they exist to meet the needs of the members. Organizations might sponsor
communities and employees might participate; however, the B2B marketer has to
relinquish some control of the brand in this context to the collective membership.

Conversation: tweets, blogs and content need to be of interest to target audiences.
If a community member is to post a 'like', participate in a discussion or share
content, then the business marketer needs to avoid the 'hard sell' (Clarke, 2015)
and enter into a conversation instead, using social media to support brand and
relationship development, signalling expertise by, for example, employees offering
professional insight and advice, resolving problems and commenting on sector-
specific issues, emerging trends or industry reports (Leek et al., 2016).

In the previous chapter and once again, in this initial consideration of social networking
sites, we underline the point that social media should be an integrative part of a business
marketer's communication strategy to ensure coherence and consistency in a customer's
experience of engaging in dialogue with a company. Take a look at B2B Scenario 8.1 to
learn of the challenge facing shipping business Maersk Line following its entry into the
world of social communication.

B2B SCENARIO 8.1   WHEN THE BOAT COMES IN

Part of the Maersk Group, Maersk Line is one of the world's largest container shipping
companies, accounting for between 15 and 17 per cent of the global market overall. The
company transports anything from manufactured goods to perishable commodities,
making 70,000 port calls annually to its 100,000 customers, of which large clients such
as Wal-Mart, Nike and Tesco represent around 25% of the company's business.

In 2011, working in the company's communications department, Jonathan Wichmann's
proposals that Maersk Line enter the world of social communication were met with
some reluctance both internally and externally, the belief being that Maersk Line was

(Continued)

(Continued)

not suitable for social media because the company was boring and nobody would like it. Leaving aside these objections, Weichman developed a social media strategy around the areas of communication, customer service, sales and internal usage. The overriding goal was to get closer to customers while at the same time using other opportunities to maximize press coverage, realize higher employee engagement and develop brand awareness. The mission of getting closer to customers made sense given that, in the words of Mette Hermund Kildahl (head of Maersk Line's channel management), those customers are really no different from B2C customers and would want to interact with the firm. So approachability and personality became Maersk Line's key social media words, involving communication (not marketing) and engagement (not pushing).

Although launching first on Facebook, Maersk Line was eventually live on a number of different social media platforms (Facebook, Twitter, Google+, LinkedIn, Instagram, Vimeo, Flickr, Pinterest and Tumblr) and the company established its own social media hub (Maersk Line Social) through which it can have more control over social media. By 2013, Maersk Line were still on Facebook, although results from a survey conducted in 2012 determined that customers preferred Twitter and LinkedIn as mediums for interaction and for accessing industry news, services updates or even co-creating products with the company.

On Twitter, Maersk Line's audience includes trade press, shipping professionals, customers and employees, the company using this micro-blogging site to share news and thus, influence the industry, to humanize the brand and to interact publicly with different stakeholders. Maersk Line tweeters include a panel of ten employees such as a chief commercial officer, a captain, a head of anti-piracy, as well as several business managers. The company's plan in using employees, is to position selected individuals as thought leaders, those employees being given advice on whom to follow, how often to tweet and how to make tweets sound more interesting and less corporate.

Maersk Line views its LinkedIn account as its most corporate platform, deliberately targeting customers as a natural extension of its brand in order to tie customers closer to the company, sharing business-related news and interacting with customers via groups or forums. These groups include the Shipping Circle, Reefer Circle and the Daily Maersk Group. The closed groups require approval to gain access, consist of shipping experts around the world (and particularly customers) who debate industry challenges and opportunities. In this way Maersk Line can monitor topics of discussion and spot trends much more effectively than might be possible by using surveys.

Similar to LinkedIn, but this time, entirely public (rather than closed), Maersk Line uses Google+ to interact openly and directly with shipping professionals and experts. Whereas the company uses LinkedIn for customer communication, interaction and collaboration, it considers Google+ as more appropriate for broader exchanges on innovation, leadership and business. To this end, Maersk Line also uses the Google+ Hangout facility to hold press briefings with small groups of journalists when it launches initiatives.

The success of Maersk Line's entry into the social media world was recognized at the European Digital Communications Awards in 2012 when the company won two awards: Community Presence in Social Media and Social Media Campaign of the Year. Beyond such external recognition, the importance of social media to the business was reflected in a budget allocation of $250,000 for 2013. This money was secured by reducing spend on print advertising, web banner advertising and sponsorships, the intention being to replace these with advertising on social networking sites. Besides this, Wichmann proposed a dedicated cross-functional social media team consisting of 1 Social Media Lead, 1 Community Manager, 1 Social Media Manager, 0.5 Customer Communications Manager and 0.5 Social Collaboration Agent (industry phd). Used to operating as a largely independent operation, there was however growing pressure from Maersk Line's marketing department to better integrate social media with the company's broader marketing efforts. However, this challenge was something that Wichmann's successor, Nina Skyum-Nielsen, was going to have to address.

Source: Based on Katona and Sarvary, 2014.

Direct mail

Direct mail consists of material sent (increasingly) online as well as offline and can be particularly effective for customer *acquisition* and *conversion* where timely, personalized messages are used. However, a challenge for the B2B marketer lies in capturing recipient attention among the multitude of messages received every day. One solution lies in using 'trigger' mail campaigns, in which the marketer only communicates with an existing or potential customer when the customer signals they are ready to engage with them – the trick then is to respond to that interest as quickly as possible (Oldroyd et al., 2011). As we saw in Chapter 7, automated marketing systems can be used to scrutinize behaviour in terms of, for example, website activity such as a prospect or customer clicking through to a company's website, downloading or viewing marketing content, responding to a survey, or it might be the anniversary of a previous purchase. Automated marketing systems mean that such events can routinely trigger email messages that are personalized according to prospect or customer profile. This is particularly important to ensure that any mail communication adds value for the customer (B2B Marketing, 2010).

Telemarketing

Telemarketing consists of communication activities performed by trained specialists. Inbound telemarketing is where contact is initiated by a potential or existing customer, and outbound is where contact is made by the vendor. Irrespective of who makes the contact, the use of marketing automation and relationship management systems means that the vendor will have data available on potential as well as existing customers to facilitate dialogue between the telemarketer and client. Compared to direct mail, telemarketing is more versatile and it can be an important tool because of the various roles that it is able to perform. These roles include the following.

Account management: when sales to a customer are insufficient to warrant field sales calls, telemarketing can be used to service accounts. Telemarketing can support online handling of low priority accounts by dealing with more complex situations, provided employees are technically skilled and have ready access to the vendor's database of product information and customer account records.

Field support: in some cases customers might require personal visits from field sales representatives, yet handling all aspects of an account can be beyond the capacity of a single salesperson. So an account manager will make personal visits to a customer's premises but will be supported by telemarketing representatives who act as a communications link between the customer and account manager.

Lead qualification: telemarketing can be used to help move leads to prospective customers. Depending on the potential, telemarketing representatives will make appointments for field sales representatives to visit prospective customers (see the section on handling leads and prospective customers).

As organizations increasingly move towards web-based platforms for market communication and some elements of relationship communication, then you might wonder whether there is still a place for telemarketing. Well the answer seems to be yes. Take a look at B2B Snapshot 8.1 to learn why.

B2B SNAPSHOT 8.1   IT'S GOOD TO TALK

Given the apparent effectiveness of inbound (and related content) marketing then you might expect telemarketing to be on its way out – but this does not seem to be the case. Content marketing can lead potential as well as existing customers to a business marketer's landing pages and digital marketing systems can give you the data that you need about your audience. But no matter how effective communications programmes and marketing systems are in creating 'marketing ready leads' and maintaining contact with existing customers, a human touch is often needed to either qualify leads or contribute to customer retention. And this is where telemarketing can step in. According to communications experts, 70 per cent of B2B purchases involve human interaction (Chumillas, 2016), while 60 per cent of communications executives view telemarketing as critical to their business (Walker, 2015) in terms of lead qualification, its capacity to generate immediate feedback from customers (potential and actual) and to help seal deals. And while Generation Y might prefer text and email contact, there are still many who would prefer a conversation rather than having to continuously go through emails and contact forms to get the information they need. Obviously, the trick is to understand what your audience needs from you and to align telemarketing with other communication tools.

PERSONAL SELLING

Personal selling involves a supplier's employees communicating directly with managers from a customer company. This direct exchange allows:

- the sharing of information and knowledge between the customer and business marketer to determine precise supply requirements;
- the negotiation of adjustments to the supplier's product offer or the formulation of a bespoke offering to match the customer's needs; and
- interaction between representatives from both organizations, which underpins the initiation, development and ongoing handling of supplier–customer relationships.

Our discussion about this form of relationship communication introduces some of the responsibilities associated with the sales function and the types of salespeople that a supplier might employ. We then move on to consider the communication process, from acquiring new customers and securing business to building relationships with customers. In doing so it should become clear that it is not just those managers with sales or relationship management responsibilities that contribute to a customer's experience of dealing with a supplier. In fact, any employee who interacts directly with managers from a customer company adds to that customer's experience of the supplier. The challenge for the marketing organization lies in coordinating activities to ensure consistency in the behaviour of its representatives and the experience of its customers.

Sales responsibilities and people

One of the principal functions of employees with sales responsibilities is to identify revenue-generating opportunities, to *secure business* with targeted customers. Getting to this point involves the salesperson in a variety of related activities. The supplier's representative has to *match* the marketing organization's problem-solving abilities with a customer's supply needs. The salesperson might be expected to *augment* the supplier's product, using technical expertise, diagnostic skills, data analytics and industry experience to determine optimum solutions to customer sourcing problems or to advise, for example, on how a customer might achieve cost reductions or productivity improvements (Porter and Heppelmann, 2015). A salesperson also assumes an important *representation* role. Clearly, they represent the *supplier* in exchanges with customers, but they also act on behalf of customers inside their own organization; that is, they represent *customer* interests and articulate their requirements when dealing internally with other functions.

Sales representatives also perform an important role in *feeding back information* (resulting from exchanges with customers) into the supplier company. Accurate information that is readily accessible to supplier employees is important in ensuring consistency in the supplier's handling of a customer. As a principal point of contact with customer companies, sales representatives might be expected to oversee the *handling of complaints* received from customers. Complaints that lie within the expertise and authority of the sales function can be resolved by the sales personnel themselves. Others, which are technically and commercially more complex, will require the involvement of other functions and levels of management authority. The salesperson might then assume responsibility for overseeing the supplier's response to the customer complaint.

The sales function can take a variety of forms within a marketing organization such that a company makes use of three different characteristic types:

Missionary salespeople. In such cases supplier representatives do not actually try to secure orders; rather they direct efforts at creating business by influencing individuals or companies who have the authority to specify particular suppliers when orders are issued. See B2B Snapshot 8.2 for an example of how one company uses its sales personnel to ensure consideration and eventual specification of its products.

Frontline salespeople. The principal responsibility of such representatives is to secure business with existing customers or to target new ones. In many relationships, companies might agree contracts to cover a specific time period. While elements such as the product specification might be fixed for the duration of a contract, other conditions such as volume, price and payment terms can require regular renegotiation. In such instances one of the salesperson's tasks is to regularly review customer requirements and renegotiate selected conditions in order to secure orders within the constraints of a broader supply agreement.

Internal salespeople. While much of the operational procedures involved in fulfilling order contracts might be handled via integrated digital business systems, internal staff can still be key to ensuring that customer requirements are met (Altman, 2015). They are likely to be in regular contact with both the customer and frontline salesperson so that contracts and individual orders are administered according to agreed specifications or, where necessary, negotiated adjustments are put in place. While they may not have responsibility for creating new business or closing deals with customers, they play an important role in ensuring that the supplier fulfils client needs.

B2B SNAPSHOT 8.2   MISSIONARY SELLING IN THE SHIP INDUSTRY

Shipbuilding involves multi-million dollar investment projects and a variety of companies, including:

- future owners that commission the construction of new vessels;
- builders that succeed in winning contracts for construction projects, such as Hellenic Shipyards SA in Europe (owned by ThyssenKrupp), Samsung Heavy Industries in Korea and Shandong Baibuting Shipbuilding Co. in China (owned by Samsung);
- power suppliers such as the Finnish company Wartsila, who design and supply marine propulsion systems for newly commissioned vessels; and
- companies such as the power transmission components supplier Renold, who vie with competitors to ensure that their components are specified in the propulsion systems for newly commissioned vessels.

Wartsila's propulsion systems are used to power a variety of ships, including bulk carriers, cargo and container vessels, defence ships, cruise liners, fishing vessels and ferries. Since it is estimated that one-third of all ships are powered by Wartsila systems, the component manufacturer Renold has identified Wartsila as a key target customer. The propulsion systems supplied by Wartsila are significant, in terms of contribution to vessel performance, technical complexity and financial value. Renold components might seem to be a small cog in an entire marine propulsion system. However, Renold's salespeople invest considerable time and effort in maintaining contact with Wartsila's project managers and systems designers. This contact means that the supplier stands a good chance of learning about the future commissioning of vessels in advance of the specification for the propulsion system being agreed. The sales representative can also work with Wartsila's managers to show how Renold's components can contribute to optimum solutions for marine propulsion systems.

Being part of the specification for a system to be contained in a new vessel has significant value for Renold. New vessels have to go through a certification process – once a specification (including the components from various named suppliers) has been agreed and a vessel has been approved by certification bodies such as DNV (Det Norske Veritas), then business for Renold is guaranteed. This includes the supply of original components for inclusion in the marine propulsion system and the servicing of those components once a new vessel is in use.

THE RELATIONSHIP COMMUNICATION PROCESS

Having considered general aspects of direct marketing and personal selling we can now go on to look at how they are used to acquire new customers and build relationships. See Figure 8.1 for the stages involved in acquiring new customers and orders.

Handling leads and prospective customers

In the previous chapter we discussed the means by which an organization might progress from a market of potential customers to developing business with those that best match the problem-solving abilities of the company. The use of digital media for customer search and supplier communication activities can speed up the lead generation and enquiry-handling process. From these leads and enquiries a company has to determine which of these might be *prospective* future clients. The marketing organization can use a simple qualification process in which customer potential is determined according to:

- whether the company is using a similar product or is considering purchasing one offered by the marketing organization;
- the timescale and value/volume for likely purchases;
- who the ultimate decision-maker is (if it is not the person with whom the company has contact); and
- whether funding for purchase has been approved.

FIGURE 8.1 New customer and order acquisition

These questions might typically feature in a company's marketing automation system as part of the lead qualification process. For leads and enquiries that appear to offer significant potential (for example, prospects that are known to be major clients in the company's target market) then qualification could be conducted via telephone by a telemarketing or even a sales representative, this allowing for additional information to be obtained.

Storing of information obtained in an organization's databases, helps refine future communication activities by making available a broader range of 'qualified' potential customers that the firm is able to target. In terms of following the customer and order acquisition process in response to specific leads and enquiries, the data obtained has to be analysed. The purpose of this analysis is to assign priority to prospects and in doing so to determine the urgency of and responsibility for making follow-up contact with prospective clients. Clearly, criteria have to be used to prioritize prospects, which would include the information obtained via the qualification process and what might already be known about the prospects. Lowest-priority prospects might be those that a firm is able to serve indirectly by using intermediaries, electronic hubs and direct mail. Others might be contacted for follow-up by a company's internal sales/telemarketing team, whereas an organization would make greater use of its external/field sales team to pursue highest-priority prospects.

Lead generation is a key priority for companies and as we noted earlier, marketing ready leads are central to sales performance. Take a look at B2B Snapshot 8.3 to learn how marketing and sales might work together to personalize communication and nurture prospective buyers with the aim of converting to sales.

B2B SNAPSHOT 8.3   UP CLOSE AND PERSONAL

GE Healthcare has recently switched their way of engaging with potential customers, choosing to adopt a more personal approach when communicating with those healthcare professionals around the world who make purchase decisions on life-saving equipment that have multimillion dollar price tags. DMU members might include a radiologist, a chief financial officer, or a technician – each with different interests. Besides these different interests (and therefore varied information needs), the situations in which such professionals operate might well differ in Brazil, India, or the UK. This means that marketing content and exchanges have to be tailored to each professional's specific situation, so that by the time a sales person gets in front of a potential customer (or should we say a marketing qualified lead), the customer is completely aware of who GE are. Not only that, the sales team is fully aware of what those interactions have been, allowing the team's discussions with a prospective customer to be more relevant and give some momentum to a potential deal (Chahal, 2015). This, however, does not mean that sales reps only get involved in exchanges with prospects in face-to-face meetings. In fact, social media channels represent one place where prospects and customers can talk to a sales rep on their own terms and without necessarily knowing that the person they are engaging with is in sales. Figures might vary in terms of the role of social channels in business, but according to LinkedIn, 75 per cent of business leaders use social media to help them make decisions, Twitter and Facebook have 'buy buttons',

Pinterest and Instagram have recently entered e-commerce, and in a report by LinkedIn and Oracle, 87 per cent of customers had a favourable first impression of a salesperson with whom they first exchanged via social networks. Social channels will likely never be used for big ticket sales, and they are best used as just another medium for interacting with prospects and customers. Social media platforms should not be used solely for sales purposes or as a conversion tool because this risks reducing engagement to zero as followers disappear. The platforms can, however, be a good place to nurture prospects, with sales reps placing tailored content to help the buyer in their decision process (Clarke, 2015).

Selling

Low-priority prospects

The basic idea behind initial contact is to determine the nature and scope of a long-term relationship with a potential customer. We might assume that where a prospect has been assigned lower priority, then exchanges have resulted in some initial judgement concerning the nature of any potential relationship and sales mode, namely that it is likely to be transactional in nature. In these instances the customer makes straightforward purchases that would equate to straight or modified re-buys, as outlined in Chapter 2. Such purchase situations for customers that a company does not normally supply might be triggered by unforeseen supply needs or problems with an existing vendor. For these types of purchases the customer is clear about the specification and application of the product required, and such purchases might not necessarily be considered as strategic by that customer (particularly if they do not impact on the customer's differentiation of its own offerings). The challenge then for the business marketer is what sales approach to adopt when dealing with a potential customer who is well informed, sees little difference in potential suppliers and might simply be looking for a business marketer's basic product at the most competitive price. Anderson et al. (2014) suggest that in such cases, the business marketer might adopt what they class as *tie-breaker selling*, whereby the sales representative includes an element, a justifier, in the offering that could make a marked difference to the customer's business. The value of this justifier has to be apparent to the customer such that it represents a stand-out reason for selecting one supplier over others, and also enables the decision maker to demonstrate to senior managers their contribution to business performance. Determining the specific form that a justifier might take necessitates exchanges with the potential customer, but might be derived from ways in which a buyer uses a product, be based on offering to integrate products with those of other companies or could emerge according to a customer's business priorities (Anderson et al., 2014).

High-priority customers

Where a prospect has been assigned a higher priority, and initial assessment suggests scope to develop a potential relationship and a supply need that has some degree of uncertainty, then the business marketer is more likely to adopt a *consultative* sales approach. The purchase situation can be classified as either a modified re-buy or new task and, as we discussed in Chapter 2, normally involves high-risk purchases (bottlenecks or critical products) for which the prospective customer is unable to articulate precise requirements and is unclear as to how its supply needs might be met. As we know from Chapter 2, these purchase situations are frequently handled by buying teams, with members of the DMU requiring a variety of information from potential suppliers during what is often an extended decision-making process.

The business marketer would typically expect to conduct numerous meetings with various members of the decision-making team, and might also need to include managers beyond the sales team in these discussions. In doing this, the business marketer is able to progress from generalities to the specific requirements that the customer's managers expect to satisfy. Instead of using sales pitches, supplier representatives must rely on questioning members of the buying team in order to uncover requirements and to determine how the supplier might use its problem-solving abilities to configure an offering that will match these needs. The salesperson draws from their own product expertise to establish supply needs, and rather than presenting the customer with a range of existing products from which to choose they will typically formulate a bespoke offering for a customer. Presentation of the offering to the buying team might include the actual features of the proposal, the functions that these features will perform and the benefits to the customer – not only in meeting the requirements of a particular supply need but also the value to the customer of the product offer.

Consultative selling might be an option for some business marketers, but for companies that provide highly bespoke services (such as engineering, project and IT consultancy; legal, financial and accounting services; or market research and communication), it can be the only way of securing business with a customer (Aarikka-Stenroos and Jaakkola, 2012). In such instances both parties engage in a collaborative process of joint problem-solving in which specialized supplier knowledge and skills are combined with customer information on requirements and goals to determine an appropriate solution.

Such a collaborative process is also used in instances where a supplier identifies some customers not as high priority but as companies with whom it would like to develop strategic partnerships. This recognition would not emerge from a supplier's procedure for qualifying prospective new customers; rather, it is more likely to result from the company's strategy development process and previous experience of having already dealt with particular customers for some time. In these instances a supplier would more likely adopt *strategic partner* selling. This approach is less about how to close a deal with a customer and more about supplier and customer companies combining resources and expertise to pursue opportunities that benefit both parties, and as with highly complex bespoke services, it typically involves managers from a variety of functions from each company (Aarikka-Stenroos and Jaakkola, 2012).

Value-based selling

In Chapter 4 we connected strategy, customer value and value proposition, and from the different sales approaches above we can see that critical for the business marketer (irrespective of customer importance or solution complexity) is the exchange of information and use of specialist technical knowledge to craft solutions that satisfy the interests of both parties. The integration of digital technology with products enables managers with sales responsibilities to move from product-based selling to advising customers on how to maximize value over time, drawing on usage data from smart products to do this (Porter and Heppelmann, 2015). For example, All Traffic Solutions (www.alltrafficsolutions.com), makes smart connected road signs that measure traffic speed and volume. The signs enable data mining of traffic patterns so that users such as law enforcement bodies and road transport authorities can monitor and manage traffic flow remotely. The company's sales reps have switched from selling signs to selling long-term services that help improve traffic safety – the signs are just the devices through which these services are customized and delivered. As we can see from this example, those with sales-related boundary-spanning roles are central to the interaction explained in Chapter 3 and product offering discussed in Chapter 10 through which supplier problem-solving abilities are aligned with customer needs to:

- understand a customer's business model;
- craft value propositions;
- communicate value (Terho et al., 2012).

In communicating value, Anderson et. al (2006) identify three possible approaches to its articulation, arguing in favour of a resonating focus in which a limited number of key points of difference are used to indicate what will best deliver value in aspects critical to the customer. Keeping with the idea that value should underpin all selling styles, Terho et al. (2012) suggest that this type of behaviour can have a variety of outcomes for the supplier and customer alike; see Figure 8.2.

Order fulfilment

Sales activity does not end with the winning of an order; rather, key to the development of business with a customer is the effective delivery of the product offering. The manager must negotiate and agree with the customer the contract details and transmit these details inside his/her own company. A variety of functions normally contribute to the order-handling process from initial receipt to final completion

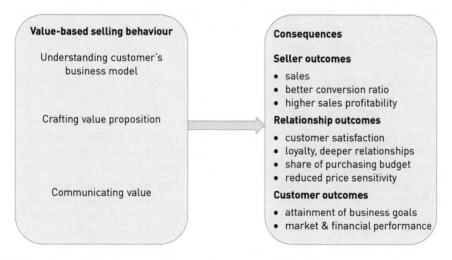

FIGURE 8.2 Value selling and consequences (Terho et al., 2012)

With permission from Elsevier.

(Shapiro et al., 2004). This means that coordination and communication are essential to ensure that necessary tasks are completed, duplication of effort is kept to a minimum and that the product is supplied as agreed with the customer. Internal sales teams are likely to oversee this, while the sales manager's interest lies in ensuring the absence of discrepancies in any element of the contracted order. If there is, then this risks undermining the credibility of the sales representative and his/her organization, and will consequently hamper any scope for the further development of business between the two companies.

Relationship building

Provided that new clients represent viable long-term prospects for a supplier, the emphasis for the business marketer switches to building an ongoing relationship with and winning repeat business from that customer. Whether the sales representative is dealing with a relatively new customer or one which the marketing organization has been trading with for some time, the principal tasks for the representative centre around:

- overseeing the handling of ongoing contracts;
- obtaining and acting on feedback from the customer regarding the supplier's performance;
- determining the scope for and negotiating the expansion of the supplier's share of the customer's existing product requirements;
- responding to and seeking to resolve new sourcing problems communicated by the customer;
- monitoring developments within the client organization and identifying new value delivery opportunities for the business marketer; and
- negotiating new contracts.

The extent to which a sales representative deals with all of the above areas is determined in part by the nature of the product supplied by the marketing organization and the type of relationship sought by both the supplier and customer companies. See B2B Snapshot 8.4 for an example of the activities of a 3M representative in handling a relationship with an IT customer.

B2B SNAPSHOT 8.4   PERSISTENCE REWARDED

3M is an internationally diversified chemicals-processing and materials company. Part of its business involves the supply of label technologies for identification, instructional and safety purposes in the electrical and electronics industries. For ICT users the labels that are displayed on products are insignificant. If you were to inspect the hardware that you use yourself, you would come across labels that identify the hardware company (and also contain producer information stored in bar codes) as well as the software and microprocessor brands that support the functioning of the hardware product. If you dismantled your laptop, you would also find additional labelling contained within the hardware items themselves. In spite of the low levels of recognition for its products, 3M works hard to ensure that its labelling technology is one of those specified by ICT customers. Technical sales engineers call periodically on ICT companies and, during discussions:

- help hardware designers select the most suitable adhesives and label designs for particular applications (after all, you would not expect a product designer to know about this sort of thing); and

- try to identify (via discussions with designers) development projects that might present 3M with product opportunities.

Persistence in maintaining contact with designers and the recognition of the company's problem-solving abilities has paid off for 3M. One of its customers approached the company for help in improving the recyclability of its hardware products. The customer was faced with increased material recycling costs because of the difficulties in removing labels and adhesives from plastic components retrieved from returned equipment. 3M drew on the expertise of its technical sales engineers, environmental experts and product development managers, and involved these managers in meetings with the customer and with a plastics supplier. This multi-company and multi-manager team worked together to understand the problem, explore various ways in which it might be resolved, identify and finally agree on a viable solution. The collaboration resulted in 3M developing a labelling and identification system for this customer which was compatible with plastic components (so did not need to be removed prior to recycling). The development of this product presented new sales opportunities with the hardware customer and provided 3M with a means of gaining access to other divisions that were part of the same customer organization.

Culture

Many organizations engage in international business markets, whether expanding beyond a domestic base for the first time or operating at the centre of a complex, global network of relationships. Whatever their stage or complexity, the development and handling of international business relationships is affected by the cultural context within which managers operate (Meyer, 2015). *Culture* can be explained as the principles which are shared by a group of people and which shape the behaviour, perceptions and emotional responses of people within that group (Goodenough, 1971). For our discussion here, we use nationality as the boundary to identify those with shared behavioural and thought patterns – it is convenient, can be readily operationalized and features prominently in relationship communication research and practice. For managers preparing to meet with customer representatives from other countries, there is a wealth of sources about appropriate etiquette for each country and behaviour to be expected from members of other cultures. Reduced to its simplest level, this can include body language such as physical greetings: firm handshakes accompanied by direct eye contact and a smile would be considered normal in Europe and Latin America, while in Asia and the Middle East, the handshake would be gentler and direct eye contact would in some instances be avoided (associated with seniority of the person being addressed) or should be short (between men and women). General etiquette is useful to avoid misunderstanding or causing offence, but it can be confusing for the company representative who has to remember the appropriate protocol to follow in different countries, and it does not necessarily provide sufficient understanding of the behaviour that a manager might experience.

One way of explaining behaviour in different countries is provided by Hall (1976), who distinguishes between high- and low-context cultures. In a *high-context* culture the meaning signalled via an individual's actions or in the dialogue during interpersonal communication is implicit; it has to be interpreted, and this interpretation will vary depending on factors such as location, the people involved (age, sex, seniority) and situation (initial meeting, negotiation of first order, annual review of established relationship). According to Hall, high-context cultures include Latin America, the Middle East and Japan. The importance of context and implicit messages contained in communications is illustrated by the fact that in Japan, for example, there are over 20 subtle adjustments which can be made in the way of speaking to someone depending on the relative positions of the participants (Usunier and Lee, 2005). The word *no* is practically non-existent in the Japanese vocabulary; instead, there are at least 16 ways in which to avoid saying it (Ueda, 1974). Managers that belong to such cultures and use implicit messages need to know their exchange partners quite well and will spend considerable time during initial exchange episodes doing just this, rather than concentrating on the commercial aspects of the meetings. By way of contrast, in *low-context* cultures behaviour and dialogue are explicit and literal, with precision and accuracy being important elements of exchanges and little interpretation of or adjustment to messages required according to the context. *Low context* is associated with North American (United States, Canada), Germanic (Germany, Switzerland, Austria), Scandinavian, Australian and New Zealand cultures, and when it comes to dealing with exchange partners, discussions will focus on the business matters for which the meeting is intended.

Developments to explain and compare behaviour across different cultures include the work by Hofstede (1980), whose survey of IBM employees around the world resulted in the grouping of countries around four dimensions – see Table 8.1 for an explanation of these. Hofstede's grouping of countries determines cultural distances between them; allows managers to identify the level of difficulty in dealing with customers from culturally distant countries; and can be used to inform inter-firm negotiations (e.g. McGinnis, 2005; Sebenius, 2002). In spite of its widespread use, Hofstede's positioning of countries has been criticized for adopting a culturally specific approach – for using a standard questionnaire to examine numerous national cultures which can result in stereotyping (Nielsen and Gannon, 2006). To avoid this and provide a broader understanding of national cultures, Gannon (2004) proposes descriptive metaphors for different cultures, arguing that the metaphors offer managers a frame of reference which can be used to better understand the behaviour of an exchange partner and to guide responses – see Table 8.2.

Broad descriptions of different cultures can be translated into behaviour that might be experienced and/or expected during negotiations; for example, Salacuse (1991, 2005) compares American and Japanese negotiation styles. Remember, however, that one style is not superior to any other – rather, being sensitive to partner behaviour can help reduce potential misunderstandings.

Although we have focused on national cultures and their relevance to the relationship communication process, the business marketer also has to be aware of the organizational

TABLE 8.1 Hofstede's four dimensions of national cultures (Hofstede, 2001; Hofstede et al, 2010. Copyright © Geert Hofstede B.V. Reprinted by permission)

Individualism	Collectivism
Emphasis on individual as resource, control and motivation	Importance given to group wellbeing; value and actions of individual directed towards collective good
Lower power distance	High power distance
Strong democratic principles; power equally distributed; superiors and subordinates are equals	Hierarchical; power is centralized at the top
Femininity	Masculinity
Caring for others; emphasis on nurturing and quality of life	Assertiveness and personal achievement are important
Low uncertainty avoidance	High uncertainty avoidance
Willingness to take risks; individual risk-taking necessary to drive change	Emphasis placed on stability, rules and procedures to reduce uncertainty and avoid risk

TABLE 8.2 Examples of Gannon's cultural metaphors (Gannon, 2004)

American football	Individualism and competitive specialization; huddling; ceremonial celebration of perfection
German symphony	Orchestra; conductors; performance; society; education; politics
Italian family opera	Pageantry and spectacle; voice expression; chorus and soloists
Swedish summer house	Love of nature; individualism through self-development; equality
Japanese garden	Wa and shikata, harmony and form; seishin, spirit of self-discipline; combining droplets
Chinese family altar	Confucianism and Taoism; roundness, harmony and fluidity
Indian cyclical Hindu philosophy	The cycle of life; the social cycle; the work cycle

culture of customer companies, as the routines and procedures for problem-solving and decision-making will shape the behaviour of those dealing with the business marketer as well as those involved (either directly or indirectly). Culture (national or organizational) will influence communication behaviour, and in preparing for negotiations, managers should:

- know with whom they are dealing;
- know what they hear; and
- know when to say what.

COORDINATING RELATIONSHIP COMMUNICATION

Relationship (and for that matter, market) communication is not just about finding the next customer or winning the next order; rather, for many organizations operating in business markets it is about managing relationships with customers, and about handling ongoing exchanges between supplier and customer companies.

These day-to-day activities can involve managers from a variety of functions as well as those with sales-related responsibilities. Our discussions in this section cover:

- the organization of functions with customer-facing responsibilities. This can centre solely on a sales department or alternatively can include other functions that also deal with customers;
- the role of communication within the vendor organization in coordinating customer relationship management;
- the contribution of relationship promoters to the processes of inter- and intra-firm communication and coordination.

Inter-firm

A variety of ways exist in which a company might organize its sales force, and this is in part determined by the nature of the product and market in which a company is involved, the marketing organization's strategy for dealing with customers in its target market, and the type of communication necessary to enable satisfactory exchanges between both parties. *Sales force organization* – the ways in which those dealing with customers can be organized – falls under three broad categories:

1. A *geographically based sales force.* This is arguably the most basic structure, in which a field salesperson is given the responsibility of selling all of the company's products to, and dealing with, all of the customers within a specified geographic area. It gives the sales representative a simple and unambiguous definition of his or her area of responsibility. The territory that can be covered by an individual manager does have to be realistic and would normally be determined by the workload involved in dealing with customers in the allocated area and the potential that they might offer. This type of design is effective when a business marketer's products are relatively simple and customers have broadly common requirements in using these products.

2. A *product-based sales force.* If a company has a diverse range of products that are based on different technologies then a supplier is more likely to use product specialists to deal with customers. Where representatives from different product divisions are dealing with the same customer, a company has to try to coordinate activities and share information to help manage the overall relationship with that client and avoid duplication of effort and/or confusion.

3. A *sector-based sales force.* In some markets, suppliers might offer the same basic product technology, but the application of that technology to solve customer supply needs in different sectors can vary significantly. This means that sales representatives will need to have considerable understanding of a particular sector and to possess sufficient expertise to enable the product technology to be configured so that it matches the needs of customers in that sector. In such cases the business marketer will organize their sales teams according to the customer industries served.

Many companies extend this customer/market-based sales force and set up structures that enable them to deal more specifically with some customers who are strategically important to them. This might be because customers are technologically demanding and stretch the vendor's problem-solving abilities, provide the vendor with access to critical resources, or account for a significant proportion of the firm's turnover. Organizing dealings with customers through account management teams is also the result of changes in the purchasing environment. For example, centralization of procurement activities (which can include sourcing requirements for various locations around the world) necessitates that a vendor is able to coordinate responses to supply needs such that there is consistency in handling a client, irrespective of the location at which the marketing organization might be dealing with that customer at any given time. As we learnt in Chapter 2, customer desire to make sourcing more efficient and to use suppliers for systems solutions means that a vendor might typically: help to reduce the costs of operational and administrative systems between the companies; use their core competencies to contribute to the customer's product development activities; and take on the responsibility of managing some of the customer's supply chain by becoming a first-tier supplier. If a company is dealing with or wishes to build business with such customers then the way in which it handles exchanges with them and organizes its 'sales efforts' can determine the effectiveness of relationship-handling and business-building endeavours. The nature of the involvement that a vendor has with a customer and the tasks that it performs for and in conjunction with that client will depend on the relationship between the firms. We discuss the development and implementation of key account management (KAM) in Chapter 9 – our interest here is simply to note the organization of communication activities as part of the handling and problem-solving at the centre of a relationship. Indeed inter-firm interaction will change as the relationship develops, from focusing on product-related issues in fairly new/distant relationships to issues of facilitation and integration in much closer relationships.

Given the scope of involvement that a vendor might have with a key customer, the company has to draw on the expertise of managers beyond the personal selling function both in its direct dealings with the customer and in the tasks that are performed internally for that customer. For this reason, companies use *key account* teams in which team members' principal responsibilities centre on the performance of tasks for that customer. An account manager typically oversees all dealings with and the successful development of a key customer relationship and will lead a team of individuals from the supplier's various functions. These individuals are also likely to deal directly with the customer and normally coordinate efforts within their own functional area such that objectives for that key account are realized. So, as well as having an account manager the team could consist of:

- field sales representatives responsible for winning new orders, and internal sales managers who administrate contracts awarded by the customer;

- product specialists who are able to advise on the configuration of product offerings for the key customer and contribute to new product development activities with them;

- commercial managers responsible for handling client credit and invoicing; and

- operations, logistics, quality and service managers.

Key account management is discussed further in the next chapter.

A vendor is likely to adopt differing strategies to reflect the importance of a customer to the firm, and this variation in strategy will be reflected in the way that the business marketer organizes sales activities. This means that while a firm might have account teams for a small number of key clients, a vendor would have other structures in place for customers who are not as strategically important to the company. Whatever structures a firm puts in place for organizing its dealings with customers, membership of those structures and contribution to the activities performed by them are not necessarily fixed. In organizing its interface with customers, a firm must decide what functions should have permanent involvement in the formulation of relationship strategies and the execution of tasks to satisfy both the vendor's and the customer's relationship requirements. The firm will also have to decide what other functions it will need to call upon more intermittently to achieve relationship objectives.

Intra-firm (vendor perspective)

Being able to access and present the necessary expertise in dealings with customers is certainly important. Whichever way a vendor organizes staff with customer-facing responsibilities, relationship objectives will be difficult to achieve unless mechanisms are in place internally that allow transactions, coordination and communication between the different functions inside the supplier company. Transactions can include:

- the release of *resources* to support marketing programmes; for example, the finance department can directly impact the allocation of funding needed to support investment in a key account;
- the allocation of 'productive' (or *work*) capacity to allow tasks to be performed; for example, without the work performed by staff in research departments the development of a new product for a customer can be hampered;
- the provision of *assistance* to support managers with customer-facing responsibilities; for example, an account manager might seek the advice of product specialists in formulating offerings for a customer, or help from IT experts to resolve problems of systems integration with a particular customer. (Ruekert and Walker, 1987)

These transactions between different functions have to be synchronized. *Coordination* is needed so that the supplier's activities operate efficiently, and the firm is able to meet the needs of its various customers. Coordination includes formal rules and procedures that managers must follow to access resources, work or assistance (Ruekert and Walker, 1987). So, for example, before 3M was able to offer the plastic-compatible labelling system to its IT customer, managers had to: seek internal authorization to initiate exploratory research; obtain agreement from the firm's European business centre to escalate the exploratory research to a formally approved product development project; and gain approval from the US corporate headquarters for inclusion of the newly developed product in the company's portfolio. Although formal systems might be in place, managers will not always rely on official lines of authority but will use informal means to influence decisions and coordinate activities.

Obviously *communication* is necessary between functions and between managers in the different departments (Ruekert and Walker, 1987). The volume (frequency) will vary depending on the contribution and complexity of transactions between departments to realizing customer-specific objectives and the need to coordinate these. Communication is not always straightforward. Dispersed geographic locations and the fact that managers from different functions do not necessarily share the same 'world view' mean that getting the message across (both in terms of it reaching the target and its meaning being correctly understood) can be particularly challenging (Hutt, 1995).

Chapter 4 clearly identified the contribution of relationships to the formulation and implementation of business and marketing strategies, and Chapter 9 discusses the strategic importance of managing portfolios of customer relationships for organizations that operate in business markets. At its core, customer relationship management has a strategic focus and is concerned with identifying and investing in valued customer relationships, matching problem-solving abilities to customer requirements, and making relationship decisions based on the vendor's performance with those customers. At an operational level, CRM presents the business marketer with numerous concerns, and these include ensuring that employees are aware of the company's strategy for a particular customer and the actions taken, or planned, to support the relationship with that customer. From our discussions in Chapters 7 and 8 it is clear that, first, vendors engage customers with multiple forms of communication over extended time periods, and second, that a variety of employees can come into contact with customers and might be responsible for internally disseminating information, performing tasks, allocating resources, or authorizing programmes of action in relation to a particular customer.

It follows that a vendor's employees must be familiar with its communication activities with a customer and have the means to share as well as access information in relation to that customer. CRM systems can provide employees with access to customer-specific information such as that relating to products (for example, new products, order quantities, scheduling or delivery), the account itself (for example, share of business, profitability data or credit performance) as well as all communication with the customer (for example, field and/or telemarketing representative reports). Given the range of employees who may deal with a customer, prior knowledge of recent interaction can avoid duplication, confusion and possibly inconsistency in discussions between managers from supplier and customer companies. Challenges for the vendor, however, lie in ensuring that common systems are used by different departments and that there is a shared understanding of how available information should be analysed and interpreted.

Relationship promoters

Internal marketing features heavily in services-marketing literature. Customer satisfaction requires coordinated action/effort among customer contact and service support personnel inside the supplier company. A key component of internal marketing is the investment by the organization in training and motivating employees to ensure a customer orientation throughout the company (Ahmed and Rafiq, 2003). This is quite a narrow view of the marketing that goes on inside a company, because in some senses managers continuously use processes of negotiation and persuasion and offer incentives to motivate other employees, managers and functions to align themselves to particular objectives or courses of action. Marketing activities and the associated interaction that takes place between supplier and customer companies and inside the vendor organization cannot be readily separated. We know that employees with various functional responsibilities (such as sales, customer service and key account management) interact with customers in order to satisfy those customers' needs and to develop relationships with them. We also know that customer satisfaction and relationship management entail the performance of tasks inside the vendor organization. Those employees that interact with customers play key *boundary-spanning* roles: they operate as relationship promoters (Walter and Gemünden, 2000), linking the customer with the supplier company and working to coordinate activities inside the supplier organization to support the development of relationships with selected customers. The principal objective of relationship promoters is to influence the attitudes, behaviour and decisions of managers so that the customer relationship can be developed and maintained. Personal attributes that relationship promoters should possess include:

> *social competence*: they must be skilled in communication, conflict management and coordination, and must be flexible and empathetic in group processes involving managers from different functions and organizations;

> *knowledge*: they must be familiar with the resources, needs and strategies of both the supplier and customer organizations;

> *portfolio of relationships*: they need to be well connected and have good personal relationships with managers in partner organizations who control resources that contribute to the development of the supplier–customer relationship (Walter and Gemünden, 2000).

Using these attributes helps:

- information sharing and communication between members of relationship teams, as well as with others who are in powerful positions and whose support can impact the relationship;
- finding the right managers who can and are willing to perform tasks as part of supplier–customer collaboration;
- facilitating relationships between managers in both companies;
- coordinating activities between companies; and
- negotiation and conflict resolution (Walter and Gemünden, 2000).

CONTROLLING RELATIONSHIP COMMUNICATION

As well as trying to synchronize inter- and intra-firm communication a company must also direct the actions of those who deal with customers, such that the endeavours of its employees contribute to relationship-specific, marketing and overall company objectives. Directing employee behaviour requires some type of control system: a 'set of procedures for monitoring, directing, evaluating and compensating its employees' (Anderson and Oliver, 1987: 76). The two principal systems associated with controlling sales force behaviour are incentive pay systems and monitoring (Menguc and Barker, 2003).

Incentive pay systems reward employees for achieving specific performance targets. In using this type of control, priority is placed on an employee realizing targeted outcomes rather than on the way in which these are achieved. So, for example, a salesperson might discuss and agree with (their manager) targets for sales revenue, market-share or specific customer-share gains, new product sales and the profitability of business won by the sales representative. Where an outcome-based control system is used a significant proportion of a salesperson's remuneration is accounted for by performance-based commission and bonus payments. Clearly in using this type of system, account has to be taken of the relative ease/difficulty, for example, in selling a particular product line or generating business with a given customer at the point when targets and resulting rewards are agreed (Oliver and Anderson, 1995). An employee might have little room for negotiation in terms of the measures against which their performance is assessed and for which they are rewarded, but they typically have considerable discretion in how they go about realizing agreed targets.

Whereas incentive pay systems direct the actions of employees by providing financial compensation for the achievement of measurable, financial, sales-related targets, a *monitoring-based system* controls employee actions by directing, evaluating and rewarding sales-related activities. The idea behind this is that effective performance in sales activities will subsequently lead to company financial objectives being realized. So, for instance, a salesperson might be evaluated and rewarded according to their technical knowledge, use of adaptive selling, teamwork, sales presentations, sales planning and sales support (Grant and Cravens, 1996). This type of control system lacks measures that can be readily observed, which affects employee remuneration (only a small proportion of employee salaries would normally be linked to individual commission and bonuses) and requires closer monitoring of employee behaviour in order to evaluate performance. If behaviour is to be monitored in this way then a company has to prescribe how various sales activities should be performed. There is an inherent tension in such prescription, in that the definition of behaviours (instructions, procedures and standards) necessary to perform specified sales-related tasks can stifle the flexibility and discretion that a salesperson would expect to have in dealing with different types of customers and purchase situations.

The two control systems that we have discussed should not be viewed as being mutually exclusive; indeed, some companies are known to use a mixture of the two, or at least to use control systems that reflect the strategies adopted for different customers and the communication activity necessary to support these strategies. So outcome measures might be used for transactional customers, for example, where emphasis lies in closing sales and winning orders, and would typically be based on individual employee performance. For high-priority customers that involve complex purchase situations and require the contribution of various functions within the supplier company, a behaviour-based control system is arguably more appropriate, with team rather than individual employee performance being rewarded.

CHAPTER SUMMARY

- Relationship communication is about the exchange of 'messages' between a vendor and *specific* prospective or actual customers.

- The principal tools used in relationship communication are direct marketing (social, mail and telemarketing) and personal selling.

- Direct marketing and personal selling can be combined in order to acquire new customers and build/manage relationships with existing ones, but in doing so the vendor must take account of the ways in which personal selling and the various direct marketing media differ.

- The main parameters differentiating direct marketing and personal selling are:
  - o the scale of communication activity for which they can be used;
  - o the breadth and depth of information that can be exchanged;
  - o the scope for tailoring communication to suit specific situations and individual client needs;
  - o the capacity for interaction between supplier and customer companies.

- Cultural backgrounds influence relationship communication, and ignorance of or inability to adjust to the negotiation style of an exchange partner can lead to difficulty in communication episodes.

- In addition to thinking about how to acquire new customers or manage relationships with existing ones, a vendor must also decide how to coordinate relationship communication activities. The organization of the firm's interface with external markets and customers might centre on staff with selling responsibilities, or may involve managers from a variety of functions that deal directly with customers.

- Whatever structure a company uses to organize inter-firm communication, internal coordination and communication are also important. CRM systems can help to ensure the dissemination of and access to customer-specific information, and relationship promoters can be used as a link between firms as a means of coordinating activities to support specific customer relationships within the vendor organization.

QUESTIONS FOR DISCUSSION

1. Do social media have a role to play in relationship communication?

2. Describe the customer/order acquisition process. What stages do you think are the most critical?

3. Value has assumed considerable prominence in marketing theory and practice. How is this reflected in selling?

4. Explain the part played by culture in shaping an individual's negotiation style.

5. What effect has account management had on personal selling?

6. What challenges does the business marketer face in trying to coordinate relationship communication activities internally?

CASE STUDY 8.1   OILING THE WHEELS OF RELATIONSHIP COMMUNICATION

The oil and gas industry consists of different activities including upstream exploration and production, midstream transportation (via for example pipeline or oil tanker), storage of crude petroleum products, the downstream refining of petroleum crude oil and the processing of natural gas. Businesses operating in this sector include BP Amoco, Chevron, Elf Aquitaine, Exxon, Shell and Total – brands that we are all familiar with – particularly because, as consumers, we buy automotive fuel from their forecourt retail services.

Companies in the oil and gas market are renowned for being conservative, which is hardly surprising given the harsh and remote conditions in which they work, the potentially catastrophic environmental consequences of errors and the fact that a single unproductive day on a platform can cost a liquid natural gas (LNG) facility as much as $25 million (Winig, 2016). LNG platforms might have five down days a year which represents a significant annual cost, but besides trying to reduce the number of down days, central to operators such as BP Amoco, Elf Aquitaine and Shell is improving the productivity of equipment (assets). Extraction rates of oil wells sit at around 35 per cent – leaving a massive amount of resource unrecovered because existing technology makes it too expensive to extract (Winig, 2016).

Engineering businesses such as General Electric, Hyundai and Schlumberger supply process equipment to a variety of industries (including oil and gas) while pump manufacturers such as Sulzer provide components which might typically be part of an OEM's integrated solution for a new oil and gas installation or replacements for customers' existing oil extraction or pipeline operations. For any engineering business, being able to guarantee maximum productive capacity for products is a key part of the commercial narrative when seeking to secure new business and when working with customers to manage the operation of an existing installed base.

Improving productive capacity in the oil and gas industry presents challenges – for both equipment suppliers and customers such as BP Amoco, Elf Aquitaine or Total. First of all, not all equipment in, for example, an extraction, transportation or processing phase is integrated. If a customer transporting gas by pipeline has a problem with a turbo-compressor (used at compressing stations to reduce gas volume) then the customer might analyse compressor data when in fact the problem lies with the heat exchanger used to cool this process. Secondly, while major capital equipment might be installed with sensors and data controls, this is not necessarily the case for less expensive pieces of equipment. This is all well and good, until the day an 'inconsequential' pump fails and shuts down an entire production process. Thirdly, companies operating in the sector invest considerable sums of money in software systems and can handle massive amounts of 'big data' for seismic modelling – used to help with oil exploration and drilling. In fact, the industry more or less invented the term 'big data' over 30 years ago. But when it comes to using data for operational processes and for monitoring equipment central to these, the industry falls over. Even if equipment is fitted with sensors (which would be used for condition monitoring), up to 40 per cent of data is lost because the sensors

(Continued)

(Continued)

are binary, that is, they just show if a specific performance parameter is above or below what it should be (Maslin, 2015). This is important but it does not give any indication of trends which could be used to help decision-making and planning (such as preventative maintenance). Fourthly, data management for condition monitoring is ad hoc and many companies lack an integrated infrastructure which would enable high-speed communication links and data storage. This means that in some processes, only 0.7 per cent of the original data generated is used (Maslin, 2015).

Companies operating in the sector are beginning to realize that they could learn much from other markets, such as the aerospace industry. Here condition monitoring is used on turbines so that potential failures are seen before they become problems. This has changed the way in which maintenance in the aerospace industry is undertaken and reduced maintenance costs by 30 per cent (Maslin, 2015). And because airline operators have more information about the performance of turbines, they are more comfortable with using different turbines, making them engine 'agnostic' – this again reducing costs.

So it looks as if big data and integrated systems made up of digital products might be finding its way into the oil and gas industry to improve machine productivity and reliability. For example, Shell's upstream business (involved in the exploration of new liquids and natural gas reserves) has been working with the software company, SAS, to help develop predictive maintenance for its deepwater assets (Schultz, 2013). Meanwhile engineering business, Siemens, has joined forces with SAP and GE has created its own software platform, 'Predix', to provide digital solutions alongside industrial machinery, so that machines are connected via the cloud and data analytics can be used to predict breakdowns and assess the overall condition of equipment (Schultz, 2013; Winig, 2016).

But what does the move towards the combination of digital solutions with equipment mean for sales reps in engineering companies such GE, Hyundai or Schlumberger? Well, looking at it from a fairly broad perspective, Porter and Heppelmann (2015) suggest that firms will create a new functional unit tasked with handling business-wide data aggregation and analytics, supporting analytics undertaken by different functions and sharing information and insights across a firm. In this vision, sales, marketing and customer service activities will be supported by a new unit which Porter and Heppelman present as 'customer success management'. The authors explain that the principle purpose of this unit is to ensure that customers get the most from a product. The unit would collaborate with (rather than replace) sales and service units, assuming responsibility for monitoring product use and performance data to gauge the value customers capture and identifying ways to increase it.

Looking more specifically at equipment supplied to customers in the oil and gas industry, then the sales process is likely to change. For a start, sales to customers in the industry have tended to be high value but transactional, i.e. customers bought machines, parts, maintenance and repair contracts at fixed prices (Wining, 2016). Having secured a sale, the sales rep's involvement with the customer would normally then be minimal. However, once suppliers start adding digital elements to the product mix alongside high value machinery, then the sales process becomes more complex. Reps have to engage in dialogue which is less product focused, moving away from discussing product features and towards more strategic conversations around solutions. As well as a sales manager normally having an application engineer in client meetings (who would know, for example, how a compressor is going to operate in a given environment), a software technician is now critical so that the 'sales team' can explain how hardware, software and service can be combined into a solution. The expansion of the sales team is just as well, given that customers in the oil and gas industry are changing who gets involved in purchase decisions. While operations or plant managers remain important (defining scope and requirements of an overall package), technology and information officers now play an important role given that the digital part of a solution might likely be managed by a customer's IT team (Winig, 2016).

This is quite a shift for sales managers who have to evolve from a transactional selling approach to one which is more solution and relationship based, involving multiple parties in the supplier and customer company. Beyond the evolution in sales approach and the development of alternative value propositions which support clients' interest in condition monitoring, the sales team might also be expected to rethink the basis of pricing. Rather than equipment being considered a capital expenditure combining equipment, software and service (and sales teams crafting negotiations and pricing models accordingly), oil and gas clients might move towards an operational expense model in which outcome-based pricing is used (Winig, 2016). Here, the equipment supplier is paid based on production performance. Obviously setting up such a programme would require close cooperation between an equipment supplier and customer, given that a client would have to share proprietary information about their oil and gas operations.

CASE STUDY QUESTIONS

1 Using Figure 10.4, how might you expect interaction and information flows involving 'sales' and 'purchasing' teams from companies such as Schlumberger and Shell respectively to evolve as suppliers and customers move from transactions to value co-creation?

2 What skills do you consider necessary for members of the sales team in crafting and implementing solutions for customers in the oil and gas industry?

3 How might social media be used internally to ensure shared understanding of and commitment to customer-specific programmes of action?

FURTHER READING

Rapp, A., Bachrach, D.G., Panagopolous, N. and Ogilvie, J. (2014) 'Salespeople as knowledge brokers: a review and critique of the challenger sales model', *Journal of Personal Selling and Sales Management*, 34 (3): 245–59.

In the last decade or so, there has been considerable interest in alternative sales approaches. This article presents a critique of one approach in particular, the 'challenger sales model'. The authors conclude that the model has considerable

(Continued)

(Continued)

weaknesses, particularly when companies are involved in solutions selling. Read this, consider the premises on which the authors present the weaknesses of the challenger model and perhaps take a look at the ideas presented by Anderson et al. (2014) on tiebreaker selling. Would this sales approach hold up to the scrutiny of Rapp et al.?

Sebenius, J.K. (2002) 'The hidden challenge of cross-border negotiations', *Harvard Business Review*, 80 (3): 76–85.

This article provides a useful overview of the well-known work on cultural differences between countries. Sebenius explains the effect of culture on negotiation behaviour, and advises managers to map out the decision process of a negotiation partner and use this to develop strategies and tactics to handle this behavioural style.

Trailer, B. and Dickie, J. (2006) 'Understanding what your sales manager is up against', *Harvard Business Review*, 84 (7): 48–56.

Taken from a *Harvard Business Review* special issue on sales, this article presents survey results from over 1,000 sales executives worldwide on challenges facing sales organizations. The principal theme is the way in which the internet enables the buyer to amass supply and product information ahead of contacting a salesperson. Read this in conjunction with Wiersema (2013, see Chapter 4) to get a sense of how things are changing in business marketing, and consider how selling might have to adapt.

9

RELATIONSHIP PORTFOLIOS AND KEY ACCOUNT MANAGEMENT

LEARNING OUTCOMES

After reading this chapter you will:

- understand the principles of portfolio management and how they can apply to the management of customer relationships;
- be able to apply the processes of relationship portfolio analysis and management;
- know a range of variables, including life-cycle concepts, that enable the marketer to classify customer relationships for portfolio management decisions;
- recognize the need for a balanced relationship portfolio and know a set of rules for establishing balance; and
- understand what is meant by key account management (KAM), and what the main issues involved in implementing KAM are.

INTRODUCTION

As we saw in Chapter 3, business-to-business marketing often involves the management of customer relationships and so necessitates a focus at the level of the relationship rather than the product. Of course, typically a company has a collection of customers with varying characteristics. A substantial task for the business marketer then is to recognize the differences between customers and to manage the collection of relationships in ways that add value to the business. Drawing from the concept of portfolio management, this chapter presents the means by which business marketers can do just that: manage the collection of relationships with which they are faced. One of the central tasks of portfolio management is to identify those key account relationships on which the company relies either for its current business, or for future business survival and growth. After outlining the principles of portfolio management, we will also discuss how companies should approach the job of managing these key accounts.

Logically, portfolio management is at a different level from decisions made about specific customer relationships (such as which product or process technology to pursue in the relationship, or how to communicate value within the relationship). It can be seen as a precursor to these decisions since the results of the relationship portfolio analysis should make it possible to make better day-to-day marketing decisions. For example, there is little point in committing substantial resources to new product variants with a customer who is clearly unreceptive and, in reality, of much lower strategic value than other customers. This is particularly true if committing greater resources to the former would mean forgoing commitment to the latter, which may be the case given finite resources. Of course, the link between the customer relationship portfolio management and day-to-day marketing management is more complex than that. For instance, as Chapter 6 indicates, one of the bases for analysing the collection of customer relationships may arise from internal characteristics of the firm (such as the extent to which a customer makes use of a new product technology from the firm).

In this chapter we will outline the principles of portfolio management and indicate how they have resonance in business-to-business marketing. Then we will consider a selection of commonly used criteria for undertaking the portfolio analysis, including the use of *relationship life-cycle* concepts that may aid the analysis. Subsequently, we will establish some guidelines for achieving a balanced relationship portfolio as a precursor to the sorts of product management decisions that are considered in greater detail in Chapter 10. Finally, this chapter discusses how to approach the task of managing those key customers, identified through relationship portfolio analysis, who are considered to be of particular strategic importance to a company.

PRINCIPLES OF PORTFOLIO MANAGEMENT

For a business marketer the relationships they forge and maintain with their customers constitute the basis for creating value for the firm. As Peter Drucker (1955: 35) pointed out over half a century ago:

> *There is only one valid definition of business purpose: to create a customer...*
> *It is the customer who determines what a business is. For it is the customer,*
> *and he alone, who through being willing to pay for a good or for a service,*
> *converts economic resources into wealth, things into goods... The customer is*
> *the foundation of a business and keeps it in existence.*

Of course, businesses do not generally have just one customer. They typically rely upon a range of customers, each bringing their own type of value. In some cases, this may be straightforward monetary value in terms of level of sales. In others, it may be in terms of the profit contribution the customer makes aside from sales volume. In yet others, it may have little to do with current monetary value and more to do with future value. It may even involve negative current value in the expectation of future revenue or profit streams, essentially up-front investments in the future of the business with the concomitant risks that accompany such investment.

When one sees the variety of relationship types, the sources of value they bring, and the time horizon over which the value may accrue, then inevitably one is drawn towards both financial investment notions and how financial managers have traditionally managed sources of risk and return. As we will see in the next chapter, marketers have long borrowed terminology from the financial management sphere to help deal with the difficulties of managing a range of different products. Just as financial managers like a balance of investments that begin and mature at different times, producing a steady stream of returns over the longer term, so marketers have seen the usefulness of such concepts for the management of products and strategic business units. Portfolio planning tools allow for the sorts of analyses that enable clear decisions to be made in order to obtain a well-balanced portfolio. A well-balanced portfolio is one that ensures that the business earns value over the long term by selectively harvesting excess current returns and ploughing them into future products. The notions of portfolio management have equal applicability to customer relationships because:

- relationships constitute sources of risk and return;
- relationships are varied in the type of risk they constitute;
- relationships vary in the level of return they bring; and
- relationships also vary in the time horizon over which they provide that return.

When seen in these terms, it is clearly appropriate to consider relationships in portfolio management terms. Indeed, we agree with Ford et al. (2002: 99; italics in original) who consider that the integrated management of the whole portfolio of relationships is a key task for the business marketer:

> *The business marketer must manage his portfolio of relationships as a totality, according to the respective contributions of each one to its corporate success, the risks that each involves, the demands that each makes on his resources and the effects that each has on his other relationships.*

Successful portfolio management requires that the marketer make the best decisions possible with the portfolio of relationships he or she has. The strategic options for specific relationships or relationship groups are typically those in Table 9.1. However, chosen options for each relationship or relationship cluster should be taken in an integrated way, rather than separately and as though they were unrelated to each other.

In order to reach the right decision the business marketer needs to be well informed about the possible risks and returns from the relationships in the portfolio. Establishing the relative standing of each relationship requires a series of analyses that essentially divide the relationships into different categories of customer. The number of categories depends upon how fine-grained the firm wants to be in identifying different customer relationship groups. Ultimately, it is possible to apply sufficient classification criteria to create a category for every single customer. However, as Chapter 6 on segmentation established, it is generally not sensible for a firm to treat every customer uniquely – often a firm has a small number of key accounts that can be treated individually, while other customers merit less special treatment. There are likely to

TABLE 9.1 Typical strategic options for a relationship

Option	Actions
Build	Build a relationship further for growth, investing where necessary to achieve this growth
Maintain	Maintain the current levels of management effort in a relationship in order to reap the benefits from the relationship now through large volumes, high profits or a greater share of the customer's purchases
Harvest	Harvest the value in the relationship by taking the current monetary value it brings while at the same time beginning to reduce the cost of servicing the relationship over time
Reduce	Reduce in the immediate future the level of management commitment to a relationship because the returns are diminishing with little prospect of reversal

be collections or clusters of customer relationships that, to all intents and purposes, require similar treatment in terms of management commitment and in terms of the level of return that they provide to the firm. Thus, as with segmentation, successful portfolio analysis requires an iterative process of breaking down the customer base into a smaller number of clusters.

A variety of classificatory criteria can be applied during the iterative deepening process in order to achieve a level of clustering that produces a meaningful set of groups in the portfolio. 'Meaningful' in this context needs to be defined by the firm itself on the basis of its own business context and the peculiarities of its customer base, and may be refined over time. However, it is likely that the number of groups for most companies will number between 8 and 14. Also, while there may be singleton relationships that are distinct, for the most part each group will contain more than one customer. While all groups will comprise customer relationships that have a degree of commonality within the group, there is also likely to be at least one set that contains a substantial number of customers where the unifying commonality has more to do with their lack of individual importance to the company (what Ford et al. (2006) call 'minor relationships'). Once a meaningful set of groups in the portfolio has been established, decisions can be taken with respect to each element in the portfolio in order to achieve balance overall.

THE RELATIONSHIP CLASSIFICATION PROCESS

An early pioneer of customer relationship differentiation, Jackson (1985b) advocated a dichotomy of the customer base into those customers where a supplier can always get a share of the business and those that want stability in their supply dealings so that they prefer to form closer relationships with suppliers. The former, 'always-a-share' customers are driven by short-term considerations like the current price and make supplier decisions based on the best deals in the market at the time. In this respect they are highly opportunistic, happy to switch supply for an immediate financial saving. If you have been supplying a customer like this and they have just switched, then the one consolation is that it is always possible to win the business back; when the next sale comes through it is merely a matter of providing a better price-based deal than the competition.

Customers who want greater stability will often subordinate short-term price-based issues to other considerations, such as continuity of supply, levels of product quality or a shared market view with their suppliers. For example, Harrington (2004) reported that Sun Microsystems (prior to its 2010 acquisition by Oracle) had reduced its supply base and consolidated 80 per cent of its spend with just 40 suppliers in an effort to manage them more strategically and long-term, recognizing that the greatest proportion of its operating costs result from sourcing. Apple uses only 17 final assembly facilities across the globe for its range of products, and 200 suppliers accounted for more than 97 per cent of its materials, manufacturing and assembly purchasing costs in 2012. The investments that companies looking for stability make in their suppliers to achieve these sorts of advantages are neither arbitrary nor transient. Cost reductions for Sun Microsystems didn't come from merely negotiating lower prices with suppliers but from involving the suppliers in ways that reduce costs for both themselves and the suppliers.

As a result of the investment that companies make in their supply base they are reluctant to switch suppliers, sometimes even preferring to work with failing suppliers to improve the situation. However, they have a breaking point in their preparedness to accept poor performance or opportunistic behaviour on the part of suppliers. While they want a close relationship with their favoured suppliers, if a supplier lets them down badly then that will be the end of the relationship. In this respect, when lost, they are lost-for-good (Jackson, 1985b).

Sako's (1992) research in the auto industry suggested a similar dichotomy between types of relationship. Her analyses of the behaviour of the car assemblers indicated a cultural predisposition among US and European assemblers to use formal and controlling mechanisms in their relationships; the relationships manifested a basic mistrust and tendency to conflict. She called this the 'arm's length' contracting approach. This approach she contrasts with a tendency in relationship management among Japanese assemblers to manifest greater amounts of trust in partners. She attributes this to a cultural tendency towards acknowledging the responsibilities that go with a relationship. The parties to a relationship understand that they are working together and that the relationship obliges them to work in particular ways that are more about mutual respect, since it is only through such attitudes and cooperative behaviour that the relationship objectives can be met. Sako (1992) calls this approach *obligational contracting*.

The sort of dichotomies to which Jackson and Sako refer are useful in distinguishing the two ends of a relationship continuum. In both cases, as the description above indicates, a whole series of indicators are at play in distinguishing both ends of the spectrum. As a first foray into splitting up the customer base into relationship types, it has merit. It is particularly useful for reducing the size of the analysis space because it is possible to discount from further analysis all those customers who are clearly not interested in a closer relationship. That is not to say that these customers are to be ignored, merely that the basis of trading with them is best focused on negotiating the best deal at any point in time.

Of course, from a managerial perspective it is not clear exactly how the split is established and what the specific variables are that should be applied in combination in order to achieve the split. It is also the case that many relationships fall into the space between the two extremes. There are not likely to be just two sets of behaviour manifested in the customer base but a whole collection, and neither are there just two ways in which a firm should manage its relationships. Consequently, the use of a broad-brush approach like the binary split can only be a starting point. It is more useful to undertake a process of sequential application of classificatory variables in order to split the customer relationship base into more than just two clusters.

A range of variables can be used to make qualitative distinctions between relationships. Some criteria are easily available and easily applied; some involve undertaking specific additional analyses in order to derive the benefit from them. We will start with the more easily undertaken analyses, which typically use the sorts of financial information that companies generate as a matter of course. As these are typically accounting based there is a sound reason for starting here anyway: a balanced portfolio needs to be financially stable. A portfolio of relationships with great potential but little current profit and which requires substantial investment will merely bankrupt the company, ensuring that the potential will never be achieved. By the same token, a portfolio of relationships that produces current cash or profits but which will dry up in two or three years is not the basis for long-run success.

CLASSIFICATION CRITERIA: MORE EASILY OBSERVED

A good starting point is analyses that draw from existing, easily obtained information sources. The accounting system constitutes the most readily available central source of information on relationships, containing, as it does, a record of the sales made to specific customers as well as company cost information. By making use of this source and undertaking some basic analyses, it is possible to start distinguishing relationships from each other without having to make deeper judgement calls about every customer. The application of criteria that require personal insight is best left until there is a need for such insight with a smaller number of relationship cases. Consequently, they are best used to further refine cluster definitions created by applying a collection of the set of criteria in this subsection.

Sales

The *value of sales* can be used directly as a means of ranking customers. In some companies it may be better to consider the *number of units sold*. It is, of course, in either case more illuminating to talk about a customer relationship in terms of *proportion of total sales*. The sales figures for the imaginary company in Table 9.2 clearly show that Acme Corp. is the biggest customer by sales. However, the sales figure percentage shows just how important a customer it is. Of course, sales alone do not say anything about the level of profitability of an account.

Profits

Sales alone do not make a relationship attractive. It may be more sensible to focus on notions of profitability. Shapiro et al. (1987) used both *net price achieved* (that is, price after all forms of discounting have been applied) and *cost-to-serve* as means of establishing relative profitability. As Figure 9.1 indicates, customers below the break-even point (Customer Y) are unprofitable, while those above it are profitable (Customer X). Using the simulated figures for SpareParts Ltd in trading year 2014/15 (Table 9.2), it becomes clear that while Acme Corp. is the biggest customer in terms of sales, it is also a highly demanding customer.

While still profitable, it is not as profitable, from a lower sales base, as Bits & Bobs plc – which generates £880,000 of profit compared to the £447,000 produced by Acme. Incidentally, Loser Ltd is ranked second in terms of sales but is unprofitable. To be a reliable depiction of the state of the customer base, net price and cost-to-serve figures need to be calculated over a fixed time span with respect to all transactions. Typically this would be the last trading year, but perhaps longer in some contexts if the cost accounting system can facilitate it. The cost accounting system also needs to enable strong tracking of the costs required to support a customer: all the sales calls, all the technical support or time taken to resolve difficulties, specific costs associated with a customer in terms of production set-ups or tooling, training or installation costs, and so on. All these need to figure if one is to establish a clear cost-to-serve. Furthermore, it is possible to extend Figure 9.1 so that the relative proportion of sales is also captured, as in Figure 9.2.

TABLE 9.2 Simulated sales and cost-to-serve figures for SpareParts Ltd, 2014/15 and 2015/16

	2014/15				2015/16			
Customer	Sales (£m)	Cost-to-serve (CTS) (£m)	Sales minus CTS (£m)	% Sales	Sales (£m)	Cost-to-serve (£m)	Sales minus CTS (£m)	% Sales
Acme Corp.	6.442	5.995	0.447	50	5.250	3.010	2.240	39
Loser Ltd	2.653	3.000	−0.347	20	4.345	3.000	1.345	33
Hodge Podge Ltd	2.351	2.110	0.241	18	2.460	1.970	0.490	18
Bits & Bobs plc	1.555	0.675	0.880	12	1.355	0.685	0.670	10
Totals	13.001	11.780	1.221		13.410	8.665	4.745	

From a portfolio management perspective, Shapiro et al. (1987) use just the two financial criteria of net price achieved and cost-to-serve in order to derive four different types of customer (based on ratings of high or low for the two criteria in a two-by-two matrix).

Bargain basement customers (low net price and low cost-to-serve) are those who are very price sensitive, but they are insensitive to levels of quality or service. They are thus much cheaper to manage than their opposites, *carriage trade* customers (high net price and high cost-to-serve). These customers may be prepared to pay premium prices but they want the levels of service and quality that go with that, so they cost more to serve.

Both of the above are balanced in terms of the demands they make for the prices they pay. With some customers there is an imbalance in respect of what they pay and what they expect for it. *Passive* customers are prepared to pay higher prices despite not commanding equivalent levels of service or quality from their suppliers.

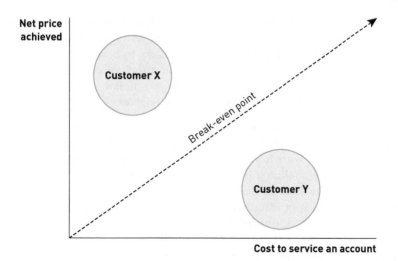

FIGURE 9.1 Customers in terms of the prices achieved and the cost to service their accounts (adapted from Shapiro et al., 1987)

Where there is a product dependence; the nature of the product does not warrant great attention by the buyer; or, there is buyer inertia, then the buyer may just pay the price demanded. These customers are at the opposite end of the spectrum from *aggressive* customers. Aggressive customers want it all: the highest levels of service and product quality at low prices. What makes them aggressive rather than carriage trade is that they generally get it; because of the relative power they have in a relationship they can command top quality at low prices. Their power may come from such characteristics as their superior access to end-markets, the volumes they purchase or their relative importance to the counterpart.

Shapiro et al. (1987) demonstrate how quickly it becomes possible to split a customer base into different clusters of customers, each with a separate management agenda.

Cost savings

Sticking with financial criteria, it may be the case that relationships can be distinguished on the basis of their potential to reduce costs for the company over time. Krapfel et al. (1991) argue that cost savings are important in generating relationship value. So, for example, a customer creates a degree of slack and therefore a cost saving for the supplier if it is prepared to carry more stock, pay its bills earlier, provide earlier and more accurate demand forecasts, or engage in forms of automated order processing. The preparedness and potential of customers to provide such cost savings can be used as the basis for distinguishing them.

Rather than being directly available from the accounting system, analysts will have to use the cost information that exists and establish in addition the potential cost savings for specific relationships. In this respect, the use of cost savings as a means of distinguishing between relationships relies upon a judgement call about the future on the basis of the historical information that already exists.

Relationship age

The age of relationships is often used to distinguish them from each other, since the concept of 'relationship' has a temporal dimension. As Table 9.3 indicates, there can be a wide range of relationship ages in a supply base. In both the examples depicted the degree of importance of the counterparts and the complexity of the exchange show a tendency to longer-lasting relationships. While not all relationships will be as important or as complex as this, age certainly enables them to be distinguished.

It is also possible to combine an element of the passing of time with the sort of financial analysis depicted in Figure 9.2. The diagram in Figure 9.3, using data from Table 9.2, shows how with financial data over as little as a two-year-period it is possible to depict the changing position. Figure 9.3 shows the trends in respect of all three of the dimensions of percentage of sales, cost-to-serve and level of sales at the same time. The appropriate time span will, of course, depend on the specific sector and what passes for normal relationship lengths in the sector. As Anderson and Narus (1991) indicate, there are natural industry bandwidths in respect of the propensity for relationships to be more collaborative or more transactional.

The concept of time has an additional relevance for relationship portfolio management. The purpose of identifying clusters of relationships is to make decisions in respect

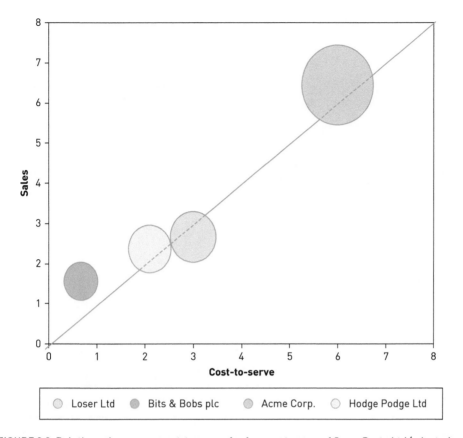

FIGURE 9.2 Relative sales versus cost-to-serve for four customers of SpareParts Ltd (adapted from Shapiro et al., 1987)

TABLE 9.3 Indication of the diversity of ages in a relationship base

For companies engaged in technical development with suppliers		Relationship age of top 17 suppliers to vehicle manufacturer (≈ 33% of purchase costs)	
Duration	No. of relationships	Duration	No. of suppliers
0–4 years	28%	1–4 years	2
5–14 years	41%	5–14 years	5
15+ years	29%	15–24 years	4
		25+ years	6
(Håkansson, 1982)		(Ford et al., 2002: 81)	

of the resulting clusters. The idea that relationships have life-cycles (Barnes, 2004; Dwyer et al., 1987; Ford, 1980) suggests that relationships change over time, and that behaviour within relationships will change. Knowing the age of a relationship and using it to define clusters provides an insight into appropriate relationship strategy.

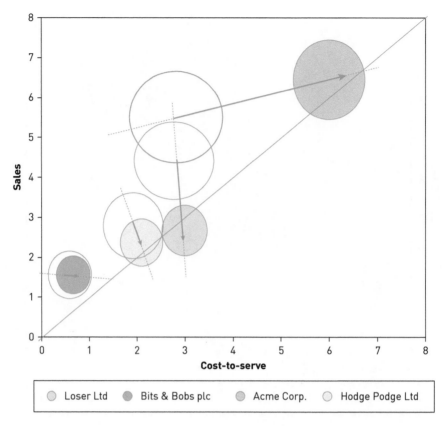

FIGURE 9.3 Extension of sales versus cost-to-serve for SpareParts Ltd, to include trend indicators over time

CLASSIFICATION CRITERIA: LESS EASILY OBSERVED

The criteria in the previous section are generally easily obtained since they emerge from standard financial information systems. However, further criteria may be useful in further refining portfolio clusters created through the application of the criteria in the previous subsection. Some of those objectively defined clusters may need further subdivision. This is done through the application of other relevant distinguishing criteria. In this section we present some variables that can be used to achieve the subdivision. They rely on non-standard evaluations, typically conducted specifically for the purposes of a relationship portfolio analysis. This makes them more difficult to conduct, relying on judgement calls from the analyst in the absence of other more objective sources of data such as accounting reports. They are thus better undertaken by someone who has sufficient strategic knowledge of the firm and its direction as well as good knowledge of the individual customer accounts.

Replaceability of a customer

One important consideration is the extent to which a customer is replaceable (Krapfel et al., 1991). The loss of some customers may be highly damaging because there are few alternatives to replace them. Other customers may be fairly easily replaced by finding alternative customers from a large set of those available. As well as the direct loss of sales, there may also be investments already made with respect to strategically important customers in terms of dedicated plant or people or procedures that need to be considered when assessing their degree of replace-ability. This assessment should also trade off any additional costs of acquiring alternative customers (even if there is a stock of substitutes available). These costs could concern potential process or material changes, higher quality standards or changes to distribution levels.

Companies will certainly want to think carefully before losing an irreplaceable customer and thus may consider the use of this variable in distinguishing between relationships.

Use of critically important products or processes

Some products or services may be more critical to a company's business than others. All other things being equal, a supplier would prefer to supply more rather than less critical products and services, because it makes the customer more dependent on the supplier. At the same time, as Krapfel et al. (1991) indicate, critical products and services typically demonstrate the supplier's specific technical and/or market competences and thus establish the relative strategic competitive position of the supplier in the market-place. In this way, criticality of a product can be the basis of value differentiation in a relationship from both the buyer and seller perspectives and may well be useful in distinguishing one relationship from another.

Because of the dynamic nature of customer markets, developments in supply markets, and decisions about changing competences within the firm, products may become more or less critical over time. Companies need to be aware of future as well as cur-rent users of these strategically important sources of differential advantage and need to be candid about their relative importance to customers.

Shared vision of the future

Companies have their own view of how their industry or sector is developing – for example, where the next big developments are going to be and where they see them-selves with respect to these changes. It is always easier to work with customers who share similar views. For that reason a portfolio analyst may use the extent to which there is a shared vision with customers as the basis for distinguishing between rela-tionships. Krapfel et al. (1991) call this *interest commonality*, where a supplier and a customer have compatible economic goals.

For example, glass manufacturer Pilkington saw that development in the glass indus-try involved more than merely cutting float glass and wrapping it in extruded UPVC. There had been growth of double-glazing companies, all pretty much substitutable, all merely buying glass for these purposes. In an effort to move the sector forward Pilkington was itself investing in product developments to provide for greater thermal efficiency performance of its glass as well as self-cleaning properties – investments that led to 'K' glass and its Activ™ range of glass respectively. At the same time, it introduced a downstream Key Processor initiative as the means of identifying and treating differently those customers that did more than just cut and wrap glass. These customers, it considered, shared the same vision of where the sector was going and in that respect these were relationships that Pilkington wanted to encourage.

By considering interest commonality (low or high) against a measure of relationship value (low or high), Krapfel et al. (1991) identified four different relationship types, each of which requires a different relationship management approach.

Acquaintance (low value, low commonality)

Customers like this should only be offered standard products and services. The low value means that there should be no customization or anything that incurs extra costs. It does not mean that such relationships should be discouraged. Apart from anything else such relationships constitute the means of reducing vulnerability that arises from being overly tied to a smaller number of relationships.

Rival (high value, low commonality)

While there is great value in the relationship currently, and relationships with such customers should be maintained for their economic value, the level of strategic interest commonality is low. Such customers are just not going in the same direction as the supplier and there is strong potential for opportunism (such as the customer trying to extract substantial price reductions at a time of excess capacity). A business marketer might want to ensure that it is protected from opportunistic action from these customers and may strive to achieve this by looking for new customers. It would certainly not be advisable to engage in additional specific investments for such customers.

Friend (low value, high commonality)

Friends show that they are clearly interested in the same things as the supplier. They might have similar views about the direction in which technology is going in the market. They might even use the supplier's products in ways that are new, and thus be a source of innovation in the sector. However, the value of the relationship itself is relatively low overall. This may be because the relationship is embryonic and yet to establish the volumes needed to be more valuable in revenue terms or operating efficiency. If such relationships are indeed embryonic then they may require the sort of attention that will lead to greater volumes and will thus incur expense in the short term. However, despite the level of interest commonality, if the investment does not lead to greater relationship value then over time this sort of customer is merely destined to become an occasional acquaintance rather than a strategic partner.

Partner (high value, high commonality)

Partners, on the other hand, are important for the economic value they represent and the alignment with the strategic interest of the seller. The volumes, criticality of the products they use, their relative irreplaceability, or the cost savings they bring, allied to the common direction they are taking, mean that specific investments in these are recommended. Calls for adaptations (to products or processes) may originate from the customer but may also be welcome to the supplier; they signal the shared interest of the two parties. While in a politically balanced relationship the extra value created by adaptations might naturally be shared equitably between the parties, in a relationship where the customer has the balance of power the marketer will need to be careful that it is not just funding value creation for the customer alone. This involves careful negotiation and a mutual understanding that the long-term strength of the business relationship depends on equitable distribution of value.

A source of learning for the company

Some customers may be considered important purely because the demands they make are valuable in increasing the problem-solving abilities of the seller. That is, these customers set the bar for requirements technically or commercially so that by reaching the threshold, the seller's abilities across the board with its customer base are enhanced. They may not even be profitable relationships financially, requiring as they do such high levels of investment in product or process improvements. However, the learning opportunities they provide compensate for the direct financial loss. For example, many automotive component suppliers have benefited greatly from working with Japanese car manufacturers such as Toyota and Nissan. By meeting the very high technical and quality standards of these companies, the supplier develops engineering skills and management processes that serve it well with other customers and in other markets. These days, many suppliers to Apple Inc. value the opportunity to work with and learn from such a technologically innovative firm.

The supplier's share of customers' purchases

The notion of share of a customer's overall purchases makes this criterion sound like it should belong among those variables that use hard data in the previous section. However, this is a judgement that the analyst makes, typically in the absence of concrete evidence. It can be a very subjective measure and analysts should be encouraged to justify the estimates that they use. They are also best advised to make conservative estimates. The quality of the estimates can, of course, be enhanced by attempts to triangulate. The most obvious way of doing this is to solicit estimates from several sources, along with evidence from each source of the validity of their estimate. These can be used to derive an average of the weighted estimates reported, based on an index of the credibility of the supporting evidence. Ford et al. (2006) show how the share of supply of the customer requirements can be combined with a measure of change in sales volume over time to help distinguish customer relationships (see Figure 9.4).

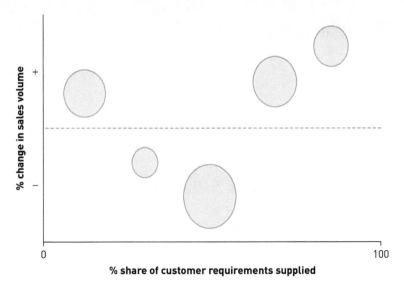

FIGURE 9.4 Customer portfolio change matrix (Ford et al., 2006: 251)

With permission from Wiley.

Short-term advantage-taking

As Ford et al. (2006) point out, business-to-business relationships are not always about being nice and are not always about mutual benefit. Where the potential to take advantage exists with companies for which the supplier has no longer-term plans, companies in a position to do so may well take the opportunities that arise. Of course, irreplaceable customers who bring special benefits to the seller are not likely to be targets of advantage-taking. However, others that are the source of short-term sales volume, profits or technical or commercial knowledge to the firm, but who offer little in the way of long-term benefit, are prime targets for relatively poor treatment at a particular point in time (for example, inflated price rises at a time of particular customer need). Ford et al. (2006) call these customers the 'fall-guys' because of this. While such behaviour from a supplier may not be seen as wholesome, it is certainly possible for companies to use their potential to take advantage as the basis for distinguishing some relationships from others.

COMBINING CLASSIFICATION VARIABLES TO PRODUCE VARIED CLUSTERS

The ultimate aim in undertaking a relationship portfolio analysis is to generate a series of different, but internally consistent, clusters of customer relationship types. Throughout the description of specific variables above there have been examples of the sorts of clusters that can be produced, typically by combining the use of classification variables – the four Shapiro et al. (1987) clusters of carriage trade, aggressive, passive

TABLE 9.4 Four-cluster portfolio analysis of the customer base (N = 222) of a packaging company and the management checks undertaken to establish appropriate resource commitments

	Yesterday's customers	Today's regular customers	Today's special customers	Tomorrow's customers
(a) Classification criteria:				
Sales volume	Low	Average	High	Low
Profitability of customer to supplier	Low	Average	High	Low
Relationship age	Old	Average	Old	New
Use of strategic resources	Low	Average	High	High
Supplier's share of customer's purchases	Low	Average	High	Low
(b) Management checks:				
Cluster size	175	38	2	7
% of sales	12	44	43	1
% of technical development expenditure	–	23	38	39

Source: adapted from Campbell and Cunningham, 1983.

With permission from Wiley.

and bargain basement customers, and the four Krapfel et al. (1991) relationship types of rival, partner, friend and acquaintance. In this section, we present other examples of how variables can be combined and the resulting clusters produced.

Campbell and Cunningham (1983) combined five different variables (see Table 9.4) to derive four categories of customer that were appropriate for a packaging company. They also indicate how companies can establish the appropriateness of their resource commitment to these clusters. In this case, where the company pursues an innovation strategy, it is appropriate to focus on the proportion of technical development expenditure that each cluster consumes. It is also appropriate that the greatest proportion of sales should come from *today's customers*. The company would not want to see any technical development resource being consumed by *yesterday's customers* and would certainly not like to see them constitute a sizeable proportion of sales.

The Campbell and Cunningham (1983) clustering shows a useful combination of the more easily derived financial measures alongside those that require a judgement call from the analyst. Turnbull and Zolkiewski (1995) advocate just such an approach, applying the hard measures (profitability of customers) before moving on to the more judgemental measures in a two-stage process. They propose the use of a three-dimensional matrix (2 × 2 × 2: net price × cost-to-serve × relationship value) with eight different categories.

You can try your hand at some analysis based on the Campbell and Cunningham (1983) approach in B2B Scenario 9.1.

B2B SCENARIO 9.1 BARBARA LEARNS ABOUT CUSTOMER PORTFOLIO ANALYSIS

Barbara Muzychuk, a marketing analyst at a large automotive components manufacturer, knew that her boss had been studying for an MBA. Usually this didn't make much difference to her working day, other than she had to tolerate his frequent use of new, fashionable management jargon. But today he had presented her with some specific analysis that one of his professors had encouraged him to undertake. So she stared at the fairly simple table he had produced (Table 9.5), and pondered the questions that he had asked.

TABLE 9.5 Customer Portfolio Analysis

	Number of customers	Percentage of sales %	Percentage of technical development expenditure %
Tomorrow's customers	3	0	12
Today's special customers	2	51	38
Today's regular customers	6	38	38
Yesterday's customers	3	11	12

(Continued)

(Continued)

Her boss said that this analysis was based on the idea of a customer relationship life-cycle, derived from the work of two professors (Campbell and Cunningham, 1983). She could see the resemblance to the product life-cycle idea that she had studied at university. That had the phases of introduction, growth, maturity and decline. This analysis was evidently applied to her firm's customer accounts, and tomorrow's customers were rather like the introduction phase, today's special customers like the growth phase, and so on.

Barbara's boss wanted her to provide him with an evaluation of the usefulness of this kind of analysis for their firm, and then wanted her to identify what kind of strategic options might be suggested from it. As far as the first question was concerned she could work out that this was basically a two-dimensional matrix for analysing the firm's customer relationships; percentage of sales was one way of measuring the current importance of the customer account, and percentage of technical development expenditure was one way of measuring how much they were investing in the customer relationship. Of course, this was just a first approximation. For example, the importance of those three firms in the 'tomorrow's customers' category certainly could not be measured by sales, because at the moment they were developing the relationships with a view to generating future sales revenue. Similarly, technical development expenditure was a useful proxy for the amount invested in a customer relationship, but it was not the whole story. For example, Barbara knew that the sales and customer service teams spent a lot of time and energy serving some customers, while other customers were much easier to serve. So, on the first question, Barbara would say that this was an interesting form of analysis but it should be handled with caution. A lot of managerial judgement would be needed to use the information appropriately. Before making any committal decisions based on the analysis one would need to consult the Key Account Management team.

Now, Barbara thought, what about the second question: what kind of strategic options did this analysis suggest?

Sources: Inspired by Campbell and Cunningham (1983) and incorporating data from research conducted by the authors.

Ford et al. (2006) take the notion of portfolio analysis further than most when they depict a series of relationship types that have proved useful (see Table 9.6).

TABLE 9.6 Indicative application of a progressive series of portfolio analysis variables and the resulting clusters, as named by Ford et al. (2006: 148–51)

Criterion applied	Resulting Ford et al. (2006) clusters	Description of cluster
Sales	'Cash cows'	Those customers currently generating the greatest proportion of sales income, typically because of higher-volume demands
	'Minor relationships'	Small customers in terms of individual sales demands and relative importance to the firm. This does not mean they are unprofitable, just not individually significant. There may be quite a lot of them and as a group they may account for a sizeable income

Criterion applied	Resulting Ford et al. (2006) clusters	Description of cluster
Profits	'Today's profits'	The most profitable customers currently
	'Yesterday's profits'	Those customers whose profitability trends indicate that they are on the wane
	'The "Old Men"'	Customer relationships that are past their heyday. There may be some residual personal interests in maintaining these relationships but generally they absorb resources that could be more profitably used
	'Tomorrow's profits'	Relationships that may currently be unprofitable and require ongoing investment but which hold the promise of substantial profits in the medium to long term
Source of learning opportunities	New technical requirements	Relationships that, because of the demands they make technically in product or process terms, force the firm to improve its game, leading to innovations that prove valuable in the business at large
	New commercial requirements	Similar to the category above but the innovation comes from commercial rather than technical operations
Source of advantage-taking	'The fall-guys'	Customers that are not of any long-term strategic import. Scope for taking advantage exists. In essence, it does not matter how badly you treat them because they are just not important to you

With permission from Wiley.

RELATIONSHIP LIFE-CYCLES

The life-cycle concept has long been used by marketers to suggest appropriate marketing strategies for a market offering. The best-known life-cycle concept is probably the *product life-cycle*. While the life-cycle concept has long been criticized for being overly idealized and of little practical help at the micro-management level, it is a concept that makes intuitive sense to most managers. We see birth, growth, maturity and decline in the living world all the time and thus suppose that human constructions like products have a life and death that correspond to the natural world in general terms. The extension of the life-cycle concept to relationships is arguably even more plausible. Relationships are constructs that actually do involve people in more direct ways than a product does, and thus the living elements are very real rather than abstractions. Unlike artefacts such as products, the social constructions that are relationships are organic: they have a life of their own as a result of the range of different people involved and the cultures and affiliations of these people. This is what can make relationships highly flexible. However, it also is what makes relationships very difficult to control. In recognition of the fluid nature of relationships, researchers have set out to establish how they develop over time. Ford (1980) examined the relationship life-cycle in terms of several variables:

- the experience of dealing with each other;
- the uncertainty associated with working with each other;
- the distance between the parties, incorporating social, geographical, time, cultural and technological manifestations;
- the commitment the parties make to each other; and
- the specific adaptations they make to what they do and how they do it that bring them closer to the counterpart (what Williamson (1979) refers to as 'transaction-specific investments').

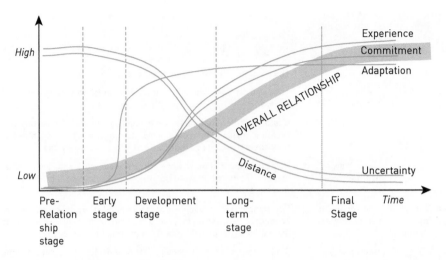

FIGURE 9.5 Ford's (1980) relationship life-cycle stages

With permission from Emerald Publishing.

Ford established that relationships that become close and enduring manifest reductions in uncertainty and distance over time. At the same time they exhibit increases in the experience of working together, in commitments to each other and in the number of adaptations that the parties make in their normal operations to avail themselves of the relationship with the other. These are depicted diagrammatically in Figure 9.5.

Relationship stages

The *pre-relationship stage* is that transient time between when there is nothing resembling a relationship at all and the point at which there could just be a relationship. It is sparked by a need for change that has a customer searching for new suppliers, whether as a result of company policy or a change in the relationship with the current supplier. In this respect the customer is in the driving seat, evaluating possible suitors against the performance of the incumbent or responding to changing marketplace information. As a largely analytical stage there is no commitment; it is only when a decision is taken on the strength of the analysis that a relationship can be said to have come into being.

The *early stage* is characterized by the need to deal with substantial unknowns. The parties have no experience of working together and thus have great uncertainty about how the relationship will unfold and the value it may bring. As the parties do not know each other well, social distance is likely to be great. There may also be great technological distance because the parties have not yet had the opportunity to see how their respective product and process technologies can work together. A contract manufacturer of office chairs to a large multinational went through nearly two years of product concept proofing with the customer before any chairs were even accepted into the customer's catalogue. Where the relationship extends across frontiers there may also be geographical and cultural distances to be reduced.

Reducing the uncertainty and the distance and increasing the experience the parties have of each other requires substantial commitment of management time in understanding each other. In the early stages there is unlikely to be much more than time committed; neither party is likely to make capital commitments until sure of the other. The commitment of time is likely to lead to reductions in the distance between the parties.

It is only during the *development stage* that the commitment of time leads to manifest reductions in uncertainty and distance between the parties. As a result of informal adaptations to what they do for each other their mutual experience of each other grows. More formal adaptations embed the practice of the relationship, and both parties start to see the benefits financially of adapting to each other more closely. When their levels of experience of each other reach their peak, during the *long-term stage*, there is little distance between them socially, technologically and culturally. There is then little more commitment that either can demonstrate, with extensive adaptation largely having taken place. At this point, the way in which the parties interact with each other starts to settle into forms of institutionalized working; established operations and working practices have become routine, without need to constantly reappraise them.

When these forms of institutionalization become the way things are done more generally in the sector, embodied in forms of industry practice, then the relationship has essentially gone full circle. From something that starts for both parties on the basis of what is common practice and then proceeds into a way of working that is singular and unique, the relationship has now become common practice again because this way of working has become the norm. This is the *final stage*, only manifest in stable markets over the long term.

Dwyer et al. (1987) also argued that there is a closing of the gap between the two parties to a relationship over time. Their model of relationship development features four phases during which the relative dependence of buyer and seller upon each other increases.

Awareness corresponds roughly to Ford's (1980) pre-relationship stage. Here the parties are looking around for potential partners but have not yet engaged in what could be construed as an interactive relationship. That is, they are essentially independently evaluating each other. The seller is communicating its strengths to the market more generally through advertisements or directly through targeted media. At the same time, the buyer may be gathering information about sources of supply or new product specifications.

Exploration corresponds roughly to Ford's (1980) early stage of relationship development. At this point some interaction between the parties takes place such that they start to learn about each other. There is still relatively little investment in the relationship and either party can walk away easily. However, already at this stage, what Dwyer et al. (1987) call the five enabling processes that underpin deepening relationship dependence are in action:

1. There is clear attraction in that both parties start to see the value to them of the relationship.

2. There is an increasing amount and breadth of communication and negotiation about how the relationship should unfold. This bargaining further deepens the communication at the same time as clarifying how the value in the relationship is to be shared.

3. The exploration of relative power dependence and the consequences of that for the relationship can start to be seen. The exercise of power by the stronger party can be just or unjust in the eyes of the counterpart, so the extent to which justice may prevail in the relationship is already being assessed. For the relationship to achieve greater deepening, power must be seen to be exercised justly.

4. As a consequence of the behaviours manifest through communication, bargaining and power and its exercise, it becomes possible to see norm development – a set of mutually agreed, accepted behaviours in the relationship.

5. All of the above give rise to development of expectations. These are the predictions of future behaviours in the relationship on the basis of what has gone before, up to the present. They are affected by the expectations companies bring into a relationship in the first place, but they also develop on the basis of how the parties see the relationship unfolding.

Expansion corresponds to what Ford (1980) calls the development stage. Here the rate and extent of dependence increase, with the parties doing more with each other and adapting what they do to enable themselves to work more closely and obtain greater benefits of the partnership. The underlying processes see more attraction, greater and wider communication, reasonable exercise of power and the development of norms that meet expectations and give rise to confidence in future expectations.

Commitment marks the point when the parties do not want an alternative partner and will happily commit resources to the continuation of a relationship, even to the point of withstanding problems that may arise in the relationship. They are prepared to make such commitments because there is a shared belief in the value of the relationship to them.

Value of the relationship life-cycle concept

Business-to-business relationship managers, such as key account managers, can assess the levels of relationship indicators over time in order to establish the extent to which the relationship has developed, and also to obtain some guidance on appropriate relationship interventions. For example, they can assess the amount and nature of the communication taking place in a relationship or gauge the level of commitment, or the degree and nature of adaptations. These indicators assist in making sound relationship decisions. For instance, where an assessment indicates levels of cultural distance that are presenting a barrier to relationship development across frontiers, alongside clear adaptations by a customer and thus a willingness for greater commitment, then the marketer can work with the customer to reduce the levels of cultural distance. Among other things in an international marketing context, this could be achieved through language study, social and cultural exchanges and workshops focused on hot topics that have specifically been seen to be sources of difficulties in mutual understanding.

Of course, there are managerial limitations to the life-cycle concept. While it describes the processes that close relationships have traversed over time, there are two major difficulties for relationship managers. First, they can never be sure the current relationship was ever destined to be a close relationship. Some relationships may develop in ways that look like they will endure, only to falter because the wider marketing environment has changed (for example, new potential partners have arrived, or competitive changes in the network more generally have rendered the relationship less significant). Some relationships may appear unpromising to begin with but develop well, either because of the conscious efforts of one party (often the marketer), or because of changes elsewhere in the business network or wider environment. Business is all about making judgement calls, and relationship managers are faced with just the same. They need to make the best call they can based upon the information they have and their own relationship objectives. Even where a relationship has been destined for greater closeness over time, since it is an idealized concept it is never clear exactly where a relationship is or should be on the life-cycle at any particular time. The measures of progress themselves are also not precise. They typically involve qualitative judgements (of level of commitment, for example, or degree of distance) rather than more objective measures.

Not knowing where you are on the life-cycle, when it is not clear where you are or even should be, may seem to make the concept of dubious managerial value. However, the value of the concept does not come from the ability to use it prescriptively. Its value is in the potential it has to inform strategic decision-making. On the basis of assessments of the relationship life-cycle position over time it becomes possible to know whether a relationship is heading towards a close and enduring future or whether it has reached its maximum potential already and so has a less close future. Knowing this enables relationship managers to make more informed relationship judgement calls. The request for capital investment to meet the demands of a customer that has manifested decreasing commitment over time can be evaluated from a more informed position. Equally, the opportunity (perhaps unsolicited by the customer) to improve a product formulation, a delivery arrangement or the payment terms for a customer (that has, say, shown a deepening commitment and preparedness to adapt to produce further value for both parties) can also be more clearly evaluated. Having now discussed the relationship manager as an abstract idea, we now turn to a managerial role that has direct responsibility for this important task, the key account manager.

KEY ACCOUNT MANAGEMENT

Key account management (KAM) involves identifying a company's most important business-to-business customers and offering them special treatment, with the goal of building trust and relationship capital in order to protect and grow long-term revenue and profits (Millman and Wilson, 1996). One of the key purposes of relationship portfolio management, discussed in the preceding sections of this chapter, is to identify customers that should be treated this way. Simply referred to as 'key accounts', these are customers of critical importance to the business which must, therefore, receive special treatment in order to maintain and develop the customer relationship. KAM has, since the 1990s, become an important topic in business-to-business marketing. There still remains some doubt about precisely what KAM means: some people argue that KAM is simply a management strategy to increase sales to selected customer accounts, but Spencer (1999) and Pardo (1999) have argued that it involves much more than this. Boles and colleagues (1999) raised several questions needing further investigation in the field – how firms decide which customers to deem key accounts, how resources are allocated to key accounts, and what the goals of a key account management programme are. In addition, Baddar Al-Husan and Brennan (2009) pointed out that although we know a substantial amount about KAM in developed economies, we still have a lot to learn about KAM in emerging economies. This is a matter of considerable concern since, as we noted in Chapter 1, emerging economies such as Brazil, China and India will represent a rapidly increasing share of global business over the next two decades.

This field can be confusing because terminology is rather fluid. Several different terms are used in the sales and marketing literature to refer to more or less the same concept – for example, national account management, strategic account management, national account marketing, major account management and key account management. Most experts agree that these are largely terminological differences that do not refer to underlying conceptual differences (Boles et al., 1999; Cardozo et al., 1987; Napolitano, 1997; Ojasalo, 2001; Weilbaker and Weeks, 1997). In this book we use 'key account management' as the general term.

Defining KAM and the KAM life-cycle

Millman and Wilson (1995: 9) defined KAM as a 'seller-initiated type of strategic alliance' identifying a key account as 'a customer in a business-to-business market identified by a selling company as of strategic importance'. The principal criterion to choose a key account is that the customer is considered by the seller to be of strategic importance. Strategic importance may go beyond the direct economic importance of the customer, including such factors as reference value and access to process or technological knowledge, or to new markets (Millman and Wilson, 1999). Because of their strategic importance, key accounts will often hold a power advantage over the supplier, and one of the jobs of the key account manager is to seek to reduce the instability associated with this power asymmetry (Millman and Wilson, 1999).

It is the key account manager's role as a facilitator and relationship developer that is particularly valued by customers. Millman and Wilson (1999) emphasized the importance of problem-solving in the role of the key account manager – he or she aims to focus the supplier organization on the resolution of customer problems, since this is expected to lead to the optimal long-term economic outcome for the supplier. Abratt and Kelly (2002) found that suppliers and customers both ranked the problem-solving ability of the key account manager as the most important success factor in a key account programme.

In highly collaborative buyer–seller relationships the pure selling function is supplanted by bilateral information sharing, joint planning and joint coordination of responsibilities and workflow (Lambe and Spekman, 1997). This has implications for organizational structure: key account managers must be able easily to talk to their own top managers. The degree of collaboration between buyers and sellers in key account relationships varies. The range of business-to-business marketing relationships can be split into five categories – spot market transactions, repeated transactions, long-term relationships, alliances and vertical integration – and key account relationships can occur in any of these except the first (spot market) and last (vertical integration). Genuine KAM relationships are characterized by very high-level buyer–seller collaboration, including joint planning, joint coordination, information sharing, avoidance of opportunism and long-term commitment; the purpose of the alliance is to work together to mutual advantage.

Both Millman and Wilson (1995) and Weilbaker and Weeks (1997) have argued that the emergence of key account management has followed a life-cycle model. Drawing inspiration from research into relationship life-cycles in business-to-business markets, Millman and Wilson (1995) proposed a six-stage model of key account relationship development:

1. Pre-KAM (identify key account candidates);

2. Early KAM (explore opportunities for closer collaboration);

3. Mid-KAM (develop a wider range of cross-boundary contacts);

4. Partnership KAM (supplier viewed as an external resource of the buyer);

5. Synergistic KAM (partners create joint value in the marketplace); and

6. Uncoupling KAM (dissolution of the KAM relationship).

Implementing KAM

There is some variation in the organization of the key account function: sometimes the key account managers are placed in the sales department, while in other firms the key account function is organizationally separated from the sales function. If key account managers are located in the sales department there is the risk that they will become simply 'super-salespeople', rather than strategic relationship managers; however, the separation of the key account function from the sales function runs the risk of poor coordination between the company's selling strategy and its strategy for key account customers.

Pardo (1999) has looked into this question; she argued that far from being a super-salesperson the role of the key account manager is to add a new dimension to how the customer is seen by people – *including the sales representative* – who work for the supplier. This conception of the key account manager is entirely as a relation-ship facilitator, and certainly not as a salesperson. The key account manager does not 'take over' the relationship, but becomes both the expert on what is happening between the supplier and customer organizations, and a privileged source of infor-mation. This role means that the key account manager has to work effectively within the supplier organization and in the external network surrounding the key account. The key account plan, a plan written separately for each key account customer to establish how the company will develop the business relationship, is central to the flow of information between key players within the firm (the internal actors' network) and key players outside (the external actors' network). It is also widely acknowledged that direct access of key account managers to the top management of their company is essential if key account relationships are genuinely to be managed strategically. Millman and Wilson (1999: 336) confirmed the importance of senior management commitment: 'Without total senior management involvement, the process is unlikely to succeed.'

KAM: benefits and risks

The effectiveness of KAM programmes has been an enduring topic of research interest (Abratt and Kelly, 2002; Colletti and Tubridy, 1987; Davies and Ryals, 2009; Millman and Wilson, 1996). While there is evidence that KAM can deliver performance gains (Homburg et al., 2002; Workman et al., 2003), there is also evidence that the implementation of KAM programmes is challenging and that the achievement of potential gains can be frustrated by implementation issues (Brehmer and Rehme, 2009; Piercy and Lane, 2006). Cardozo et al. (1987) reported that the benefits of national account management to suppliers were found in increased/retained market share, improved customer service and enhanced customer satisfaction. However, they also warned that a company should not focus its attention and resources on key accounts to the exclusion of the traditional sales role: it is necessary as well to develop and maintain profitable relationships with customers who are not key accounts. Foster and Cadogan (2000) showed that successful 'relationship selling' is correlated with increased trust, enhanced loyalty, enhanced purchase intentions and greater likelihood that the buyer will recommend the supplier to other firms.

Subsequently, Abratt and Kelly (2002) identified a number of factors important to key account programme success:

- knowledge and understanding of the key account customer's business;
- proper implementation and understanding of the key account programme;
- commitment to the key account programme (the key account manager has a key role in bringing about commitment);
- suitability of the key account manager (suppliers highlighted the key account manager's skills, ability and competence, while customers highlighted the importance of integrity, interpersonal skills and sensitivity to the customer);
- trust.

There are also risks associated with a KAM strategy. Cardozo et al. (1987) discussed the opportunity-loss risk, meaning the risk that, by concentrating scarce resources on a few key customers, other customers may receive less attention (and be attracted away by competitors) and customer prospecting may be neglected (leading to lower growth of the customer base). The risk of opportunism in key account relationships has also been raised (Lambe and Spekman, 1997): this is a risk that is created, in particular, where the seller invests more in relationship-specific assets than the buyer. Piercy and Lane (2006) elaborated on the risks of relying too heavily on a few large customers and the risk of opportunism, and, additionally, discussed the risk that KAM relationships could attract the attention of anti-trust regulators in certain markets. Sharma and Evanschitzky (2016) confirmed that there are both benefits and costs associated with KAM programmes. On the benefits side, Sharma and Evanschitzky (2016) found that relationships with a key account had significantly better chances of long-term survival than relationships with regular customers, so that there could be greater certainty about future business flows, and lower transaction costs, in doing business with key accounts. On the other hand, the profitability of key accounts appeared to decline over time; it seems that key accounts tend to become more demanding and to ask for more price reductions the longer the KAM relationship endures. Consequently, firms that implement KAM programmes should monitor the performance of their key account relationships carefully to keep an eye on the balance between the benefits and the costs.

CHAPTER SUMMARY

- This chapter has introduced an important task in strategic business-to-business marketing management, that of relationship portfolio analysis.

- The management of customer relationships as strategic assets requires an analysis of the differential value of each relationship in the customer base as a precursor to formulating differential strategies for the management of the relationships.

- This does not mean that all relationships are treated completely differently. Rather, a sensible collection of relationship types can be derived that are the basis of differential treatment.

- Differential treatment of customer relationships is not merely 'better' or 'worse'. By identifying the different types of relationships it becomes possible to specify a whole range of relationship strategies, some involving reducing distance while others may involve adding to it; some involving investments in new processes, products or other technology; and some involving merely demonstrating commitment through words, others through actions. The overall objective is to arrive at a notion of balance in the relationship portfolio, recognizing that it is not possible for all relationships to be close and the subject of substantial investment.

- To aid the analysis process a series of criteria were introduced that can help differentiate customer accounts from each other, from broad binary splits to the application, singly or in combination, of a series of variables. The variables range from those that are relatively easy to apply because they are financial in nature and use accounting data as their basis, to those that require judgement calls from the portfolio analysts on the basis of the wider knowledge they have of the future company strategy, relationship histories and the potential of those relationships.

- The dynamic nature of relationships and the continuing need for strategic realignment mean that portfolio analysis is not done on a once-and-for-all basis. Rather, it needs to be conducted regularly, typically yearly, and needs to accommodate the changing needs of the company and the changes in relationships over time. For that reason, relationship life-cycles have an impact on this process. In the chapter we describe the stages of relationship development and what these mean for relationship variables over time. Further, we indicate the value that the relationship life-cycle concept can bring in informing relationship decisions.

- The role of strategic key accounts as part of the relationship portfolio was given special consideration because of their relative importance to the firm. In addition to dealing with how to define a key account, the benefits that key account management can bring, and how to implement a key account strategy, we also point to the demands such a strategy makes and ultimately the risks inherent in following such a strategy.

QUESTIONS FOR DISCUSSION

1. Explain the process of portfolio management and its value.

2. Compare and contrast the use of financially derived criteria for portfolio analysis with those relying on the judgement of the analyst.

3. For a company that you know well, describe four criteria that you would use for analysing its portfolio of relationships.

4. Should all customers be key accounts?

CASE STUDY 9.1   RESELLER RELATIONSHIP PORTFOLIO MANAGEMENT AT O_2

O_2 is the customer brand name of one of the biggest mobile phone service providers in the UK (second only to EE). Originally a spin-off joint venture between BT and Cellnet in the UK, the company is now a wholly-owned subsidiary of the global telecoms giant Telefonica and goes under the name of Telefonica Europe plc. It has a presence in the UK, Ireland, Germany, Slovakia and the Czech Republic.

In a competitive marketplace like the UK, where there is an increasing number of mobile phone providers (those who sign customers up to a service rather than the company who owns the network) and where market growth has slowed from the heady days of the early 1990s (penetration levels are well above 100 per cent), acquiring customers becomes more difficult for providers. Churn rates that were sources of inconvenience to the providers in the 1990s have become much more pressing. This is doubly so when one calculates the costs of providing increasingly feature-laden smartphones, and yet this cannot guarantee that customers will stay beyond the contract tie-in period. Like the other operators, O_2 has put greater efforts into managing its relationships with end-customers in order to improve this situation.

The intention was to ensure that the relationship with the end-customer was embedded as early as possible and managed so that the customer felt no compulsion (or even motivation) to leave. It introduced customer relationship management programmes underpinning its commitment in this respect that attempted to integrate all the contacts that customers have with the service provider. This strategy ultimately proved effective with O_2 claiming the lowest levels of churn in the market by March 2009, and it has been helped by arrangements such as exclusive partnering with Apple Inc. for the initial iPhone release in the UK and Ireland. It is still managing to maintain contract churn rates of lower than 1 per cent and remains ahead of the sector.

Of course, like its competitors, O_2 does not always get to deal directly with its individual or corporate end-customers. In fact, its own direct retail channel accounted for little more than 50 per cent of its connections before 2006. The rest were recruited through independent sales channels and, while customers sign up to contracts with O_2, they often have strong personal relationships with the independent intermediary who recruited them. This strength of relationship may not seem so obvious when one considers only the big national retailers of mobile services in the UK (such as Carphone Warehouse or Phones 4u): they are highly visible to individual end-customers and while they may be natural sources for the general public to pick up a handset and a contract, the relationship may not be that strong. However, up until 2002 O_2 had about 30 direct independent sales intermediaries working for it, all with the rights of distributors, particularly in the corporate sales market. Some were large with wide geographic spread (for example, 20:20 Mobile in the business-to-business market), while others were small and local, providing phones and connections for business and private customers.

This variety made it difficult to ensure the consistent high-quality customer experience that was then starting to drive O_2 strategy. O_2 may have had little visibility to some end-customers because there may in fact have been two or more intermediaries in the channel between it and the end-customer. The strong relationship with an intermediary may also have meant that the account with the end-customer was more fragile; if an intermediary decided to switch to another service provider then O_2 would often lose the individual or corporate end-customers with them.

Unsurprisingly, the relationship thinking O_2 had been doing with its end-customers had also extended to management of its channels to market. A major issue for O_2 marketers has always been the relative efficacy of the different routes to market, and key to this is the management of the relationships it builds with channel members. The first efforts at managing its portfolio of channel customers were aimed at creating a channel that was more responsive to O_2's 'customer experience' strategy. Up to that point, O_2 had been happy to have any company undertake channel sales as long as they were financially sound and could get 250 connections per month. Delivering a new connection always got the intermediary an upfront connection bonus plus a flat 5 per cent share of the customer's bills. Of course, the connections could have been obtained by a company further down the channel, so involving little effort by the direct independent, and for some independents the upfront fee itself was often the only value they were interested in obtaining. It mattered little to them that a customer left at the earliest opportunity; they could always get signing-on fees from new customers.

O_2 was keen to create greater stability in the channel and to provide incentives for their independents to obtain their own connections, particularly connections that would endure. They took the view that if the independents were getting paid for acquiring phone customers then they should actually demonstrate the commitment to doing just that. So they changed the five different contract types they had with the 30 or so direct independents (often up to 300 pages in length) to one standard contract. They recognized that the previous 30-day contracts could perhaps have bred some of the instability so they changed the contracts to rolling 30-day contracts with a 12-month minimum duration. The requirement was now also for a minimum of 50 connections a month. This may seem small compared to 250 but it was still considered challenging for some (and it removed the impetus to obtain connections through onward sales via second- or third-level intermediaries). Those who were able to could, of course, go beyond 50 per month. They also moved from a flat 5 per cent fee to a tiered mechanism: there was no commission at all for the first six months, at which time the 5 per cent rate applied, rising to 10 per cent for contracts lasting over 24 months. The intention was to obtain lower churn rates and higher ARPU (average revenue per user). All the existing customers were moved over to the new contract terms. Those who wanted and were able to achieve the target of 250 connections per month had the opportunity to become proper 'distributors' with a different set of terms and conditions. Full distributors had to demonstrate that they had their own field sales team and clear channel management objectives.

With the established new arrangements for the direct independent channel, a new phase of channel development could then occur. Over the next couple of years the number of direct independents grew from 30 to 150 and the business grew accordingly, at the same time reducing the degree of exposure to any individual account. In portfolio management

(Continued)

(Continued)

terms, this brought its own set of problems. All were classed as 'direct independents' and all were subject to the same standard commercial contracts, all getting paid the same regardless of how much effort they were putting in and regardless of how much better they could perform. O_2 recognized that there were opportunities to support different independents differently, depending on their relationship value. A series of analyses (including financial measures, total connection numbers, churn rates, ARPU and customer lifetime value) were undertaken. This revealed substantial diversity among the direct independents. Some were delivering 1,500 connections per quarter, while others were only delivering 100 per quarter – yet their treatment was essentially the same. There had always been some marketing funds that O_2 used to help some customers with communications activities (for example, mailshots), and those delivering the most connections typically tendered for and obtained these, but this was about the limit of the differential treatment.

A new O_2 Advance programme aimed to deal differently with those that performed demonstrably better. For those who could provide lower churn rates and higher ARPU, O_2 was prepared to share customer data, guarantee a share of marketing funds and provide a dedicated contact (rather than the usual helpline), with increased access to these extras over time. For some, additional resources for further business development could also be available. Membership of the scheme required that the independent continued to meet targets (though one lapse over a two-quarter period is allowed). The terms of the contracts were also changing to become more relational.

Additionally, O_2 has been very active in discussing difficulties in meeting targets for the accounts. It has been envisaged that the group of direct independents can be further split into a relatively small number of big accounts (though still doing less business than the full distributors), with a greater proportion of smaller accounts. For the smallest accounts the level of O_2 support will increasingly be provided by technology, through automated telephone systems. Some might even be encouraged to move their accounts to the distributors rather than dealing directly with O_2.

When it comes to making decisions about where to invest efforts, account managers at O_2 are now having those discussions with their sales directors armed with greater in-depth knowledge of particular accounts because they have been involved in investigating what has been happening with the customers. The account managers will know the history and will have been finding out from the customer what exactly has been happening in their business, and will know when it can grow further and what it requires as input from O_2. By the same token they will also know more intimately when further investment in an account will not generate greater returns and will thus be able to make better resource allocation decisions. Overall, they will have the right level of knowledge of a variety of different accounts so that they can achieve the balance of connection and revenue targets that are best for O_2.

CASE STUDY QUESTIONS

1 What variables would you use to analyse O_2's independent sales channels?
2 What relationship clusters would you identify and how would you manage each to achieve a balanced portfolio for O_2?
3 How could the life-cycle concept be used effectively by O_2 in its portfolio management?

Sources: the assistance of Brian Latham at O_2 in the preparation of this case study is gratefully acknowledged. See also www.telefonica.com and www.O2.com.

FURTHER READING

Baddar Al-Husan, F. and Brennan, R. (2009) 'Key account management in an emerging economy: a case study approach', *Journal of Business & Industrial Marketing*, 24 (8): 611–20.

This article contains a strong summary of the literature on key account management, including the important issue of key account management in developing countries.

Ford, D. (1980) 'The development of buyer–seller relationships in industrial markets', *European Journal of Marketing*, 14 (5/6): 339–54.

This seminal article provides a strong introduction to the concept of relationship life-cycles and the stages through which relationships evolve.

Zolkiewski, J. and Turnbull, P. (2002) 'Do relationship portfolios and networks provide the key to successful relationship management?', *Journal of Business and Industrial Marketing*, 17 (7): 575–97.

This article provides a very insightful use of the concept of relationship portfolios, and incorporates good summaries of the contributions of other portfolio thinkers.

PART IV

MANAGING MARKETING PROCESSES

10

MANAGING PRODUCT OFFERINGS

LEARNING OUTCOMES

After reading this chapter you will:

- know what the concept of a product offering means;
- be able to apply portfolio planning techniques to decisions about offering investment, development or divestment of products;
- be able to apply life-cycle and portfolio approaches to the management of product offerings;
- understand how innovation can be managed in the business-to-business context to ensure enduring success in creating offerings for customers; and
- be familiar with the process and activities associated with the development of new offerings.

INTRODUCTION

The success of a company's marketing only materializes at the point where a customer is prepared to buy its products and services. As Chapters 2 and 3 indicated, it is the problem-solving abilities of the marketer that constitute a source of value to customers. Therefore, the problem-solving abilities of the supplier are very important. It does not really matter how well the marketer has undertaken all the tasks up to this point; if the firm cannot create an offering that satisfactorily meets customer needs then everything else is pointless. If the marketer wants to continue to meet customer needs then the offering must adapt to changing needs. Clearly this is a dynamic process. It implies that there is a development cycle for product offerings, from conception through to deletion, and that they are not just made once and for all but need constant reappraisal. It implies a need to adjust to changes in market circumstances, such as competitive action, over and above changing customer needs. This chapter considers just what needs to be done throughout this dynamic process. We start by examining the offering concept, its nature and extent. We then look at the offering management tasks that face the business marketer: making the right interventions throughout the life of an individual offering and managing each individual offering as part of a balanced portfolio. Subsequently, we focus on the process by which offerings can be conceived and brought to market in the first place. The long-term health of the firm depends on how successful it is at bringing new products to market and managing

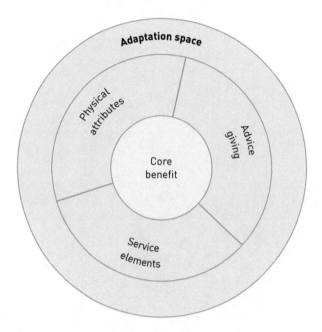

FIGURE 10.1 Elements of business-to-business offering

them throughout their life, so we focus on creating the environment within which innovation can be managed successfully as well as the process for developing new offerings themselves.

BUSINESS-TO-BUSINESS PRODUCT OFFERINGS

It may seem pedantic, but it is always more precise to use the term 'product offering' rather than the more generic word 'product'. It is for this reason that this chapter talks of 'managing product offerings' rather than the more usual 'product management'. This is because the word 'product' is more often considered as something relatively physical, which you can point to and/or handle. Consequently, 'product' may only capture a part of an overall offering, namely its *physical attributes* (see Figure 10.1). In many cases there is certainly a physical aspect to the offering that is transferred to a customer. That is the case, for instance, when the customer is buying MRO supplies, raw materials or components. It is, after all, these physical goods that are used, consumed or transformed by the customer's own value-adding activities. It is also very easy to talk about these products in terms of their physicality. They have a size, shape, material composition and other particular physical properties, including performance levels (for example, tensile strength). In cases like this the *physical attributes* are of the utmost importance in creating the *core benefit* that all offerings have to provide to be of value. Without the ability to deliver the fundamental customer benefit, the offering will never be considered as a viable choice. This core benefit may or may not arise largely out of its physical attributes. Certainly, as the case study in Chapter 1 demonstrates, Rolls-Royce's customers are paying for a lot more than the physical characteristics of an aero-engine. In fact, they are obtaining a hybrid offering that combines physical goods with a service element. These *service elements* have a massive role in creating the value of the offering for Rolls-Royce customers, and these elements also need to be considered as an intrinsic part of the product offering. Adding forms of service innovation to physical products appears to have a positive impact on a supplier's profitability (Mathieu, 2001; Wise and Baumgartner, 1999), though Eggert et al. (2011) have shown that increased profitability depends upon the type of service innovation and the level of product innovation that the supplier already engages in. When a supplier already engages in substantial amounts of physical product innovation, service innovation to support that activity is best addressed at supporting the physical products themselves to ensure that they function fully and properly (through, for instance, equipment inspection, maintenance and repair, spare part delivery, providing a hotline). On the other hand, when the supplier does not engage in much physical product innovation, the service innovation activity is best aimed at supporting the activities of the customer more broadly. This could be through forms of business consultancy for the customer, or research and development activity, but could extend to operating processes on the customer's behalf.

Many developed economies generate most of their wealth not from tangible product manufacturing but from intangible services, which are increasingly information intensive (see Chapter 1 for a discussion of the structure of developed economies). In a service and information economy, much of the value of the offering may be highly intangible even though the results of the delivery of the offering are tangible. For example, the UK water companies that make use of the engineering skills of a company like Black and Veatch will obtain a design document and drawings for an asset such as a waste-water pumping station, and ultimately the station itself. However, the service that they want most is the design abilities of the engineers, including their speed of design and their ability to respond flexibly to customer requirements. It is this service performance that leads to the physical artefacts; but separating out the tangible and the intangible aspects of the offering is often difficult.

At a time when many manufacturing companies are recognizing the value of hybrid offerings (that is, physical goods and service aspects rolled together to create additional value), Ulaga and Reinartz (2011) have established the supplier resources and capabilities that are critical in the competitive context to being able to create such offerings. The following resources are key:

1. product usage and process data from the company's installed base of physical goods that enable its offerings to be more differentiated;

2. product development and manufacturing assets that can be used differentially to introduce innovations that can reduce a customer's cost of ownership;

3. an experienced product sales force and distribution network whose understanding of the strengths and capabilities of the products they are selling is such they are able to gain privileged access to customers and build strong links with key contacts, typically in purchasing and technical positions;

4. a field service organization that is focused on more than just delivery and installation, but is strong at after-sales service and can spot opportunities for pursuing new and more complex hybrid offerings with customers.

A set of capabilities can be used in combination with these resources in the deployment of hybrid offerings:

1. Service-related data processing and interpretation capability. This is the supplier's capacity to analyse and interpret the installed base product usage and process data so that customers can be helped to achieve productivity gains and/or cost-reductions.

2. Execution risk assessment and mitigation capability. This is the supplier's capacity to use the product and process usage data to assess the uncertainty of whether agreed outcomes will be met and put in place mechanisms to handle it.

3. Design-to-service capability. This is the supplier's capacity to use its product development and manufacturing assets to come up with integrated tangible and intangible elements that are meaningful and likely to be attractive to customers such that they generate new income and/or reduce costs.

4. Hybrid offering sales capability. This is the supplier's capacity to use its product sales force and distribution network effectively to reach key customer staff and work with both parties to sell hybrid offerings, which often demand approaches that are different to purely physical product sales and may even require forms of co-creation activity with customers.

5. Hybrid offering deployment capability. This is the supplier's capacity to use its product development and manufacturing assets alongside its field service organization to successfully deploy hybrid offerings, trading off the need to provide the offering in the way that the customer needs with the internal requirement to do these things efficiently through forms of standardization.

For some offerings where the physical product itself is highly substitutable, because all competitors can achieve much the same standard, the sole basis for differential advantage may be the additional elements of the service. A construction material like float glass is largely a commodity and is readily available from a range of global suppliers (for example, Asahi of Japan, Pilkington of the UK, Saint-Gobain of France, and Guardian of the USA). While price will undoubtedly play a strong role for highly substitutable products, Pilkington works hard to differentiate itself by providing a range of services to customers over and above the glass itself, including applications advice and market forecasts. A regional sales representative may even pass on possible sales leads to customers. This sort of *advice-giving* constitutes another relevant element of the design of offerings (Ford et al., 2006). Those companies that recognize the nature of the uncertainties that a customer faces (see Chapter 3), and are able to help to provide solutions to those uncertainties, put themselves in a stronger position competitively, and these solutions can draw from any or all of the elements of the offering.

Product offering management is not a once-and-for-all activity. Both customers and marketers improve their abilities over time, even with respect to individual offerings. A supplier may be able to introduce materials changes in a component that has economic benefits to itself without compromising performance for the customer, for example. Changes in downstream customer needs may mean that a customer is happy to reduce the performance demands made of a supplier and obtain economic benefits in doing so. Further, if the parties work together they may be able to simplify production processes or product formulations that provide additional economic value to both. These examples typically concern reductions in offering complexity and hence cost reductions. It is equally possible to engage in changes that add extra cost but that are seen as economically valuable to either or both parties over the longer haul because of improved performance. Consequently, it is possible to talk about an *adaptation space* that surrounds an offering, and the sorts of changes just described are facilitated within that space. In conceiving of new offerings, a marketer may have some understanding of what is possible with the offering. However, the full extent of what is really possible can only become known through interaction with the customer. Indeed, lots of potential adaptations may become evident. The degree to which the marketer or customer is prepared to engage in any adaptive behaviour with respect to the offering will be a function of how they feel about the relationship with the counterpart. Ford et al. (2006) argue that an adaptation in relationship terms is really only worth the name when it involves doing something in a relationship that is not intended to be replicated for all customers. The example cited in Chapter 3 of the plastic blow-mould bottling company that introduced an additional line to cater for all sizes of bottles required by its major customer can clearly be seen in these terms; it involved a capital investment on the company's part to add the extra line. We concur with this view in terms of the consequences of adaptation for relationships between buyer and seller. However, from an offering management perspective, it serves to demonstrate the value of considering what is sometimes called the 'potential product offering', even from inception.

STRATEGIC TOOLS FOR MANAGING PRODUCT OFFERINGS

Two of the most useful strategic management tools that can aid the business marketer when making decisions about market offerings have been introduced in Chapter 9 in our coverage of relationship management. These are the life-cycle tool and portfolio analysis. In the following discussion we will consider their application to offering management in more detail. They can be applied at different levels of abstraction when it comes to offering management. A company may have several product ranges, and several different technologies or technology platforms may be manifested in the product mix – see B2B Snapshot 10.1 for an illustration.

B2B SNAPSHOT 10.1   MULTIPLE TECHNOLOGIES AND MULTIPLE PRODUCTS AT NATIONAL GUMMI

For over 70 years, National Gummi AB of Sweden has been producing a range of extruded, moulded and punched rubber and plastic products for use as seals and dampeners in a range of sectors, including the automotive industry, construction, and shipping. Its brochure captures very simply what it does as a capability, without limiting the specific products or sector within which those products could be used: 'WE SEAL, DAMP, INSULATE & PROTECT'. It can make these different products using solid rubber, cellular rubber, cellular plastics with open cells, or cellular plastics with closed cells. All these technologies have different properties in terms of the hardness of the product that is produced, its tensile strength, its weight and the working temperature at which it should be used. Decisions about the range of technologies it needs to offer,

(Continued)

MANAGING PRODUCT OFFERINGS USING THE LIFE-CYCLE CONCEPT

The principle that different strategies are appropriate at different life-cycle stages was introduced in the last chapter when discussing relationships. The use of the concept, however, originates in the management of product offerings, where it has been most often described. The classic idealized model of a product life-cycle (Figure 10.2) depicts a series of stages through which products notionally proceed during their life. Recognition of the life-cycle stages and the different management needs at those various stages prepares managers to act in ways that are most appropriate for the product at any point in time. As Figure 10.2 shows, a life-cycle is typically described as four major stages, with those stages occurring once a product is released to the market.

From a managerial perspective, of course, there is substantial activity before launch in development and in preparation for launch (the *pre-launch* stage), which we have chosen to include in our diagram. In business markets, the time from product concept to market launch may be substantial, even when working directly with a customer that has a particular product need in mind. In one example, a UK manufacturing company

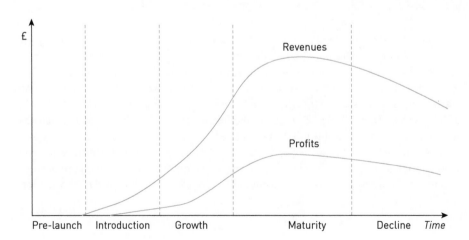

FIGURE 10.2 Stages in the life-cycle of an offering

was commissioned to make an office chair for a large office furniture maker. After several iterations of product concept testing, and then value engineering activities to ensure it could be made at an acceptable price point, almost two years had elapsed before the chair was even ready to enter the customer's catalogue. Two years, of course, seems a short time when one considers the amount of time required for the design and manufacture of a new aircraft such as the Airbus A380 (see B2B Snapshot 10.2).

B2B SNAPSHOT 10.2   A380 QUEEN OF THE SKIES?

The research and development costs of a new offering, along with costs of bringing it to market such as production costs (possibly involving new processes and equipment or additional tooling), are all incurred prior to launch, of course, with the intention that they will be recouped by the product after its introduction. While making a commitment in principle to the much-heralded A380, Airbus needed the assurance of advance orders for the aircraft to confirm that it was worth the investment. It set a viability threshold of 50 aircraft and a break-even point of 270 units, although a little more than 18 months after the reveal ceremony in Toulouse on 18 January 2005, that figure was revised to 420 airframes.

There can, of course, be major differences between planned schedules and operational reality. Wiring-layout problems and difficulties in integrating designs (produced using two different variants of the CAD software) beset the production such that it fell about two years behind schedule. Despite a planned delivery of the first aircraft to Singapore Airlines in late spring 2006, the first plane was delivered about 18 months later on 15 October 2007. Further problems with wing cracks and the need to repair them added more delays and additional MRO costs.

By August 2016, Airbus had total cumulative orders for 319 aircraft, at a 2016 list price of about $433 million each, with 194 having been delivered and in service. Emirates accounts for a large part of Airbus' order book (over 200) and with other customer orders being relatively small in comparison, it remains to be seen whether the company will ultimately recoup the development cost. Certainly, production delays and resulting cancellations, notably by carriers FedEx and UPS in 2006 and 2007 respectively for freighter versions of the aircraft put a hole in Airbus' order book in the early days. And this has not really changed. There is no freight version of the aircraft despite initial estimates that there was a potential demand of up to 400 aircraft. In the commercial sector, Airbus has been praised by airline operators and customers for raising the bar in terms of passenger comfort and service reliability targets are now being met. Nevertheless, a slow order book in the last couple of years puts into question the medium term program for this aircraft – particularly bearing in mind that the original business case for the aircraft was predicated on sales of 750 aircraft over 20 years and a development budget of around $15m (which had increased to $25m come 2005). Operator reluctance to place further significant orders is partly due to uncertainty over what Airbus has in mind for the future of the A380 (evolving to the A380neo and A380-900 for example) as well as debate surrounding smaller alternatives to such aircraft. Nevertheless, alongside continued improvements to the existing A380 such as changes to the internal configuration to enhance operational efficiency of the aircraft, Airbus has recognized changing market need and responded with the smaller but more efficient and environmentally-friendly A350, a strong example of how network capabilities can be pulled together to drive technological innovation (see B2B Snapshot 10.4).

Introduction stage

No value is made from a product offering until it is brought to market. It is only at this point that any contribution to the development costs can be generated. However, during the introductory phase it may still be costing more money than it is bringing in, since there is a series of marketing tasks to be carried out. Up to and beyond the launch of the new offering, customers need to be made aware of it, so there will be a series of communications activities: public demonstrations, exhibitions, trade shows or other publicity. If it is a completely new concept to the market, there may be a need to generate primary demand for this type of offering. There may be trial offers with existing key customers, particularly if they are important reference customers. In addition, field sales time is likely to be invested in communicating its value (advice-giving), and the sales force must be trained in the product and shown how to demonstrate its benefits to customers. Where indirect channels are being used, distribution channels must be secured. These activities are likely to continue until sales start to rise, indicating a degree of market acceptance. By this time early problems with the offering can also be identified and resolved, and even more specific examples of the product in use will have been obtained that can enhance sales training.

Growth stage

As the offering is increasingly accepted by the market (assuming it is), and sales and profits begin to increase more rapidly than before, the nature of the demands on the business marketer change. Competition is likely to increase, with consequent pressure on prices, and this pressure creates greater demand and thus fuels further growth. For particularly innovative market offerings, competition is most likely to be from copycat products, tapping into the same primary demand but from a lower cost base (without the costs of development in creating the primary demand in the first place). Defending market share through attempts to differentiate may be successful in achieving secondary demand. This may involve incurring additional costs in expanding production, increasing the product line, adding product extensions or securing additional distribution. It may involve adding some additional service elements or working with some specific key customers to consider how adaptations to the product might benefit both parties. In all cases the business marketer will want to ride the growth wave as long as possible and achieve the best margins possible.

Maturity stage

Ultimately, the rate of sales growth slows. Profits may continue to rise in the aftermath of the growth phase. To maintain the profit trend requires cost reductions. They can be achieved by cutting the amount of sales force time spent on pioneering activities such as determining new applications for the product. A shift from more personal forms of marketing to forms of telemarketing may also reduce costs. This may be combined usefully with a promotion focus on trade customers rather than end-customers, with the aim of maintaining availability levels, and it could accompany price-based promotional activities aimed at increasing the loyalty of heavy users. These are exactly the sort of activities that a company such as Lafarge in the construction industry undertakes in order to continue securing availability for its plasterboard through important builders' merchants while at the same time negotiating favourable deals with large developers such as national house builders. Where the offering needs maintenance and repair it is important to have sufficient capacity for this, and if spare parts are needed then there should be good availability. Reductions in other cost sources may also be worthy of consideration, such as logistics/transportation.

Decline stage

The efforts at maintaining price levels and reducing the cost base that have been initiated in a mature market will work for a limited time (unless a product can find a completely new primary demand source). Profit margins will decline and the business marketer must look for ways to extract further value. Even where the degree of competition has declined so that there is less direct price competition, the drop in the level of demand means that sustaining levels of profitability typically requires cost reductions. Marketing expenses should be at a minimum. In terms of relationship portfolio management (see Chapter 9) the business marketer should drop unprofitable customers and channels. There should be no further development of the offering. Where specific profitable customers continue to use the offering and where strategic value exists for the marketer, then there may be a case for adaptations with this customer. These may be in respect of the product attributes or the service elements. Such adaptation comes at a cost, though, and the customer needs to bear it, unless the adaptation opens up new market or technology possibilities for the marketer so that new offerings or markets become obtainable.

CRITICISMS OF THE LIFE-CYCLE APPROACH

The life-cycle concept has not gone without criticism. As an idealized pattern for the development of an offering, it is certainly possible that an offering may not necessarily correspond to the life-cycle shape depicted in Figure 10.2. In fact, through the latter stages much marketing endeavour is committed to ensuring that the profile does not follow the idealized shape. In an ideal world the marketer would see demand for an offering just grow and grow and there would be no real need for defensive strategies. Such cases are truly exceptional, and thus marketers must have a strong view about what marketing actions are appropriate at any point in the life-cycle. However, the life-cycle concept is criticized in respect of this latter point as well. The life-cycle alone does not provide a day-by-day prescription for how to manage an offering. It can be difficult for a marketer to be clear about exactly where the offering is in its life-cycle. However, this is perhaps to misunderstand the purpose of the life-cycle concept. It is at its most valuable when it is seen as a conceptual tool for strategic management rather than as a tactical or operational prescription.

MANAGING OFFERINGS USING PORTFOLIO ANALYSIS

In Chapter 9 the principles and practice of portfolio management were introduced, specifically in the context of managing a portfolio of customer relationships. Just as the portfolio approach was seen to be useful for analysing a set of customer relationships, so it can be useful for analysing a set of market offerings. There is an enduring need to consider all sources of potential value in order to determine which specific marketing responses are required. At a given time some product offerings will require money to be invested in them to help unlock further value. Some may be generating good returns as they stand and may require little additional marketing intervention. Meanwhile, some may not be producing good returns and may show little potential for future profitability; the firm will want to consider cutting back investment in these offerings and perhaps deleting some.

Two well-established frameworks for analysing product portfolios are the Boston Consulting Group (BCG) market share/growth matrix and the General Electric (GE) market attractiveness/strength matrix. The former, also known as the Boston Box, uses two measurement scales to position offerings on a 2 × 2 matrix. These are *relative market share* and *relative market growth* respectively (Figure 10.3). The GE framework, often used to position strategic business units within a multi-divisional business, acknowledges that market share and market growth on their own are not necessarily sufficient to give a clear indication of relative performance. Consequently, two composite dimensions are used:

Market attractiveness: This includes variables such as size of the market, its growth rate, competitive structure, market diversity and the impact of market environmental factors (socio-cultural, political, legal, technological). It gives a firm indication of the relative possibilities in the various market segments where its offerings may be present.

Business strength: This includes variables such as the firm's relative share of the market and its growth rate, along with profitability and the quality of the specific resources it can bring to the market, such as company image and human and technological resources. It provides a clear idea of how well the firm is doing in the market.

The Boston Box is clearly easier to use and for many product offerings is sufficient to provide the firm with good intelligence from which to undertake marketing decision-making. The decisions taken are a function of the relative position of offerings within the framework. Relative market share is calculated as a proportion of the market share held by the market leader, and is often presented on a logarithmic scale. Market growth is expressed as an annual percentage rate.

Those offerings that have a relatively low share in a fast-growing market, labelled *question marks* (see Figure 10.3), pose particular difficulties for the marketer. New offerings typically start in this position (a new and growing market presenting a strong marketing opportunity in the first place) and so inevitably take time to establish themselves and to achieve profitability (as the life-cycle concept indicated). Supporting these offerings in the early stages of the life-cycle is necessary and this would be seen as a reasonable investment. However, if the development of an offering positioned in this quadrant of the matrix fails to head to the left (increased relative share) and preferably upwards (as part of a growing market) over time, then it may be that the offering is not as successful as was expected at launch. At this point decisions need to be taken about whether to continue with the offering at all, or whether to reposition it.

A product offering that has followed a path downwards and to the right will invariably end up in the bottom right quadrant of the Boston Box. Such products are termed *dogs*. They may have been successful products at one time, or may just have been question marks that quite quickly failed to achieve their potential. Either way, there is little point in committing additional resources to dogs; they are candidates for deletion, unless a value-creating strategy can be devised.

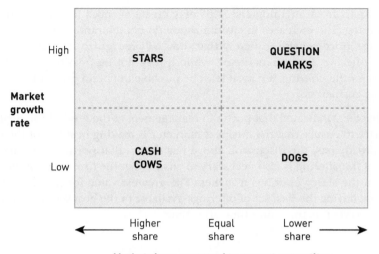

FIGURE 10.3 Boston Consulting Group market share/market growth matrix

When an offering has captured the largest share of the market, it has clearly arrived in the left-hand side of the box (see Figure 10.3). An offering that has managed to become market leader in a growing market is clearly successful and will generate positive cash flows. However, these *stars* also need money invested in them to maintain or enhance their position. They are likely to be at the growth stage of the life-cycle and, while awareness amongst customers may already be strong, there may also be new market segments to develop.

When growth in a market starts to slow, the market is getting to its most competitive stage; there are few new customers to reach. Companies competing in a market of this kind are typically competing against each other for a share of relatively static customer demand. This demand may be quite stable and so a firm with high market share, achieving economies of scale and with no further product development requirement, is likely to be generating substantial positive cash flows. This can be used to sustain the development of new offerings or question marks that have recently just been brought to market. At the same time, these *cash cows* will make the greatest contribution to company profits. Of course, as the growth slows even more and the market starts to contract, profit margins will decline. This requires vigilance, since market leaders are the natural target for competitive action, and losing share in a contracting market will diminish the cash generation from cash cows. While efforts need to be made to protect share, and these are likely to be price based, the choice of price reductions or additional costs needs to be taken with a clear view as to their impact on specific customer relationships within the wider customer portfolio. As Chapter 9 indicates, it may be necessary to accept margin erosion with some customers on the basis of their relative value within the portfolio of relationships, but the same principle may not apply to all. Even in a contracting market some customization of the offering may be possible for some customers, perhaps through service elements or advice giving, or through forms of adaptation, which reduce the level of price competitiveness by creating relationships where the level of substitutability is reduced. Apart from anything else, this may create avenues for further innovation in the offering. The increases in customization do not guarantee that customers will become less price sensitive, merely that they will recognize the value that comes from this offering. For the marketer, while it may not be possible to obtain price premiums for the offering, it may at least be possible to obtain greater levels of share from these customers.

While Chapter 9 indicated that portfolio management at the level of the relationship is necessary to ensure that the business marketer is making best use of the relationships it already has, the discussion above has shown that portfolio management at the level of the offering is also necessary to ensure that the firm is obtaining the best value from the set of offerings it makes. The greatest value for the firm ultimately comes from having the best set of offerings available to the best set of customers and being able to do this time after time after time.

MANAGING INNOVATION IN THE BUSINESS-TO-BUSINESS CONTEXT

Relevance of innovation management

It is perhaps a cliché that companies need to keep adapting in order to keep ahead of the competition. More than that, in the extreme circumstances of global economic recession as witnessed in recent years, adaptive innovation became a necessity for survival. This consideration of business activities is crucial to what we understand by innovation and its management. It is not just new product development (which is, of course, very important as an aspect of innovation, and is thus considered separately in greater detail below), but concerns '... *all the activities involved in the process of idea generation, technology development, manufacturing and marketing of a new (or improved) product or manufacturing process or equipment'* (Trott, 2012: 15, italics in original). Products themselves are innovation outputs, arising from having the right processes and structures in place. And, of course, these things do not really happen by accident. Even the serendipitous discovery of the non-sticky adhesive technology in the Post-it Note was not entirely accidental, since it relied on 3M's existing pedigree in materials and product development, organizational structures that allowed individuals the space to experiment, and the necessary commercial exploitation abilities to make it highly successful. As the 3M example shows, the source of value for businesses may not necessarily be the end product itself. Rather, a firm's value-creating potential may stem from any of a number of areas: its production innovations, its process innovations, its marketing innovations and its organizational or management innovations. So, for example, Black & Decker's technological innovations in small electrical motors created the basis for a core competency that was not easily copied, while Pilkington's float glass manufacturing process innovation established a whole new way of creating high-quality sheet glass for the industry.

When it comes to managing innovation to create advantage, the key questions for the business-to-business marketer centre both on how the firm should be organized to encourage innovation and on the role that relationships with external partners have in aiding the process.

ORGANIZING FOR INNOVATION

Trott (2012) argues that 'innovation is invariably a team game' (p. 11). Rather than relying on the lone researcher coming up with the next big thing, companies typically need to create an environment where creative individuals can operate within an inter-organizational context that harnesses their creativity and which provides an architecture and set of links externally that enable them to recognize market needs and opportunities such that their efforts can gain some traction in use.

To create the right environment, Trott (2012) argues that the innovative firm requires the following characteristics:

- commitment to long-term growth rather than short-term profit;
- a general acceptance within the firm of the value of innovation;
- ability to be aware of its threats and opportunities;
- willingness to invest in the long-term development of technology;
- willingness to include risky opportunities within a balanced portfolio of activities;
- mutual respect amongst individuals and a willingness to work together across functions;
- ability both to become aware of and take effective advantage of externally developed technology;
- ability both to manage the tension between the need for stability within the firm and the need for creativity, and to provide room for creativity;
- readiness to accept change; and
- combination of suitable specialization as well as diversity of knowledge and skills.

Using the dichotomy proposed by Burns and Stalker (1961), these sorts of characteristics are more likely to emerge when companies adopt more 'organic' rather than 'mechanistic' organizational structures. Organic structures tend to be more decentralized, with less formal and hierarchical control, and thus are more flexible and adaptable. Mechanistic structures tend to emphasize stricter task differentiation and specialization, with more centralized and hierarchical control.

ROLE OF BUSINESS-TO-BUSINESS RELATIONSHIPS IN INNOVATION MANAGEMENT

The basic premise of this book is that value in business-to-business markets results from the relationships companies have with their customers and others. This means that the innovation team game also extends beyond the single firm to the supply network, customer base or other agencies (such as universities or government bodies). The external linkages should make the firm aware of opportunities and threats as well as the essential characteristic of knowing about and making use of external technology to bring the relationship context into innovation management very directly. Suppliers and customers can be sources of ideas as well as capability that when harnessed with a company's own expertise can create the basis of substantial innovation. As Cox et al. (2002) indicate, the ability of a company like Marks & Spencer to coordinate its latent customer demand for ready meals along with its suppliers' ability to meet that demand without excess waste (despite the short shelf life) proved critical in establishing a key development in food retailing in the UK in the 1980s, which was quickly copied by the sector. The pioneering coordination of process innovations needed to accompany these chilled ready meal developments (typically using electronic data interchange technology), had a similarly revolutionary impact on the food distribution sector, leading to the emergence of regional distribution centres and growth in the number of specialist independent food distributors working with the large grocery retailers.

This raises the question of how to encourage the external linkages to add value to the innovation processes of the firm. There are several aspects to consider:

- *Type of innovation project and degree of innovativeness required.* Bonner and Walker (2004) found that the type of innovative activity should affect which customers to involve and how much involvement to solicit. When looking to incrementally innovate, for example extending or enhancing an existing product, the use of embedded, homogeneous large customers seems to be the way to greater advantage. However, for completely innovative endeavours the choice of new, largely heterogeneous customers seems to be preferable because the use of such a varied group brings a diversity of experiences, perspectives and competencies.

- *Degree of knowledge sharing.* Inter-organizational knowledge sharing is positively associated with supplier contribution to development outcomes, which, in turn, improves buyer product development performance and, ultimately, financial performance (Lawson et al., 2009).

- *Formality of the mechanisms for knowledge sharing.* Lawson et al. (2009) also reveal that informal mechanisms such as communication guidelines or social events play an important role in facilitating knowledge sharing between firms. While formal mechanisms (e.g. cross-functional teams, matrix reporting structures) also influence knowledge sharing they are seen to do so indirectly through informal mechanisms.

The business-to-business marketer must of course avoid the trap of just seeing the customer as a recipient of product-based solutions (a product-centric view that's largely about customizing and integrating goods and services as currently conceived). Tuli et al (2007) argue for a change that recognizes the relational processes through which customers expect to receive solutions to their needs (from requirements definition, through customization and integration, to deployment, and on to post-deployment support). Tuli et al. (2007) maintain that a focus on the product-centric view risks missing the customer perspective to a large extent and as a consequence misses the full extent of the possible customer solution. Take a look at B2B Snapshot 10.3 to learn how technology business Honeywell is rethinking its approach to product innovation.

B2B SNAPSHOT 10.3   HONEYWELL USER EXPERIENCE: HUE OF A DIFFERENT COLOUR

Honeywell is a $40bn technology business whose mission is to make the world cleaner and more sustainable, more secure, connected, energy efficient and productive. You might not necessarily be that familiar with the company, but the chances are that you will have benefited (even if indirectly) from their products, which range from intelligent airplane cockpits to connected thermostats to safety products. In 2012, Honeywell announced its ambition to become the 'Apple of the industrial sector' by offering high fit and finish products which are intuitively easy to use, install, and repair. The company recognized that it was not always easy to work with and that many of its products, while highly engineered and competitive, were somewhat dated in design. Furthermore, the company was hearing business customers question why websites for industrial suppliers such as Honeywell were unable to match the ease of use of consumer sites such as Amazon or Apple.

To this end the company introduced the Honeywell User Experience (HUE), a key process initiative that involves a human-centred design perspective and is intended to help Honeywell best understand the needs of customers, installers, maintenance operatives, channel partners and employees. HUE is driven mainly by the company's Experience Design Group, which has studios in various major cities around the world including Austin, Minneapolis, Shanghai and Sydney and is responsible for making each Honeywell product as beautiful and functional as possible by taking colour, shape and ergonomics into account.

The Honeywell User Experience is guided by touchpoint analysis in which each detail of a product's pathway to market is examined, including end-user experiences, as well as the process for upgrading or replacing a product. The design, sales and marketing teams also analyse market trends, and draw from observational research and discussions with customers to understand how users interact with Honeywell products as well as the features that they would like or prefer not to have. Using techniques which have been common practice for consumer branded companies for some time, Honeywell discovered traditional hard hats (part of its safety products division) are designed for Euro-American head sizes. So the company introduced a modified version for the Chinese market. And when it comes to product installation, Honeywell redesigned the product and packaging of its industrial fire-sensing systems which meant that the installation of these complicated sensors could be completed by one rather than two people – thus cutting service costs in half.

HUE is important to channel partners, particularly those such as ADT or Lowe who deal in end-consumer markets and whose competitors stock similar products. Honeywell's design improvements are proving critical to reseller sales and customer loyalty while the introduction of end-user dashboards is providing Honeywell and its partners with insight into product performance across systems and locations.

Source: Hosford (2015).

Looking more specifically at services and one of the few empirical studies to adopt a truly dyadic approach to understanding how offering value can be co-created in knowledge intensive business-to-business relationships (those involving application of the specialist knowledge of a supplier to the benefit of a customer, such as IT services, R&D services, technical consultancy, and legal, financial and management consultancy), Aarikka-Stenroos and Jaakkola (2012) provide a framework that captures how value co-creation occurs through a dyadic problem-solving process (see Figure 10.4). Their joint problem-solving framework features the following activities: (a) diagnosing needs; (b) designing and producing solutions; (c) implementing the solution; (d) organizing

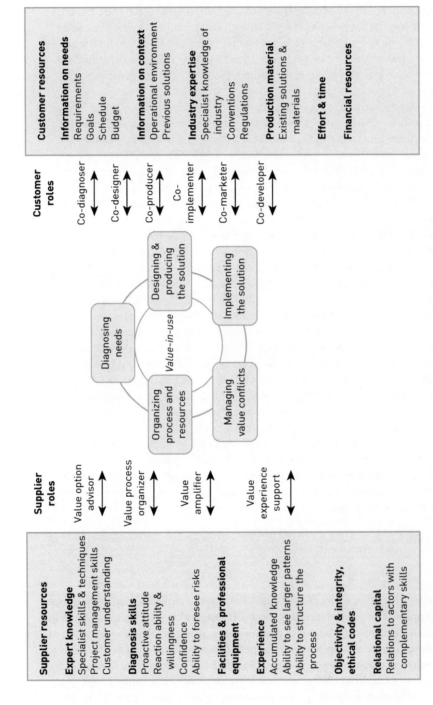

FIGURE 10.4 Joint problem solving as value co-creation in knowledge intensive services (Aarikka-Stenroos and Jaakkola (2012), Figure 3, p. 22)

With permission from Elsevier.

the process and resources; (e) managing value conflicts. The first three are typically task-focused, related directly to the technical or other aspects of the supplier and customer contributions to problem-solving. The last two are more about managing the interactive process itself. Supplier and customer bring their respective resources to the co-creation and along the way play a variety of different but complementary roles. The supplier may be: value option advisor, value experience supporter, value amplifier, value process organizer. The customer may be: co-diagnoser; co-designer; co-developer; co-marketer; co-implementer; co-producer.

The value of the framework managerially is that recognizing the activities, resources, and roles means that both customer and supplier can become attuned to dealing with the process and have a greater ability to determine the critical resources needed at any point in time and a clearer understanding of the respective roles to be played and therefore greater clarity about how the role can be played most appropriately. It also highlights the need to deal with the process aspects effectively and particularly to recognize that value conflicts are almost inevitable; the key to successful joint problem-solving is to find ways of managing the conflict. Aarikka-Stenroos and Jaakkola (2012) urge customers and suppliers to view the conflicts as opportunities for each side to recheck their assumptions and expectations and to adopt frank discussions throughout the process as the basis for establishing whether relative objectives are being met.

NEW PRODUCT OFFERING DEVELOPMENT

While the earlier sections of this chapter considered the management of offerings once they get to market, the firm also needs to develop successful new offerings. Indeed, global surveys by McKinsey consistently point to new product or service creation as the primary focus for companies over the immediate 1–3 year time horizon, with 33 per cent of the 2,927 executive respondents in 2012 indicating that this remains a priority for them (McKinsey, 2012). As we established in Chapter 9, portfolio management is intended specifically to ensure that a continued balance of investments exists over the longer term. New offerings need to be added to the portfolio as existing offerings go into decline. These new offerings will begin the cycle once more as question marks but the firm will hope that they in turn will become the stars and cash cows of the future.

NEW PRODUCT OFFERINGS: AN UNAVOIDABLE RISK

This takes us directly to new product offering development, generally considered to be a risky undertaking. Research indicates that most new product offerings fail with estimates of the percentage of all new products and services realizing a return ranging from 10 per cent (Clancy and Krieg, 2003) to 67 per cent (Schilling and Hill, 1998). With such variable figures, company reluctance to get involved in new offering development is perhaps understandable. However, ultimately they have no choice. Failure to engage in forms of new offering development leads inexorably to a portfolio that over time will come under greater pressure and ultimately produce less value for the firm. Even the mightiest of firms recognize this need and it is certainly critical to pharmaceuticals and biotechnology companies. Take a look at B2B Scenario 10.1 to get a sense of the development challenges facing the pharma giant Astra-Zeneca.

B2B SCENARIO 10.1   THE PHARMA CHALLENGE

Astra-Zeneca is one of the top ten global biopharmaceuticals businesses, investing $5.6bn (equivalent to 25 per cent of its turnover) in R&D activities in 2015. Drugs developed by the company are used by millions of patients around the world. Getting treatments to end-users involves not only considerable resource investment from both Astra-Zeneca and its collaborators, but also necessitates approval and financial support from health governing bodies in different countries.

One area targeted by pharmaceutical companies, research institutions and health authorities alike is the treatment of cancer. Between 2011–16, 70 new cancer medicines entered the market and with global spending on treatments predicted to reach $150bn by 2020, the number of people worldwide living beyond a cancer diagnosis is expected to reach almost 19 million by 2024. This is clearly an important research area and there are more than 500 companies engaged in final-stage research and development, including Astra-Zeneca. One if its recent projects is the introduction of the drug *olparib* (known under the brand name Lynparza) which can be used as part of treatment for ovarian cancer. Initially developed by the Cambridge-based oncology research company KuDos in the late 1990s, the project was taken over by Astra-Zeneca when the pharmaceuticals giant bought KuDos in 2005.

By 2014 Astra-Zeneca had secured Federal Drug Agency (FDA) approval in the US for the branded version, Lynparza, and recommendations for approval from the European Medical Agency (EMA), with public health bodies across Europe (other than England and Wales) subsequently reviewing and giving all patients access to the drug. Alongside this approval success, Astra-Zeneca continues with related developments, entering into partnership with Foundation Medicine (a molecular information company) to develop diagnostic procedures intended to enable physicians to identify those patients most likely to benefit from the drug, *olparib*.

The sticking point for Astra-Zeneca, however, has been in England and Wales, where until December 2015, NICE (National Institute for Health and Care Excellence) had refused to approve *olparib*. The decision in late 2015 now allows treatment for women who have already undergone three or more rounds of chemotherapy. But this success comes at a considerable price for Astra-Zeneca, who have agreed to heavily subsidize the use of the drug across England and Wales, including reducing the sales price to the NHS and covering the medication costs of those women who remain on the drug for more than 15 months.

Such a situation presents Astra-Zeneca with considerable dilemmas. Firstly there is the question of whether the company should subsidize the NHS when in other countries this is not necessary – does it make sense to do this. And more broadly, like other biopharmaceutical businesses, if NICE's reluctance to approve new drugs continues, might the firm consider relocating R&D activities to places that appreciate innovations more. Which is some irony given the UK's reputation as a leader in the discovery and development of groundbreaking medicines.

Often, the proportion of sales revenue spent on R&D is a good indicator of the level of new product activity. Table 10.1 shows that sectors such as pharmaceuticals, software and technology continue to attract most R&D spend. In fact, even during periods of global recession, these sectors continue to attract research investment. Bowonder and Yadav (1999) showed that US firms dominated spending in the major categories of industry, with particular dominance in sectors such as software.

Table 10.2 shows that it remains largely true in 2015, with US firms occupying 11 of the top 25 accounting for 38.2 per cent of world R&D investment in 2014, with Japan second in the rankings but quite a way behind at 14.3 per cent (2014 EU IRI Scorecard). Published indices such as the EU IRI Scoreboard are useful benchmarks managerially. Individual companies can compare their own spend with the standard for their sector or with respect to key competitors to see the extent to which their own spend exceeds or fails to meet the sector trends.

The risk in offering development is compounded by the costs of development that often accompany it in the first place. The large development costs in some sectors for completely new product offerings make this point very clearly. For example, we saw in B2B Snapshot 10.2 that the cost of bringing the Airbus A380 to market went well beyond calculations used in the initial business case for its development. And Boeing had pretty much the same experience with their wide-bodied jet, Dreamliner, which cost $32bn (instead of the estimated $6bn) by the time it took to the skies in 2011. As B2B Snapshot 10.4 shows, Airbus was even more reluctant to take on the development costs of the A350, although the potential for it to drive substantial sales through the innovations of members of the Airbus consortium ultimately set those concerns aside. Drug development is another area that demands considerable investment and as we saw in B2B scenario 10.1 this is hardly surprising given the

TABLE 10.1 Median R&D spending as a proportion of sales in 2014 for Top 15 business sectors, with the median figure for all companies in the dataset for comparison (distilled from 'The 2015 EU Industrial R&D Investment Scoreboard'; European Commission 2015, iri.jrc.ec.europa.eu)

	Business Sector	Median R&D spend as % of sales
1	Software and Computer Services	16.9%
2	Technology Hardware and Equipment	11.6%
3	Pharmaceuticals and Biotechnology	11.3%
4	Financial Services	7.7%
5	Media	7.7%
6	Health Care Equipment and Services	7.6%
7	Real Estate Investment and Services	6.9%
8	Mobile Telecommunications	6.4%
9	Travel and Leisure	6.4%
10	Leisure Goods	5.9%
11	Electronic and Electrical Equipment	5.1%
12	Aerospace and Defence	4.9%
13	Equity Investment Instruments	4.4%
14	Support Services	4.2%
	Average:	3.7%

TABLE 10.2 Major R&D spenders in 2014 (distilled from 'The 2015 EU Industrial R&D Investment Scoreboard'; European Commission 2015, iri.jrc.ec.europa.eu)

Rank	Company	Country	Industry	R&D spend (€m)	Sales (€m)	R&D as % sales
1	GOOGLE	US	Software and computer services	8 098	54 362	14,9
2	MICROSOFT	US	Software and Computer Services	9 922	77 078	12,9
3	JOHNSON & JOHNSON	US	Pharmaceuticals and Biotechnology	6 996	61 223	11,4
4	SAMSUNG	South Korea	Electronic and Electrical Equipment	12 187	154 501	7,9
5	VOLKSWAGEN	Germany	Automobiles and Parts	13 120	202 458	6,5
6	SIEMENS	Germany	Electronic and Electrical Equipment	4 377	71 920	6,1
7	AIRBUS	The Netherlands	Aerospace and Defence	3 616	60 713	6,0
8	PANASONIC	Japan	Leisure Goods	3 122	52 673	5,9
9	BMW	Germany	Automobiles and Parts	4 566	80 401	5,7
10	IBM	US	Software and Computer Services	4 336	76 429	5,7
11	SONY	Japan	Leisure Goods	3 170	56 093	5,7
12	HONDA	Japan	Automobiles and Parts	4 577	90 996	5,0
13	FORD	US	Automobiles and Parts	5 683	118 670	4,8
14	GENERAL MOTORS	US	Automobiles and Parts	6 095	128 432	4,7
15	NISSAN	Japan	Automobiles and Parts	3 456	77 663	4,4
16	DAIMLER	Germany	Automobiles and Parts	5 650	129 872	4,4
17	PEUGEOT	France	Automobiles and Parts	2 260	53 607	4,2
18	UNITED TECHNOLOGIES	US	Aerospace and Defence	2 170	53 620	4,0
19	FIAT CHRYSLER	The Netherlands	Automobiles and Parts	3 665	96 090	3,8
20	TOYOTA	Japan	Automobiles and Parts	6 858	185 940	3,7
21	HITACHI	Japan	Electronic and Electrical Equipment	2 286	66 737	3,4
22	APPLE	US	Technology Hardware and Equipment	4 976	150 560	3,3
23	HEWLETT-PACKARD	US	Technology Hardware and Equipment	2 839	91 800	3,1
24	BOEING	US	Aerospace and Defence	2 272	74 757	3,0
25	GENERAL ELECTRIC	US	General Industrials	3 487	122 386	2,8

time and procedures necessary to get new medicines to the commercialization stage. In fact DiMasi et al. (2003) estimated drug development costs to be in the region of $802 million for each successful new product. Adams and Brantner (2006) put the figure at between $839 million and $868 million, though more recent estimates have increased that substantially; Adams and Brantner (2010) arrived at a figure in excess of the $1 billion mark, though the costs are different for different therapeutic areas, while the Office for Health Economics in the UK estimate that the cost at 2011 prices was above $1.5 billion (Mestre-Ferrandiz et al., 2012).

These examples are obviously at the extreme end of the scale of development costs. Many smaller business-to-business companies will not face such high costs, though in comparison to their size the commitment may seem just as great, because typically they will face a capital investment cost. For example, the concept of a new offering may well need changes in production processes and material or distribution arrangements to make it a reality. Caddie (see Case study 10.1) could come up with lots of shapes, sizes and configurations of shopping trolley. However, to produce a new shape, size and configuration requires that a series of production processes change, including the creation of new jigs. To justify the commitment of costs for a new offering the company will want to be sure that there will be sufficient demand to obtain a return that easily covers the development cost and makes an acceptable contribution to profits.

Given these costs and risks it is inevitable that many companies choose to develop incrementally, in the sense that they just add new variants to existing product lines, or add sufficient changes to create a wider range of product lines. This seems to be a lower-risk approach because there is at least a clear indication that the marketplace already accepts the product concept. It may also deliver incremental sales. However, the risk is that the portfolio of offerings becomes ever more complex and difficult to manage. The potential for economies of scale may diminish. For companies producing manufactured goods it also increases the number of set-ups required (with associated retooling and swapping of product jigs) and thus reduces operating efficiencies; less time is spent adding value in production compared with getting ready to add value. Such a situation would perhaps be acceptable if individual customers were prepared to pay the large premiums required to make this situation economically valuable (if not efficient). In practice, few are.

B2B SNAPSHOT 10.4   AIRBUS A350: TAKING AIRCRAFT CO-CREATION TO NEW HEIGHTS

The A350 had been described as the 'aircraft that Airbus did not want to build' (BBC, 2013a). Originally proposed in 2004 as a direct competitor to Boeing's 787 Dreamliner, Airbus was already enmeshed in a large-scale development of the A380, itself seen as a natural competitor, and heir apparent, to the aging fleet of Boeing 747s that were coming to the end of their useful service lives. As the B2B Snapshot 10.2 indicates, the A380 project has been beset by a series of problems that have occupied Airbus management for over ten years.

However, the Dreamliner attracted a lot of customer attention, particularly in respect of the lightweight carbon composite materials used in its manufacture and its more advanced aerodynamic capabilities. This sector of the market also looked as if it was set for the greatest amount of growth. Initial Airbus proposals, based merely upon upgrading its existing A330 craft to add better fuel efficiency to compete with the Dreamliner, were not well received by prospective customers. So Airbus went back to the drawing board and with the help of its supply base came up with a new aircraft design that it felt would not just keep pace with the Dreamliner, but would surpass it in the drive for fuel efficiency. As with the Dreamliner, carbon composite materials featured heavily in the revised A350 design. However, as the following partial list indicates, Airbus and its suppliers pushed

(Continued)

(Continued)

the materials technology, aeronautics and power envelopes further to produce a craft that uses 25 per cent less fuel than older craft and with less noise and lower emissions:

- GKN Aerospace created a new purpose built production facility in the UK to make the rear wing spars for the A350. The spars are the backbone on which the wings are made. The $300 million facility uses advanced automated tape laying technology to lay about half a million metres of carbon fibre tape to make each spar, has extra long ovens to 'cook' them, and advanced robotics to finish them.

- Spirit AeroSystems opened a 500,000 square foot manufacturing facility in North Carolina to design and manufacture the carbon composite centre fuselage section and front wing spar for the A350.

- Using advanced materials, coatings, engine architecture, and cooling technologies, Rolls-Royce designed and built a completely new engine for the A350 that is 15 per cent lighter. It uses blades made of hollowed titanium and the diameter of the set of blades is 299 cm, making it the largest the company has ever built. The 50:1 compression ratio is also the highest Rolls-Royce has ever achieved, large enough to suck in enough air to fill a squash court every second and then squeeze it to the size of a fridge-freezer (BBC, 2013b), ensuring a burn temperature that's higher than Roll-Royce has ever achieved before. With these features the fuel burn for the weight of the engine and the airframe generates a 25 per cent saving.

- Messier-Dowty, which makes the main landing gear for the 800 and 900 variants of the new craft, also introduced new materials technology to reduce weight ratios, including the use of titanium for structural strength alongside stainless steels. Both materials provide greater corrosion resistance and reduce service on costs.

- Honeywell devised a new integrated test bed for mechanical and environmental control systems on the A350 so that for the first time ever it was able to test the auxiliary power unit and all the air generation and conditioning systems together and as a consequence reduce the weight of the systems and lower the power demands by 10 per cent.

The new A350 certainly looks like it has the Wow factor with customers; by the end of August 2016 orders for 810 craft had been received from 44 customers. Although 35 units have been delivered since Qatar took receipt of the first A350, Airbus's own problems with the A380 and Boeing's with the Dreamliner served as a salutary warning to Airbus. It was more cautious in the development of the A350, choosing for example not to rush development in order to feature at the 2013 Paris Air Show (though its maiden flight occurred the week before to ensure that it was at least the ghost at the feast) and it also avoided specifying the exact date of delivery of the first craft to Qatar Airways, other than to indicate that it was going to be before the end of 2014.

Given the difficulties that both Boeing and Airbus have experienced in the last decade or so in producing their new craft designs, there was recognition of the need to do things differently with the A350 particularly as 70 per cent of the production work is outsourced. Didier Evrard, who runs the A350 programme, reportedly indicated that Airbus had worked in an entirely different way with its partners based on greater trust (Economist.com, 2013). And as Boeing's experience with in service Dreamliner craft goes to show, such trust is critical when it comes to resolving issues with airline customers: from overheating lithium ion batteries in 2013, to cracks in turbine blades on aircraft fitted with Rolls-Royce Trent 1000 engines in 2016.

NEW PRODUCT OFFERING DEVELOPMENT PROCESS

Because of the inherent risk, much research has been conducted into the new offering development process, and over the years substantial efforts have been made to enhance the process in order to reduce this risk. Typically, efforts have gone into establishing a clear development process whereby consideration can be given to the issues that are important at each stage of the process. By managing the process well and taking appropriate decisions at each stage, the risk becomes manageable. There are a variety of different stage models of the new offering development process. For example, Crawford and DiBenedetto (2003) proposed five phases: opportunity identification, concept generation, concept evaluation, development, and launch. Gross et al. (1993) proposed seven steps to the process: idea generation, screening, business analysis, concept development, prototype development, test marketing, and commercialization. Dwyer and Tanner (2002) likewise proposed a seven-stage process, albeit slightly different to Gross et al. (1993): idea generation, screening and preliminary investigation, specifying features, product development, beta-testing, launch, and evaluation. While similar to other stage models, we propose that the business marketer consider eight different elements of the process (see Figure 10.5).

FIGURE 10.5 The new offering development process. Reprinted with permission from Pearson Education Limited. Trott, P. (2005) *Innovation Management and New Product Development* (3rd edn). Harlow: FT/Prentice-Hall.

Identifying opportunities/generating ideas

New offering development is a creative process. It requires the seeds of creation and these seeds are ideas, the more of them the better. The more ideas that can be generated the greater the prospect of finding one or more that will lead to a successful new product offering. They can come from many sources: for example, through talking to end-customers, distributors and suppliers; by examining what competitors are doing; and by allowing staff to make suggestions. They can come out of the blue or they can be solicited. They might be solicited in particular areas (for example, identifying opportunities that a particular target market would welcome, or ideas for extensions to an existing product line).

Regardless of where they come from, there is a need to establish a repository of ideas and to establish someone as the keeper. That person might readily be charged with promoting the generation of new ideas in the firm more generally. They could do this in a variety of ways. For example, they could actually organize workshops that bring people together to brainstorm ideas. The workshop participants might be lead users within customer companies feeding ideas of 'what I'd really like is …'. Or they might be cross-departmental staff groupings providing ideas on how elements of an offering could change or how its production could change and reduce costs.

Screening ideas and making preliminary investigations

Having a strong stream of ideas is a good starting point. The more ideas that can be generated the lower the cost per idea produced. Beyond this, the effectiveness of a company in spotting good and bad ideas comes into play. The earlier it can discard ideas that have no real potential, the better. For this reason there is value in having a screening process for each idea that establishes it very quickly as good or bad. There are some criteria that are fundamental and that can be applied first:

- company's ability to make the offering;
- the fit with company production capabilities or technical expertise;
- the fit with company objectives and image;
- the market sales and profit potential; and
- the fit with current offerings and distribution channels.

By getting managers' assessments of these, using rating systems such as five-point scales (with scores ranging from +2 to −2, with 0 as the midpoint) it becomes possible to arrive at aggregate scores and a ranking for each idea.

This initial screening will remove the weakest ideas from further scrutiny in the most efficient way. The remaining ideas can then be subjected to further screening. This incorporates preliminary investigations of how customers will react to the offering and how competitors will respond. As far as customer reactions are concerned the focus will be on which particular segments will be interested and what it is about the offering concept that will be attractive to them. Again, on the basis of rating managers' evaluations, it becomes possible to discard further ideas.

Analysing the business case

Analysing the business case takes the screening process further. However, rather than looking specifically for the fastest route to discard the weakest ideas, which was the previous focus, the emphasis shifts to trying to establish which ideas have the greatest business potential. The business analysis needs to involve careful financial estimates of the market size, growth rate and potential for each product offering idea. This data may be available from secondary data sources. As well as trying to determine market potential, the business case needs to establish what the development costs are likely to be for each new idea offering before it can be brought to market. These costs may include the nature of the capital investment needed, the staff costs, and the break-even level and payback period, along with the rate of return on the investment. When each new offering proposal can be seen in these financial terms it becomes possible to compare them as prospective projects.

Developing the concept and specifying the features

During the preliminary investigations the offering concept starts to become better developed. The closer identification of the likely targets and their reactions to the offering starts to allow for the features to be specified. This knowledge can be used with the small number of proposed offerings that have emerged with a sound business case in order to start specifying them. It then becomes possible to state what the concept is and the benefits it brings to customers, as well as how the offering will be used. A likely price can be estimated. Concept boards or drawings may be used to communicate all this information, and may also be employed to solicit the continuing support of management on the one hand as well as to convey the concept to suppliers where there are specific implications for the sourcing of materials or components for the offering.

Developing prototypes and developing marketing support

Having arrived at a clear concept statement for the new offering and having received a positive response, the offering can be prototyped. A prototype is a facsimile of the final offering that enables evaluation of form, design, performance and material composition. The intention is to develop a series of working prototypes that can be successively fine-tuned towards the final offering. The fine-tuning may involve slight performance enhancements or layout changes that progressively improve the offering. At the same time as the prototyping is moving towards the final offering, the marketing support activities for the offering need to commence. These activities are likely to revolve around packaging and labelling designs, pricing and distribution strategy, and the promotional plans that will see the offering up to and beyond commercial launch.

Undertaking limited-scale trial marketing

At some point the successive refinements of the offering will lead to fewer and fewer changes; it is at this point that the offering is ready to be used by customers. It is only through use by customers that the value in use of the offering can really be established (see B2B Snapshot 10.4). However, it is generally best to identify any remaining adjustments and the cost of production that might be entailed before full-scale launch. Where feasible, test marketing in a small market area will also be beneficial in obtaining feedback on the whole offering, including the marketing activities that accompany it (such as communications materials, marketing approach and prices). Of course, this kind of approach makes less sense where the size of the market segment for the offering is estimated to be small.

Taking the offering to commercial launch

On the basis of a successful trial, final changes can be made to the offering and the strategy for bringing it to market. The launch itself could be planned as a big bang. However, depending on the size of the company, the nature of the offering and its innovativeness, and the readiness of the market itself, it may be more sensible to roll the offering out sequentially, often on a geographical basis. Smaller companies are likely to need to do this anyway because of the resources required for a big launch. If the product is novel then customer education may be needed concerning the offering's function, the benefits it brings and how it can be used. If there is an ongoing service need associated with the product then the support personnel need to be trained.

Evaluating the offering development process and drawing lessons for the next time

While not strictly an element of the offering development process itself, it is good practice each time an offering is launched to reflect upon the process, the sound-ness of decisions and the effectiveness of implementation. The intention is to learn lessons that can be used for subsequent products. What matters is to establish if the next offerings need to proceed through all the stages of the process in the same way. The criteria that determine when the offering is ready to be moved on through the stages can be fine-tuned. In some cases steps in the process might be missed out for future development processes. For example, for extensions to earlier offerings where the market is familiar with the technology and the use of the product offering, it may be that trial marketing is unnecessary. By following a strong new product offering development process, the prospect of a good series of new offerings adding value to the offering portfolio is increased. By managing each of these in ways that are appropriate to their stage in development and in respect of the value they bring to the portfolio overall, the firm is in the strongest position to solve customer problems as effectively as it can and thus to grow and bring value to its shareholders.

CHAPTER SUMMARY

- This chapter has focused upon the activities that business marketers need to undertake in the management of offerings to business customers. It has described the elements of the product offering, arguing that it is often more than just a physical good.

- We saw that the product offering incorporates service and advice components that often enable an otherwise standardized product to become a more customized offering.

- We then turned our attention to the major product offering management tasks that face business marketers: ensuring that the right marketing interventions are made with offerings throughout their life-cycle so that they add the greatest value they can to the firm, and ensuring that the portfolio of product investments that the firm has made are managed to ensure balance and thus greater value over the longer term.

- Recognizing that offerings do not just materialize from thin air, we then argued for the necessity to build innovation into the organization systemically. Successful product offerings require an organizational environment that prioritizes innovation, a culture that underpins this, and structures and processes to make it happen.

- Finally, having considered the environment within which innovation can occur, we focused in particular on one of the riskiest activities for business marketers, specifically, the task of bringing the next generation of product offerings to market so that they too can add to the portfolio over time. During consideration of new offering development we described a well-established process for ensuring that the inevitable risk involved in the task of bringing offerings to market is as low as possible.

QUESTIONS FOR DISCUSSION

1. What are the elements of a product offering and why do we need to identify them?

2. Describe the product offering life-cycle stages for an industrial offering with which you are familiar, and indicate how you would have managed the offering through the stages.

3. Choosing a mature business offering, indicate how you propose to manage it to avoid decline.

4. What is the value of a portfolio analysis approach such as the Boston Box?

5. What characteristics facilitate innovation within an organization?

CASE STUDY 10.1   TROLLEY'S UP FOR CADDIE

The business brand 'Caddie' has existed for some time, yet it represents one of many companies that most people have never heard of, despite the fact that products sold under the 'Caddie' brand are supplied to airport, healthcare, hospitality, logistics and retail customers. The Caddie brand is owned by the French firm 'Les Ateliers Réunis' S.A.S., who has its head office and main production facility at Drusenheim, France. Founded in 1928, the company first used its wire processing skills to supply the poultry industry. Its core expertise is still based on steel wire, but this has been extended to the manipulation of and combination with other materials, such as plastics, to create for example carts, roll cages and trolleys which can be used to move and store, amongst other things, retail merchandise (not chickens!). Though you might not recognize the name, the 'Caddie' brand is registered in over 70 countries and the company uses a network of 130 agents to target potential customers around the world. Major retail clients include Aldi, Carrefour and Weldom and if you happen to fly via Paris Charles de Gaulle or Orly airports then you will likely push one of the trolleys that the company designed and built. And further afield, as you make your way through Cairo airport, you will find yourself offloading your case from the luggage belt onto one of Caddie's trolleys in the arrivals lounge.

Caddie's retail interests extended beyond trolleys into retail shelving and displays, into technology for moving merchandise around. Looking at trolleys themselves, they may seem quite simple but they are important in the retail experience; try carrying

(Continued)

(Continued)

more than six items in your arms and you see the need. The facilitating role can be particularly acute at an airport; after the car park, the trolley may be the first real contact that a traveller has with the airport and it is certainly what brings them from the outside world right into the heart of the airport experience. The facilitating role at its most functional, of course, is embodied in those work-horses of retail replenishment, the roll cage. The alternative to transporting upwards of 500 kg of merchandise is many trips to and from the stock room– not a recipe for retail efficiency.

Caddie's range of products for storing and transporting items serve different needs, according to sector. For example,

- retail
  - ○ shopping trolleys with different sizes, shapes, capacities, castors, child seating configurations and stacking space requirements;
  - ○ garden and DIY trolleys, with different shapes, basket or tray configurations and load capacities;
  - ○ shopping baskets with different materials, sizes, weights and capacities;
  - ○ roll cages with different finishes, chassis bases, numbers of sides and stacking space requirements;
- *airport*
  - ○ airport luggage trolleys with different sizes, shapes, weights, stacking space requirements and customer purposes;
- *hospitality*
  - ○ hotel reception, housekeeping and room service trolleys with different sizes, shapes and stacking or storage space as well as, in the case of the latter, the capacity to keep items cool or warm;
- hospitals
  - ○ units to transport sterile materials/equipment, to evacuate medical waste, to handle staff and patient linen.

When it comes to retail, a perennial issue for Caddie is where to take its merchandise handling technology next. When you are selling to the big names in retail, where do you go if you are interested in growing the business further – particularly if the technology itself is well established? Of course, it is always possible to look for additional markets – for example, secure material handling for governmental organizations, residential uses such as recycling, or extend hospitality activities beyond land-based hotels to cruises (as has done Wanzl, one of Caddie's competitors). It is also possible to do more for existing customers, for example by offering a full 'cradle-to-the-grave' solution for all trolley needs, that is, a full-service contract, selling use by the hour or leasing by the day. And this is increasingly what Caddie's major clients are expecting. For example, airports are adopting a systems approach to purchasing trolleys – just selling trolleys to them is not enough. As a consequence, trolley companies need to ensure they have the supply partners and alliances with the right systems technology firms to create a total offering that satisfies their airport customers' requirements completely.

While this is a mature technology it is possible to find additional innovations to the existing technology itself that will meet the needs of business-to-business customers, delivering even greater value from trolleys, as well as providing a functionality that continues to meet the needs of end-users. There are specific areas which have seen innovation in recent years. For example, Caddie introduced a design which replaces the normal trolley 'cage' with a rack from which shoppers can hang their shopping bags. Combining this with self-scanning systems removes the need to transfer items for instore trolleys to shopping bags at the checkout. Trolley security has been improved with the introduction of 'smartwheels' which block automatically once a trolley reaches the perimeter of a specified area. And when you think about the number of pairs of hands that get hold of trolleys and storage equipment, then hygiene can be important. The introduction of wrap-around handles made of anti-bacterial plastic and the embedding of silver ions in the handle material inhibits the spread of germs and bacteria for the lifetime of the equipment.

In addition to such functional improvements, advertising also presents innovation opportunities, particularly when combined with airwave and display technology, the possibilities for income from renting advertising space could be very attractive to retailers – the equivalent of the Formula 1 trolley! Beyond its physical characteristics, developments to integrate the checkout and trolley continue and maybe one day soon the combined use of intelligent shelving and trolleys connected to a shopper's store account or bank card will eliminate the need for checkouts and queuing completely. As you take the product from the shelf into the trolley it self-scans and upon exit automatically charges the goods to your card.

As far as roll cages are concerned, the design has changed little in 30 years. Often companies will also buy exactly the same trolley for all logistics needs. However, a company like Carrefour has a variety of store formats, each with slightly different needs for the product. Recognizing the different segment needs and meeting the more diverse needs more precisely also present opportunities.

The potential for all these adaptations raises the question of the limit to standardization and the extent to which it is sensible to do different things for special customers. Establishing those customers that warrant special attention could become the cornerstone of offering management for Caddie. Of course, the payback for such investment may not necessarily be cash right now. Rather, some customers may be sources of adaptations to offerings that could ultimately lead to changes in the technology that spawn a whole new generation of market-leading offerings.

CASE STUDY QUESTIONS

1 Describe how the life-cycle concept might apply to shopping trolleys, and discuss the extent to which the life-cycle for roll cages is the same as for shopping trolleys.

2 On the basis of your view of the life-cycle stages of (a) airport trolleys and (b) roll cages, describe the marketing activities you would undertake, assuming strong market share in both product markets.

3 Generate some ideas for new product development that extend the existing technology platform for trolleys (you could refer to www.caddie.com or even its competitor www.wanzl.com to help broaden your knowledge of this technology).

(Continued)

(Continued)

4   Generate some ideas for novel new product developments that might appeal to end-customers and retailers (again, you could refer to www.caddie.com to broaden your knowledge of this technology).

5   On the basis of screening in a group, take one of the ideas generated in (3) and (4) and develop it further, establishing end-customer acceptance for the concept.

FURTHER READING

Ford, N., Trott, P., Simms, C. and Hartmann, D. (2014) 'Case analysis of innovation in the packaging industry using the cyclic innovation model', *International Journal of Innovation Management*, 18, 5.

In this chapter we present product development as a linear process, more to introduce you to the different activities involved rather than to suggest that these are in fact sequential. This article provides an alternative, cyclical perspective of innovation activities which is increasingly used to understand product development. Furthermore, the article illustrates how innovation is just as important in low technology industries such as packaging as it is in sectors like aerospace and pharmaceuticals.

La Rocca, A. and Snehota, I. (2014) 'Relating in business networks: Innovation in practice', *Industrial Marketing Management*, 43 (3): 441–7.

This article allows you to look in more depth at the importance of relationships in the development and commercialization of innovation. The role of relationships is a key theme in this chapter, just as it is elsewhere in the book. Besides showing how relationships are critical for knowledge development and the commercialization of new technology, the illustration of innovation failure featured in the article offers insight into some of the reasons for the relatively low level of innovation success that we allude to in this chapter.

Steiner, M., Eggert, A., Ulaga, W. and Backhaus, K. (2016) 'Do customised service packages impede value capture in industrial markets?', *Journal of the Academy of Marketing Science*, 44: 151–65.

Capturing the value of industrial services is a growing concern for companies operating in business markets, particularly for traditional manufacturing-based organizations who might create customized service packages to overcome difficult price negotiations. This article reports that customers can be unwilling to pay for service elements integrated into the overall product offer, whereas if kept separate and provided the business marketer can document and communicate value to customer, then supplier profitability can be enhanced.

11

ROUTES TO MARKET

LEARNING OUTCOMES

After reading this chapter you will:

- know about the interface between supply chain management, logistics and routes to market;
- understand the tasks performed by intermediaries in reconciling the interests of supplier and customer companies;
- know about the different types of intermediaries and kinds of exchanges that they handle;
- be able to explain conditions under which companies will choose to use the different types of intermediaries;
- be able to describe the various channel structures and reasons for the use of multiple routes to market;
- know about the effect of market and company factors on the role of intermediaries and on channel structures; and
- be able to describe the challenges involved in managing relationships and coordinating activities between the parties involved in a marketing channel.

INTRODUCTION

This chapter looks at the means by which a business marketer might try to reach target markets and gain maximum market coverage for their problem-solving abilities. For many organizations the only way that they can maximize market coverage is by making use of third parties, that is, intermediaries. Intermediaries such as agents and distributors help companies achieve marketing objectives by handling some of the exchanges involved in business transactions and by connecting suppliers with customers. As companies outsource non-value-adding activities and use various forms of digital business to ease coordination between the different parties involved in reaching and satisfying end-customers, so the role of the intermediary and the way in which a company might work with an agent or distributor can change.

The business marketer and intermediaries with whom it might work do not operate in isolation to reach and satisfy target customers. Rather, they are likely to be part of a supply chain, the management of which determines the success of those within it and their collective ability to deliver value to end-customers. While our principal interest lies in the handling of *routes to market*, we start this chapter by examining the nature and role of *supply chain management* (SCM) and logistics. This provides the context in which to revisit the types of exchanges conducted between supplier and customer companies, and the contribution that intermediaries might make in handling some of these exchanges. We introduce the routes that can be used to bring suppliers and customers together, and take account of the complexity and flexibility that can feature in channel structures. Effective channel performance requires that companies minimize the transaction costs associated with coordinating activities between the various channel members. We consider the contribution of relationship management and the means of controlling behaviour to channel coordination.

SUPPLY CHAIN MANAGEMENT AND LOGISTICS

Critical to the success of any organization is its ability to maximize customer value while minimizing the costs incurred in doing this. Very few companies deal directly with end-customers while at the same time performing all tasks in-house to deliver value to that end-customer. Instead, we know that a variety of firms are involved in this process, including extractors of raw materials, producers (of components and of assembled products), providers of transportation, warehousing, distribution, material handling, logistics and IT services. These various parties represent a supply chain, the management of which involves the planning and coordination of all activities of parties within a specific supply chain to provide the end-customer with a product which adds value (Chartered Institute of Purchasing and Supply, 2013). Fundamental to SCM is the responsiveness of a supply chain and the integration of all organizations that are a part of it. Responsiveness involves the monitoring of and adjustment to end-user demand, keeping the flow of 'product' (ranging from raw materials to finished product) to a minimum, thus reducing inventory costs throughout that supply chain. A key factor fuelling the growing importance of supply chain management is its contribution to an organization's competitive advantage because of its capacity to reduce costs, improve asset utilization and reduce order cycle times. Companies who excel in the management of their supply chains draw from new technologies, innovations and process thinking, resulting in a significant gap between industry leaders and average performers. If we look at the consumer goods firm Proctor and Gamble (P&G), essential to the evolution of this company's performance is its focus on customer centricity and supply chain responsiveness. The firm has 130 manufacturing sites and 200 distribution centres around the world and through which it reaches its retail customers. Critical to satisfying the needs of those customers is P&G's ability to take an uninterrupted thread from point-of-sales (POS) data to the supplier base and on through to its distribution network. The company's focus on customer centricity and supply chain responsiveness is transforming its own activities as well as those of its suppliers. For example, placing importance on responsiveness is translated into a target of being within a single day's transit from 80 per cent of its retailer customers. This means setting up mega-distribution centres in key geographic locations and reconfiguring its manufacturing operations so that they are demand (based on POS information) rather than forecast driven. Alongside this, P&G is also asking its suppliers to create 'supplier villages' next to its plants, similar to the just-in-time delivery model used in the automotive industry (Trebilcock, 2015). From this example of P&G, we can see that SCM extends beyond individual organizational performance to include all parties connected with a particular supply network and, as we learned in Chapter 4, this is also the case when it comes to reduced environmental impact. In fact, improved environmental performance can necessitate the complete rethinking of supply chains (Lee, 2010). See B2B Snapshot 11.1 to learn how supply chains might be overhauled to realize sustainability objectives.

B2B SNAPSHOT 11.1   DOING THINGS DIFFERENTLY

Reduced environmental impact can be more effective where organizations in a supply chain adopt an integrated rather than an independent and piecemeal approach to sustainability initiatives. Obviously some actions can be taken internally – so for example, by looking at and aligning every stage in its fabric and shirt manufacturing process, the Chinese producer Esquel cut energy consumption by 26.4 per cent and water use by 33.7 per cent. At the same time Esquel worked with independent farms and others that it owned to introduce drip irrigation and natural pest- and disease-control programmes for cotton production. In other instances companies, such as the South Korean steel producer POSCO, were driven to radically rethink their operational processes. Collaborating with its equipment supplier Siemens, the company created a radically new technology (FINEX) for steel production that both eliminates the need for coking and sintering and allows for cheaper bituminous coal and lower-quality iron ore. The net result is substantially reduced carbon emissions and a 15 per cent reduction in operating costs. Looking beyond immediate suppliers to other parties elsewhere in the same supply chain and also beyond a firm's own supply network can be critical to improved environmental performance. Take, for example, Starbucks' Coffee and Farmer Equity (CAFE) programme. The company has no direct contact with coffee producers (the product is sourced from cooperatives, food processors, exporters and importers) but uses this scheme to encourage suppliers to farm more sustainably. Meanwhile, faced with the onerous task of dealing with European legislation (WEEE) and producer responsibility for electronic waste, Hewlett-Packard, Electrolux, Sony and Braun created a joint venture, the European Recycling Platform (www.erp-recycling.org). This operates as an independent business and handles electronic waste for companies across Europe, offering operational scale and geographic reach that other providers have difficulty in matching. So in a nutshell, improved supply chain sustainability performance requires:

- managing sustainability as a key operational issue;
- coordinating operations both internally and with immediate suppliers;
- examining the extended supply chain; and
- looking beyond an organization's own enterprise network.

Source: Lee, 2010.

Whatever the purpose, improved supply chain performance requires close working partnerships to enable the coordination of (and quite likely changes in) activities performed by firms and the material and informational flow between organizations that are part of the same supply chain (or indeed elsewhere). The high degree of integration needed to ensure the effective movement of product to market typically involves both the use of multi-functional teams that cut across organizational boundaries and, most critically, the sharing of sensitive information between companies (for example, strategic and product development plans, point-of-sale transactions and customer data). Linked to this integration and information sharing is the synchronization of activities and the negotiation of profit sharing among supply chain members: for savings and profits to be realized requires long-term and open relationships between those involved. The importance of such collaboration is reflected in the way in which firms might use sensitive data (such as customer demand, product cost breakdown and asset utilization) for future business development. For example, a global fast-food chain built a data 'cleanroom' with its key capital equipment suppliers. The fast-food company shared projected future demand and outlet expansion data, while the equipment suppliers provided information on their global manufacturing footprint and total landed cost for products. Sharing data in the legal and secure environment of a cleanroom gave the parties a more accurate view of how a fully optimized supply chain of the future might look, offered an indication of the potential business opportunity, while protecting sensitive margin and cost information (Hu and Monahan, 2015).

Supply chain management performance is underpinned by the following goals:

Waste reduction: keeping duplication to a minimum, aligning operational processes and information systems, and reducing inventory levels allow waste to be reduced.

Time compression: more accurate market-demand predictions and faster response times are made possible by the improved information flow between supply chain members. Reduced cycle times improve the cash flow and therefore financial performance of an entire supply chain.

Flexible response: supply chain flexibility means that all members can adjust more quickly to changing market conditions. Flexible response to specific customer requirements (for example, order handling) means that unique customer needs can be met more effectively. Flexible response can contribute to competitive advantage.

Unit cost reduction: reducing unit costs means operating the supply chain so that it reduces the cost per unit for the end-customer. To do this companies have to determine the performance level required by a customer and the cost to deliver that service level. Unit cost reduction is achieved by eliminating activities that do not add value.

An increasingly critical contributor to the achievement of these objectives are technological developments which combine both tangible products, IT hardware (e.g. radio frequency identification tags, microprocessors, sensors, communication and monitoring equipment) and software programs (e.g. resource planning and management systems). Such technology has existed for quite a number of years, take for example, Otisline®, the remote electronic monitoring system which the firm, Otis, uses to manage its installed base of over 1.5 million elevators worldwide. Introduced in the early 1990s, the system allows Otis to continuously track elevator performance, detect servicing needs as well as trigger planned maintenance, all of which contributes to the company's diagnostic capabilities and customer satisfaction. Likewise organizations have used software-based resource planning systems for some time to more effectively manage internal operations, handle sales-driven demand and coordinate upstream requirements with suppliers. While such practices are commonplace in a variety of industrial markets, a significant development in recent years has been the application of such technology along entire supply chains, across different sectors and its evolution into smart, connected product systems. This has the potential to drive change along supply chains (rather than just the operations of individual companies), including the activities that different parties perform as well as the nature and sharing of data amongst supply chain members (A.T. Kearney/WHU, 2015; Porter and Heppelmann, 2014, 2015). The digitization of product systems and the sharing of data via web-based computing resources integrates functions such as sales, procurement, operations and customer service, connecting these through the supply chain. Such digitization can improve supply chain processes, while at the same time enabling flexibility in solutions offered to customers and transforming the activities of those parties in a product system (Fawcett et al., 2011; Porter and Heppelmann, 2015; Zelbst et al., 2010). A critical point remains however, namely that such connected systems are only of value if they make business sense, provide data and analytics that allow companies to make quicker and more informed decisions and contribute to competitive advantage (A.T. Kearney/WHU, 2015; Hinchcliffe, 2014).

While supply chain management is the overall mechanism for integrating all business processes that add value for the end-customer, *logistics management* covers the coordination of activities that contribute to the forward and reverse flow of information, goods and services between the point of origin and point of consumption to satisfy customer requirements. These activities can include the management of transport (inbound and outbound), warehousing, materials handling, order fulfilment and inventory (Council of Supply Chain Management Professionals, 2010). Given what we learned in Chapter 3 about issues associated with food traceability, then supply chain transparency and information flow associated with this will perhaps become an important logistical issue in some sectors (see B2B Snapshot 11.2 to learn more).

B2B SNAPSHOT 11.2   KEEPING TRACK

Being able to assure the provenance of items such as aerospace components, pharmaceutical ingredients and medical equipment is standard practice for organizations operating in these sectors, in spite of the cost and complexity associated with ensuring authenticity. However, technological developments mean that organizations in other industries can now readily show material origin and identify specific product components or ingredients. So, for example, *radio frequency identification* (RFID) tags, a cornerstone of inventory management, are becoming smaller and cheaper and are being used for other purposes. For example, Selinko a Belgian specialist in digital product authentication and NXP Semiconductors have partnered to provide digital connectivity for vintners. This means that estates such as Geantet-Pansiot in Burgundy can safeguard its wines from counterfeiting and combat grey markets. Meanwhile, Hitachi's sand-grain sized chip can be embedded in paper or plastic which, besides

(Continued)

(Continued)

indicating material or product provenance, can help business customers ensure that suppliers are not substituting components with inferior alternatives. When such technology is combined with other data sources and with RFID readers in mobile devices, even consumers can retrieve information about a firm and the route of its products from raw materials to finished item. Beyond miniature RFID tags, further developments include 'radio-dust' and DNA markers. So if a customer wanted to know about food safety then they can find out about the type of chicken as well as a particular chicken!

Sources: Labels and Labelling, 2016; New, 2010.

Logistics management is a key element in business marketing strategy because of:

- the significant cost savings which can be achieved through improved logistics performance;
- the explosion in product variety that in turn heightens the complexity of handling the movement of products; and
- improvements in information technology such as web-based logistics systems, digital methods for tracking products (uniform bar codes, RFID, radio-dust, DNA tags) and electronic handling of order and payment data, all of which can increase logistical efficiency.

The importance of logistics as a competitive weapon and its effect on customer operations means that some business marketers provide customers with integrated logistics programmes, drawing from contributions of sales, marketing and logistics to do this. Critical to the provision of such programmes and their competitive performance is the balancing of cost against service level and the management of those elements of the logistics system over which organizations have control (Bygballe et al., 2012). Firms within a supply chain will obviously want to keep total distribution cost to a minimum, but as service levels (and associated costs) increase, there will come a point at which the value of these do not warrant the extra cost incurred. Managers responsible for the formulation of logistics programmes have to determine costs, customer willingness to pay and performance levels expected of service components such as delivery time, delivery reliability, order accuracy, information access, damage, ease of doing business and value-added services (Byrnes et al., 1987). Whether managers are responsible for the formulation or actual operation of a system, the ability to deliver to specific service levels and to cost is dependent on their ability to effectively manage the controllable elements of the logistics system, namely customer service, order processing, logistics communication, transportation, warehousing, inventory control, packaging, materials handling, production planning and plant and warehouse location. As we see in B2B Snapshot 11.3, investments in digital supply chains are expected to improve up and downstream logistics.

B2B SNAPSHOT 11.3   CONNECTED SUPPLY CHAINS

A.T. Kearney and WHU Business conduct an annual survey amongst managers of leading European companies. The 2015 survey determined that the key drivers towards digitalization of the supply chain centred on:

- *IT integration*: an area in which 70 per cent of supply chain managers are planning significant investment and where the greatest impacts are expected. Realizing this can be challenging, particularly for companies such as engineering and technology firm ABB, whose businesses and supply chain span multiple countries. Besides the potential complexity of internal integration, streamlining IT systems and sharing sensitive data with suppliers and customers requires a special degree of trust between partners. This is certainly the case for aluminum and material composite component producer Avanco Gmbh who has seen its raw material suppliers start downstream activities and effectively become its competitors. Despite such challenges, benefits resulting from investments in IT integration centre on significantly lower inventory levels, as well as more flexible delivery times and batch sizes.

- *Demand forecasting and planning*: this will require investment in systems that support integrated, automated data gathering, tactical planning, purchasing and execution. For example, the Finnish production engineering company, Fortaco, has combined a forecasting system with its enterprise resource planning (ERP) system which covers downstream customers and suppliers.

- *Advanced big data analytics:* over 70 per cent of firms surveyed confirmed that big data is capable of delivering marked improvements in supply chain performance, particularly those companies who currently make products to stock (rather than to order). The key challenge for firms, is not data generation, rather its appropriate use and evaluation so that potential process disruptions can be identified and changes implemented quickly. The principal benefits that supply chain managers expect from big-data analytics centre on substantial reductions in inbound inventory, improvements in the optimization of batch sizes and reduced supply chain risk.

While these might drive the evolution of digital supply chains, managers who participated in the survey expect less of smart tagging and 3D printing. In terms of the tracking of materials, components and products via digital communications and radio transmitters, the current level of systems integration with supply chain partners is such that it does not favour investment. Added to this is the fact that while tagging can greatly improve provenance and authenticity (as we noted in B2B Snapshot 11.2), knowing the precise location of a product does not generate sales. With regards 3D printing, in the medium term, this might well offer potential for local and customized product or component supply. However in the immediate future, the technology has not reached a stage of development capable of replacing traditional production techniques because the range of printable raw material is limited.

REACHING AND SATISFYING CUSTOMERS: THIRD-PARTY INVOLVEMENT

Wherever it might be in a supply chain, included in an organization's objectives will be the intention to use its core competencies and capabilities to deliver superior customer value and to gain maximum market coverage for its problem-solving abilities. Maximum market coverage could mean targeting a broad range of customer groups, having as extensive a geographic scope as possible (involving regions, countries and continents) or indeed both. Herein lies the problem: few organizations have the resources to simultaneously and independently deliver superior value to all customers in all locations. So at some point a company has to decide whether to involve third parties in helping to reach and satisfy customers, the form that this 'intermediary' role might take, and how to allocate responsibility for handling the flow of communication, information exchange, product/service delivery and payment.

Traditionally the composition of routes to market has been approached from a linear/hierarchical perspective, with the principal company (the organization with the product capability) deciding on the type of intermediaries to use and the channel structure to enable products to reach target customers. It is clear from our discussion of supply chain management that many industries are unlikely to have such a straightforward structure, but for the time being let us adopt this approach in order to introduce variations in intermediary types, activities and channel design (while taking into account the product technology being used and the control sought by the marketing organization).

Bespoke/complex offerings

Where the risk/uncertainty associated with a customer's supply needs is high, and it involves a complex solution, the marketing organization may choose to deal directly with customers. This could be used for goods and services alike, allowing the principal company to have complete control of exchanges with customers. A concentrated customer base and the high-value contracts typically associated with such complex offerings can normally support the investment of the supplier's own resource to trigger interest and formulate product offerings, as well as negotiate and administer contracts, even when customers are geographically dispersed. The technical expertise used to devise an optimum solution and 'assemble' the finished product is normally contained within the marketing company. The high value of tangible forms of these products can also sustain necessary physical transportation of the finished item from the supplier's to the customer's premises, whatever the distance might be.

The challenge for an organization arises when it wants to enter new markets (product or geographic) with which it is unfamiliar. In such instances a company might rely in part on a *sales agent*. In Chapter 8 (B2B Snapshot 8.2) we described how the company Renold uses its own sales team to maintain contact with target customers involved in the design and supply of marine propulsion systems. The company cannot use its sales force in this way around the world so, for example, in South Korea it uses appointed agents to maintain its profile with potential customers such as the marine engine builder Hyundai Machinery. Agents essentially operate as independent sales representatives for a company, using their product, customer and market knowledge to generate business for a supplier. These representatives act as a link between the supplier and end-users, make contact with customers, introduce the supplier's capabilities to potential customers, and act as a mediator in the formulation and presentation of product offerings to customers and the negotiation and handling of contracts.

Uniform product offerings

Where the risk/uncertainty associated with the solution sought by a customer is somewhat lower and involves a rather more standard product offering, the marketing organization will be less inclined to want to control all exchanges with all customers. The customer base is likely to be more fragmented as well as being geographically dispersed, and contract value will vary significantly. The marketing organization's expertise centres on the design and efficient production of products that match end-customer needs. To make these available to customers, a company that produces tangible goods would use distributors. Distributors can act as a key link between a company and its end-customers and will normally handle related products from a range of suppliers, generating volume sales from a large number of customers. A distributor's income is derived from the difference between the price at which products are sourced from the original supplier and the price at which those same products are then sold on to the end-customer. This margin has to allow for some net profit once the distributor's operating costs have been deducted. These costs are incurred as a result of the distributor taking title to the original supplier's products and assuming principal responsibility for initiating and handling all exchanges with end-customers in a specified geographic territory. Activities associated with these exchanges include:

Communication: handling all communications activities with targeted customers in an allocated territory. This could include the use of impersonal tools such as advertising and sales promotion as well as the more obvious use of sales teams responsible for initiating and handling contact with and orders from customers.

Modification and assembly: standard products might be supplied unchanged to customers. In other instances a distributor might adapt a supplier's product or assemble elements from a variety of sources to meet a customer's individual product specification.

Product supply: ensuring local product availability (by carrying necessary stock) and facilitating transactions. This facilitation could include advice on product specification and selection as well as necessary commercial and logistical support such as the provision of credit/finance terms, order processing and product delivery.

Service and repair: distance from, and the geographic dispersion of, end-customers can mean that distributors play an important role in maintaining the supplier's products at customer locations.

While this might work for products that can be physically transported and stored, distributors are of no use to companies that supply service-based products that require the physical presence of the service operation in close proximity to customers to ensure ready availability of the service. Where the product is essentially a standard offering, the marketing organization can opt to enter into franchise arrangements. *Franchising* is essentially a form of licensing whereby the principal (the franchiser) allows another organization (the franchisee) the right to conduct business in a specified manner. The right might include selling the principal's product and using its name, or operational or marketing methods. As with licensing, the franchisee pays royalties for this right and in return is able to use the principal's trademark, and they may also benefit from training programmes as well as the franchiser's experience, credit facilities and marketing communications programmes. Franchising is an important means of extending market coverage (without major capital investment) for organizations involved in service sectors where a physical presence is necessary to enable customers to access a company's service. See B2B Snapshot 11.3 for a description of Rolls-Royce's use of franchising and how this connects with other channels used by the company.

At a very basic level it can be argued that in order to exploit its own operational efficiency, a supplier's principal interest is to have as narrow a product range as possible and to maximize the sales of those products. By contrast, customers do not necessarily have high-volume requirements and would want to choose from as broad a range of alternative products as possible. Therefore intermediaries can reconcile the needs of suppliers and end-customers by sourcing relatively high volumes of products from a number of suppliers and offering customers a broader product choice and order levels that suit their specific requirements.

If we think about the variety and number of exchanges that can occur between a supplier and customer to get to the point of agreeing a contract, and about those associated with the subsequent fulfilment of that contract, it is clear that many companies cannot realistically deal directly with all of their customers (or, for that matter, customers with their suppliers) and operate efficiently in their marketplaces. If a supplier uses different types of intermediaries, its dealings are directed towards a reduced number of contacts, to their chosen third parties, who then handle some

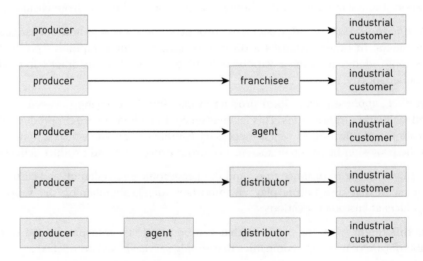

FIGURE 11.1 Routes to business markets

or all exchanges and transactions with end-customers (depending on whether they are sales agents, distributors or franchisees). This allows the supplier to concentrate on its areas of expertise and simplifies the means by which supplier and customer companies gain access to their output and input markets respectively.

From single to multiple routes to market

Figure 11.1 shows the various permutations that we have discussed so far. While some firms may start out by relying on one principal route to market, the reality is that most organizations are likely to operate a number of alternative channels. This might be because market conditions change (requiring a company to rethink its channel strategy), because a firm is trying to serve a variety of target customers (each require different levels of servicing) or because the nature of the solution provided and customer location necessitates a variety of ways to delivery that solution. Take a look at B2B Snapshot 11.4 to learn how Rolls-Royce delivers service programmes to its customers

B2B SNAPSHOT 11.4   STAYING AIRBORNE

We saw in chapter one the nature of Rolls-Royce's business and the range of sectors in which it competes using its engineering expertise, relying increasingly on service contracts rather than engine sales for revenue generation and profitability. For the company to deliver competitive service solutions to customers, it needs to have good geographic coverage and the ability to manage service, maintenance and repair activities as quickly as possible and according to strict technical procedures. Let's look at helicopter aircraft, for which Rolls Royce provides original equipment (OE) and service solutions. One of the smaller engines supplied by the company is the M250 (along with its recently rebadged equivalent the RR300) – this is a turbine engine used on lighter helicopters. Civilian and defence helicopters that operate using these engines can be anywhere in the world, so that Rolls-Royce uses a mixture of fully owned and franchised operations to handle servicing as part of its 'FIRST network' facility. See Table 11.1 for an overview of different types of members.

Specialized major/critical and minor repair services are only undertaken by RROF/AMROC and ASC members respectively, while ASC repair and maintenance activities are carried out in coordination with AMROC or AMC members. Take a look at Figure 11.2 to get an idea of how Rolls-Royce structures the worldwide delivery of after sales service for its M250 engines to helicopter clients. In running service, repair and maintenance operations, all of its members need timely access to replacement parts. And for this FIRST network members have access to API aftermarket supply chain operator (www.apiworldwide.com) as well as Aviall, the aftermarket arm of aircraft manufacturer Boeing (www.aviall.com).

Source: Rolls-Royce (2015a).

(Continued)

(Continued)

TABLE 11.1 Rolls Royce M250 FIRST Network: types of service operation

FIRST Network Members	Operations	Component repair	Services				
			Repair and maintenance	Complete overhaul	TotalCare programme (flying hours agreement)	Engine, component and accessory exchange	Warranty administration
RROF Rolls-Royce Repair and Overhaul Facility (wholly-owned)	test cell for diagnostic and acceptance testing	specialized major and critical repairs	◆	◆	◆	◆	◆
AMROC Authorized Maintenance, Repair and Overhaul Centre (independent)	test cell for diagnostic and acceptance testing	specialized major and critical repairs	◆	◆	◆	◆	◆
AMOF Authorized Military Overhaul Facility (independent)	test cell for diagnostic and acceptance testing		◆	◆	◆	◆	◆
AMC Authorized Maintenance Centre (independent)	test cell for diagnostic and acceptance testing	basic book and minor repairs	◆	◆	◆	◆	◆
ASC Authorized Servicer Centre (independent)	regional operation maintenance and support		◆				
ARC Authorized Repair Centre (independent)	overhaul and repairs	repair of specific piece parts					

Source: Rolls Royce, 2015a.

FIGURE 11.2 Rolls-Royce M250 First network map (Rolls-Royce 2015a).

IMPROVING CHANNEL PERFORMANCE

So far we have given a relatively straightforward account of the types of intermediaries that operate in business markets and the alternative means by which a company might make its problem-solving abilities available to target customers. However, we know from our initial discussion of supply chain management and logistics that the reality for many organizations is much more complex, as they seek to marry firm-specific objectives and resources with the opportunities and constraints of the markets in which they operate. In this section we take a more detailed look at how external and internal factors can determine the structure of routes to market, the types of parties involved and the contributions that they make.

Customer expectations

In many industries, customers have increasingly higher expectations of the value that they seek to derive from products purchased and the sources used to obtain them. For the products themselves, standard items are no longer guaranteed to meet customer needs, principally because customers have become used to being able to purchase products that have been customized according to their own individual specification. In addition to the tailoring of products to individual needs, customers are also more demanding of services offered to support purchases, including ready availability and rapid order fulfilment via their preferred channel (Anderson et al., 1997). Clearly such product and service expectations place particularly exacting demands on supply/distribution chains as companies seek to simultaneously meet market demands and remain cost competitive. We look at how some of these demands impact on the channel structure and the activities of those involved.

The rethinking of value/distribution chain activities

In response to customers' increasing demands (but also in an effort to eliminate activities that do not contribute to delivering superior value), many companies have rethought their internal operations and transferred activities to other points in the value chain where organizations are able to perform those activities better (Anderson et al., 1997). Some organizations have successfully used production postponement (delaying the differentiation of a product for an individual customer until the latest point possible in the value chain) to deal with market demands for mass customization (Feitzinger and Lee, 1997). For this to work a company has to rethink product design and the supply network. The design of products changes so that they consist of independent modules that can be easily and inexpensively assembled into different product formats. The supply network changes in terms of the positioning of stock and the location, amount and structure of production and distribution facilities. The network is designed so that the basic product is readily available at locations performing the customization, and the network has to have sufficient flexibility and responsiveness to receive, process and subsequently deliver orders for customized products quickly. So while the basic products might be produced centrally, these are subsequently shipped to local distribution centres and subsequently customized for differentiation.

As well as rethinking activities to enable a firm to accommodate market demand for mass customization, we know that many organizations outsource non-value-adding activities. So in the automotive industry, for example, a company such as Honda uses its expertise in engine and power-train design to compete. It completes final assembly of the automotive product and invests considerable effort in handling relationships with its dealership network. In addition to this it relies on a tiered supply chain of companies for sub-assemblies and components that make up the finished product, and also logistics companies to manage the movement of cars between its manufacturing plants and dealers. Like many other companies, Honda buys in activities to which it is unable to add value. So the organization has to handle a number of relationships up and down the value chain in order to reach and satisfy target customers. (See Trappey et al. (2007) for an example of changes in the supply chain for Taiwanese automotive OEMs and assemblers.)

Outsourcing has had a significant effect on the role of the parties that contribute to the value chain that delivers product to the end-customer, and this includes intermediaries. Outsourcing is not restricted to items that might be contained in a company's own finished product; rather it can also include the management of supplies for items such as MRO products. Expenditure on MRO items can represent less than 1 per cent of a firm's revenue split across the various budget-holders in a company. Given the transaction costs involved in sourcing what are typically low-value/low-importance items, some companies have opted to transfer the management of their MRO supply needs to distributors (Anderson and Narus, 1996). Although this can present distributors with significant opportunities for building business, it can stretch their resources, as customers typically expect a broader product offering than that normally supplied by an MRO distributor. To deal with this challenge, W.W. Grainger set up Grainger

Integrated Supply Operations. This organization consists of the company's own distribution business, a series of best-in-class suppliers for a variety of products, and an internal sourcing group. When the company receives an order from a customer, it can either supply directly from its own distribution business, or if it cannot fulfil the order it will look to the best-in-class suppliers or its sourcing group (Anderson et al., 1997). So the distributor is effectively covering some of the transaction costs associated with searching for and securing supplies that would previously have been incurred by the customer.

What should be clear from our discussion of postponement and outsourcing is that it is difficult to think of routes to market as simply being associated with a firm's decision about whether to use an intermediary, what type to use and what activities the selected intermediary might perform. Instead, supply/distribution chains frequently consist of a network of organizations, of 'a confederation of specialists that are flexible and specialised, and [which] pool complementary resources and skills to achieve shared goals' (Anderson et al., 1997: 61).

Digital coordination

Prices charged for products consist of three elements: product costs, coordination costs and profit margin. A key challenge for any supply/distribution chain, or for any group of organizations involved in activities that contribute to addressing end-customer needs, lies in trying to minimize the costs of coordination between the various parties in that chain. At each point in the chain, costs are incurred as a result of having to identify appropriate partners, allocate tasks between partners and specify contracts, exchange information to ensure timely and accurate task performance, and administer financial settlements in line with contract specifications (Malone et al., 1987). We noted earlier that SCM required close working partnerships, and entering into long-term relationships with channel partners is one way in which to reduce transaction costs. The repeated exchanges associated with such relationships result in structures, and processes and norms that link firms becoming institutionalized. This means that patterns of behaviour between firms in a distribution channel become routine and the various parties in that channel do not have to invest time and effort in repeatedly searching for and learning about/accommodating new exchange partners. Indeed, as we noted in our earlier discussion, the routinization of tasks performed by channel members and the sharing of information between them to support these activities is increasingly enabled through digitization of product systems. This does, however, raise some interesting and apparently contradictory issues.

The integration of the systems of the various parties in a supply chain, and the closer coordination of activities and the information sharing it seeks to realize, require significant commitment in the form of resource investment by channel members. To realize the potential offered by digital business tools and minimize possible conflict between channel partners requires that companies engage intermediaries in discussions regarding the type of tools and their manner of use (Osmonbekov et al., 2009). Besides conflict, such systems can shift the balance of power in channel relationships and even challenge the role of channel members. In fact, it might be argued that in some markets the role of the intermediary can be diminished or at least transformed as digital business systems enable suppliers to perform some of the functions for which they usually relied on distributors. For example, one of the expected benefits of companies investing in the continued digitization of their supply chains, is the reduction in the number partners needed for the supply chain to function effectively and to realize the flexibility and responsiveness necessary to meet customer needs (A.T. Kearney/WHU, 2015). Such responsiveness is a key aspect of the after-sales service that Otis provides direct to its elevator customers through its remote electronic monitoring systems. Companies, such as equipment supplier, Caterpillar, include remote monitoring as part of solutions to construction and mining customers, but this does not eliminate their need for intermediaries in the marketplace. Take a look at B2B Scenario 11.1 to discover the expected role of dealers in Caterpillar's future plans.

B2B SCENARIO 11.1   HUNGRY CATERPILLAR

In 2012, Caterpillar, the global supplier of equipment to the construction, energy and mining sectors, posted global sales of $65.9 billion and set itself the objective of reaching $100bn revenue by 2020. However, the three years that followed saw sales decline (rather than grow) with the company reporting income of $55bn for 2015. Slowing economic activity in key geographic regions around the world has had a knock on effect on the sales that Caterpillar can generate in its target sectors of construction, energy and mining. Added to this are changes, for example, in the construction market, where sales of equipment to rental companies now outnumbers sales to contractors. This is an important development given that the switch to rental moves the financial pressure from the customer to the dealer (and ultimately Caterpillar), particularly as a rental business requires a considerable amount of working capital.

Facing such challenges, Caterpillar is relying on its distribution system for improved business performance and its 178 independently owned dealers for revenue growth. And it expects this to be realized through means other than new equipment sales. Firstly, Caterpillar wants more dealers to re-orientate operations towards the potentially more lucrative fleet-management business. Distributors already offer a tiered fleet-management programme (marketed as CAT Equipment Management Solutions), but Caterpillar wants dealers to move more customers onto higher levels of EMS, where the dealer handles equipment monitoring and at the highest level, actually takes over the management of customers' fleets of equipment. Beyond increasing market share in fleet management, Caterpillar is also asking distributors to increase its share of the global parts and service market. As a way to monitor revenue growth in this area, the company is setting dealers new absorption rates of over 100. The absorption rate measures how long a dealer could stay in business if they had to rely solely on parts and service revenue generated from equipment already in use. Where gross profit from parts and service sales covers total overhead and interest costs for a year, then a dealer scores 100. For some years, a score of 100 was considered good enough, but Caterpillar is now expecting higher absorption rates from its distributors.

The company believes that dealers can make more of technology deployed in Caterpillar's machines to not only move more towards equipment monitoring solutions but also to support parts and service revenue growth. The best distributors are using digital technology to help customers manage their fleets more efficiently and know around 90 per cent of both parts demand by customer and where opportunity exits. However, Caterpillar considers that average or lower performing dealers could easily realize up to 8 per cent share increase in the aftermarket by making better use of the data transmitted by the 3.5 million pieces of Caterpillar equipment in the field. Besides better use of data analytics, Caterpillar also thinks that billions of sales could be realized through better coordination between dealers and the provision of a consistent customer experience, particularly for those global clients who use different Caterpillar distributors around the world.

Faced with slowing markets and declining sales figures since 2012, the challenge for Caterpillar lies in working out how to make best use of a distribution system and a dealer network which have been a key part of its competitive advantage and on which it relies for future revenue growth.

(*Sources*: www.cat.com; Kellaher, 2014)

Coordination: handling channel partners

Whatever the structure and functioning of the routes to market used by an organization, a number of factors have to be taken into account to ensure the effective management of channel operations and the relationships with other parties in the channel system. These factors include:

- selection of channel members;
- support provided to channel partners;
- means of controlling channel behavior; and
- dealing with channel conflict.

Selection of channel members

Given the obvious contribution that intermediaries can play in a company's ability to reach and satisfy target customers, identifying and selecting suitable channel partners are important activities for the business marketer. This process can be time-consuming, yet it is important to get it right, bearing in mind that an ineffective distributor can set you back years; it is almost better to have no distributor than to have a bad one in a major market. For some companies, it is not necessarily a question of going through a search-and-selection process in appointing intermediaries; rather, more often it is one in which they try to persuade key channel players to represent them and to carry their products. However, for the purposes of the ensuing discussion, we will assume that the principal company has some scope for selecting specific intermediaries.

Before a company can make a selection decision, it has to be able to find potential intermediaries. Sources used for identifying possible channel members include trade sources and intermediaries themselves. Government bodies can, for example, conduct preliminary searches and provide lists of possible agents or distributors in overseas markets that a company may wish to develop. A particularly useful means of finding potential intermediaries is via trade fairs and exhibitions. Companies participating in trade fairs might be approached by agents/distributors looking to build their supplier/product base, and likewise a supplier might visit an event specifically to identify likely channel partners who themselves could be exhibiting.

However a company locates possible intermediaries, the criteria used to select eventual channel partners have to be clear. Selection will normally depend on a partner's resources, product and marketing capabilities, and commitment. If a company is going to enter into agreement with an intermediary, then it needs to be certain that the channel partner has the necessary *resources* to support its marketing plans. For example, if a company wanted to pursue an aggressive growth strategy, it would need representatives that had sufficient financial resources to expand with the business, and a sales team that was big enough to support target growth rates and the capacity to formulate marketing plans that reflect both the intermediary's objectives as well as the principal's sales targets. A company also needs to ensure that an intermediary's *product* range complements its own, and that it has the necessary physical facilities to handle stock and (where production postponement or customization is part of the supplier's strategy) perform some light manufacturing or assembly. In the case of technically complex products then the quality of an intermediary's sales and service personnel would be particularly important for a supplier. In addition to product capability, a supplier would be interested in a channel partner's *marketing* capability, its market coverage (customer and geographic) and its aggressiveness in developing market demand, its expertise in market and relationship communication, and the level of its after-sales support provided to customers. A potential intermediary might score favourably in these areas, but a company also has to be certain of a channel partner's *commitment* to building business with the supplier. A company might determine this based on an intermediary's willingness: to keep minimum stock levels; invest in equipment, advertising and personnel training specifically to support the development of sales of the supplier's products; and to provide market, customer and competitor information where it is representing the company (Tamer-Cavusgil et al., 1995).

FIGURE 11.3 Criteria for evaluating distributors (adapted from Tamer-Cavusgil et al., 1995)

TABLE 11.2 Influences on industrial distributor's choice of supplier

Influence	Ranking
Economic	
Product quality	1
Service delivery quality	2
Product range	3
Product superiority compared to competitors	5
Product replacement service	13
Prices, discounts, commission	14
Channel partnership	
Receptive to complaints and advice	4
Quality of working relationship	6
Regular communication	8
Long-term business commitment	11
Regular personal contact	15
Intermediary support	
Image	7
Product information service	9
Quotation service	10
Well-known products	12

Source: adapted from Shipley and Prinja, 1988: 183.

Figure 11.3 lists these various criteria – clearly the suitability of these would differ depending on whether a company is looking to recruit an agent or a distributor. Partner selection is not one-sided: intermediaries also consider conditions under which they would agree to enter into partnership with a supplier. Criteria that inform an intermediary's selection decision can be grouped according to whether they contribute to the economic conditions needed to satisfy end-customer need, channel partnership or intermediary support (Shipley and Prinja, 1988). These criteria are listed and ranked in order of importance according to research by Shipley and Prinja (1988) in Table 11.2.

Channel support

In addition to recruiting intermediaries, a company has to develop programmes of activity to support channel members, including methods of motivating and training intermediaries as well as reviewing performance. Incentives and behaviour that can be used to encourage an intermediary to devote necessary resources and commitment to a particular company's products include:

- financial incentives in the form of attractive commission rates or margins, and bonuses for realizing or exceeding target sales or winning business with specific customers;
- territorial exclusivity;
- provision of supplier resources such as: sales team involvement in dealings with selected customers; sharing of market research information; market communication support; and training of intermediary staff;
- the working relationship approach to intermediary dealings, such as: joint planning of strategies for regions, customers or products handled by an intermediary; demonstrable understanding and appreciation of intermediary efforts to handle supplier products; regular communication including information exchange and interpersonal contact; and signaling of supplier long-term commitment by, for example, having a sales team responsible for handling dealer relationships. (Adapted from Shipley et al., 1989.)

While the above represent a variety of ways in which a supplier might try to motivate channel members, those actually used would depend on the requirements of the intermediaries themselves. The use of training to support channel activities will depend on intermediary expertise but also on the complexity of the product offering and rate of new product introduction. Given the potential contribution of intermediaries to a supplier's position in target markets, the evaluation of channel member performance is important. Table 11.3 details criteria against which intermediary performance might be evaluated. Evaluation should allow a company to spot weaker intermediaries, to identify gaps in necessary capabilities (offering training to help close these gaps) and where necessary to terminate contracts. Assuming that a supplier is using a working relationship approach as a means to motivate intermediaries, then it might be expected that criteria and actual measures would be agreed by both parties. As we saw in B2B Scenario 11.1, in seeking to stay declining sales, the equipment supplier Caterpillar needs to support its distributors to enable them to transform their operations, develop more equipment management solutions with customers and align themselves with the performance metrics proposed by the company.

TABLE 11.3 Evaluating intermediary performance

Criterion	Factors to consider
Intermediary contribution	supplier profitability, sales growth
Intermediary competence	experience, product knowledge, administrative and supervisory skills, strategic thinking of senior management
Loyalty	commitment and motivation towards supplier
Compliance	acceptance of supplier channel policies and programmes
Adaptability	innovation in handling supplier products
Customer satisfaction	measures in terms of level and quality of services

Source: adapted from Kumar et al., 1992.

© American Marketing Association, AMA.org. Reproduced by permission.

Channel 'control': power, contracts and trust

From our discussions in this chapter it should be clear that channel activities can provide companies with a means to create both strategic advantage and end-customers with an important source of value-added benefit (Weitz and Jap, 1995). The mechanisms by which activities between various channel partners are coordinated are therefore key concerns, and interest has been devoted to determining the contribution of *power-*, *contractual-* and *trust-*based means of controlling inter-firm behaviour (Weitz and Jap, 1995).

Of these three means of organizing routes to market, the one that has attracted considerable attention in channels research (Gaski, 1984) is the means and effect of a single organization using its position of *power* to control the activities of other channel members. The ability to do this occurs as a result of the more powerful organization having more resources that are valued by the less powerful channel member. So, for example, a supplier that has a strong brand or product that is highly valued by target customers could use incentives to encourage dealers to invest more effort in supporting its products. The supplier could rate dealers according to effort expended, and link this to price discounts, marketing assistance and credit terms available to the dealer. Using such influence with channel members can result in a dealer eliminating products available from other companies and allow the favoured supplier to improve its position by restricting competitor access to markets by the same distribution channels (Mohr et al., 1999). Power lies not only with suppliers, however, since intermediaries can enjoy considerable positions of influence over producers, particularly where they have large volume requirements and provide suppliers with significant market coverage and access to a fragmented and dispersed customer base (Kumar, 1996). A dealer can use its power over producers to dictate terms and conditions of supply, and might readily switch between alternative sources if companies are unwilling to accept dealer-specified conditions.

The use of power in channel relationships can be viewed negatively if one party is coerced into acceding to the demands of the more powerful party. It can also lead to conflict in relationships where coercion restricts the ability of the weaker organization to achieve objectives that it might seek from involvement in a channel relationship (Gaski, 1984). However, if the more powerful company uses its influence to improve channel coordination and then shares the benefits equitably with channel members, conflict will not necessarily arise and weaker organizations may be satisfied with the relationship outcomes (Weitz and Jap, 1995).

An alternative to one organization using its position of authority to coordinate activities in a channel relationship is for companies to use *contractual arrangements* as the principal means of control. In a channel setting this is typically associated with franchising, and requires companies to agree on the activities to be performed by each party, the policies and procedures that both companies will follow, and the rewards for carrying out activities and complying with policies (Weitz and Jap, 1995).

Rather than using power or contracts to control actions, coordination might be based on *trust*, where companies develop norms – patterns of behaviour as a result of repeated interaction and ongoing dealings with channel partners. These 'rules' of behaviour guide each party's behaviour and expectations of the other in terms of: tradeoffs between long- and short-term profit opportunities; the extent to which the other party's interests are considered in reaching decisions; the nature and extent of the sharing of proprietary information; and the degree to which previously agreed arrangements can be altered (Weitz and Jap, 1995). One of the principal mechanisms for facilitating such relationship norms is through *collaborative communication* between channel members. This consists of:

- a high frequency of interaction across all communication mediums (face-to-face, telephone, email, etc.);
- extensive two-way communication consisting of ongoing dialogue between supplier and intermediary;
- the use of formal policies guiding communication behaviour; and
- the use of influence tactics that place priority on common goals. (Mohr et al., 1996)

Using such collaborative communication can improve an organization's commitment, satisfaction and perceived coordination with a channel partner (Mohr et al., 1996, 1999), and is particularly effective where a manufacturer lacks power over a dealer and both parties are independent of each other (so there is no form of vertical integration or franchise agreement in operation) (Mohr et al., 1996, 1999).

While collaborative communication reflects the apparent shift in many industries from competitive to collaborative relationships between suppliers and intermediaries, it is not necessarily suited for all market or relationship conditions. Indeed an organization is likely to draw from each of these coordination mechanisms to control activities with channel partners (Weitz and Jap, 1995).

Channel conflict

Whatever approach is used to coordinate activities, conflict between the channel parties is inevitable and can vary from minor disagreements that are easily forgotten to significant disputes that can lead to acrimonious relationships between companies. For the business marketer, it is important to understand both the potential sources of conflict and the ways in which it might be handled.

The principal causes of conflict include the following:

Differences in objectives. Disagreement can occur between channel partners because a supplier would typically prefer to offer intermediaries low margins and limited allowances, and expect a dealer to carry a large inventory and invest heavily in communication activities to support the supplier's products, while an intermediary is interested in improving its profit performance by being able to operate with high margins, carry a small inventory and keep expenses incurred in supporting a supplier to a minimum.

Differences in desired product lines. One way in which an intermediary can achieve growth objectives is to expand the product lines that it handles. This can cause dissatisfaction among its original suppliers, who may view the intermediary as disloyal and be concerned about any reduced support caused by the dealer's product expansion.

Multiple routes to market. We know that the business marketer might use multiple channels to maximize market coverage. Intermediaries may become frustrated when they are restricted from targeting certain customers because the principal company wishes to deal with those customers directly. Difficulties can also occur when the various channels are competing for the same business – a dealer might spend time dealing with potential customers or building a case for a major contract with a customer, only to be rewarded by the customer opting to deal with or place the order with an alternative channel partner used by the supplier.

Inadequate performance. Conflict is inevitable when, for example, an intermediary fails to hit agreed sales targets or does not carry necessary inventory, or support services do not meet necessary performance standards. Likewise, poor delivery performance or product quality and inadequate financial incentives or promotional support on the part of the supplier can trigger conflict in a channel relationship (McGrath and Hardy, 1989).

What, then, can channel members do to avoid and manage conflict? We discussed previously the contribution of collaborative communication to channel relationships. We also talked about how frequent interaction that results in shared understanding, mutually agreed objectives (to be achieved via the channel) and performance targets (for each party in achieving these objectives) can help avoid conflict occurring in the first place. Where an intermediary is not reaching set targets, a supplier can try to understand the underlying causes and in consultation with the intermediary determine and agree on ways to *improve performance. Training* in how to handle high-conflict situations can help managers deal with difficult problems without resorting to emotional or blaming behaviour. Where companies are using multiple channels, conflict can be avoided by *partitioning markets* between the various intermediaries based on geographic area, industry, application, customer size or product group. For this to be effective, channel members have to agree to the basis for the partition and operate according to their individual allocation. A supplier can also try to eliminate conflict by taking *control* of the channel relationship; this might be via forward integration or, as we have previously discussed, by using power or contractual arrangements such as franchising (McGrath and Hardy, 1989).

CHAPTER SUMMARY

- Supply chain management involves the planning and coordination of all activities of parties within a specific supply chain to provide the end-customer with a product which adds value.

- Coordination between the various channel parties should be such that a customer gets the actual product that they want as well as support services, spatial convenience and time utility from an intermediary – benefits that a supplier could not ordinarily supply to all of its customers.

- Configuring routes to market requires a company to take account of customers' preferred means of accessing products and the tasks that different types of intermediary can perform.

- The use of multiple parties and channels provides customers with choice and allows a company to accommodate the capabilities of various types of third party.

It also presents challenges in terms of added complexity and transaction costs as the number of parties and channels that contribute to reaching and satisfying customer needs increases.

- Digital systems and approaches to handling inter-firm relationships provide the means by which costs can be contained, behaviour managed and channel performance improved.

QUESTIONS FOR DISCUSSION

1. How might supply chain management affect the business marketer's design and operation of routes to market?

2. Compare and contrast the tasks performed by distributors and agents.

3. Are franchise operations a suitable route to accessing business customers?

4. How are market- and firm-specific factors affecting routes to market?

5. How might a company go about recruiting intermediaries?

6. Does the growth in partnerships mean that channel conflict is a thing of the past?

CASE STUDY 11.1   ROUTES TO MARKET IN THE TOYS AND GAMES INDUSTRY

Established in 1982 the German toy group Simba-Dickie realized a turnover of €602m in 2014 (Spielwarenmesse, 2015). Although organic growth had a part to play, acquisition has been key to the company's development, supported by a concentrated number of production centres and an extensive sales, marketing and warehousing network around the world. By 2013, the company had 15 toy brands in its portfolio, production facilities in six different countries, subsidiaries in 26 and agencies in a further six countries (see Table 11.4 for an indication of some of the group's key brands, products and manufacturing locations). Few toy producers have global presence (think Hasbro, Lego and Mattel), and as a medium-sized business, operating in this way allows Simba-Dickie to extend geographic market coverage for all its brands and perhaps most importantly to offer retailers an extensive product range.

Germany, France, Italy, Spain, Belgium, Russia and the UK represent the group's most important markets and while the company plans to reduce its reliance on sourcing from the Far East (including investment in Brazil to serve the South American region), over 70 per cent of Simba-Dickie's toys are supplied from manufacturing sites in China. Items produced in Europe might be shipped direct to retailers or to the group's various distribution centres while Chinese production and delivery to Simba-Dickie's distribution network is coordinated by the group's offices in Hong Kong and sales headquarters in Fürth. So for example, in scheduling deliveries from China to Simba-Dickie's logistics centre in Sonnenberg, planners have to factor in production time as well as the 25 days that it takes for shipments to reach Germany. This is quite an enterprise when you consider that one or more containers (each one filled with up to 800 cases of toys) arrive five or six times a day (Simba-Dickie Group, 2010).

TABLE 11.4 A taste of Simba-Dickie Group activities

Brand	Toy	Age group	Development	Production
Simba (incl. Filly Beauty Queen; Chi Chi Love)	soft toys, dolls	0+ years	Germany/ Hong Kong	China
Nicotoy	soft toys	babies, toddlers	Belgium	China
Eichhorn	wooden toys	0–6 years	Germany	Czech Republic
Heros	wooden toys	0–6 years	Germany	Germany
Big	ride-on plastic toys	1+ years	Germany	Germany
Smoby	role-play plastic toys	0+ years	France	France/China
Dickie (incl. Eat My Dust; Kids Mate)	action, farm, utility vehicles	3+ years	Germany/ Hong Kong	China
Majorette (incl. Majo Teams; Rockerz)	metal vehicles	3+ years	Germany	Thailand
Schuco	metal classic vehicles	collectors	Germany	Germany
Solido	metal classic vehicles	collectors	Germany/ Hong Kong	China
Dickie-Tamiya (Tamiya; Carson)	remote-controlled models	8+ years	Germany/ Hong Kong	China
Märklin (LGB; Märklin)	model trains	8+ years	Germany	Hungary
Noris-Spiele (Norris; Zoch; Schipper)	board games; arts and crafts	1+ years	Germany	Germany

Source: collated from publicly available information sources.

Just as many toy brands have tended to offer region-specific products (other than well-known international brands that we mentioned earlier), distribution infrastructure equally varies by country. In France, for example, hypermarkets (Carrefour, Auchan, E.Leclerc) account for 70 per cent of all toy sales and, in the UK, supermarkets are responsible for 12 per cent of all toy sales. In France, the UK and Germany there are 1,600, 450 and 2,800 independent toy retailers respectively. While the major retailers in France and the UK will deal directly with toy producers, because of the number of independent retailers in Germany, product supply is handled by buying groups.

Toy producers such as Simba-Dickie deal with retailers in different countries through the group's various sales offices (visit www.simba-dickie-group.de to get an idea of its sales operation), and many of the larger intermediaries (or buying groups in Germany) use buying teams to handle supplies of different products. The structure of buying teams varies depending on the retailer, but typically includes a number of buyers (supported by assistant buyers) responsible for various product categories such as girls' and boys' toys respectively, as well as preschool, media (TV games etc.), electronic games and board games. Within any product category, the buying team is faced with a significant task: having to process up to 300 quotes from suppliers for one product item. Given the scale of this, retailers keep the number of vendor accounts in any one category to the minimum.

(Continued)

(Continued)

RETAILER PURCHASING AND ORDER CYCLE

An intermediary's purchasing cycle is driven by seasonality, with the decision-making process being initiated as much as 18 months before a product appears in-store. So in preparing for Christmas 2016, for example, buying teams will have spent summer/early autumn 2015 visiting trade fairs around the world in search of ideas, trends and new toy products that might have sales potential in national European markets. As well as attending trade fairs, buying teams will review products offered by existing suppliers. For toy producers such as Simba-Dickie, this may include the following:

- Buying teams from the principal intermediaries in key geographic markets visit the company's head office in Fürth in autumn 2015 to view product proposals for Christmas 2016. Discussions also include a review of existing products and which of those will be carried forward to the next season, as well as others that the retailer is likely to delete, with reasons for their removal.
- Based on the business meeting held at the company's head office, 'photo-quotations' are sent to the retailer for every item viewed by the buying team and for which the retailer signalled interest and desire to evaluate the product further.
- For each item, the supplier sends a one-page quotation to the retailer. Information sent includes: cost price, a photographic image, size (disassembled and assembled), size of packaging, size of outer packaging, weight of product, country of origin, battery needs, and accessories that can accompany the product. Among other things, such detail enables the retailer to calculate handling and storage costs.
- Evaluations using the photo-quotations lead to sample requests for some of those items by early December 2015. Samples are used by larger retailers in their 'dummy stores', allowing in-store planograms to be used for further product evaluation.
- The combined photo-quotations and presentation of the samples in the retailer's 'dummy stores' contribute to the retailer's internal approval process. Buying teams evaluate competing products and present this evaluation, along with recommended product selections, to merchandise managers/directors for approval.
- During this internal evaluation process, discussions between buyers and the supplier are ongoing. Areas might include scope for price reductions, changes to the product specification, or own-label options.
- If successful, the toy producer receives confirmation of final product selection by March 2016; this then leads to the onset of negotiations regarding price/product contribution and volumes for product delivery in July 2016, with in-store availability by autumn 2016.

Retailers select from the entire product range offered by a supplier. Criteria used for product selection might include:

- profitability;
- communication campaigns planned by suppliers to drive customer demand;
- dealer support provided by a supplier, such as tag advertising, pricing promotion and funding of in-store displays and catalogues; and
- 'exit plans' for product supplies (previously known as sale-or-return).

Toy producers typically do not receive orders before shipping products; rather a retailer will confirm items that have been selected from the supplier's product range. Once an item has been selected the toy company provides product and packing details and requests a supplier order number. The dealer then advises order number and volume requirements, which both allows companies such as Simba-Dickie to calculate the delivery schedule and results in it requesting appointments for delivery of products to retailer warehouses. Only after an item has been purchased by a consumer and its details have gone through the retailer's EPOS system does the toy supplier actually receive order confirmation from the retailer.

Larger retailers expect toy producers to manage supply logistics on their behalf. For example, in the UK, Simba-Dickie would be required to use Argos's extranet facility to key in product information, generate order numbers and invoices and trigger payment on the retailer's behalf for the group's products that have been sold through Argos channels.

RELATIONSHIP MANAGEMENT

The principal points of contact between toy producers and retailers are the sales representatives and purchasing managers. However, other managers would regularly deal with each other (including the point-of-sale personnel, display managers, marketing communications staff, and warehouse and quality control managers) to facilitate relationship administration. In addition to this, senior managers from both the supplier and retailers (such as sales and purchasing/merchandise directors) meet periodically to reinforce the relationship.

Face-to-face meetings normally occur every two to three months, principally to review ongoing contracts, negotiate future contracts and present product ideas for future business. These meetings would normally involve the category buyer and possibly senior buyers/purchasing directors. As well as meeting with the purchasing team, the supplier would also make a point of seeing other managers in the retailer's business centre.

Toy producers who deal with retailers on a regular basis are subject to periodic reviews of their 'serviceability'. The review would typically feature as part of the supplier–retailer meetings, and consists of:

- *Profit performance.* This assesses the extent to which a supplier is contributing to targets set by the buying team in terms of profit return per linear metre.

- *Delivery performance.* Contracts are agreed using an initial estimated figure that the retail business believes it can sell during a season. Once the product has gone to a store, sales are monitored, and estimated volume requirements are adjusted on a weekly basis. Supplier delivery performance is evaluated in terms of the accuracy of information provided on lead times (which is used by the retailer for forecasting and order fulfilment) and accuracy of completed deliveries (in terms of volume and timing).

- *Quality of contact.* In a broad sense the administration of a relationship is helped when both the supplier and dealer have a good understanding of each other's business, and this contributes to the dealer's evaluation of the quality of contact with a supplier. More specifically, the retailer will use comments/feedback from managers across the business to evaluate the supplier in terms of flexibility, responsiveness and problem-solving abilities.

(Continued)

(Continued)

CASE STUDY QUESTIONS

1   Based on the information in the case study, outline the structure of the supply chain of which Simba-Dickie is a part, identifying key parties and their role in the supply of products to end-consumers.

2   Describe what you consider to be the main elements of the logistics service programme that retailers expect of Simba-Dickie. Do the locations of the toy producer's activities present it with any difficulties in meeting these expectations?

3   Using the case study, and additional internet research, identify the principal differences in the distribution structure of the toy industry in France, Germany and the UK. What are the key implications of these differences for toy producers wanting to sell their products in these countries?

Sources: Simba-Dickie Group, 2010; Spielwarenmesse, 2015.

FURTHER READING

Bairstow, N. and Young, L. (2012) 'How channels evolve: a historical explanation', *Industrial Marketing Management*, 41 (3): 385–93.

This article provides an interesting account of the way in which routes to market in the Australian IT industry have evolved. While some characteristics are unique to the Australian marketplace, the industry has also been affected by other factors common to the sector worldwide. Particularly useful in giving a flavour of tensions that can exist in routes to markets are the authors' accounts of (and reasons for) the transformation of channel arrangements that were previously transaction-orientated, but highly profitable, into relational exchanges dominated by conflict.

Kashyap, V. and Sivdas, E. (2012) 'An exploratory examination of shared values in channel relationships', *Journal of Business Research*, 65 (5): 586–93.

This article moves thinking beyond the constructs of power and conflict frequently associated with channel relationships, to consider the role of shared values in contributing to partner behaviour. The authors suggest that shared values (in relation to, for example, annual sales, measures for determining organization effectiveness and methods of behaviour enforcement and performance monitoring) affect partner behaviour and are determined by perceived fairness and relationship quality (trust, commitment and satisfaction).

Porter, M.E. and Heppelmann, J.E. (2015) 'How smart connected products are transforming companies', *Harvard Business Review*, October: 96–114.

This paper provides a useful overview of the way in which digital products might change individual companies as well as all parties in a product system. The authors touch on both consumer and business markets, in doing so it is easy to see the basic ideas behind connected products. The article is generally positive about the potential offered by digitalization, although the reader might refer to other sources (such as A.T. Kearney/WHU annual survey of supply chain managers) to judge the immediate/medium business potential which can be pursued through 'connected' product systems.

12

PRICE-SETTING IN BUSINESS-TO-BUSINESS MARKETS

LEARNING OUTCOMES

After reading this chapter you will:

- understand how cost analysis, competitor analysis and customer analysis are essential elements of well-informed price decisions in business markets;
- be able to apply sales break-even analysis (cost–volume–profit analysis) to business pricing decisions;
- understand the different price positioning strategies that can be used in business-to-business markets;
- know what types of inter-departmental conflict can arise in pricing decisions;
- understand how long-term buyer–supplier relationships affect pricing in business markets;
- understand why bidding processes are important in business-to-business markets;
- know what types of bid process may be encountered;
- be able to draw up a strategy for key decisions in the bidding process, including whether or not to bid for a given contract, and the analytical procedures involved in deciding on a bid price;
- know how online auctions work and what influence they are likely to have on business markets; and
- appreciate that pricing decisions may have an ethical dimension.

INTRODUCTION

In previous editions of this book we remarked that pricing is both one of the most important and yet one of the most neglected aspects of business-to-business marketing. Rather surprisingly, the relative neglect of pricing as a research topic in B2B marketing seems to persist (Liozu and Hinterhuber, 2013; Liozu, 2015), even though the financial impact of price decisions is undeniable. A great deal of marketing effort is spent on trying to increase market share and sales volume, but in relative terms if a firm can manage to increase its prices this will have a far greater effect on profitability than an increase in sales. On average, a 5 per cent increase in price increases earnings before interest and taxes (EBIT) by 22 per cent, whereas a 5 per cent increase in sales turnover increases EBIT by 12 per cent, and a 5 per cent reduction in the cost of goods sold increases EBIT by 10 per cent (Hinterhuber, 2004). Price has a direct and substantial effect on profitability. Despite this, there is evidence that relatively few companies do systematic research on pricing, and pricing has received comparatively little attention from marketing scholars (Malhotra, 1996). According to Hinterhuber (2004), managers suffer from some pervasive misconceptions about pricing: that industrial buyers are highly price sensitive, that pricing is fundamentally a zero-sum game and that firms are generally price-takers who must follow the prices set in the market. Yet there is research evidence to show that industrial buyers often regard price as a comparatively unimportant decision criterion (Avila et al., 1993), suggesting that managers may have greater discretion than they think when setting price.

The business environment in which companies have to set their prices is growing ever more challenging. There are deflationary pressures in world markets, meaning that in many sectors prices are declining from one year to the next (Christopher and Gattorna, 2005). Some of this can be explained by normal cost-reduction processes such as the experience effect (unit costs tend to decline in a predictable way as accumulated experience rises), but other factors are also at work. These factors include the availability of new low-cost manufacturing capacity in emerging economies such as China, reductions in international trade barriers, the deregulation of many markets, and the impact of the internet, which has made price comparisons so much easier. Although rising labour costs in China mean that it is no longer quite the source of low-cost manufacturing that it once was, other countries such as Indonesia, India and Mexico are filling this gap (*The Economist*, 2014). In addition, business-to-business customers are increasingly sharing pricing information, and as business buyers and purchasing managers become better trained and qualified, so they gain improved negotiation skills in dealing with their suppliers (Lancioni, 2005). These pressures have put a growing emphasis on business-to-business organizations to get their pricing strategy right.

In this chapter we begin with the classic 'three Cs of pricing' – costs, customers and competitors – and then move on to consider strategic aspects of pricing, including price positioning, the pricing plan and the role of different departments in the pricing process. Two key aspects of business-to-business pricing are addressed in the middle sections of the chapter, dealing respectively with the impact of long-term buyer–supplier relationships on pricing and the bidding process under competitive tendering conditions. As the chapter unfolds a number of ethical issues in pricing emerge, and the final section of the chapter directly addresses ethical issues in business-to-business pricing.

COSTS, CUSTOMERS AND COMPETITORS

Clearly it is the case that costs, customers and competitors – the three Cs of pricing – all have an important part to play in pricing decisions. However, it would be misleading to think that any one of these factors necessarily *determines* price. To put it succinctly, the relevant costs associated with making a product or delivering a service determine the *price floor*; the benefits that the customer perceives the product or service to deliver determine the *price ceiling*; while the intensity of competition and the strategies of competitors affect the *feasible pricing region* that lies between the costs floor and the customer benefits ceiling.

Costs and break-even analysis

Cost-plus pricing is a common approach to pricing in business markets. The price is determined by calculating the average cost of production and then adding on a standard profit mark-up – a method illustrated in Figure 12.1.

This approach to pricing creates the illusion of security, since at first sight the firm will necessarily both cover its costs and make a respectable profit. However, cost-plus pricing completely ignores both competitors and customers, and so must therefore be flawed. In fact, cost-plus pricing contains a fundamental logical flaw at its very heart:

- in order to set price one must know average costs of production;
- one cannot know the average cost of production without knowing production and sales volume;
- sales volume is expected to vary with price; and
- therefore, in order to set price one must first know ... price!

In order to calculate the full average cost of production the fixed overheads of the business have to be allocated, and this allocation is based on a sales volume estimate. If sales volume is overestimated then the fixed costs per unit of production will be higher than expected, and the firm will make less than its target profit margin. If sales volume is underestimated then fixed costs per unit will be lower than expected, and the profit margin will be above target. A particular danger of cost-plus pricing arises where sales fall below forecast so that profits are lower than expected, which encourages the firm (using cost-plus logic) to increase price in an attempt to capture the desired profit margin. Elementary economic theory suggests that raising price in these circumstances is likely to reduce sales further, leaving the firm even further away from its target profit goal.

FIGURE 12.1   Cost-plus pricing

To calculate the price of a manufactured component	£
Variable costs of production (e.g. materials, direct labour)	5.75
Allocated overhead costs (see below)	3.49
Full cost of production	9.24
Desired profit margin (20%)	1.85
Final selling price	11.09
Calculation of allocated overhead	
Total overhead cost for factory	£150,000.00
Expected sales volume	43,000 units
Overhead cost per unit	£3.49
Complicating factors	
How to allocate overhead between multiple products manufactured using the same facilities? What happens if sales volume is higher or lower than target?	

There are two key questions that managers will invariably be interested in concerning pricing decisions, and for which an understanding of costs is essential. They are:

1. If we cut price, then by how much must sales volume increase so that we increase our profit?

2. If we raise price, then by how much can sales decline before we incur a loss?

These questions can be answered with the help of *break-even sales analysis* (cost–volume–profit analysis), which is illustrated in B2B Snapshot 12.1.

B2B SNAPSHOT 12.1   BREAK-EVEN SALES ANALYSIS: BRICOLAGE MANUFACTURING

Table 12.1 and Figure 12.2 show the level of costs, revenues and profits for a small firm, Bricolage Manufacturing, for a typical month. Fixed costs amount to £7,500 per month, while variable costs are £2.50 per unit manufactured. These two amounts combine to give the total cost per month at different volume levels. Two revenue lines are shown in Figure 12.2, one for each of two price levels of £10.00 per unit and £12.00 per unit. Table 12.1 shows the complete data for the month, while the graph in Figure 12.2 shows a classic graphical linear break-even analysis.

Notice that the gradient of the revenue curve depends on the price; technically, revenue equals price multiplied by volume $[R = PV]$, the gradient of the revenue curve is the first differential of revenue with respect to volume, and for a linear function the first differential is a constant $[d/dV (PV) = P]$. From the graph we can see that the break-even point for Revenue 1 is around 1,000 units and the break-even point for Revenue 2 is around 800 units. A simple calculation can be used to find the precise break-even volume for each revenue curve; the break-even volume equals fixed costs divided by the difference between price and variable costs.

$$BEV \quad \frac{FC}{(P-VC)}$$

Hence for Revenue 1, the break-even point is [7500/(10.00 – 2.50)], which is exactly 1,000 units, and for Revenue 2 the break-even point is [7500/(12.00 – 2.50)], which is 789 units.

Suppose that the price is currently £10.00 per unit and the sales volume is 1,400 units, so that the current profit level is £3,000. If Bricolage were to raise the price to £12.00 per unit, by how much could volume decline before profits were reduced? An approximate answer can be derived from Table 12.1. At a price of £12.00 Bricolage makes £2,950 profit on a sales volume of 1,100 units, so if sales volume declines by less than 300 units (21.4 per cent) then profits will increase as a result of the 20 per cent price increase.

Suppose that the price is currently £12.00 per unit and the sales volume is 1,200 units, so that the current profit level is £3,900. If Bricolage were to reduce the price to £10.00 per unit, by how much would sales volume have to increase if profits were not to decline? Again, an approximate answer can be found from Table 12.1 – at price £10.00 and volume 1,500, Bricolage makes profits of £3,750, which is reasonably close to £3,900. This means that if sales volume increases by over 300 units (25 per cent) then profits will increase as a result of the 16.7 per cent price cut. This indicates that the price cut will only increase profits if sales are reasonably elastic with respect to price; strictly, Bricolage is looking for an own-price demand elasticity value of in excess of 1.5 to make the price cut profitable (price elasticity of demand is discussed further in the next section).

As with the break-even sales volume, it is quite straightforward to calculate exact break-even sales changes associated with specific price changes when one has the data shown in Table 12.1. The percentage break-even sales change can be calculated from the price change and the change in contribution margin (CM) (Nagle and Holden, 2002):

$$\% \text{ Break-even sales change} = \frac{-\text{ Price change}}{CM + \text{Price change}}$$

For the price increase from £10.00 to £12.00 this equation gives:

$$\% \text{ Break-even sales change} = \frac{-2.00}{7.50 + 2.00} = -21.05\%$$

For the price cut from £12.00 to £10.00 this equation gives:

$$\% \text{ Break-even sales change} = \frac{-2.00}{9.50 + (-2.00)} = 26.7\%$$

In summary, on grounds of profitability (and neglecting other issues that may affect the pricing decision) Bricolage should consider increasing the price from £10.00 to £12.00 if research tells it that its sales volume will fall by less than 21.05 per cent. If its price was already at £12.00, then it should consider cutting the price to £10.00 only if its sales volume will increase by more than 26.7 per cent.

TABLE 12.1 Break-even sales analysis

Volume	Variable cost	Fixed cost	Total cost	Revenue 1	Revenue 2	Profit 1	Profit 2
0	0.00	7,500.00	7,500.00	0.00	0.00	−7,500.00	−7,500.00
100	250.00	7,500.00	7,750.00	1,000.00	1,200.00	−6,750.00	−6,550.00
200	500.00	7,500.00	8,000.00	2,000.00	2,400.00	−6,000.00	−5,600.00
300	750.00	7,500.00	8,250.00	3,000.00	3,600.00	−5,250.00	−4,650.00
400	1,000.00	7,500.00	8,500.00	4,000.00	4,800.00	−4,500.00	−3,700.00
500	1,250.00	7,500.00	8,750.00	5,000.00	6,000.00	−3,750.00	−2,750.00
600	1,500.00	7,500.00	9,000.00	6,000.00	7,200.00	−3,000.00	−1,800.00
700	1,750.00	7,500.00	9,250.00	7,000.00	8,400.00	−2,250.00	−850.00
800	2,000.00	7,500.00	9,500.00	8,000.00	9,600.00	−1,500.00	100.00

(Continued)

(Continued)

Volume	Variable cost	Fixed cost	Total cost	Revenue 1	Revenue 2	Profit 1	Profit 2
900	2,250.00	7,500.00	9,750.00	9,000.00	10,800.00	−750.00	1,050.00
1000	2,500.00	7,500.00	10,000.00	10,000.00	12,000.00	0.00	2,000.00
1100	2,750.00	7,500.00	10,250.00	11,000.00	13,200.00	750.00	2,950.00
1200	3,000.00	7,500.00	10,500.00	12,000.00	14,400.00	1,500.00	3,900.00
1300	3,250.00	7,500.00	10,750.00	13,000.00	15,600.00	2,250.00	4,850.00
1400	3,500.00	7,500.00	11,000.00	14,000.00	16,800.00	3,000.00	5,800.00
1500	3,750.00	7,500.00	11,250.00	15,000.00	18,000.00	3,750.00	6,750.00

Notes:

1. Variable cost per unit = £2.50
2. Price 1 = £10.00
3. Price 2 = £12.00

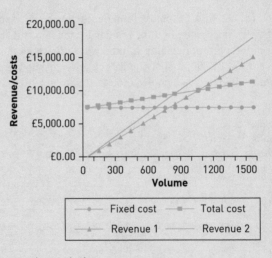

FIGURE 12.2 Break-even sales analysis

Customers and demand analysis

It is clear from the preceding analysis that the responsiveness of demand to price changes is a critical issue in pricing decisions. One of the elementary flaws in cost-plus pricing is that this factor is completely ignored. In making pricing decisions managers are forced to make assumptions about demand responsiveness, which is

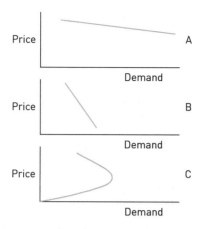

FIGURE 12.3 The demand curve and price elasticity of demand

most conveniently measured using the elasticity of demand with respect to price – this is usually simply referred to as *demand elasticity*. Demand elasticity can be readily understood graphically by considering the shape of a firm's demand curve.

Figure 12.3 illustrates three forms of the demand curve. Curves A and B fall under the general heading of 'normal' demand, meaning that the quantity demanded declines continuously as the price rises. Curve C is an example of perverse demand – above a certain price the demand curve is 'normal' and demand declines as price increases, but below that price, demand declines as the price decreases. The lower section of this curve (the 'perverse demand' section) indicates that firms wish to buy more of the product as the price rises. This may be because price is seen as a clear indicator of quality, so that buyers steer clear of very cheap products in the belief that they cannot be of high quality. (Shipley and Jobber (2001) suggest that nobody would want to buy the services of a very cheap management consultant, and that industrial buyers would be deeply suspicious of truck tyres that were offered at a price far below the prevailing market price.)

Most of the time and in most market segments business marketers are dealing with conditions of normal demand – the conditions implied by demand curves such as A and B. Curves A and B have been constructed to illustrate quite different circumstances however. The market segment illustrated in curve A exhibits *elastic demand*, meaning that a 1 per cent change in price causes a change in demand of more than 1 per cent. In general terms demand elasticity can be calculated as the percentage change in demand caused by a 1 per cent change in price. An examination of the demand curve for segment B will show that a substantial change in price is needed to cause much change at all in demand – a 1 per cent change in price will cause far less than a 1 per cent change in demand. Market segment B shows *inelastic demand*. The following conditions relate demand elasticity to the firm's revenue:

- where demand is *elastic*, a price increase will reduce revenue and a price cut will increase revenue; and
- where demand is *inelastic*, a price increase will increase revenue and a price cut will reduce revenue.

According to Shipley and Jobber (2001: 305), demand will tend to be inelastic for industrial brands that:

- customers need urgently;
- are strongly differentiated;
- compete against few alternative customer solutions;
- are complex and difficult to compare;
- are complementary to other highly priced products;
- involve high switching costs;
- customers see the price as being a quality indicator;
- customers buy for ostentatious motives;
- account for a small proportion of the buyer's total expenditure; and
- where the price can be shared by multiple buyers.

In addition, it is generally the case that the elasticity of demand for the products of a single company is lower (more inelastic) than the elasticity of demand for the products of the industry as a whole. The reason for this is that demand will be more inelastic where many close substitute products are available – within an industry the products of competing suppliers are normally regarded as fairly close substitutes for each other. Another important issue upon which some light has recently been shed is whether customer demand sensitivity is affected by investments in customer service designed to maintain and develop the supplier–customer relationship; in short, does customer relationship-building through improved service deliver lower customer price sensitivity? There is some evidence to suggest that it does (Zeng et al., 2011). We return to this issue below when discussing relational aspects of business-to-business pricing, and particularly in B2B Snapshot 12.2.

The ultimate form of customer-based price-setting occurs where the firm aims to set price based on customer-perceived value. This is known as value-based pricing, and it is used infrequently in practice (Töytäri et al., 2015). A difficulty associated with value-based pricing is that it requires the supplier to have a good understanding of the customer-perceived value that each customer obtains from the use of their product offering. Customers themselves often resist attempts by suppliers to quantify customer-perceived value and prefer to focus instead on the supplier's costs, particularly where cost-based pricing has been commonly used and so is considered to be the norm (Töytäri et al., 2015). It is important to understand that customer perceptions about value and price are not fixed, and that marketing managers can influence how customers perceive these factors (Hinterhuber, 2015). Furthermore, as Andreas Hinterhuber has amusingly pointed out, neither customers nor marketing managers always act with perfect rationality in B2B pricing decisions: 'Rationality is not merely resting, it may never have existed in the first place … We need a replacement' (Hinterhuber, 2015: 72).

Take a look at B2B Scenario 12.1 and give some thought to how you would go about trying to convert enhanced customer value into premium prices in a competitive B2B market.

B2B SCENARIO 12.1   HOW TO CAPITALIZE ON ENHANCED CUSTOMER VALUE AT PRINTCO?

A characteristic challenge facing business to business firms these days is that they have to invest in new technology to deliver enhanced value to customers, but find it very difficult to raise prices because of global competition. So on the one hand investment costs money and delivers additional customer benefits, but on the other hand the B2B firm struggles to achieve a return on their investment in new technology because customers have so many competing suppliers to choose between. Nowhere has this been truer in recent years than in the printing industry. Globally, the commercial printing market is worth around $380 billion. The market is characterized by a large number of printing companies, most of which are small. Even the largest commercial printing company only has around 2.8 per cent of the total market. Over-capacity in the market is putting downward pressure on prices, while the adoption of new digital printing technology requires firms to invest in new equipment. It is common for commercial printing jobs to be awarded following a competitive bidding process.

Printco is a small Swedish commercial printing company that is experiencing the effects of these global market trends. Printco was an early adopter of digital printing technology, foreseeing that the industry would eventually become dominated by digital. Over the last seven years Printco has continued to invest substantially in digital printing equipment, while the prices it has been able to charge commercial companies have been steady or declining. Consequently, the customers have benefited from the investment in new technology, but Printco's profits have been squeezed. For example, digital technology enables Printco to respond very quickly to customer requirements by offering short delivery times, but it has not been possible to charge more for this service. On the other hand, there is little doubt that the ability to offer short delivery times on critical commercial printing jobs has benefited Printco in two ways: first, it makes it easier to win orders; and, second, it helps to build good relationships with customers who are impressed by the excellent service. Nevertheless, the management at Printco are determined to seek out ways of capitalizing on their substantial investments in new technology to improve their profit margins by charging a premium over the offerings of less technologically advanced competitors.

The management team have got together to consider how to make a price premium acceptable to their customers.

Sources: Hultén et al. (2009); MarketLine (2012).

Competitor analysis

Shipley and Jobber (2001) make the point that most business-to-business firms operate in *oligopolistic markets*, while Nagle and Holden (2002) make the important and related point that in terms of game theory, pricing should generally be considered a zero-sum game (although notice that Hinterhuber (2004) argues that managers should avoid thinking of pricing as necessarily a zero-sum game). In the hypothetical, perfectly competitive market (this entails some very unrealistic assumptions such as zero entry and exit barriers and perfect information) all firms are price-takers, which means that they can either sell their product at the market price or not sell it at all. In a pure monopoly (which is, of course, very uncommon but not as unrealistic as perfect competition) the firm has a great deal of discretion over price.

In practice, virtually all markets lie nowhere near the extremes of perfect competition or monopoly, and most are dominated by a few substantial competitors, each with a substantial market share (a point that we also made in Chapter 1, when discussing market concentration in business markets). These are the conditions of oligopoly. The key feature of oligopoly, is that the decisions of each competitor directly affect its rivals (interdependence), which means that in terms of economic theory there is no determinate solution to the strategic problems of oligopoly, and oligopoly can be conveniently analysed as a formal game (hence 'game theory'). Under oligopoly, pricing is generally a zero-sum game because the gains of one 'player' are the losses of another. If one firm cuts its price and increases its market share, then that market share (and associated revenue and profits) must have been lost by one or more rival firms. Under conditions of oligopoly there is always a danger of a price war that will see prices spiralling downwards as the rival firms try to grab market share from each other, with profits for individual firms and for the industry as a whole declining as a result.

Two types of legal price behaviour, characteristic of oligopoly, are designed to avoid the risk of a price war. First, there is price leadership, where the acknowledged leader in the industry (probably the firm with the highest market share) is closely watched by rivals who follow its lead on pricing decisions. When demand is slack and there is overcapacity, the price leader is the first to cut prices, which provides rival firms with a signal about the appropriate magnitude of price reductions. When the industry is operating near to capacity, the price leader will be the first to raise price, with rival firms following shortly after. The price leadership mechanism introduces discipline into the market and reduces the risk of a destructive price war. The second mechanism is price stability. Where there is no acknowledged price leader, prices can become very 'sticky', and the firms in the industry adjust their production volume rather than their price to adapt to changing market conditions. If one of the competitors cuts its price, then the other firms can be expected to follow, but there is no similar guarantee that rival firms will follow when one of their number raises price. The result will tend to be lengthy periods of price stability interspersed with brief periods of price cutting by all firms in the industry.

While the circumstances described in the previous paragraph are the common legal methods of handling price-setting under oligopoly, this type of market structure lends itself to illegal and unethical practices of price fixing and collusion. These issues will be discussed further in the final section of this chapter on ethical issues in pricing.

PRICING: STRATEGY AND ORGANIZATION

Shipley and Jobber (2001) have argued that it is essential to adopt a systematic and well-organized approach to pricing. They proposed a comprehensive, multi-stage pricing process that takes account of all of the relevant factors affecting pricing effectiveness – a process that they called the 'pricing wheel'. The pricing wheel is illustrated in Figure 12.4.

FIGURE 12.4 The pricing wheel (Shipley and Jobber, 2001: 303)

With permission from Elsevier.

The point of the pricing wheel is to emphasize that pricing is not a decision that is taken once and then forgotten about. Rather, pricing is a more or less continuous process, in which pricing decisions must be constantly updated to take account of factors within the control of the firm, such as new product features, and factors outside of the control of the firm, such as new competitor pricing strategies. The first decision to be made is how great a role that pricing is to play in the overall marketing strategy. In industries with highly customized products that are designed specifically to meet the needs of each individual customer, price is a comparatively unimportant component of marketing strategy. Naturally, there are other industries, such as the office-cleaning sector, for example, where price is a much more important factor. Even within a single industry sector, there is scope for a firm to put more or less emphasis on price as a component of its marketing strategy – if the firm positions itself as a differentiator offering enhanced customer value, then it will de-emphasize price as a factor in its marketing strategy.

Although business-to-business organizations may pursue a very wide range of price objectives, research has shown that the most common objectives are concerned with profits, survival, sales volume, sales revenue, market share, image creation, competitive parity or advantage, barriers to entry and perceived fairness. Of these, profit targets are the most common. Survival pricing usually only arises in industries with chronic overcapacity, where firms are desperate to make as much use as possible of their fixed assets. Pricing to maximize sales or market share will generally imply lower prices than profit-driven pricing, and may indicate a longer-term orientation (with the strategic aim of building a dominating position in the market) or a belief that higher market share will inevitably bring about higher profits. It is well known that there is a correlation between profitability and market share (Buzzell and Gale, 1987), but there is no obvious reason to suppose that this shows that higher market share *causes* higher profitability – it is equally likely that firms that pursue effective competitive strategies achieve both higher profitability and higher market share (Nagle and Holden, 2002). Image-based pricing associates the price with the desired value position of the product in the mind of the business buyer; a premium price will be associated with above-average customer value, which may be delivered through product characteristics such as enhanced quality or additional customer service. Competitor pricing may be aimed at achieving price parity, at aggressively undercutting competitor prices, or at deterring new market entrants by keeping price sufficiently low that the prospects of profitable market entry are minimized. Whatever pricing objective is adopted, fairness will often be an additional consideration. For example, a shortage of a particular type of computer memory chip might encourage suppliers to raise their prices sharply (a practice known as 'price gouging') in the knowledge that personal-computer OEMs have no ready substitute and must pay the higher prices if they are to maintain production. Such a pricing strategy would very likely be seen as unfair by the OEMs, would encourage them to seek alternative products or alternative manufacturers of similar products, and would reduce the loyalty of the OEMs to their suppliers once supplies of the memory chip became more plentiful.

Price positioning

Price-positioning strategy takes account of three elements: the price itself, the customer benefits derived from using the product or service, and competitor positioning. Figure 12.5 illustrates an approach to price-positioning strategy recommended by Shipley and Jobber (2001). In a particular market segment, nine possible price positions are defined in terms of relative customer value. Remember that we have defined customer value as the tradeoff between customer-perceived benefits and customer-perceived sacrifices (see Chapter 4).

In Figure 12.5 we are using price as a proxy to represent customer-perceived sacrifices. The strongest price–benefits tradeoff is offered by the *market ruler* position. This position is difficult to achieve, since delivering enhanced benefits to the customer generally involves additional costs, making it difficult to offer a low price while also achieving an acceptable profit margin. In any case, a firm trying to establish itself in the market ruler position would probably find it difficult to convince customers that

Perceived benefits of competing suppliers' offerings

		Low	Med	High
P R I C E	Low	Chancer	Thriver	Market ruler
	Med	Bungler	Also-ran	Thriver
	High	No-hoper	Bungler	Chancer

FIGURE 12.5 Alternative price–benefit positioning strategies (Shipley and Jobber, 2001: 308)

With permission from Elsevier.

the customer value offering was genuine – buyers would need to be convinced that this firm could deliver above-average benefits for below-average prices. The market ruler makes sense when there is a long-term goal, such as becoming the established market leader and maximizing long-term market share, associated with forgoing potential short-term profits. If there is no such long-term goal then a firm that can genuinely offer above-average customer benefits is probably better off in the *thriver* (medium price/high benefits) position. This position is more sustainable than the other *thriver* (low price/medium benefits) position because rival firms generally find it easier to cut price and accept smaller margins than to deliver enhanced customer benefits.

The *chancer* positions become viable where the thriver and market ruler positions are unoccupied. Both chancer positions are vulnerable – the low price/low benefits chancer is particularly vulnerable to a rival who offers higher customer benefits for a similar price, and the high price/high benefits chancer is vulnerable to a rival who offers equivalent customer benefits at a lower price. In addition, Anderson and Wynstra (2010) discuss the issue of *ambiguity about superior value*, meaning that customers are often uncertain whether they will be able to reap the cost reductions or the revenue increases that are promised by a product that supposedly offers enhanced value. This means that chancers who offer a high value/high price product may have difficulty persuading customers to buy; Anderson and Wynstra (2010) suggest that using 'reference customers' who will confirm the higher value of the product is a way to convince customers.

Of the remaining four positions in Figure 12.5 it is clear that the *bungler* and *no-hoper* positions offer poor customer value and are unlikely to be sustainable other than in the very short term and in unusual market conditions (for example, during an acute shortage of supply of a key industrial component). The *also-ran* position too is very vulnerable to attack, since rivals can attack it on price or customer benefits alone (the two thriver positions), or on both simultaneously (the market ruler position).

The pricing plan and the pricing committee

The pricing plan comprises seven components:

- overall summary
- overview of the current marketing situation
- pricing SWOT analysis
- pricing strategy
- pricing objectives
- pricing programmes
- pricing control and review.

These seven components are characteristic of many types of planning process. In essence, they can be reduced to an analysis of the current situation (overview and SWOT analysis), strategy determination (strategy and objectives), and an implementation and control process (programmes, control and review).

According to Lancioni (2005: 177), 'Building value-added into a pricing program requires that a company develop a comprehensive pricing plan that integrates all of the components of the pricing process into a single document that details how the value-added strategy of the company will be implemented.' The two major hurdles to establishing a pricing plan are, first, the perception that pricing is too interdependent with other elements of the marketing mix and, second, difficulties in establishing a pricing organization in the firm (Cravens, 1997). Clearly, marketing strategy involves a wide range of elements such as target market selection, positioning, distribution strategy, product features and quality, many of which interact with price. While it is true that there are interactions between many of the elements of the marketing mix, the contention is that price in particular depends upon a very large number of other mix elements.

Similarly, just as price affects and is affected by so many other elements of the marketing mix, a wide range of different functions within the company have a legitimate interest in pricing decisions. For example, one could argue that in addition to senior management the sales, marketing, finance, operations and customer service functions all have a legitimate interest in pricing decisions. Pricing is inherently a cross-functional activity that involves people from several different departments. For this reason, many firms have a pricing committee which oversees the pricing process. The principal functions of the pricing committee are to administer pricing policy, to respond to competition and to develop the pricing strategy for the firm (Lancioni, 2005). Membership of the pricing committee is likely to include finance, accounting, marketing, sales, operations and senior management personnel. Each department brings its own perspective. For example, the concerns of the sales department tend to be the impact of price upon customers and the opportunities to use price as a tool to increase sales; the finance department tends to focus on the analysis of profit margins and return on investment.

Intra-organizational aspects of pricing

Despite the obvious importance of pricing decisions, there is evidence that the pricing function receives insufficient attention from top managers, and that inadequate consideration is given to internal organizational factors affecting pricing (Liozu, 2015). Obstacles to the development of effective pricing strategies can arise from internal organizational factors (Lancioni, 2005). Each department tends to have its own perspective on pricing decisions, and these perspectives may conflict. Lancioni et al. (2005) even refer to internal 'roadblocks' getting in the way of strategic pricing decisions. The finance department often seeks to control the whole of the pricing process and tends to have a short-term perspective on pricing. This leads the finance department to insist that all products must always make profits. This can cause conflict because the marketing department may wish to sell one or more products at a loss in the short term for a variety of reasons – for example, to respond to a competitor's strategy, to build a customer relationship or to increase demand for complementary products in the product line. The accounting department tends to emphasize traditional costing methods and, in particular, cost-plus pricing (that is, setting price equal to fully allocated costs plus a target profit margin). In general, the finance and accounting departments are far less inclined than the sales and marketing departments to respond quickly to competitor action and customer preferences.

Obstacles to price-setting arise out of these conflicts between departmental positions. While it would be wrong to see one department or another as the 'problem' in the pricing process, there is no doubt that B2B marketing managers can become frustrated by what they perceive to be roadblocks to pricing constructed by other departments. Strikingly, Lancioni et al. (2005) surveyed 125 American B2B firms and found that in 45 of them the finance department was considered to raise pricing roadblocks, while in 37 the accounting department did the same. The tendency within finance and accounting departments is to emphasize the importance of costs and short-term considerations in pricing – such considerations are important, but if considered paramount can lead to pricing inflexibility. The tendency within sales and marketing departments is both an emphasis on the importance of customer relationships and competitor actions in pricing, and an inclination towards optimism regarding the responsiveness of demand to price (price elasticity of demand). Clearly, although a concern for customers and competitors is essential, it must be tempered by a realistic assessment of the impact of pricing decisions on short- and long-term profitability.

The role of the sales force in pricing

Chapter 8 addressed the principal functions of the sales force from the point of view of relationship communications. The sales force has a particularly important role to play in mediating between the company and its customers with respect to pricing decisions (Liozu, 2015). Business-to-business sales executives can carry more or less responsibility for pricing, depending on how much authority is delegated to them from the company generally and from the sales manager specifically. The conventional view is that since salespeople are the closest to the customer, it follows that they understand the customer's valuation of the company's product offerings better than anyone else and so they should have considerable delegated authority to make pricing decisions for individual customers. As long as the remuneration structure for the sales force is based on gross margin rather than simply on sales revenue – so that the salesperson is rewarded according to profits generated and not just on sales – one would expect the salesperson to make informed decisions about making profitable sales. However, in a study of 108 business-to-business marketing organizations, Stephenson et al. (1979) found that those firms that gave salespeople the least pricing authority generated the highest levels of gross margin. They suggested that five factors caused salespeople to make pricing decisions that resulted in sub-optimal profits:

1. Salespeople may use price discounting to avoid the work or time involved in creative selling or customer problem-solving. They may offer discounts rather than try to overcome customer objections during the selling process.

2. Salespeople may not have sufficiently objective knowledge of the customer's response to price; they may overestimate customer price sensitivity because of their high motivation to make a sale.

3. When salespeople are given greater price discretion this may alter competitive behaviour in the market. Competitors may feel compelled to give their salespeople more price discretion as well. The result may be an industry-wide decline in profit margins, rather than increased sales.

4. Greater price discretion for salespeople may alter buyer behaviour – when they know that the salesperson has price discretion, buyers may adopt more aggressive price negotiation tactics.

5. Using a sales incentive scheme based on gross profit margin may not be sufficient to ensure that salespeople make optimal price decisions for the company as a whole. First, salespeople may not completely understand the implications of such an incentive scheme, and may prefer to use sales revenue as a simpler measure of success. Second, on any one deal the loss of commission resulting from giving the customer an extra discount may appear insignificant, compared to the sense of satisfaction arising out of making the sale.

For these reasons Stephenson et al. (1979) recommend *against* giving the sales force substantial pricing authority. Joseph (2001) developed a formal model of price delegation and suggested a contingency approach for sales managers. An important feature of this model is the inclusion of the difficulty of making a sale (the 'effort cost' of the sale) as well as the remuneration associated with the sale. Joseph (2001) concluded that salespeople should be given high pricing authority when the effort cost of making the sale is either relatively low or relatively high, but should be given limited pricing authority for intermediate levels of effort cost. This suggests that salespeople should have high pricing authority in market segments where sales are either fairly easy to achieve or are hard to achieve, but they should have limited pricing authority in market segments where the difficulty of making sales is intermediate. Where sales are easy to achieve, the salesperson does not need to abuse the delegated pricing authority in order to make the sale; where sales are hard to achieve the salesperson needs to have extra pricing discretion as a tool in the armoury. However, in intermediate sales situations, limited pricing authority removes the possibility that the salesperson will take the easy route to making the sale and simply offer a discount.

RELATIONAL ASPECTS OF BUSINESS-TO-BUSINESS PRICING

The pricing effects of long-term buyer–supplier relationships

We know that buying and selling in business-to-business markets often takes place within relatively stable inter-firm relationships, which can last for many years. The processes of developing and managing inter-firm buyer–seller relationships were discussed earlier in the book. The reader might reasonably wonder what the implications of long-term buyer–seller relationships are for pricing strategy. Clearly, in a business world where long-term relationships are a fact of life, one must take account of them when considering price. Research in business markets has suggested that there are both costs and benefits to suppliers from entering into long-term buyer–seller relationships with customers (Kalwani and Narayandas, 1995).

The advantages arise from increased sales and greater sales stability, and from using loyal customers as a source of new product ideas, as a test-bed for new product development and as showcase accounts – long-term customers can be used to help attract new business. In addition, long-term customers may be locked into the relationship through the creation of switching costs that make it far more economical for the customer to do business with their long-term supplier than with a potential rival. On the other hand, there are costs associated with being tied into a long-term customer relationship. Customers that are willing to enter into such relationships may be particularly demanding and difficult to serve (Jackson, 1985b); they may demand short-term price concessions from the supplier while continuing to expect a long-term orientation towards the relationship, so that it is not clear that the investment in the relationship pays an economic rate of return. Certainly, there is plenty of evidence that major manufacturing firms expect their long-term suppliers to deliver continuous price reductions. Of course, the justification for price reductions is that the greater volume and stability of business with a major customer generate long-term cost savings for the supplier (through the experience effect and economies of scale).

In a study carried out in the American manufacturing sector, Kalwani and Narayandas (1995) found that supplier firms involved in long-term customer relationships generally benefited from higher sales growth and reduced inventory costs when compared to similar firms pursuing a transactional approach to marketing. However, they also had lower gross profit margins, indicating that their long-term customers had benefited most from the cost reductions achieved – the cost benefits had been passed on to the customers in the form of reduced prices. Nevertheless, the firms engaging in long-term customer relationships had performed better than comparable transactional marketing firms in terms of return on investment. In short, long-term customer relationships brought the benefits of lower costs to the suppliers, who, despite seeing their gross profit margins shrink, had also benefited in terms of return on investment. Long-term customer relationships commonly place suppliers under price pressure, but the benefits of being involved in such relationships mean that customer relationship building in business-to-business markets can be expected to pay off in terms of profitability. Argouslidis and Indounas (2010) studied the export pricing practices of 243 UK manufacturing firms to find out if they were implementing a relationship-based approach to export pricing. They found that relationship pricing is more likely to be used by firms that have greater experience of exporting and by firms that have a formal and systematic approach to pricing. Although the work of Argouslidis and Indounas (2010) was exploratory, it provides considerable encouragement for the idea that relationship pricing – that is to say, taking account of desired relationship maintenance and development goals in pricing – is a promising pricing strategy. Further evidence for this proposition is provided in B2B Snapshot 12.2.

B2B SNAPSHOT 12.2   CUSTOMER SERVICE, RELATIONSHIP BUILDING AND PRICING IN CHINA

There are many good reasons to build relationships with your B2B customers. However, if we could establish that relationship-building activities reduced the price sensitivity of customers, it would provide a great incentive for relationship building as a marketing strategy in B2B markets. In the fast-moving world of the Chinese mobile phone industry, four Chinese researchers seem to have shown that relationship building using enhanced customer service leads to lower customer price sensitivity. The customers involved in this study were no pushovers – 233 Chinese mobile phone retail businesses, operating in a highly competitive market. But the evidence is clear that retailer price sensitivity is significantly affected by the quality of the relationship with the supplier (the suppliers are companies like Motorola, Samsung and local Chinese manufacturers). Suppliers that deliver better customer

(Continued)

(Continued)

service experience lower customer price sensitivity. Consequently, the Chinese researchers advise suppliers trying to sell mobile phones in China to strive to build better relationships with retailers based on superior customer service, customer satisfaction and customer perceived value, in order to reduce price sensitivity. Five key dimensions of service quality all play a part: the way customer-service staff handle customer interactions, the efficiency with which orders are fulfilled, the ease with which orders can be placed, the product range that is offered, and how well order discrepancies are handled when they arise. The most direct way of reducing customer price sensitivity is to have excellent processes for fulfilling orders and for handling order discrepancies. Not surprisingly, these busy mobile phone retailers place considerable value on getting the right products as quickly and easily as possible, enabling them to deliver a great service to their own customers.

Source: Zeng et al., 2011.

Supply chain pricing

Changes in the environment of global business have encouraged companies to concentrate on their core competencies and to outsource an increasing number of business activities. This means that companies find themselves relying on suppliers for an increasing proportion of their business activities. Under these circumstances supply chain management becomes a critically important management process, and companies seek to build partnerships with preferred suppliers. When this becomes the case, the traditional role of price must change. Traditionally, pricing has been regarded as the way in which the value associated with a transaction is divided up between the buyer and the seller – thus, price has primarily a 'distributive' function. In this traditional view, price is seen as the means of dividing up a fixed 'pie' of value that is created during a business transaction, and the predominant approach to pricing is win/lose or a zero-sum game, meaning that if one party is better off then the other party must be worse off.

In *supply chain pricing*, the various companies involved at the different stages of the production process (companies located at different links in the chain of derived demand) are seen as collaborators in the production of an end product, rather than as rivals in a single transaction. Logically it is plainly the case that the value accruing to all of the companies in the supply chain can only be turned into cash when the end product is sold to a final customer. When this idea is applied to pricing, we have the concept of supply chain pricing. First, the participants in the supply chain should collaborate to ensure that the realized value from the sale of the end product is optimized, and then a second, and subsidiary, question is how that value is distributed between the members of the supply chain.

Under most circumstances the aggregate profits accruing to the members of the supply chain will be maximized when supply chain pricing is employed rather than any other pricing method (Voeth and Herbst, 2005). This means that a more collaborative approach to pricing by members of the supply chain will increase their overall profitability. Of course, the key dilemma associated with this idea is that the benefits of supply chain pricing must subsequently be distributed between the companies involved. Powerful members of the supply chain may use their position to appropriate more than a fair share of the overall profit; there is also an incentive for members of the supply chain to act deceitfully (for instance by exaggerating their costs) in order to claim a higher share of the profits. Supply chain pricing relies on open-book costing, meaning that all of the suppliers involved provide full, honest details of their costs to the final manufacturer (the company that will convert the end product into cash). Clearly there is a risk of dishonesty.

BID PRICING

Types of bidding process: four basic auction mechanisms

The four basic auction mechanisms are the English, Dutch, first-price sealed-bid and second-price sealed-bid auctions. The English auction is the most familiar auction format – an ascending-price auction in which the last remaining bidder receives the good and pays the amount of their bid. In a Dutch auction a public price starts at a very high level and the price falls until the first participant finds the price low enough to submit a bid. The first bidder is the winner and receives the good at the price prevailing when the clock was stopped. Both of these auction types are 'real-time' auctions. *Sealed-bid auctions* are not real-time auctions. Each bidder submits a single sealed bid, and all of the bids are opened at a stipulated time. The bidder submitting the highest bid price is the winner. In a first-price sealed-bid auction the winner pays the price of their own bid. In a second-price sealed-bid auction the winner pays the amount of the second-highest bid.

That branch of economics concerned with auctions – auction theory – shows that where bidders are revenue neutral and their valuations of the good are independent of each other ('independent private values') then all four auction types yield the same expected revenue to the auctioneer. Under these conditions the English auction is *strategically equivalent* to the second-price sealed-bid auction, and the Dutch auction is strategically equivalent to the first-price sealed-bid auction. Strategic equivalence means that an identical bidder would follow the same bidding strategy in the two different auction types (Lucking-Reiley, 1999).

Internet auctions

Estimates of the scale of B2B e-commerce vary. It is clear that the business-to-business sector pioneered e-commerce, that e-commerce is of greater importance in the business sector than in the consumer sector, and that the value of B2B e-commerce transactions exceeds the value of B2C e-commerce transactions by a large amount. Although B2B e-commerce pre-dates the internet, the internet has brought the advantages of common standards, resulting in lower costs and ubiquitous adoption by business organizations (Timmers, 1999). As a result, e-commerce is available to small firms as well as large, and has become an important part of both marketing and procurement practices in firms of all sizes (Wilson and Abel, 2002).

The *internet auction* is an important mechanism for facilitating B2B transactions. Major companies started to investigate the use of internet auctions in the mid-1990s (Sashi and O'Leary, 2002). General Electric was a pioneer in developing its own in-house auction site, which became one of the most successful internet auction sites. Today, General Electric uses the Oracle Sourcing system, a component of Oracle's E-Business Suite. An ex-employee of GE developed the pioneering independent B2B internet auction site www.freemarkets.com. Subsequently, many other large firms developed their own in-house auction sites, while auction software is now available as a component of business software packages provided by global software firms. Freemarkets.com itself merged with the software company Ariba in 2004, and then Ariba was acquired by the business software giant SAP in 2012. These days, B2B online auctions have become mainstream. You might think of eBay as no more than a great place to sell books and DVDs you no longer want, but eBay also offers a wide range of B2B auctions, as we see in B2B Snapshot 12.3.

B2B SNAPSHOT 12.3　EBAY (BUSINESS & INDUSTRIAL) AND ALIBABA.COM

These days, for many people who are looking to buy or sell household items the first place to look is eBay, the online auction site. The fact is, eBay has become something of an institution: for some people it is a great place to look for designer clothing at really low prices; other people are on the lookout for retro fashions; then of course there are the enthusiasts looking for exactly the right thing that is more or less impossible to find in the shops... model railway enthusiasts, photography enthusiasts, book collectors, and so on.

However, there is another side to eBay, which you only find if you take the trouble to click through to the eBay Business & Industrial website at www.ebay.com/rpp/business-industrial (or www.ebay.co.uk/rpp/business-office-industrial if you are in the UK). You would be amazed what you can find there. For example, how about a 2001 John Deere 9100 Tractor, sporting new tyres, with a reserve price of $80,000? Or, perhaps you would prefer a Case IH Cotton Picker CPX610 (2004 model) at a reserve of $135,000? Or you can find just about anything you might need to run a substantial construction project: a Mack triaxle dump truck with only 300,000 miles on the clock ($15,000), a Case backhoe industrial digger ($34,000), a vibratory pile hammer/pile driver (whether or not this is good value at the reserve price of $225,000 we really cannot say)... anyway, you get the picture!

A rival to eBay in B2B online auctions is Alibaba.com, whose mission statement is 'To make it easy to do business anywhere'. Have some fun – take a look around! In particular, look how easy it is to search for suppliers from a specific part of the world. See if you can find a supplier of electronic components from Malaysia, a coal supplier from Australia, and (this one we couldn't resist) a coffee supplier from Brazil.

Source: www.ebay.com/rpp/business-industrial; www.alibaba.com.

Internet auctions can be conveniently categorized into the English (or ascending-price) auction and the Dutch (or reverse) auction. In both cases the internet acts as a medium to bring together buyers and sellers and to exchange information about product specifications, terms and conditions and, most importantly, price.

In an English auction, as mentioned previously, firms offer goods for sale and buyers offer to buy those goods. The seller starts the bidding at a reserve price and the buyers offer higher and higher prices until no one is willing to go any higher. The buyer with the highest bid wins the auction. This is a very suitable mechanism for companies to sell off excess stocks. The ubiquity of the internet means that sellers can reach a much larger number of potential buyers than in the past.

A Dutch auction, as explained earlier, is a descending-price auction. The original meaning of a Dutch auction arose where a seller offered a good for sale at a very high price, with that price then gradually declining until a willing buyer could be found and a bargain struck. In the case of B2B e-commerce the Dutch auction has come to refer to reverse auctions of contracts by buying organizations. The buying organization specifies exactly what it wants to buy, makes this information publicly available, and invites bids from qualified suppliers. The buyer posts an RFQ describing the detailed requirements at an auction website, and sellers respond to the RFQ. The sellers provide details of how they propose to respond to the bid, including technical and commercial details as well as the price at which they are prepared to sell. As the auction proceeds, the price at which potential suppliers are prepared to accept to undertake the contract declines – hence the expression 'reverse auction'. The buyer will generally apply several criteria when choosing between the competing sellers, and will choose the bid that best matches those criteria. A particular problem that can arise with reverse auctions is the *winner's curse*. Reverse auctions often take place in conditions of uncertainty, where neither the buyer nor the seller can be sure of the true costs of fulfilling the contract. The purpose of the auction is to ensure that the buyer does not pay a much higher price than is justified. However, if price is used as the most important criterion to judge between the competing sellers, then it follows that the winning seller will be the one that has made the lowest estimate of the costs of fulfilling the contract *under conditions of uncertainty*. It is entirely possible that the winner has underestimated the costs, and therefore stands to make a loss on the contract – the winner's curse. For this reason, some authorities have suggested that further contract negotiation between the buyer and the seller should be allowed even after the auction has been completed (Daly and Nath, 2005).

Of course, auctions pre-date the internet by many centuries! However, the internet has created a particular set of conditions that are favourable to the auction approach. The costs involved in buying and selling (the 'transaction costs') are lower; geographical proximity is no longer an issue so that businesses have easy access to many more potential buyers and sellers; and the timing of the auction can be more flexible – buyers and sellers can join at any point in the auction process. Internet auctions may have a rigidly specified closing time (a hard close) or may be allowed to continue as long as there is a substantial amount of continuing bidding activity (a soft close). If an auction has a hard close, then participants may use 'sniping' tactics – that is, they may try to win the auction by putting in a bid at the very last minute.

Bidding decisions

Figure 12.6 outlines in a simplified way the decisions that face a company which has the opportunity to bid for a contract through a competitive tendering process. First, there is the decision of whether to proceed with a bid or to refrain from bidding. If the decision is made to proceed with a bid, then a bidding strategy must be determined.

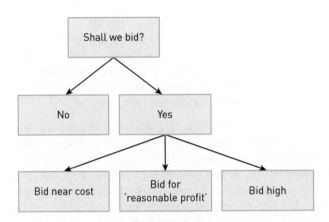

FIGURE 12.6 A simplified view of the bidding decision process

In Figure 12.6 the bidding strategy decision has been simplified into three categories – to bid at or near cost, to bid for a normal level of profit for the industry, or to bid at a price that would yield a much higher level of profit than normal.

The very process of bidding for a contract can be time-consuming and costly. This applies particularly in the case of major industrial contracts but it also applies to business-to-business services such as marketing research. For example, when buying marketing research services a firm will typically prepare a brief and then invite between three and five qualified market research firms to submit proposals – that is, detailed specifications of the methods that will be used to gather and analyse the data to answer the specified research questions. In order to put together a competitive research proposal each market research firm has to conduct some preliminary secondary research and expend considerable managerial time. Clearly, there are costs associated with submitting a bid. These costs are much greater with a major industrial project such as the construction of a warehouse or factory. Because of the costs associated with bidding, business-to-business firms have to be selective concerning the bids to which they respond. Firms will be more inclined to bid where they believe they have a good chance of winning and where the contract is 'attractive'.

Clearly, expected profitability is an important criterion in deciding on how attractive a contract is. However, other factors are also relevant. In particular, there are relational aspects to the bidding decision. Where a supplier believes that it has a long-term partnership with a particular customer, then it is more likely to bid even though the individual contract may not appear lucrative. Equally, where a supplier wishes to try to establish a business relationship with an important buying organization – so that future contracts will flow out of the relationship – then it may be rational to enter into the bidding process even though the first contract looks relatively unattractive.

Having made the decision to submit a bid, the bidding strategy may be to bid low (near cost), to bid high, or to bid at a price that will yield a normal level of profit. All other things being equal a higher bid price will reduce the probability of winning the contract. It follows that making a bid at or near cost should maximize the probability of winning the contract. However, such a strategy also runs the risk of suffering the winner's curse, since in most cases it is not possible to calculate the costs of delivering a contract with complete accuracy, and when the price quoted is at or near cost then there is clearly a real chance that the costs involved in delivering on the contract will exceed the revenue generated. A low-price bidding strategy makes sense where the bidding firm has spare capacity, or where there is a good chance that by winning one contract with the customer there will be further, more lucrative contracts to follow from the same customer.

A high-price bidding strategy (bidding at a price that will yield a profit in excess of industry norms) may make sense where the bidder believes that they have certain special competencies that make their bid more attractive to the customer on non-price grounds – for example, a management consultancy firm that believes that it employs the best legal experts on corporate mergers. That is to say, the bidder believes that they can deliver enhanced customer benefits so that their value proposition will be attractive to the customer despite the relatively high bid price. Where there are no such enhanced benefits then a high-price bid may be used simply to signal that the bidding firm is working close to capacity and really does not need the extra business. For example, when an automotive components supplier is invited to bid for a contract by a major automobile OEM such as Ford, it may feel compelled to respond positively in order to demonstrate a desire to do business with an important player in the industry. Submitting a high-price bid may be considered a wiser response than simply not submitting a bid, since the latter response could be treated as evidence that the supplier is simply not interested in business with the OEM.

Under most normal business conditions a supplier responding to a competitive tender will aim to achieve a standard rate of profit on the contract. This still provides fairly wide scope for variations in the quoted bid price. If one makes the convenient simplifying assumption that the contract will always go to the lowest bidder, then the probability of winning a bid depends on how many other bidders there are and how close to the estimated costs of delivering the contract one bids (Nagle and Holden, 2002). For example, suppose that experience within the industry has demonstrated that when you bid for an expected profit margin over costs of 10 per cent, there is a 50 per cent chance that your price will be lower than a single bidding rival, whereas when you bid for a 20 per cent profit margin, there is only a 10 per cent chance that your price will be lower than a single rival. It follows that if you know that there will only be one bidding rival, then pricing for 10 per cent over costs will give you a 50 per cent chance of success, while pricing for 20 per cent over costs will give you only a 10 per cent chance of success. However, the chance of success falls sharply as the number of rivals increases. With two rivals, at a price of 10 per cent over cost your chance of success is now 25 per cent (50 per cent chance of beating rival A, 50 per cent chance of beating rival B, hence a 25 per cent chance of beating them both). With two rivals, at a price of 20 per cent over costs, your chance of success is now 1 per cent (10 per cent chance of beating rival A, 10 per cent chance of beating rival B, 1 per cent chance of beating them both). The method of calculating the probabilities against more than one rival is to express the probabilities as a decimal, and then multiply the probabilities together (hence, $0.25 = 0.5 \times 0.5$, while $0.01 = 0.1 \times 0.1$). The key message is that both the competitiveness of the proposed bid price *and* the expected number of rival bidders must be taken into account when evaluating the likelihood of success in a competitive tender.

Pricing: common ethical concerns

Pricing is an aspect of the marketing mix within which ethical issues often arise. Stohs and Brannick (1999) carried out interviews with the managing directors of 348 Irish businesses to investigate their perceptions of the importance and frequency of various unethical practices. They found that 'unfair price' was perceived to be the second most common out of a list of ten unethical practices – 39.5 per cent of their respondents thought that it occurred 'very commonly'.

The principal ethical issues that arise concerning business-to-business pricing decisions are *anti-competitive pricing*, price fixing, price discrimination and predatory pricing or *dumping* (Schlegelmilch, 1998; Smith and Quelch, 1993). Anti-competitive pricing arises where a group of producers collude to raise prices above the level that would apply in a freely operating market. Such behaviour is regarded as unfair and damaging to the free enterprise system and so is often prohibited by law; these are known as anti-trust laws. Such laws apply, for example, in the USA (the Sherman Act of 1890 and later legislation known as anti-trust law), in the EU (Article 81 of the EC Treaty) and Japan (Act on Prohibition of Private Monopolization and Maintenance of Fair Trade). Article 81 of the EC Treaty states that it is prohibited to 'directly or indirectly fix purchase or selling prices or any other trading conditions'.

Companies may be tempted to enter into explicit price-fixing arrangements because they believe that otherwise there is the risk of a price war leading to financial losses, and eventually to job losses and potential bankruptcy. However, price fixing is illegal in all of the major economies of the world. For example, price fixing was alleged in the American explosives market during the 1980s and 1990s. The allegation was that explosives manufacturers had artificially raised and fixed prices, allocated customers between themselves and rigged commercial bids between 1988 and 1992. Following legal action instigated by the US Department of Justice under the Sherman Act, several companies were found guilty on price-fixing charges and were fined. In 1995, ICI Explosives USA Inc. received a $10 million criminal fine for conspiring to fix the prices of commercial explosives sold in western Kentucky, southern Indiana and southern Illinois. Dyno Nobel, the world's second largest commercial explosives manufacturer, was fined $15 million for similar offences (Schlegelmilch, 1998; US Department of Justice, 1996). The case study at the end of this chapter provides another example of B2B pricing that was found to be illegal.

Unethical pricing practices arise particularly in industries where competitive tendering is in common use. Collusive tendering occurs where there is 'an exclusive agreement between [competitors] either not to tender, or to tender in such a manner as not to be competitive with one of the other tenderers' (Zarkada-Fraser, 2000: 270). It is sometimes found in the construction industry, the defence industry and in a wide range of government procurement arrangements (Zarkada-Fraser, 2000). The essence of collusion in tendering is that there is an agreement between the bidders to win the contract for one bidder, with the other parties receiving some other benefits – these may be direct financial benefits, or agreements that they will win future contracts. Collusion aims to undermine the rationale for competitive tendering by avoiding direct price competition between the bidders. In commercial contracts this means that the buyer is disadvantaged by paying more than they otherwise would, while in government contracts the ultimate loser is the taxpayer. Collusion is illegal in all of the world's major economies but nevertheless is by no means an uncommon practice (Zarkada-Fraser, 2000).

Dumping is 'the selling of exported goods in a foreign market below the price of the same goods in the home market'. Claims of dumping have been made in a range of industrial markets including computer chips, nylon yarn, semiconductors, steel, transformers and vinyl (Delener, 1998: 1747). The General Agreement on Tariffs and Trade (GATT) of the World Trade Organization (WTO, 1994) permits countries to take measures against dumping.

Allegations of dumping are increasing, because the independent nation-state remains the key building block of international politics while at the same time major corporations prefer to see the world as a single, global market. In ethical terms dumping is a troublesome concept. On the one hand, it can be seen as an aggressive action that will cause harm to a domestic industry and threaten the jobs of those who work in it; on the other hand, it is offering consumers lower-priced products. In many cases of dumping, a consequentialist (for example, a utilitarian) approach to ethics (see Chapter 4) would suggest that dumping creates net *benefits* when the interests of all parties are taken fully into account. Indeed, Delener (1998: 1751) concludes as follows:

> *There is little justification in theory or in practice to say that predatory pricing or dumping is wrong... There are no persuasive economic, business or consumer welfare arguments for why dumping should be illegal... Ethically, then, one could argue that a marketer involved in low or discount pricing in another country is not violating any moral law, breaking a promise or causing injury.*

Responding to ethical issues in pricing

Nagle and Holden (2002) provide a spectrum of ethical behaviour concerning price that is a useful basis for understanding one's own ethical position in pricing matters. They arrange their five ethical levels from the least restrictive ethical principle, upon which virtually everyone would agree, to the most restrictive ethical principle, with which most people would disagree:

- Pricing is ethical where the buyer *voluntarily* pays the agreed price.
- Pricing is ethical where both parties have equal information.
- Pricing is ethical where there is no exploitation of a buyer's 'essential needs'.
- Pricing is ethical where it is justified by costs.
- Pricing is ethical where everyone has equal access to goods and services regardless of ability to pay.

In capitalist economies there would be near-universal agreement with level 1 – coercing the buyer into paying a price they would not pay willingly is more consistent with criminal activity than with commerce. Level 2 is more restrictive, and requires that the seller should disclose all information that is relevant to the purchase; in their study of Irish managing directors, Stohs and Brannick (1999) found that 'mislead buyer' was considered to be the second worst unethical business practice, and 30.1 per cent of the respondents believed that it occurred 'very commonly'. In business-to-business markets the development of long-term supplier–customer relationships (see Chapter 3) depends on this kind of information flow; a trusting relationship between the buyer and the seller cannot be established if important items of information are withheld. At level 3 the seller is urged *not* to exploit opportunities for 'price gouging' (defined by Laczniak and Murphy (1993: 128) as 'taking advantage of those who must have your product and are willing to pay an inordinately high price for it'). Then level 4 generalizes from level 3 and asserts that prices must be justified by costs for *all* products and not just for essential products. Finally, level 5 moves well beyond the ethical considerations that are normally observed in capitalist economies, towards a communist perspective.

For most business-to-business exchanges within capitalist economies there would be near-universal agreement with ethical level 1 and near-universal disagreement with level 5. No doubt there would be substantial debate about the levels in between, which would depend upon the ethical preferences of the people concerned and the specific aspects of any particular exchange process. For example, some people might argue that it is fair to withhold key information from a powerful buying organization that has extensive resources and employs professionally trained buyers (whose job it is to uncover all relevant information), but that it is unfair to withhold key information from a small business with limited resources and no trained buyers. Some people would argue that it is legitimate to make very high profits on, say, a critical electronic component when there is a shortage of supply – and, indeed, that this makes up for the lean times when the price is driven down to cost or below by the forces of supply and demand. Each individual manager has to make his or her own decisions, and these five ethical levels provide a useful framework within which to do so.

CHAPTER SUMMARY

- A basic framework for approaching pricing decisions is the three Cs of costs, customers and competitors. Although cost-plus pricing is often used in business markets it is fundamentally flawed since it does not take account of customer price sensitivity. Sales break-even analysis (or cost–volume–profit analysis) is a useful technique for understanding how profitability is affected by pricing decisions, and for informing decisions about price changes. Customer price sensitivity is usually measured using the price elasticity of demand – the percentage change in demand for a 1 per cent change in price. Most business markets are oligopolies, so there is an ever-present risk of a price war, leading to price stickiness and price leadership and also providing an incentive for firms to engage in such illegal practices as price fixing and price collusion.

- Pricing is a continuous process rather than a one-off decision; prices need to be constantly rethought in the light of factors within the firm's control and factors outside the firm's control. The two long-term viable price positioning strategies are the market ruler (low price/high customer benefits) and the thriver (low price/medium benefits or medium price/high benefits). The chancer position (low price/low benefits or high price/high benefits) is a short-term viable position although it is dominated by the thriver and market ruler positions.

- Many different departments have an input into the pricing process, and members of different departments tend to have different pricing priorities. For example, the finance department may insist that all products should always make a profit, while the marketing department may see strategic advantage in occasionally taking a loss on one or more products. The role of the sales force in pricing is particularly problematic – the key question being how much pricing latitude should be given to the individual salesperson. The best advice seems to be that salespeople should have considerable pricing authority in market segments where selling is either particularly difficult or particularly easy, but only limited authority in market segments that fall between these categories.

- Buyer–supplier relationships in business markets influence pricing decisions. Suppliers that are involved in long-term relationships with customers benefit from higher sales growth and lower inventory costs, but also have to deliver lower prices than suppliers that do not engage in long-term partnering.

- Bid pricing (competitive tendering) is common in business markets. The internet has facilitated business-to-business auctions. When offered the opportunity to bid, a firm must first decide whether it is worthwhile taking part at all (since there are substantial costs associated with bidding), and subsequently decide on a bidding strategy. The likelihood of success in a bidding process depends on the cost base of the bidder, the desired profit margin and the number of other bidders taking part. As the number of other bidders increases, the probability of success declines.

- Pricing is an aspect of business marketing that often raises ethical concerns, such as anti-competitive pricing, price fixing, price collusion, price discrimination, predatory pricing (dumping) and price gouging. Both ethical and legal issues are relevant.

QUESTIONS FOR DISCUSSION

1. Discourse Products makes electrical components that have multiple uses in industrial manufacturing. The Marketing Director is considering whether or not to implement a price cut, and has asked for your advice. You have been provided with the following data:

Current price = £2.50

Variable costs = £1.00

Fixed costs = £12,500

2. What is the break-even sales volume at the current price of £2.50 per unit? If Discourse Products cuts the price to £2.25 per unit, by how much would sales need to increase for profits to be maintained at the current level? Given the further information that Discourse Products believes that demand for its products is inelastic with respect to price, do you think that it should proceed with a price cut?

3. What are the characteristics that differentiate an oligopoly from a perfectly competitive market and from a monopoly? What difference does this make to pricing strategy?

4. Explain why, in an oligopolistic industry that faces inelastic demand and in which there is no acknowledged price leader, it is inadvisable for a firm to pursue a price-cutting strategy aimed at increasing market share.

5. What are the arguments for and against giving salespeople a high level of price discretion during their negotiations with customers?

6. From the point of view of costs, prices, revenues and profitability, what are the pros and cons of engaging in long-term partnerships with major customers?

7. A business colleague to whom you have shown Nagle and Holden's (2002) 'five ethical levels' (see the final section of this chapter) simply cannot understand why any of them is relevant except for the first – 'Pricing is ethical where the buyer voluntarily pays the agreed price.' What arguments can you provide in favour of going beyond level 1? What is your own view on the five ethical levels?

CASE STUDY 12.1   COVER PRICING IN THE UK CONSTRUCTION INDUSTRY

Adam Smith (1723–90) was a Scottish philosopher and one of the most famous economists who ever lived. His work is often cited today as the place where many of the ideas of modern economics were first clearly and comprehensively explained. Many important concepts to which we pay great attention in this book, such as the concept of exchange value, and the principles of supply and demand that underlie pricing decisions, were developed in the book for which Smith is best remembered – *An Inquiry into the Nature and Causes of the Wealth of Nations* – usually shortened to simply *The Wealth of Nations*. In the very same book, Smith warned against the ever-present danger in market economies that producers would strive to avoid full and fair competition in order to load the dice against consumers, or as Smith himself more elegantly put it: 'People of the same trade seldom meet together, even for merriment and diversion, but the conversation ends in a conspiracy against the public, or in some contrivance to raise prices' (Butler, 2007: 7).

The evidence is that the tendency of producer groups to use 'contrivances' to raise prices has not diminished since Smith's day, and governments around the world put in place laws and regulations to dissuade producers from any 'conspiracy against the public' and to ensure that competition is fair. A prominent case from the UK illustrates why such laws and regulations are necessary. In September 2009, after a five-year investigation, the UK's competition watchdog the Office of Fair Trading (OFT) announced that it had imposed fines totalling £129.5 million on 103 construction firms in England, which had been found guilty of colluding with competitors on building contracts. Technically, the nature of the offence was considered to be *cover pricing*, but the news media (and even the OFT itself) used a variety of different and more colourful terms for the practice: illegal bid rigging, price rigging, price fixing and scam. *The Times* newspaper proclaimed that 'the scale of the offences is breathtaking … all the signs are that bid-rigging was endemic across the industry' (Wighton, 2009), while the *Daily Mail* identified the UK's favourite entrepreneur, Lord Alan Sugar, as a victim of the 'price-rigging scam' (Poulter, 2009). In many cases it was public-sector bodies, such as local authorities, which were the victims of cover pricing by construction firms, leading to the inevitable accusation that taxpayers' money had been ripped off.

So, everything seems quite straightforward: Adam Smith warned of the dangers of contrivances to raise prices centuries ago; laws were put in place to prevent such practices; but many firms in the British building industry flouted those laws, were found out and subsequently fined. What exactly were those firms found guilty of? Cover pricing, which, according to the OFT's press release on the case 'is where one or more bidders in a tender process obtain an artificially high price from a competitor ... cover bids are priced so as not to win the contract but are submitted as genuine bids, which gives a misleading impression to clients as to the extent of competition' (OFT, 2009). In other words, one or more of the firms that appear to be bidding for a contract (that is, submitting a price at which they are prepared to deliver the work) submit unreasonably high prices with no genuine intention of winning the business. Firms may collude to do this on a rota basis (so that each firm in turn submits the winning bid) while in some cases the firm winning a bid under such collusive circumstances actually makes a compensatory payment to the firm that submitted a cover price.

However, is everything as simple as first it seems? Industry commentator Tony Bingham, while agreeing that the law had been and must be correctly applied, has pointed out that cover pricing can be an entirely innocent practice (Bingham, 2009). Suppose that a building firm is already working at full capacity and is asked for a price by a major customer. It has to decide whether to make a realistic bid (and possibly win a contract that it will struggle to deliver), or to turn the bidding opportunity down (and possibly upset an important customer from whom it will want to win business in the future). Under these circumstances a bid pitched far too high to win the contract might seem to the building firm a reasonable solution: a polite way of saying 'no thanks' to the client. However, in the light of the 2009 cover pricing case, might this kind of bidding practice bring suspicion of illegal anti-competitive behaviour on the firm concerned?

(Note: When the events described took place responsibility for regulation of competition lay with the Office of Fair Trading. Today it lies with the Competition & Markets Authority.)

CASE STUDY QUESTIONS

1 What is the fundamental purpose of legislation designed to prohibit anti-competitive behaviour by businesses? What are the wider benefits to society that are expected from such legislation?

2 On the one hand, some commentators were appalled at the extent of cover pricing in the UK building industry, and on the other hand, Tony Bingham suggested that cover pricing could be a reasonable business practice. In your opinion, is there a dividing line between acceptable and unacceptable forms of cover pricing? Would it be possible to distinguish between them in practice?

Sources: Bingham, 2009; Butler, 2007; OFT, 2009; Poulter, 2009; Wighton, 2009.

FURTHER READING

Hinterhuber, A. (2004) 'Towards value-based pricing – an integrative framework for decision making', *Industrial Marketing Management*, 33 (8): 765–78.

While Nagle, Hogan and Zale's (2010) book will give you an extensive treatment of all of the issues involved in pricing in both B2B and B2C markets, this substantial article focuses on the key issues for pricing decision-makers in B2B markets. The approach adopted by Hinterhuber is a value-based perspective.

(Continued)

(Continued)

Hinterhuber, A. (2015) 'Violations of rational choice principles in pricing decisions', *Industrial Marketing Management*, 47 (May): 65–74.

This article addresses an important question relevant to all aspects of B2B marketing, in the specific context of B2B pricing. That question is the extent to which it makes sense to assume fully rational behaviour in B2B exchange processes. Surprisingly, the article also includes an extended quotation from a Monty Python comedy sketch! Intriguing.

Nagle, T.T., Hogan, J. and Zale, J. (2010) *The Strategy and Tactics of Pricing: A Guide to Growing More Profitably* (5th edn). Upper Saddle River, NJ: Prentice Hall.

For a comprehensive yet compact introduction to all of the important issues in pricing decisions this is the book to read. So, whether you are a student with an essay to write or a manager with a practical pricing problem to solve, if you are looking for a more extended discussion of many of the issues that are explained in this chapter, this is the place to look.

GLOSSARY

3-D printing   Also known as additive manufacturing (AM), in which synthesized objects of almost any shape or geometry are produced from digital model data.

4Ps model   Synonym for 'marketing mix approach' (q.v.).

accelerator effect   In industries buying investment goods, relatively small fluctuations in demand can lead to large fluctuations in their need for new investment; the accelerator effect refers to the ratio of the demand for capital equipment to the demand for the output of the customer industry.

activity links   The connections between the activities that the parties in a network undertake. May be a source of network advantage.

actor bonds   The connections between people and organizations in a network context. Strong bonds make for strong connections.

adaptation space   In reference to a business-to-business offering, the scope for development or changes to the offering, typically to customize for the needs of a particular relationship.

after-market   The market for repair and upgrade components and services for products originally sold by an OEM (q.v.).

'always-a-share' customers   Category of customers who will always be happy to do business as long as the price is right.

anti-competitive pricing   Where a group of producers collude to raise prices above the level that would apply in a freely operating market.

application uncertainty   The fundamental difficulty that a supplier faces of knowing what to make or do for the marketplace.

ARA analysis   Consideration of the actor bonds, resource ties and activity links that join the parties in a network.

'arm's length' contracting   An approach to relationship management that is distant, typically focused upon the demands of the current transaction, and subject to substantial opportunism.

B2B   Acronym for 'business-to-business'.

B2C   Acronym for 'business-to-consumer'.

Boston Box/Boston Matrix   An approach to portfolio management that originates from the Boston Consulting Group (also known as the growth/share matrix).

brand   A mixture of tangible features and intangible associations, or alternatively functional and emotional values, associated with a product offering.

break-even sales analysis   A method of calculating the break-even point, at which revenue equals costs – from information about price, sales volume, and fixed and variable costs.

BRIC economies   The emerging-market economies of Brazil, Russia, India and China.

business market   Synonym for 'business-to-business market' (q.v.).

business-to-business market   A market in which the customers are organizations rather than individual consumers.

capacity uncertainty   The fundamental difficulty that a supplier faces of knowing how much to make and therefore what capacity to plan.

catalogue purchasing   Where an organization collates a wide range of items within a particular product category from a range of suppliers. Business buyers will normally use catalogue purchasing to handle a wide range of casual and routine re-buys of direct and indirect product/MRO items (q.v.).

collaborative exchange   Very close information, social and process linkages, and mutual commitments between buyer and supplier.

communication automation   The use of software which enables the systemizing of repetitive communication tasks such as the creation of targeted email lists, campaign execution, tracking of email and website activity as well as lead qualification.

communications mix   The tools and the importance attributed to them, reflecting an organization's marketing communications objectives and the way in which information is used by its target audience.

competitive bidding   The process in which a buying organization obtains competing bids from potential suppliers to undertake some work, and then evaluates the bids received to determine the winner, to whom the contract is awarded.

concentrated targeting   A focus upon meeting the needs of one or a small number of target segments exclusively.

concentration ratio   The combined market share of the top few firms – usually the top three, four or five – in a market.

consultative selling   Used where a customer is uncertain of actual supply requirements; involves the questioning of members of the DMU and numerous discussions to formulate bespoke offering.

content marketing   The creation and sharing of information (in various formats) that is of value to potential and existing customers.

contingent   Depending on circumstances; in this book, it is used to mean that appropriate marketing strategies and tactics depend on the particular circumstances of markets and customers and there is no single right way to design a B2B marketing programme.

corporate brand expression   An organization's signalling of its identity to the marketplace via visual identity, brand purpose, personality and communication.

corporate brand identity   The expression and stakeholder images of an organization's identity.

corporate brand image   The way in which stakeholders describe, remember and relate to an organization resulting from brand experience, relationships and communities.

corporate brand reputation   Closely linked to image, and represents stakeholder judgements of a firm's actions and achievements.

cost-plus pricing   The price is determined by calculating the average cost of production and then adding on a standard profit mark-up.

cost-to-serve   The aggregation of the costs of all the activities involved in meeting the needs of a customer.

cover pricing   In a competitive bidding process, cover pricing occurs when one or more of the bidders submits an unreasonably high price in order to have no chance of success.

culture   The principles which are shared by a group of people and which shape the behaviour, perceptions and emotional responses of people within that group.

customer lifetime value   The net discounted cash flow that a supplier expects to receive from all transactions conducted with a single customer throughout the customer life-cycle.

customer perceived value   The customer's overall assessment of the utility provided by a product based on an assessment of what is received (benefits) and what is given up (costs, including selling price).

decision-making unit (DMU)   Also known as the 'buying team' or 'buying centre', will involve a range of managers who assume different roles in a purchase decision.

demand elasticity (elasticity of demand with respect to price)   The percentage change in demand for a 1 per cent change in price (with everything else assumed constant).

deontological ethics   The ethical position that moral dilemmas should be resolved by acting in accordance with established systems of duties or rules.

derived demand   Demand for a good or service which originates from the use of that good or service in a production or service-delivery process.

differentiated targeting   The provision of different offerings for different target segments.

direct demand   Demand for a good or service which originates from the immediate value obtained by the customer.

direct marketing   Communication and transactions between individual customer and the marketer where activity is recorded and the data used for relationship management programmes.

distributor   Takes title to goods and assumes responsibility for making the product available to customers in a specific area.

dumping   The selling of exported goods in a foreign market below the price of the same goods in the home market.

Dutch auction   A public price starts at a very high level and the price falls until the first participant finds the price low enough to submit a bid; the first bidder is the winner and receives the good at the price prevailing when the clock was stopped.

elastic demand Where a 1 per cent change in price leads to a demand change of more than 1 per cent.

electronic procurement Use of internet technology to support the purchasing process, enabling companies to reduce this process cost.

English auction An ascending-price auction in which the last remaining bidder receives the good and pays the amount of their bid.

firmographics Characteristics of a company, for example size, location and industry classification.

franchising The principal (franchiser) allows an organization (franchisee) the right to conduct business in a specific manner.

IMP Group International group of researchers who collaborate on business-to-business relationships research. The IMP interaction approach emanates from the founding collaborators in this group.

IMP interaction model (approach) An approach to describing and understanding business-to-business exchange which is relationship based and interactive in nature, arguing that management of exchange must come through relationship processes such as communication, negotiation and adaptation.

inbound marketing (communications) Activities that direct leads and customers to a business when those customers are ready to engage with an organization.

incentive pay system Rewards employees for achieving specific performance targets which for a salesperson might include revenue, market/customer share, new product sales, and profitability targets.

industrial marketing An older term for business-to-business marketing.

inelastic demand Where a 1 per cent change in price leads to a demand change of less than 1 per cent.

integrated communications strategy Planning, implementation and control of the various communications tools used by a business marketer so that the message presented to target audiences is consistent.

interaction An inherently two-way process by which parties exchange to construct a relationship.

interest commonality Shared economic goals.

logistics management The coordination of activities that contribute to the forward and reverse flow of information, goods and services between the point of origin and point of consumption, to satisfy customer needs.

'lost-for-good' customers Category of customers which show a preference for enduring relationships with suppliers they trust and from whom they switch unwillingly.

macro-segmentation The use of relatively easily observed aggregate-level data to differentiate between companies as a basis for establishing different groups that require different market responses.

maintenance, repair and operating (MRO) supplies   Individually minor items of expenditure by a buying organization, necessary to ensure the smooth operation of the business.

managerial egoism   The ethical position that a firm should act within the law so as to maximize its financial returns.

market uncertainty   The fundamental difficulty a buyer faces when it comes to knowing from which seller to buy. It is typically a function of the number of alternatives and how differentiated the suppliers are from each other.

marketing ethics   The systematic study of how moral standards are applied to marketing decisions, behaviours and institutions.

marketing mix approach   A managerial approach to marketing based on the ideas that the buyer and seller operate independently, and that an active marketer creates markets (using the marketing mix) while customers are relatively passive recipients of the offerings that the seller brings to market. (Also frequently referred to as the 4Ps model.)

micro-segmentation   The use of less easily observed, typically company-specific, data in order to differentiate between companies as a basis for establishing different groups that require different market responses.

monitoring-based system   Rewards employees based on effective performance of sales activities such as technical knowledge, adaptive selling, teamwork, sales presentations, planning and support.

NACE   Nomenclature statistique des activités économiques dans la Communauté Européene (the European Union standard industrial classification).

NAICS   North American Industrial Classification Scheme (a standard industrial classification, q.v.)

need uncertainty   The fundamental difficulty a buyer faces of knowing what or how much to buy. Where need uncertainty is high a buyer is likely to adopt more protracted buying processes in order to help reduce the uncertainty.

needs-satisfaction selling   Questioning by the salesperson to determine actual customer needs and the matching of these to supplier products.

net price achieved   The price a customer actually pays, after all forms of discounting have been taken into consideration.

network embeddedness   The extent to which a relationship and its participants affect or are affected by other relationships or relationship actors.

niche targeting   A focus upon meeting the needs of one or a small number of target segments exclusively.

non-probability sampling   A sample in which the units in the population do not have a known, non-zero probability of being included.

obligational contracting   Category of customer relationship management that sees the relationship as bringing a set of responsibilities that extend to behaving in the interests of the relationship at large and the counterpart in particular.

oligopolistic market   A market in which there are only a few competitors, so that each firm is directly affected by the decisions of its rivals.

original equipment manufacturer (OEM)   A business that buys component goods and services from suppliers, and combines these components into an end product for sale under a brand name of the OEM.

outbound marketing (communications)   Activities through which the marketer drives communication directed at target audiences.

perceptual map   A pictorial mechanism for representing the relative positioning of providers and products in a marketplace.

personal selling   Involves a supplier's employees communicating directly with customers, and can involve handling enquiries, winning business, administering orders and handling complaints.

probability sampling   A sample in which every member of the target population has a known, non-zero probability of being included.

problem-solving abilities   Those abilities that a supplier or buyer can manifest that are sources of the reduction of uncertainties for the counterpart. Any claimed ability is only as valuable as the uncertainties it helps to reduce.

product life-cycle   A consideration of the development of a product as a series of distinct stages which place different demands upon the product manager.

purchase process   Series of linked activities that culminates in a purchase decision and may include need/problem recognition, determining specification, supplier and product search, proposal evaluation and supplier selection, selection on order routine, performance feedback and evaluation.

purchasing orientation   A company's approach to acquiring resources and capabilities from external supply markets.

quota sampling   A non-probability sampling method which divides the relevant population into subgroups, such as manufacturing and service firms, or small, medium and large firms.

RFID   Radio frequency identification. RFID systems consist of a tag (made up of a microchip with an antenna) and a reader (also with an antenna). Used by firms to make the flow of goods more efficient by tracking the movement of items from production facilities, through distribution centres to retail outlets.

rational planning approach   The idea that strategy is best conducted by following a series of logical, analytical steps designed to match the strategic actions of the business to the opportunities and threats in the business environment.

reciprocal value proposition   A more sophisticated version of the value proposition (q.v.) that applies in complex exchange processes.

relationship life-cycle   A model of the development of a relationship as a series of distinct stages which place different demands upon the relationship manager.

relationship portfolio management   Set of tasks intended to obtain a balance of customer relationships that will create stability and value over the long term.

relationship promoter   Employee in a boundary-spanning role, linking the customer with the supplier company and coordinating supplier internal activities to support a specific customer relationship.

relationship spectrum   The range of types of exchange that can occur in B2B markets, from *transactional exchange* (q.v.) to *collaborative exchange* (q.v.).

resource-based view   The idea that a sustainable competitive advantage can best be achieved by concentrating on firm resources that are valuable, rare, inimitable and non-substitutable.

resource ties   The connections in relationships that emerge as a consequence of the parties creating and/or sharing resources that are deemed to add value to the relationship.

response rate   The proportion of the members of a sample who reply to a survey.

reverse auction   The buyer offers the opportunity to satisfy a product requirement to a range of interested suppliers, with the order going to the company that makes the lowest-priced bid.

route to market   The means by which the business marketer tries to reach target markets and gain maximum market coverage for its products.

sales agent   Independent sales representative; uses market, customer and product expertise to generate business, and earns commission on orders won.

sales force organization   Types of structure used to coordinate revenue generation, customer acquisition and relationship management.

sampling frame   A list of the units (such as firms, managers or industry associations) that are eligible to be included in a survey.

script-based selling   A standard sales presentation or dialogue used when there is little difference in product use.

sealed-bid auction   Auction in which each bidder submits a single sealed bid, and all of the bids are opened at a stipulated time.

search engine marketing   Internet marketing intended to promote websites through increased visibility in search engine results pages.

simple random sampling   Every unit within the sampling frame has an equal chance of being selected for the sample.

smart product system   Cyber-physical product/system (CPS) that uses and integrates internet based services to perform a particular functionality. Capable of communicating and interacting with other CPS via different channels i.e. internet or LAN.

snowball sampling   A sampling method where the researcher relies on previously identified members of the target population to identify other sample members.

social-exchange theory   View of exchange that recognizes that the economic dimension does not completely determine participant behaviour. Rather, it recognizes that relationships are socially constructed and embedded and thus that a whole set of social norms and expectations may affect participants' actions.

social media Internet-based platforms that enable creation and exchange of user-generated content.

standard industrial classification A systematic, official method of classifying economic activity.

strategy Policies and key decisions adopted by management that have major financial implications, involve substantial resource commitment, and are not easily reversible.

stratified random sampling The population and sampling frame are divided up into meaningful groups or 'strata' and then samples are taken from each of the strata according to their representation in the population.

supplier value The supplier's overall assessment of the utility obtained from a sale based on an assessment of what is received (benefits, including selling price) and what is given up (costs).

supply chain management (SCM) The planning and coordination of all activities of parties within a specific supply chain to provide the end-customer with a product which adds value.

supply chain pricing Cooperation among members of a supply chain to optimize the price paid by the final buyer.

sustainability The principle that global economic development must be conducted in such a manner that it can be supported indefinitely by planet Earth, and the related idea that individual businesses must act in accordance with this principle.

tie-breaker selling The inclusion of an element, a justifier, in the offering that could make a marked difference to the customer's business.

total cost of ownership (TCO) Looks at the true cost of obtaining a product from a given supplier and involves a company measuring costs that are most significant for that product in terms of its acquisition, use, and in the case of tangible goods, subsequent disposal.

trade mission A government-sponsored promotional activity intended to facilitate the economic growth of a particular region or country, typically via international trade in overseas markets.

trade show A temporary event at which sellers exhibit and which can provide a close match between supply markets and target audiences.

transaction uncertainty How vulnerable a buyer feels after a sale has been agreed; a function of the potential for something to go wrong before an acceptable product is available for use by the buyer.

transactional exchange The timely exchange of standard products at competitive prices, where there is no continuing business relationship.

transfer abilities Those abilities post-sale that a supplier can manifest that reduce potential for problems or provide means for limiting the effect of unforeseen problems.

undifferentiated targeting Providing the same offering to all target segments.

utilitarianism   The ethical position that moral dilemmas should be resolved by selecting the course of action that creates the greatest net utility for all of those affected by the decision.

value-adding exchange   A position on the relationship spectrum (q.v.) where the supplying firm emphasis shifts from making sales to retaining customer business.

value-based pricing   An approach to price-setting that starts with the customer-perceived value (q.v.) associated with using the supplier's product offering.

value proposition (also customer value proposition)   The supplier's statement of the benefits that the customer can expect to receive in return for the price paid.

virtual trade show   An electronic and more permanent alternative to the physical and temporary event.

virtue ethics   The ethical position that individuals should cultivate within themselves an understanding of the 'right' way to behave, and should tackle moral dilemmas using this cultivated moral integrity.

REFERENCES

Aarikka-Stenroos, L. and Jaakkola, E. (2012) 'Value co-creation in knowledge intensive business services: a dyadic perspective on the joint problem solving process', *Industrial Marketing Management*, 41: 15–26.

Abratt, R. (1993) 'Market segmentation practices of industrial marketers', *Industrial Marketing Management*, 22 (2): 79–84.

Abratt, R. and Kelly, P.M. (2002) 'Customer–supplier partnerships: perceptions of a successful key account management program', *Industrial Marketing Management*, 31: 467–76.

Abratt, R. and Kleyn, N. (2012) 'Corporate identity, corporate branding and corporate reputations: reconciliation and integration', *European Journal of Marketing*, 46 (7/8): 1048–63.

Achrol, R., Reve, T. and Stern, L. (1983) 'The environment of marketing channel dyads: a framework for comparative analysis', *Journal of Marketing*, 47 (4): 55–67.

Adams, C. and Brantner, V. (2006) 'Estimating the costs of new drug development: is it really $802 million?', *Health Affairs*, 25 (2): 420–8.

Adams, C. and Brantner, V. (2010) 'Spending on new drug development', *Health Economics*, 19 (2): 130–41.

AHDB (2016) *UK Producer Numbers*. Available at: //dairy.ahdb.org.uk/market-information/farming-data/producer-numbers/uk-producer-numbers (accessed 10 September 2016).

Ahmed, P.K and Rafiq, M. (2003) 'Commentary: Internal marketing issues and challenges', *European Journal of Marketing*, 37 (9): 1177–86.

Air Products (2012) *Commit to Integrity: Code of Conduct for Employees of Air Products and its Companies*. Available at: www.airproducts.com/~/media/Files/PDF/company/en-IE-conduct- brochure-english-2012.pdf (accessed 1 June 2013).

Altman, I. (2015) 'Why do companies with great solutions and salespeople still fail?' *Forbes*, 22 September. Available at www.forbes.com (accessed 1 August 2016).

Andersen, P.H. (2005) 'Relationship marketing and brand involvement of professionals through web-enhanced brand communities: the case of Coloplast', *Industrial Marketing Management*, 34: 285–97.

Anderson, E. and Oliver, R.L. (1987) 'Perspectives on behaviour-based versus outcome-based sales force control systems', *Journal of Marketing*, 51 (4): 76–88.

Anderson, E., Day, G.S. and Rangan, V.K. (1997) 'Strategic channel design', *Sloan Management Review*, 38 (4): 59–69.

Anderson, J.C. and Narus, J.A. (1984) 'A model of the distributor's perspective of distributor–manufacturer working relationships', *Journal of Marketing*, 48 (Fall): 62–74.

Anderson, J.C. and Narus, J.A. (1990) 'A model of distributor firm and manufacturer firm working partnerships', *Journal of Marketing*, 54 (January): 42–58.

Anderson, J.C. and Narus, J.A. (1991) 'Partnering as a focused market strategy', *California Management Review*, 33 (3): 95–113.

Anderson, J.C. and Narus, J.A. (1996) 'Rethinking distribution', *Harvard Business Review*, July–August: 112–20.

Anderson, J.C. and Narus, J.A. (1999) *Business Market Management: Understanding, Creating, and Delivering Value*. Upper Saddle River, NJ: Prentice Hall.

Anderson, J.C. and Narus, J.A. (2004) 'Gaining new customers', in *Business Market Management* (2nd edn). Upper Saddle River, NJ: Prentice Hall, pp. 315–60.

Anderson, J. and Wynstra, F. (2010) 'Purchasing higher-value, higher-price offerings in business markets', *Journal of Business & Industrial Marketing*, 17 (1): 29–61.

Anderson, J.C., Narus, J.A. and van Rossum, W. (2006) 'Customer value propositions in business markets', *Harvard Business Review*, March: 1–9.

Anderson, J.C., Narus, J.A. and Wouters, M. (2014) 'Tiebreaker selling', *Harvard Business Review*, March: 91–6.

Anderson, M.G. and Katz, P.B. (1998) 'Strategic sourcing', *International Journal of Logistics Management*, 9 (1): 1–13.

Ansoff, H.I. (1965) *Corporate Strategy*. New York: McGraw-Hill.

Argouslidis, P.C. and Indounas, K. (2010) 'Exploring the role of relationship pricing in industrial export settings: empirical evidence from the UK', *Industrial Marketing Management*, 39 (3): 460–72.

Arjoon, S. (2000) 'Virtue theory as a dynamic theory of business', *Journal of Business Ethics*, 28: 159–78.

Arndt, J. (1979) 'Toward a concept of domesticated markets', *Journal of Marketing*, 43 (Fall): 69–75.

Arrow, K. (1985) 'The economics of agency', in J. Pratt and R. Zeckhauser (eds), *Principals and Agents: The Structure of Business*. Boston, MA: Harvard Business School Press, pp. 37–52.

A.T. Kearney/WHU-Otto Beisheim School of Management (2015) Digital supply chains: increasingly critical for competitive advantage. European A.T. Kearney/WHU Logistics Study 2015. Available at: www.atkearney.com (accessed 29 June 2016).

AUMA (2013) *German Trade Fair Industry Review 2012*. Berlin: AUMA (Association of the German Trade Fair Industry). Available at: www.auma.de/en/DownloadsPublications/PublicationDownloads/AUMA_Review2012.pdf (accessed 25 November 2013).

Australian Commission on Safety and Quality in Health Care (2015) Review of operational clinical and patient care at Fiona Stanley Hospital. 26 June 2015. Available at http://ww2.health.wa.gov.au (accessed 7 August 2016).

Avila, R., Dodds, W., Chapman, J., Mann, K. and Wahlers, R. (1993) 'Importance of price in industrial buying', *Review of Business*, 15 (2): 34–48.

Axelson, B. (2001) 'Virtual trade shows await their turn', *B to B*, 86 (5): 23.

B2B Marketing (2010) 'Get trigger happy', *B2B Marketing Magazine*, 4 May. Available at: www.b2bmarketing.net (accessed 16 January 2013).

Baddar Al-Husan, F. and Brennan, R. (2009) 'Key account management in an emerging economy: a case study approach', *Journal of Business & Industrial Marketing*, 24 (8): 611–20.

Bailey, C., Baines, P., Wilson, H. and Clark, M. (2009) 'Segmentation and customer insight in contemporary services marketing practice: why grouping customers is no longer enough', *Journal of Marketing Management*, 25 (3–4): 227–52.

Bairstow, N. and Young, L. (2012) 'How channels evolve: a historical explanation', *Industrial Marketing Management*, 41 (3): 385–93.

Baker, M.J. and Hart, S. (1989) *Marketing and Competitive Success*. Oxford: Philip Allan.

Ballantyne, D., Frow, P., Varey, R.J. and Payne, A. (2011) 'Value propositions as communication practice: taking a wider view', *Industrial Marketing Management*, 40 (2): 202–10.

Ballantyne, D. and Varey, R.J. (2008) 'The service-dominant logic and the future of marketing', *Journal of the Academy of Marketing Science*, 36 (1): 11–14.

Bals, L., Hartmann, E. and Ritter, T. (2009) 'Barriers of purchasing departments' involvement in marketing service procurement', *Industrial Marketing Management*, 38: 892–902.

Bandler, J. and Burke, D. (2012) 'How Hewlett Packard lost its way', *Fortune*, 8 May. Available at: www.fortune.com (accessed 17 July 2016).

Barnes, B.R. (2004) 'Is the seven year hitch premature in industrial markets?', *European Journal of Marketing*, 39 (5/6): 560–84.

Barney, J.B. (1991) 'Firm resources and sustained competitive advantage', *Journal of Management*, 17 (1): 99–120.

Barry, J. and Weinstein, A. (2009) 'Business psychographics revisited: from segmentation theory to successful marketing practice', *Journal of Marketing Management*, 25 (3/4): 315–40.

Barry, N. (2001) *Ethics, Conventions and Capitalism*. London: Institute of Economic Affairs.

Bayer, (2016) Bayer: Science for a better life. Available at: www.bayer.com/en/focus-life-sciences-article.aspx. (accessed 12 July 2016).

BBC (2013a) 'A350: The aircraft that Airbus did not want to build', Theo Leggett. Available at: www.bbc.co.uk/news/business-22803218 (accessed 5 November 2013).

BBC (2013b) 'A350 marks new phase in aero-engines', David Shukman. Available at: www.bbc.co.uk/news/science-environment-22889969 (accessed 5 November 2013).

Bergen, M., Dutta, S. and Walker, O. (1992) 'Agency relationships in marketing: a review of the implications and applications of agency and related theories', *Journal of Marketing*, 56 (July): 1–24.

Bevilacqua, M. and Petroni, A. (2002) 'From traditional purchasing to supplier management', *Internal Journal of Logistics: Research and Applications*, 5 (3): 235–55.

Bingham, T. (2009) 'Is it still cover pricing without the phone call?' Available at: www.building.co.uk (accessed 23 September 2009).

Blois, K. (2003) 'Using value equations to analyse exchanges', *Marketing Intelligence and Planning*, 21 (1): 16–22.

Blythe, J.W.D. (1997) 'Does size matter? Objectives and measures at UK trade exhibitions', *Journal of Marketing Communications*, 3 (1): 51–9.

Blythe, J.W.D. (2002) 'Using trade fairs in key account management', *Industrial Marketing Management*, 31: 627–35.

Boejgaard, J. and Ellegaard, C. (2010) 'Unfolding implementation in industrial market segmentation', *Industrial Marketing Management*, 39: 1291–9.

Boles, J., Johnston, W. and Gardner, A. (1999) 'The selection and organization of national accounts: a North American perspective', *Journal of Business & Industrial Marketing*, 14 (4): 264–75.

Bonner, J.M. and Walker, O.C. (2004) 'Selecting influential business-to-business customers in new product development: relational embeddedness and knowledge heterogeneity considerations', *Journal of Product Innovation Management*, 21: 159–69.

Bonoma, T.V. (1983) 'Get more out of your trade shows', *Harvard Business Review*, January–February: 75–83.

Bowonder, B. and Yadav, S. (1999) 'R&D spending patterns of global firms', *Research Technology Management*, 42 (6): 44–55.

Brakus, J.J., Schmitt, B.H. and Zarantonello, L. (2009) 'Brand experience: what is it? How is it measured? Does it affect loyalty?', *Journal of Marketing*, 73: 835–55.

Brehmer, P-O. and Rehme, J. (2009) 'Proactive and reactive: drivers for key account management programmes', *European Journal of Marketing*, 43 (7–8): 961–84.

Brennan, R. (2012) 'The industrial/consumer dichotomy in marketing: can formal taxonomic thinking help?', *Journal of Customer Behaviour*, 11 (4): 311–24.

Brennan, R. and Croft, R. (2012) 'The use of social media in B2B marketing and branding: an exploratory study', *Journal of Customer Behaviour*, 11 (2): 101–15.

Brennan, R. and Turnbull, P. (1995) 'Adaptations in buyer–seller relationships'. *Proceedings of the 11th Annual IMP International Conference, Manchester, 7–9 September*.

Brennan, R., Baines, P., Garneau, P. and Vos, L. (2008) *Contemporary Strategic Marketing*. Basingstoke: Palgrave Macmillan.

Browning, J.M. and Adams, R.J. (1988) 'Trade shows: an effective promotional tool for the small industrial firm', *Journal of Small Business Management*, October: 31–6.

Brownlie, D. and Saren, M. (1992) 'The four Ps of the marketing concept: prescriptive, polemical, permanent and problematical', *European Journal of Marketing*, 26 (4): 34–47.

Bruell, A. (2012) 'Another wrench in the pitch: agencies lament the rise of e-auctions', *Advertising Age*, 10 September. Available at: www.adage.com (accessed 26 March 2016).

Bruhn, M. (2003) *Relationship Marketing*. Hemel Hempstead: Prentice Hall.

Bruhn, M., Schnebelen, S. and Schäfer, D. (2014) 'Antecedents and consequences of the quality of e-customer-to-customer interactions in B2B brand communities', *Industrial Marketing Management*, 43: 164–76.

Bunn, M.D. (1993) 'Taxonomy of buying decision approaches', *Journal of Marketing*, 57 (January): 38–56.

Burns, T. and Stalker, G. (1961) *The Management of Innovation*. London: Tavistock.

Butler, E. (2007) *Adam Smith – A Primer*. London: Institute of Economic Affairs.

Buyersphere (2015) *A Comprehensive Survey into the Attitudes and Behaviours of the B2B Buyer*, Base One (January). Available at: www.baseone.co.uk (accessed 15 March 2016).

Buzzell, R.D. and Gale, B.T. (1987) *The PIMS Principles: Linking Strategy to Performance*. New York: Free Press.

Bygballe, L.E., Bø, E. and Grønland, S.E. (2012) 'Managing international supply: the balance between total costs and customer service', *Industrial Marketing Management*, 41: 394–401.

Byrnes, J.L.S., Copacino, W.C. and Mets, P. (1987) 'Forge service into a weapon with logistics', *Transportation and Distribution*, 28 (9): 46.

Campbell, C., Papania, L., Parent, M. and Cyr, D. (2010) 'An exploratory study into brand alignment in B2B relationships', *Industrial Marketing Management*, 39: 712–20.

Campbell, N. and Cunningham, M. (1983) 'Customer analysis for strategy development in industrial markets', *Strategic Management Journal*, 4: 369–80.

Carbon Trust (2004) *The Climate Change Challenge 1: Scientific Evidence and Implications*. London: Carbon Trust.

Cardozo, R.N., Shipp, S.H. and Roering, K.J. (1987) 'Implementing new business-to-business selling methods', *Journal of Personal Selling and Sales Management*, 7 (August): 17–26.

Carter-Morley, J. (2013) 'How Zara took over the high street', *The Guardian*, 16 February. Available at: www.guardian.co.uk/fashion/2013/feb/16/how-zara-took-over-high-street (accessed 5 November 2013).

Cater, B. and Zabkar, V. (2009) 'Antecedents and consequences of commitment in marketing research services: the client's perspective', *Industrial Marketing Management*, 38 (7): 785–97.

Chaffey, D. (2014) 'B2B marketing automation briefing. An introduction to the benefits and options for marketing automation', *Smart Insights*, July. Available at: www.smartinsights.com (accessed 15 July 2016).

Chahal, M. (2015) 'GE Healthcare on how to humanise. B2B marketing', *Marketing Week*, 29 October. Available at: www.marketingweek.com (accessed 26 July 2016).

Chartered Institute of Purchasing and Supply (2013) 'P&SM: Supply Chain Management', CIPS Knowledge, Procurement Topics and Skills. Available at: www.cips.org (accessed 25 June 2016).

Chisnall, P.M. (1989) *Strategic Industrial Marketing*. Hemel Hempstead: Prentice Hall.

Choffray, J.M. and Lilien, G. (1978) 'A new approach to industrial market segmentation', *Sloan Management Review*, 19 (3): 17–29.

Chopra, S. and Sodhi, S.M. (2014) 'Reducing the risk of supply chain disruptions', *MIT Sloan Management Review*, 55 (3): 72–80.

Christopher, M. (1996) 'From brand values to customer value', *Journal of Marketing Practice: Applied Marketing Science*, 2 (1): 55–66.

Christopher, M. (2000) 'The agile supply chain: competing in volatile markets', *Industrial Marketing Management*, 29: 37–44.

Christopher, M. and Gattorna, J. (2005) 'Supply chain cost management and value-based pricing', *Industrial Marketing Management*, 34: 115–21.

Christopher, M. and Peck, H. (2001) 'Moving mountains at Marks & Spencer'. Available at: http://old.cba.ua.edu/~grichey2/SCS/MarksandSpencer.pdf (accessed 25 November 2013).

Chumillas, A. (2016) 'Marketing automation or telemarketing in the race for leads?', 14 January. Available at: www.celciusinternational.com (accessed 26 July 2016).

CIA (2012) *The CIA World Factbook*. Available at: www.cia.gov/library/publications/the-world-factbook/docs/guidetowfbook.html (accessed 1 December 2012).

Clancy, K. and Krieg, P. (2003) 'Surviving innovation', *Marketing Management*, March/April: 14–20.

Clarke, A. (2015) 'How to link social media to sales', *B2B Marketing Magazine*, 21 September. Available at: www.b2bmarketing.net (accessed 7 March 2016).

Coleman, D.A., de Chernatony, L. and Christodoulides, G. (2015) 'B2B service brand identity and brand performance: an empirical investigation in the UK's B2B IT services sector', *European Journal of Marketing*, 49 (7/8): 1139–62.

Colletti, J.A. and Tubridy, G.S. (1987) 'Effective major account sales management', *Journal of Personal Selling and Sales Management*, 7 (2): 1–10.

Cook, K. and Emerson, R. (1978) 'Power, equity and commitment in exchange networks', *American Sociological Review*, 43: 721–39.

Copeland, M.T. (1924) *Principles of Merchandising*. Chicago, IL: A.W. Shaw.

Council of Supply Chain Management Professionals (2010) 'Supply chain management definitions'. Available at: cscmp.org/about-us/supply-chain-management-definitions (accessed 19 January 2010).

Cox, H., Mowatt, S. and Prevezer, M. (2002) 'The firm in the Information Age: organizational responses to technological change in the processed foods sector', *Industrial and Corporate Change*, 11 (1): 135–58.

Cox, W.E.J. and Dominguez, L.V. (1979) 'The key issues and procedures of industrial marketing research', *Industrial Marketing Management*, 8: 81–93.

Crane, A., Matten, D. and Spence, L.J. (2008) *Corporate Social Responsibility: Readings and Cases in a Global Context*. London and New York: Routledge.

Cravens, D. (1997) *Strategic Marketing*. New York: Irwin/McGraw-Hill.

Crawford, C. and DiBenedetto, A. (2003) *New Products Management* (7th edn). Boston, MA: McGraw-Hill.

Cunningham, M.T. and Homse, E. (1997) 'Controlling the marketing–purchasing interface: resource development and organizational implications', in D. Ford (ed.), *Understanding Business Markets: Interaction, Relationships and Networks* (2nd edn). London: Dryden.

Cutler, B.D. and Javalgi, R.G. (1994) 'Comparison of business to business advertising: the United States and the United Kingdom', *Industrial Marketing Management*, 23: 117–24.

Daly, S.P. and Nath, P. (2005) 'Reverse auctions for relationship marketers', *Industrial Marketing Management*, 34: 157–66.

Datamonitor (2004) *Liquid Petroleum Gas in Europe*. London: Datamonitor.

Datamonitor (2009) *Rolls-Royce Group plc: Company Profile*. London: Datamonitor.

Datamonitor (2011) *Global Heavy Electrical Equipment: Industry Profile*. London: Datamonitor.

Datamonitor (2012a) *Company Profile: Air Products and Chemicals, Inc.* London: Datamonitor.

Datamonitor (2012b) *Global Environmental Services and Facilities Services: Industry Profile*. London: Datamonitor.

Davies, I.A. and Ryals, L.J. (2009) 'A stage model for transitioning to KAM', *Journal of Marketing Management*, 25 (9–10): 1027–48.

Dawe, K. (2015) 'Best practice in business-to-business email', *Journal of Direct, Data and Digital Marketing Practice*, 16 (4): 242–7.

Day, G.S. (2000) 'Managing market relationships', *Journal of the Academy of Marketing Science*, 28 (1): 24–30.

Delener, N. (1998) 'An ethical and legal synthesis of dumping: growing concerns in international marketing', *Journal of Business Ethics*, 17: 1747–53.

Desarbo, W.S., Jedidi, K. and Sinha, I. (2001) 'Customer value analysis in a heterogeneous market', *Strategic Management Journal*, 22: 845–57.

Deshpande, R. and Zaltman, G. (1982) 'Factors affecting the use of market research information: a path analysis', *Journal of Marketing Research*, 19: 14–31.

Deshpande, R. and Zaltman, G. (1984) 'A comparison of factors affecting researcher and manager perceptions of market research use', *Journal of Marketing Research*, 21: 32–8.

Deshpande, R. and Zaltman, G. (1987) 'A comparison of factors affecting use of marketing information in consumer and industrial firms', *Journal of Marketing Research*, 24: 114–18.

Diamantopoulos, A. and Schlegelmilch, B. (1996) 'Determinants of industrial mail survey response: a survey-on-surveys analysis of researchers' and managers' views', *Journal of Marketing Management*, 12 (6): 503–31.

DiMasi, J., Hansen, R. and Grabowski, H. (2003) 'The price of innovation: new estimates of drug development costs', *Journal of Health Economics*, 22: 151–85.

Dobler, D.W. and Burt, D.N. (1996) *Purchasing and Supply Management* (6th edn). New York: McGraw-Hill.

Dowst, S. (1988) 'Quality suppliers: the search goes on', *Purchasing* (28 January): 94A4–12.

Doyle, P. (2000) *Value-Based Marketing*. Chichester: Wiley.

Doyle, P. and Saunders, J. (1985) 'Market segmentation and positioning in specialized industrial markets', *Journal of Marketing*, 49 (2): 24–32.

Drozdowski, T. (1986) 'At BOC they start with the product', *Purchasing* (13 March): 62B5–1.

Drucker, P. (1955) *The Practice of Management*. London: Heinemann Professional Publishing.

Dwyer, F. and Tanner, J. (2002) *Business Marketing* (2nd edn). Boston, MA: McGraw-Hill.

Dwyer, F.R., Schurr, P.H. and Oh, S. (1987) 'Developing buyer–seller relationships', *Journal of Marketing*, 51 (April): 11–27.

Eatwell, J., Milgate, M. and Newman, P. (eds) (1987) *The New Palgrave: A Dictionary of Economics*. London: Macmillan.

Eborall, C. and Nathan, L. (1989) 'Caveat Emptor, or ours not to reason why? A look at client/agency relationships in business research'. *Proceedings of the Market Research Society Conference*, London: MRS.

The Economist (2009) 'Briefing: Rolls-Royce – Britain's lonely high-flier', 10 January: 62–4.

The Economist (2014) 'Rethinking "low-cost" and "high-cost" manufacturing locations'. Available at: www.economist.com/news/business-and-finance/21614076-rethinking-low-cost-and-high-cost-manufacturing-locations-when-cheap-not-so-cheap (accessed 28 April 2016).

Economist.com (2013) 'The Airbus A350: up and away'. Available at: www.economist.com/blogs/schumpeter/2013/06/airbus-a350 (accessed 5 November 2013).

Eggert, A., Hogreve, J., Ulaga, W. and Muenkhoff, E. (2011) 'Industrial services, product innovations, and firm profitability: a multiple-group latent growth curve analysis', *Industrial Marketing Management*, 40: 661–70.

El-Ansary, A. and Stern, L. (1972) 'Power measurement in the distribution channel', *Journal of Marketing Research*, 9: 47–52.

Ellis, S.C., Henke, J.W. and Kull, T.K. (2012) 'The effect of buyer behaviors on preferred customer status and access to supplier technological innovation: an empirical study of supplier perceptions', *Industrial Marketing Management*, 41: 1259–69.

Erevelles, S. and Stevenson, T.H. (2006) 'Enhancing the business-to-business supply chain: Insights from partitioning the supply side', *Industrial Marketing Management*, 35: 481–92.

Erevelles, S., Stevenson, T.H., Srinivasan, S. and Fukawa, N. (2008) 'An analysis of B2B ingredient co-branding relationships', *Industrial Marketing Management*, 37: 940–52.

European Commission (2011) *A Renewed EU Strategy 2011–14 for Corporate Social Responsibility*. Brussels: European Commission. Available at: http://eur-lex.europa.eu/LexUriServ/LexUriServ.do?uri=COM:2011:0681:FIN:EN:PDF (accessed 1 June 2013).

European Commission (2015) *EU R&D Scoreboard. The 2014 EU Industrial R&D Investment Scoreboard*. Available at: http://iri.jrc.ec.europa.eu (accessed 25 August 2016).

Evans, M., O'Malley, L. and Patterson, M. (2004) *Exploring Direct and Customer Relationship Marketing* (2nd edn). London: Thomson.

Faria, A.J. and Dickinson, J.R. (1992) 'Mail survey response, speed, and cost', *Industrial Marketing Management*, 21: 51–60.

Fawcett, S.E, Wallin, C., Allreed, C., Fawcett, A.M. and Magnan, G.M. (2011) 'Information technology as an enabler of supply chain collaboration: a dynamic capabilities perspective', *Journal of Supply Chain Management*, 47 (1): 38–59.

Feitzinger, E. and Lee, H.L. (1997) 'Mass customization at Hewlett Packard: the power of postponement', *Harvard Business Review*, January–February: 116–21.

Fern, E.F. and Brown, J.R. (1984) 'The industrial/consumer marketing dichotomy: a case of insufficient justification', *Journal of Marketing*, 48 (Spring): 68–77.

Ferrin, B.G. and Plank, R.E. (2002) 'Total cost of ownership models: an exploratory study', *Journal of Supply Chain Management*, 38 (3): 18–29.

Fleming, P. and Jones, M.T. (2013) *The End of Corporate Social Responsibility*. London: Sage.

Foedermayr, E.K. and Diamantopoulos, A. (2008) 'Market segmentation in practice: review of empirical studies, methodological assessment, and agenda for future research', *Journal of Strategic Marketing*, 16 (3): 225–63.

Ford, D. (1980) 'The development of buyer–seller relationships in industrial markets', *European Journal of Marketing*, 14 (5/6): 339–54.

Ford, D. (ed.) (1990) *Understanding Business Markets: Interaction, Relationships, Networks*. London: Academic Press.

Ford, D. (ed.) (1997) *Understanding Business Markets: Interaction, Relationships, Networks* (2nd edn). London: Dryden.

Ford, D. (ed.) (2002) *Understanding Business Marketing and Purchasing* (3rd edn). London: International Thomson.

Ford, D. and McDowell, R. (1999) 'Managing business relationships by analyzing the effects and value of different actions', *Industrial Marketing Management*, 28 (5): 429–42.

Ford, D., Håkansson, H., Lundgren, A., Snehota, I., Turnbull, P. and Wilson, D. (1998) *Managing Business Relationships*. Chichester: Wiley.

Ford, D., Berthon, P., Brown, S., Gadde, L.E., Håkansson, H., Naudé, P., Ritter, T. and Snehota, I. (2002) *The Business Marketing Course*. Chichester: Wiley.

Ford, D., Gadde, L.E., Håkansson, H. and Snehota, I. (2003) *Managing Business Relationships* (2nd edn). Chichester: Wiley.

Ford, D., Gadde, L.E., Håkansson, H. and Snehota, I. (2006) *The Business Marketing Course: Managing in Complex Networks* (2nd edn). Chichester: Wiley.

Ford, N., Trott, P., Simms, C. and Hartmann, D. (2014) 'Case analysis of innovation in the packaging industry using the cyclic innovation model', *International Journal of Innovation Management*, 18 (5). Available at: https://researchportal.port.ac.uk/portal/en/publications/case-analysis-of-innovation-in-the-packaging-industry-using-the-cyclic-innovation-model(ddd51f20-9184-4409-bdeb-51a9d2a37817).html (accessed 23 January 2017).

Foster, B.D. and Cadogan, J.W. (2000) 'Relationship selling and customer loyalty: an empirical investigation', *Marketing Intelligence and Planning*, 18 (4): 185–99.

Frazier, G., Spekman, R. and O'Neal, C. (1988) 'Just-in-time exchange relationships in industrial markets', *Journal of Marketing*, 52 (October): 52–67.

Frederick, J. (1934) *Industrial Marketing*. New York: Prentice Hall.

Freeman, R. (1984) *Strategic Management: A Stakeholder Approach*. Marshfield, MA: Pitman Publishing Inc.

Freytag, P. and Clarke, A. (2001) 'Business to business market segmentation', *Industrial Marketing Management*, 30 (6): 473–86.

Friedman, M. (1979) 'The social responsibility of business is to increase profit', in T.L. Beauchamp and N. Bowie (eds), *Ethical Theory and Business*. Englewood Cliffs, NJ: Prentice Hall.

Gadde, L.-E. and Håkansson, H. (2001) *Supply Network Strategies*. Chichester: Wiley.

Ganesan, S. (1994) 'Determinants of long-term orientation in buyer–seller relationships', *Journal of Marketing*, 58 (2): 1–19.

Gannon, M. (2004) *Understanding Global Cultures: Metaphorical Journeys Through 28 Nations, Clusters of Nations and Continents* (3rd edn). Thousand Oaks, CA: Sage.

Gaski, J. (1984) 'The theory of power and conflict in channels of distribution', *Journal of Marketing*, 48 (Summer): 9–28.

Gaski, J.F. (1999) 'Does marketing ethics really have anything to say? A critical inventory of the literature', *Journal of Business Ethics*, 18: 315–34.

Gaski, J.F. (2001) 'Normative marketing ethics redux, incorporating a reply to Smith', *Journal of Business Ethics*, 32: 19–34.

Gassenheimer, J.B., Houston, F.S. and Davis, J.C. (1998) 'The role of economic value, social value, and perceptions of fairness in interorganizational relationship retention decisions', *Journal of the Academy of Marketing Science*, 26 (4): 322–37.

Gates, B. (1996) *The Road Ahead: Revised and Updated*. London: Penguin.

Geigenmüller, A. (2010) 'The role of virtual trade fairs in relationship value creation', *Journal of Business and Industrial Marketing*, 25 (4): 284–92.

Gelderman, C.J. and van Weele, A.J. (2003) 'Handling measurement issues and strategic directions in Kraljic's purchasing portfolio model', *Journal of Purchasing and Supply Management*, 9 (5/6): 207–16.

Ghingold, M. and Wilson, D.T. (1998) 'Buying centre research and business marketing practice: meeting the challenge of dynamic marketing', *Journal of Business and Industrial Marketing*, 13 (2): 96–108.

Gilliam, D.A. (2015) 'Trade show boothscapes', *Journal of Marketing Management*, 31 (17–18): 1878–98.

Gilliland, D.I. and Johnston, W.J. (1997) 'Toward a model of business-to-business marketing communications effects', *Industrial Marketing Management*, 26: 15–29.

Giunipero, L.C., Hooker, R.E. and Denslow, D. (2012) 'Purchasing and supply management sustainability: drivers and barriers', *Journal of Purchasing and Supply Management*, 18 (4): 258–69.

Goodenough, W.H. (1971) *Culture, Language and Society*, Modular Publications 7. Reading, MA: Addison-Wesley.

Gopalakrishna, S. and Lilien, G. (1995) 'A three-stage model of industrial trade show performance', *Marketing Science*, 14 (1): 22–42.

Granovetter, M. (1985) 'Economic action and social structure: the problem of embeddedness', *American Journal of Sociology*, 91 (3): 481–510.

Grant, K. and Cravens, D.W. (1996) 'Examining sales force performance in organizations that use behaviour-based sales management processes', *Industrial Marketing Management*, 25: 361–71.

Greer, T.V. and Lohtia, R. (1994) 'Effects of source and paper color on response rates in mail surveys', *Industrial Marketing Management*, 23: 47–54.

Griffith, R. and Pol, L. (1994) 'Segmenting industrial markets', *Industrial Marketing Management*, 23 (1): 39–46.

Grönroos, C. (1997) 'From marketing mix to relationship marketing – towards a paradigm shift in marketing', *Management Decision*, 35 (4): 322–39.

Gross, A.C., Banting, P.M., Meredith, L.N. and Ford, I.D. (1993) *Business Marketing*. New York: Houghton Mifflin.

Guimarães, C.M. and de Carvalho, J.C. (2010) 'Outsourcing in the healthcare sector – a state of the art review', *International Conference on Logistics and SCM Research, BEM Bordeaux Management School, September–October*.

Gummesson, E. (1987) 'The new marketing – developing long-term interactive relationships', *Long Range Planning*, 20 (4): 10–20.

Hadjimatheou, G. and Sarantis, N. (1998) 'Is UK deindustrialisation inevitable?', in T. Buxton, P. Chapman and P. Temple (eds), *Britain's Economic Performance* (2nd edn). London: Routledge.

Håkansson, H. (ed.) (1982) *International Marketing and Purchasing of Industrial Goods: An Interaction Approach*. Chichester: Wiley.

Håkansson, H. and Ostberg, C. (1975) 'Industrial marketing: an organizational problem?', *Industrial Marketing Management*, 4 (2/3): 113–23.

Håkansson, H. and Snehota, I. (1989) 'No business is an island: the network concept of business strategy', *Scandinavian Journal of Management*, 4 (3): 187–200.

Håkansson, H. and Snehota, I. (1995a) *Developing Relationships in Business Networks*. London: Routledge.

Håkansson, H. and Snehota, I. (1995b) 'The burden of relationships or who is next?', *Proceedings of the 11th Annual IMP International Conference, Manchester, 7–9 September*.

Håkansson, H., Johanson, J. and Wootz, B. (1976) 'Influence tactics in buyer–seller processes', *Industrial Marketing Management*, 5 (5): 319–32.

Hall, E.T. (1976) *Beyond Culture*. New York: Doubleday.

Hallén, L., Johanson, J. and Seyed-Mohamed, N. (1991) 'Inter-firm adaptation in business relationships', *Journal of Marketing*, 55 (April): 29–37.

Harrington, L. (2004) 'Building the sense and respond company', *Inbound Logistics*, September. Available at: www.inboundlogistics.com/articles/features/0904_feature03.shtml (accessed 5 November 2013).

Harrington, R.J. and Tjan, A.K. (2008) 'Transforming strategy one customer at a time', *Harvard Business Review*, March: 62–72.

Hart, N. (1988) *Practical Advertising and Publicity*. Maidenhead: McGraw-Hill.

Hart, S.L. (1997) 'Beyond greening: strategies for a sustainable world', *Harvard Business Review*, January–February: 66–76.

Hartley, K. and Hooper, N. (1997) 'Industry and policy 1: theory and competition policy', in P. Curwen (ed.), *Understanding the UK Economy*. Basingstoke and London: Macmillan.

Harvey, F. (2006) 'Ribena loosens grip on blackcurrant farmers', *Financial Times*, 5 September. Available at: www.ft.com (accessed 18 March 2016).

Heide, J. and John, G. (1990) 'Alliances in industrial purchasing: the determinants of joint action in buyer–supplier relationships', *Journal of Marketing Research*, 27 (1): 24–36.

Helm, S.V. and Özergin, B. (2015) 'Service inside: the impact of ingredient service branding on quality perceptions and behavioural intentions', *Industrial Marketing Management*, 50: 142–9.

Hinchcliffe, D. (2014) 'Is the internet of things strategic to the enterprise?', 31 May. Available at: www.zdnet.com (accessed 28 June 2016).

Hinterhuber, A. (2004) 'Towards value-based pricing – an integrative framework for decision making', *Industrial Marketing Management*, 33 (8): 765–78.

Hinterhuber, A. (2015) 'Violations of rational choice principles in pricing decisions', *Industrial Marketing Management,* 47: 65–74.

Hlavacek, J.D. and Ames, B.C. (1986) 'Segmenting industrial and high-tech markets', *Journal of Business Strategy*, 7 (2): 39–50.

Ho, W., Xu, X. and Dey, P.K. (2010) 'Multi-criteria decision-making approaches for supplier evaluation and selection: a literature review', *European Journal of Operational Research*, 202: 16–24.

Hoffman, M.W. and Moore, J.M. (1990) *Business Ethics.* New York: McGraw-Hill.

Hofstede, G. (2001) *Culture's Consequences: Comparing Values, Behaviors, Institutions and Organizations Across Nations*. 2nd Ed. Thousand Oaks, California: SAGE Publications, Inc.

Hofstede, G., Hofstede, G.J. and Minkov, M. (2010) *Cultures and Organizations: Software of the Mind*. 3rd Ed. McGraw Hill Education.

Hofstede, G. (1980) *Culture's Consequences: International Differences in Work-Related Values*. Beverly Hills, CA: Sage.

Høgevold, N.M. and Svensson, G. (2012) 'A business sustainability model: a European case study', *Journal of Business & Industrial Marketing*, 27 (2): 142–51.

Homburg, C., Workman, J.P., Jr and Jensen, O. (2002) 'A configurational perspective on Key Account Management', *Journal of Marketing*, 66 (2): 38–60.

Hooley, G.J. and Jobber, D. (1986) 'Five common factors in top performing industrial firms', *Industrial Marketing Management*, 15: 89–96.

Hosford, C. (2015) 'Honeywell user experience', *BMA Buzz*, 15 March. Available at: www.marketing.org (accessed 14 September 2016).

Hu, M. and Monahan, S.T. (2015) 'Sharing supply chain data in the digital era', *MIT Sloan Management Review*, 57 (1): 95–8.

Hultén, Peter, Viström, Magnus and Mejtoft, Thomas (2009) 'New printing technology and pricing', *Industrial Marketing Management*, 38 (3): 253–62.

Hunt, S.D. and Vitell, S. (1986) 'A general theory of marketing ethics', *Journal of Macromarketing*, 6 (1): 5–16.

Hurkens, K., van der Valk, W. and Wynstra, F. (2006) 'Total cost of ownership in the services sector: a case study', *Journal of Supply Chain Management*, 42 (1): 27–37.

Hutt, M.D. (1995) 'Cross-functional working relationships in marketing', *Journal of the Academy of Marketing Science*, 23 (4): 351–7.

Jackson, B.B. (1985a) 'Build customer relationships that last', *Harvard Business Review*, 63 (6): 120–8.

Jackson, B.B. (1985b) *Winning and Keeping Industrial Customers: The Dynamics of Customer Relationships*. Lexington, MA: Lexington Books.

Järvinen, J.J. and Karjaluoto, H. (2015) 'The use of web analytics for digital marketing performance measurement', *Industrial Marketing Management*, 50: 117–27.

Järvinen, J.J. and Taiminen, H. (2016) 'Harnessing marketing automation for B2B content marketing', *Industrial Marketing Management*, 54: 164–75.

Jean, R.-J., Sinkovics, R. and Cavusgil, S.T. (2010) 'Enhancing international customer-supplier relationships through IT resources: a study of Taiwanese electronic suppliers', *Journal of International Business Studies*, 41 (7 September): 1218–39.

Johanson, J. and Mattsson, L.G. (1992) 'Network positions and strategic action – an analytical framework', in B. Axelsson and G. Easton (eds), *Industrial Networks: A New View of Reality*. London: Routledge, pp. 205–17.

Joseph, K. (2001) 'On the optimality of delegating pricing authority to the sales force', *Journal of Marketing*, 65 (January): 62–70.

Julius, D. and Butler, J. (1998) *Inflation and Growth in a Service Economy*. London: Bank of England.

Kalwani, M.U. and Narayandas, N. (1995) 'Long-term manufacturer–supplier relationships: do they pay off for supplier firms?', *Journal of Marketing*, 59: 1–16.

Kang, M.-P., Mahoney, J.T. and Tan, D. (2009) 'Why firms make unilateral investments specific to other firms: the case of OEM suppliers', *Strategic Management Journal*, 30 (2): 117–35.

Kantrowitz, A. (2014) 'B2B marketing budgets set to rise 6% in 2014', *Advertising Age*, 21 January. Available at: www.adage.com (accessed 18 July 2016).

Kapferer, J.N. (2008) *The New Strategic Brand Management* (4th edn). London: Kogan Page.

Kashyap, V. and Sivdas, E. (2012) 'An exploratory examination of shared values in channel relationships', *Journal of Business Research*, 65 (5): 586–693.

Katona, Z. and Sarvary, M. (2014) 'Maersk Line B2B social media – "It's communication not marketing"', *California Management Review*, 56 (3): 140–56.

Keaveney, S.M. (2008) 'The blame game: an attribution theory approach to marketer–engineer conflict in high-technology companies', *Industrial Marketing Management*, 37 (6): 653–63.

Kellaher, J.B. (2014) 'From dumb iron to big data: Caterpillar's dealer sales push', *Business*, 20 March. Available at: www.reuters.com (accessed 1 July 2016).

Keller, K.L. and Richey, K. (2006) 'The importance of corporate brand personality traits to a successful 21st century business', *Journal of Brand Management*, 14 (1/2): 74–81.

Koslowski, P. (2000) 'The limits of shareholder value', *Journal of Business Ethics*, 27: 137–48.

Kothandaraman, P. and Wilson, D.T. (2001) 'The future of competition: value-creating networks', *Industrial Marketing Management*, 30 (4): 379–89.

Kotler, P. (1972) *Marketing Management: Analysis, Planning, and Control.* Englewood Cliffs, NJ: Prentice Hall.

Kotler, P. and Pfoertsch, W. (2007) 'Being known or being one of many: the need for brand management for business-to-business companies', *Journal of Business and Industrial Marketing*, 23 (1/2): 123–35.

KPMG (2013) *Something to Teach, Something to Learn: Global Perspectives on Healthcare.* London: KPMG International. Available at: www.kpmg.com/healthcare (accessed 1 May 2013).

Kraljic, P. (1983) 'Purchasing must become supply management', *Harvard Business Review*, September: 109–17.

Krapfel, R., Salmond, D. and Spekman, R. (1991) 'A strategic approach to managing buyer–seller relationships', *European Journal of Marketing*, 25 (9): 22–32.

Kumar, N. (1996) 'The power of trust in manufacturer–retailer relationships', *Harvard Business Review*, November–December: 92–106.

Kumar, N., Stern, L.W. and Achrol, R.S. (1992) 'Assessing reseller performance from the perspective of the supplier', *Journal of Marketing Research*, 29 (May): 238–53.

Labels and Labelling (2016) 'Selinko, NXP partner for connected wine bottles', 21 June. Available at: www.labelsandlabelling.com (accessed 26 June 2016).

Laczniak, G.R. and Murphy, P.E. (1993) *Ethical Marketing Decisions: The Higher Road.* Upper Saddle River, NJ: Prentice Hall.

Lambe, C.J. and Spekman, R.E. (1997) 'National account management: large account selling or buyer–supplier alliance?', *Journal of Personal Selling and Sales Management*, 17 (4): 61–74.

Lancioni, R.A. (2005) 'A strategic approach to industrial product pricing: the pricing plan', *Industrial Marketing Management*, 34: 177–83.

Lancioni, R., Schau, H.J. and Smith, M.F. (2005) 'Intraorganizational influences on business-to- business pricing strategies: a political economy perspective', *Industrial Marketing Management*, 34 (1): 124–31.

Lapierre, J. (2000) 'Customer-perceived value in industrial contexts', *Journal of Business & Industrial Marketing*, 15 (2/3): 122–40.

La Rocca, A. and Snehota, I. (2014) 'Relating in business networks: innovation in practice', *Industrial Marketing Management*, 43 (3): 441–7.

Lawson, B., Petersen, K.J., Cousins, P.D. and Handfield, R.B. (2009) 'Knowledge sharing in interorganizational product development teams: the effect of formal and informal socialization mechanisms', *Journal of Product Innovation Management*, 21: 156–72.

Leavy, B. (2004) 'The concept of learning in the strategy field', in K. Starkey, S. Tempest and A. McKinlay (eds), *How Organisations Learn.* Oxford: Blackwell, pp. 51–70.

Lee, H.L. (2010) 'Don't tweak your supply chain – rethink it end to end', *Harvard Business Review*, October: 62–9.

Leek, S., Naudé, P. and Turnbull, P.W. (2003a) 'Interactions, relationships and networks in a changing world', *Industrial Marketing Management*, 32: 87–90.

Leek, S., Turnbull, P.W. and Naudé, P. (2003b) 'How is information technology affecting business relationships? Results from a UK survey', *Industrial Marketing Management*, 32: 119–26.

Leek, S.H., Canning, L.E. and Houghton, D.J. (2016) 'Revisiting the task-media-fit model in the era of Web 2.0. Twitter use and interaction in the healthcare sector', *Industrial Marketing Management*, 54: 25–32.

Lilien, G.L. (1987) 'Business marketing: present and future', *Industrial Marketing and Purchasing*, 2 (3): 3–21.

Lilien, G.L. (2016) 'The B2B Knowledge Gap', *International Journal of Research in Marketing*. Available at: http://dx.doi.org/10.1016/j.ijresmar.2016.01.003 (accessed 16 January 2017).

Lindgreen, A. and Wynstra, F. (2005) 'Value in business markets: what do we know? Where are we going?', *Industrial Marketing Management*, 34 (7): 732–48.

Liozu, S.M. (2015) 'Pricing superheroes: how a confident sales team can influence firm performance', *Industrial Marketing Management*, 47: 26–38.

Liozu, S.M. and Hinterhuber, A. (2013) 'CEO championing of pricing, pricing capabilities and firm performance in industrial firms', *Industrial Marketing Management*, 42 (4): 633–43.

Lockett, A. and Blackman, I. (2004) 'Conducting market research using the internet: the case of Xenon Laboratories', *Journal of Business and Industrial Marketing*, 19 (3): 178–87.

Lohtia, R., Johnston, W.J. and Aab, L. (1995) 'Business-to-business advertising: what are the dimensions of an effective print ad?', *Industrial Marketing Management*, 24: 369–78.

Lucking-Reiley, D. (1999) 'Using field experiments to test equivalence between auction formats: magic on the internet', *American Economic Review*, 89 (5): 1063–80.

Magee, K. (2015) 'IPA slams Heinz pitch process and "the long hand of procurement"', *Campaign*, 22 June. Available at: www.campaignlive.co.uk (accessed 27 March 2016).

Malhotra, N. (1996) 'The impact of the academy of marketing science on marketing scholarship – an analysis of the research published in *JAMS*', *Journal of the Academy of Marketing Science*, 24 (4): 291–8.

Malone, T., Yates, J. and Benjamin, R. (1987) 'Electronic markets and hierarchies', *Communications of the Association of Computing Machinery (CACM)*, 30 (6): 484–97.

Manser, K., Hillebrand, B., Woolthuis, R.K., Ziggers, G.W., Driessen, P.H. and Bloemer, J. (2016) 'An activities-based approach to network management: an explorative study', *Industrial Marketing Management*, 55, 187–99.

MarketLine (2012) *Global Commercial Printing*. London: MarketLine.

Marshall, A. (1920) *Principles of Economics* (8th edn). London and Basingstoke: Macmillan.

Marshall, M. (2012) 'Research news: procurement saves money but hinders marketing campaigns', *B2B Marketing Magazine*, 17 April. Available at: http://b2bmarketingleaders.net/news/archive/research-news-procurement-saves-money-hinders-marketing-campaigns (accessed 5 November 2013).

Maslin, E. (2015) 'Big data gets even bigger', *OE Offshore Engineer*, 1 August. Available at: www.oedigital.com (accessed 4 August 2016).

Mathieu, V. (2001) 'Service strategies within the manufacturing sector: benefits, costs and partnership', *International Journal of Service Industry Management*, 12 (5): 451–75.

McCorkle, D.E. and McCorkle, Y.L. (2012) 'Using LinkedIn in the marketing classroom: exploratory insights and recommendations for teaching social media/networking', *Marketing Education Review*, 22 (2): 157–66.

McDonald, C. (2015) 'Creative focus: how would you make pitching better?', *AdNews*, 14 October. Available at: www.adnews.com\au (accessed 28 March 2016).

McDonald, M. (1996) 'Strategic marketing planning: theory, practice and research agendas', *Journal of Marketing Management*, 5 (1): 5–27.

McDougall, D., Wyner, G. and Vazdauskas, D. (1997) 'Customer valuation as a foundation for growth', *Managing Service Quality*, 7 (1): 5–11.

McGinnis, M.A. (2005) 'Lessons in cross-cultural negotiations', *Supply Chain Management Review*, April: 9–10.

McGrath, A.J. and Hardy, K.G. (1989) 'A strategic paradigm for predicting manufacturer–reseller conflict', *European Journal of Marketing*, 23 (2): 94–108.

McGreal, J. (2014) 'Campaign of the month: HP making it matter', *B2B Marketing Magazine*, 27 October. Available at: www.b2bmarketing.net (accessed 17 July 2016).

McKinsey (2012) *Making Innovation Structures Work: McKinsey Global Survey Results*. Available at: www.mckinsey.com/insights/innovation/making_innovation_structures_work_mckinsey_ global_survey_results (accessed 5 November 2012).

McWilliams, R.D., Naumann, E. and Scott, S. (1992) 'Determining buying center size', *Industrial Marketing Management*, 21: 43–9.

Menguc, B. and Barker, A.T. (2003) 'The performance effects of outcome-based incentive pay plans on sales organizations: a contextual analysis', *Journal of Personal Selling and Sales Management*, 23 (4): 341–58.

Mestre-Ferrandiz, J., Sussex, J. and Towse, A. (2012) *The R&D Cost of a New Medicine*, Office of Health Economics. Available at: www.ohe.org/publications/article/the-rd-cost-of-a-new-medicine-124.cfm (accessed 5 November 2013).

Meyer, E. (2015) 'Getting to Si, Ja, Oui, Hai and Da', *Harvard Business Review*, December: 74–80.

Michaelidou, N., Siamagka, N.T. and Christodoulides, G. (2011) 'Usage, barriers and measurement of social media marketing: an exploratory investigation of small and medium B2B brands', *Industrial Marketing Management*, 40 (7): 1153–9.

Miles, R.E. and Snow, C.C. (1978) *Organizational Strategy, Structure and Process*. New York: McGraw-Hill.

Millman, T. and Wilson, K. (1995) 'From key account selling to key account management', *Journal of Marketing Practice: Applied Marketing Science*, 1 (1): 9–21.

Millman, T. and Wilson, K. (1996) Developing key account management competencies. *Journal of Applied Marketing Science*, 2 (2): 7–22.

Millman, T. and Wilson, K. (1999) 'Processual issues in key account management: underpinning the customer-facing organisation', *Journal of Business and Industrial Marketing*, 14 (4): 328–37.

Mintel (2012) *Laundry Detergents and Fabric Conditioners – UK*. London: Mintel.

Mintzberg, H., Ahlstrand, B. and Lampel, J. (1998) *Strategy Safari*. London: FT/Prentice Hall.

Mitchell, V.W. (1995) 'Organizational risk perception and reduction: a literature review', *British Journal of Management*, 6: 115–33.

Mohr, J.J., Fischer, R.J. and Nevin, J.R. (1996) 'Collaborative communication in interfirm relationships: moderating effects of integration and control', *Journal of Marketing Management*, 60 (July): 103–15.

Mohr, J.J., Fischer, R.J. and Nevin J.R. (1999) 'Communicating for better channel relationships', *Marketing Management*, Summer: 39–45.

Monzcka, R.M., Handfield, R.B., Guinipero, L.C. and Patterson, J.L. (2015) 'Supply chain information systems and electronic sourcing', ch. 18 in *Purchasing and Supply Chain Management* (6th edn). Boston, MA: Cengage Learning, pp. 700–45.

Moorman, C., Deshpande, B. and Zaltman, G. (1993) 'Factors affecting trust in market research relationships', *Journal of Marketing*, 57 (January): 81–101.

Morgan, R. and Hunt, S. (1994) 'The commitment–trust theory of relationship marketing', *Journal of Marketing*, 58 (July): 20–38.

Moriarty, R.T. and Spekman, R.E. (1984) 'An empirical investigation of the sources of information used during the industrial buying process', *Journal of Marketing Research*, 21 (May): 137–47.

Morley-Fletcher, G. (2011) 'Using the right tone of voice to suit your audience: B2B marketing seminar – taking it to the next level' (10 March). Available at: www.b2b marketing.net (accessed 12 August 2013).

Murphy, P.E. and Enis, B.M. (1986) 'Classifying products strategically', *Journal of Marketing*, 50 (July): 24–42.

Nagle, T.T. and Holden, R.K. (2002) *The Strategy and Tactics of Pricing: A Guide to Profitable Decision Making* (3rd edn). Upper Saddle River, NJ: Prentice Hall.

Nagle, T.T., Hogan, J. and Zale, J. (2010) *The Strategy and Tactics of Pricing: A Guide to Growing More Profitably* (5th edn). Upper Saddle River, NJ: Prentice Hall.

Napolitano, L. (1997) 'Customer–supplier partnering: a strategy whose time has come', *Journal of Personal Selling and Sales Management*, 17 (4): 1–8.

Naudé, P. and Holland, C. (1996) 'Business-to-business relationships', in F. Buttle (ed.), *Relationship Marketing: Theory & Practice*. London: Paul Chapman Publishing/Sage, pp. 40–54.

Needles, A. (2010) 'The "new" B2B buyer', *B2B Marketing Magazine*, September.

New, S. (2010) 'The transparent supply chain', *Harvard Business Review*, October: 76–82.

NHS (2009) 'Revised healthcare cleaning manual', National Patient Safety Agency. 9 June. Available at: www.npsa.nhs.uk/cleaning (accessed 30 March 2016).

Nielsen, C.S. and Gannon, M.J. (2006) 'Cultural metaphors, paradoxes, and cross-cultural dimensions', *International Studies of Management and Organisation*, 35 (4): 4–7.

Nowak, L.I., Boughton, P.D. and Pereira, A.J.A. (1997) 'Relationships between businesses and marketing research firms', *Industrial Marketing Management*, 26: 487–95.

Oakley, J. and Bush, A.J. (2016) 'The role of suspicion in B2B customer entertainment', *Journal of Business & Industrial Marketing*, 31 (5): 565–74.

OECD (1993) *United Kingdom*. Paris: OECD.

OECD (2003) *United Kingdom*. Paris: OECD.

OECD (2008) *Labour Force Statistics: 1987–2007*. Paris: OECD.

OECD (2011) *Labour Force Statistics: 1999–2009*. Paris: OECD.

OFT (2009) 'Construction firms fined for illegal bid-rigging'. Available at: www.oft.gov.uk/news-and-updates/press/2009/114-09.UnjvpHDwnGg (accessed 23 September 2009).

Ojasalo, J. (2001) 'Key account management at company and individual levels in business-to-business relationships', *Journal of Business and Industrial Marketing*, 16 (3): 199–218.

Oldroyd, J.B., McElheran, K. and Elkington, D. (2011) 'The short life of online sales leads', *Harvard Business Review*, 89 (3): 28.

Oliver, R.L. and Anderson, E. (1995) 'Behaviour- and outcome-based sales control systems: evidence and consequences of pure-form and hybrid governance', *Journal of Personal Selling and Sales Management*, 15 (4): 1–15.

O'Neal, C.R. (1989a) 'JIT procurement and relationship marketing', *Industrial Marketing Management*, 1 (1): 55–64.

O'Neal, C.R. (1989b) 'The buyer–seller linkage in a just-in-time environment', *Journal of Purchasing & Materials Management*, 25 (1): 34–41.

Osmonbekov, T., Bello, D.C. and Gilliland, D.I. (2009) 'The impact of e-business infusion on channel coordination, conflict and reseller performance', *Industrial Marketing Management*, 38: 778–84.

Palmer, R.A. and Millier, P. (2004) 'Segmentation: identification, intuition, and implementation', *Industrial Marketing Management*, 33: 779–85.

Papacharissi, Z. (2009) 'The virtual geographies of social networks: a comparative analysis of Facebook, LinkedIn and ASmallWorld', *New Media & Society*, 11 (1/2): 199–220.

Pardo, C. (1999) 'Key account management in the business-to-business field: a French overview', *Journal of Business and Industrial Marketing*, 14 (4): 276–90.

Peattie, K. (1995) *Environmental Marketing Management: Meeting the Green Challenge*. London: Pitman Publishing.

Peppers, D. and Rogers, M. (2004) *Managing Customer Relationships: A Strategic Framework*. Hoboken, NJ: John Wiley & Sons, Inc.

Peterson, R.A. and Kerin, R.A. (1980) 'The effective use of marketing research consultants', *Industrial Marketing Management*, 9: 69–73.

Petrick, J.A. and Quinn, J.F. (1997) *Management Ethics: Integrity at Work*. Thousand Oaks, CA: Sage.

Pfeffer, J. and Salancik, G. (1978) *The External Control of Organizations: A Resource Dependence Perspective*. New York: Harper & Row.

Piercy, N. and Lane, N. (2006) 'The hidden risks in strategic account management strategy', *Journal of Business Strategy*, 27 (1): 18–26.

Porter, M.E. (1980) *Competitive Strategy: Techniques for Analyzing Industries and Competitors*. New York: Free Press.

Porter, M.E. (1985) *Competitive Advantage: Creating and Sustaining Superior Performance*. New York: Free Press.

Porter, M.E. and Heppelmann, J.E. (2014) 'How smart connected products are transforming competition', *Harvard Business Review*, November: 64–85.

Porter, M.E. and Heppelmann, J.E. (2015) 'How smart connected products are transforming companies', *Harvard Business Review*, October: 96–115.

Poulter, S. (2009) 'Lord Sugar among victims of builders' price-fixing that brings £130m in fines for the swindlers', *Daily Mail*, 22 September. Available at: www.dailymail.co.uk/news/article-1215207/More-100-building-firms-fined-130million-construction-bid-rigging-scandal.html (accessed 23 September 2009).

Power, J., Whelan, S. and Davies, G. (2008) 'The attractiveness and connectedness of ruthless brands: the role of trust', *European Journal of Marketing*, 42: 586–602.

Power, R. and Chaffey, D. (2012) *Brilliant B2B Digital Marketing*, Smart Insights ebook. Available at: www.smartinsights.com (accessed 5 November 2013).

Powers, T.L. and Sterling, J.U. (2008) 'Segmenting business-to-business markets: a micro-macro linking methodology', *Journal of Business & Industrial Marketing*, 23 (3): 170–7.

Raman, A.P. (2009) 'The new frontiers: how the global slowdown is reshaping competition from emerging markets', *Harvard Business Review*, July–August: 130–7.

Ravald, A. and Grönroos, C. (1996) 'The value concept and relationship marketing', *European Journal of Marketing*, 30 (2): 19–30.

Rawnsley, A. (ed.) (1978) *Manual of Industrial Marketing Research*. Chichester: Wiley.

Reichheld, F.F. (1996) *The Loyalty Effect: The Hidden Force Behind Growth, Profits, and Lasting Value*. Boston, MA: Harvard Business School Press.

Rhodes, C. (2015) 'Manufacturing: statistics and policy'. House of Commons Library. Available at: www.parliament.uk/briefing-papers/sn01942.pdf (accessed 22 July 2016).

Ries, A. and Trout, J. (2001) *Positioning: The Battle for Your Mind*. New York: McGraw-Hill.

Rinallo, D., Borghini, S. and Golfetto, F. (2010) 'Exploring visitor experiences at trade shows', *Journal of Business and Industrial Marketing*, 25 (4): 249–58.

Ritter, T. and Walter, A. (2012) 'More is not always better: the impact of relationship functions on customer-perceived relationship value', *Industrial Marketing Management*, 41 (1): 136–44.

Ritter, T. and Geersbro, J. (2015) *Challenging Customers*. Copenhagen: Copenhagen Business School (The CBS Competitiveness Platform). Available as an e-book under a Creative Commons License at: http://openarchive.cbs.dk/handle/10398/9253 (accessed 16 January 2016).

Robinson, P.J., Faris, C.W. and Wind, Y. (1967) *Industrial Buying and Creative Marketing*. Boston, MA: Allyn & Bacon.

Rolls-Royce (2009) 'Rolls-Royce Group plc: Annual Report 2008'. Available at: www.rolls-royce.com/reports/2008/ (accessed 5 November 2013).

Rolls-Royce (2012) 'Rolls-Royce Holdings plc: Annual Report 2011'. Available at: www.rolls-royce.com/reports/2011/ (accessed 5 November 2013).

Rolls-Royce (2015a) M250 Rolls-Royce FIRST Network. 2015 Customer support directory. 22 February. Available at: www.rolls-royce.com/products-and-services/civil-aerospace/products/helicopter-engines/helicopter-services.aspx#first-network (accessed 7 August 2016).

Rolls Royce (2015b) 'Rolls Royce Holdings plc: Annual Report'. Available at: http://ar.rolls-royce.com/2015/ (accessed 1 August 2016).

Ruekert, R.W. and Walker, O.C. (1987) 'Marketing's interaction with other functional units: a conceptual framework and empirical evidence', *Journal of Marketing*, 51 (January): 1–19.

Rust, R.T., Zeithaml, V.A. and Lemon, K.N. (2000) *Driving Customer Equity: How Customer Lifetime Value is Reshaping Corporate Strategy*. New York: Free Press.

Sako, M. (1992) *Prices, Quality and Trust – Inter-Firm Relations in Britain and Japan*. Cambridge: Cambridge University Press.

Salacuse, J. (1991) *Making Global Deals*. Boston, MA: Houghton Mifflin.

Salacuse, J. (2005) 'Negotiating: the top ten ways that culture can affect your negotiation', *Ivey Business Journal*, 69 (4): 1–6

Sandel, M. (2010) *Justice: What's the Right Thing to Do?* Harlow: Penguin.

Sashi, C.M. and O'Leary, B. (2002) 'The role of internet auctions in the expansion of B2B markets', *Industrial Marketing Management*, 31: 103–10.

Schilling, M. and Hill, C. (1998) 'Managing the new product development process: strategic imperatives', *Academy of Management Executive*, 12 (3): 67–81.

Schlegelmilch, B. (1998) *Marketing Ethics: An International Perspective.* London: International Thompson Business Press.

Schmidt, K., Adamson, B. and Bird, A. (2015) 'Making the consensus sale', *Harvard Business Review*, March: 106–13.

Schroeder, H. (2013) 'The art of social relationships through social media', *Ivey Business Journal*, March/April. Available at: http://iveybusinessjournal.com (accessed 27 July 2016).

Schultz, B. (2013) 'Shell cautions patience on analytics adoption', *All Analytics*, 10 March. Available at: www.allanalytics.com (accessed 4 August 2016).

Schultz, D.E. (1996) 'The inevitability of integrated communications', *Journal of Business Research*, 37: 139–46.

Schultz, D.E. (2006) 'Media synergy: the next frontier in a multimedia marketplace', *Journal of Direct, Data and Digital Marketing Practice*, 8 (1): 13–29.

Sebenius, J.K. (2002) 'The hidden challenge of cross-border negotiations', *Harvard Business Review*, 80 (3): 76–85.

Seringhaus, F.H.R. and Rosson, P.J. (1998) 'Management and performance of international trade fair exhibitors: government stands vs. independent stands', *International Marketing Review*, 15 (5): 398–412.

Seyed-Mohamed, N. and Wilson, D.T. (1989) 'Exploring the adaptation process', *Research in Marketing: An Interactive Perspective, Proceedings of the 5th IMP Conference*, Pennsylvania State University.

Shapiro, B. and Bonoma, T. (1984) 'How to segment industrial markets', *Harvard Business Review*, 62 (3): 104–10.

Shapiro, B., Rangan, V., Moriarty, R. and Ross, E. (1987) 'Manage customers for profits (not just sales)', *Harvard Business Review*, 65 (5): 101–8.

Shapiro, B.P., Rangan, V.K. and Sviokla, J.J. (2004) 'Staple yourself to an order', *Harvard Business Review*, 7 (8): 162–71.

Sharma, A. and Evanschitzky, H. (2016) 'Returns on key accounts: do the results justify the expenditures?', *Journal of Business & Industrial Marketing*, 31 (2): 174–82.

Sharma, S. and Henriques, I. (2005) 'Stakeholder influences on sustainability practices in the Canadian forest products industry', *Strategic Management Journal*, 26 (2): 159–80.

Sheehan, K.B. (2001) 'Email survey response rates: A review', *Journal of Computer-Mediated Communication*, 6(2). Available at: http://onlinelibrary.wiley.com/doi/10.1111/j.1083-6101.2001.tb00117.x/full (accessed 16 January 2017).

Sheth, J.N., Sharma, A. and Iyer, G.R. (2009) 'Why integrating marketing with purchasing is both inevitable and beneficial', *Industrial Marketing Management*, 38 (8): 865–71.

Shipley, D. and Jobber, D. (2001) 'Integrative pricing via the pricing wheel', *Industrial Marketing Management*, 30: 301–14.

Shipley, D. and Prinja, S. (1988) 'The services and supplier choice influences of industrial distributors', *Service Industries Journal*, 8 (2): 176–87.

Shipley, D. and Wong, K.S. (1993) 'Exhibiting strategy and implementation', *International Journal of Advertising*, 12: 117–30.

Shipley, D., Cook, D. and Barnett, E. (1989) 'Recruitment, motivation and evaluation of overseas distributors', *European Journal of Marketing*, 23 (2): 79–93.

Simba-Dickie Group (2010) 'Lord of the racks', News, 31 May. Available at: www.simba-dickie-group.de/en/news/2010/logistics_centre_sonneberg.2.shtml (accessed 16 August 2013).

Simkin, L. (2000) 'Marketing is marketing – maybe!', *Marketing Intelligence and Planning*, 18 (3): 154–8.

Simões, C. and Mason, K.J. (2012) 'Informing a new business-to-business relationship: corporate identity and the emergence of relationship identity', *European Journal of Marketing*, 46: 684–711.

Skeels, M.M. and Grudin, J. (2009) 'When social networks cross boundaries: a case study of workplace use of Facebook and LinkedIn'. *Proceedings of the ACM 2009 International Conference on Supporting Group Work, Florida, 10–13 May*.

Smeltzer, L.R. and Carr, A.S. (2003) 'Electronic reverse auctions: promises, risks and conditions for success', *Industrial Marketing Management*, 32: 481–8.

Smith, N.C. and Quelch, J.A. (1993) *Ethics in Marketing*. Homewood, IL: Irwin.

Smith, P. (2015) 'Heinz means unhappy agencies – suppliers rebel over procurement process, Spend Matters', 25 June. Available at: www.spendmatters.com (accessed 26 March 2016).

Smith, W.R. (1956) 'Product differentiation and market segmentation as alternative marketing strategies', *Journal of Marketing*, 21 (1): 3–8.

Spekman, R. (1988) 'Strategic supplier selection: understanding long-term buyer relationships', *Business Horizons*, 31 (4): 75–81.

Spencer, R. (1999) 'Key accounts: effectively managing strategic complexity', *Journal of Business & Industrial Marketing*, 14 (4): 291–309.

Spielwarenmesse (2015) 'Toy manufacturer Simba-Dickie Group publishes annual results for 2014', 27 January. Available at: www.spielwarenmesse.de (accessed 5 July 2016).

Stacey, N.A.H. and Wilson, A. (1969) *Industrial Marketing Research: Management and Technique* (2nd edn). London: Hutchinson.

Steiner, M., Eggert, A., Ulaga, W. and Backhaus, K. (2016) 'Do customised service packages impede value capture in industrial markets?', *Journal of the Academy of Marketing Science*, 44: 151–65.

Stephenson, R.P., Cron, W.L. and Frazier, G.L. (1979) 'Delegating pricing authority to the salesforce: the effects on sales and profit performance', *Journal of Marketing*, 43 (Spring): 21–8.

Stern, L. and Reve, T. (1980) 'Distribution channels as political economies: a framework for comparative analysis', *Journal of Marketing*, 44 (3): 52–64.

Stohs, J.H. and Brannick, T. (1999) 'Codes and conduct: predictors of Irish managers' ethical reasoning', *Journal of Business Ethics*, 22: 311–26.

Tamer-Cavusgil, S., Yeoh, P.L. and Mitri, M. (1995) 'Selecting foreign distributors', *Industrial Marketing Management*, 24: 297–304.

Tapp, A., Whitten, I. and Housden, M. (2014) *Principles of Direct, Database and Digital Marketing* (5th edn). Harlow: Pearson Education.

Terho, H., Haas, A., Eggert, A. and Ulaga, W. (2012) '"It's almost like taking the sales out of selling" – towards a conceptualisation of value-based selling in business markets', *Industrial Marketing Management*, 41: 174–85.

Timmers, P. (1999) *Electronic Commerce*. Chichester: Wiley.

Töytäri, P., Rajala, R. and Alejandro, T.B. (2015) 'Organizational and institutional barriers to value-based pricing in industrial relationships', *Industrial Marketing Management*, 47: 53–64.

Trailer, B. and Dickie, J. (2006) 'Understanding what your sales manager is up against', *Harvard Business Review*, 84 (7): 48–56.

Trappey, C.V., Trappey, A.J.C., Lin, G.Y.P., Liu, C.S. and Lee, W.T. (2007) 'Business and logistics hub integration to facilitate global supply chain linkage', *Proceedings of the Institute of Mechanical Engineers, Part B: Engineering Manufacture, Journal of Engineering Manufacture*, 221 (7): 1221–33.

Treacy, M. and Wiersema, F. (1993) 'Customer intimacy and other value disciplines', *Harvard Business Review*, January–February: 84–93.

Trebilcock, B. (2015) 'What does it take to remain a supply chain leader?', 2 January. Available at: www.Supplychain247.com (accessed 25 June 2016).

Treleven, M. (1987) 'Single sourcing: a management tool for the quality supplier', *Journal of Purchasing and Materials Management*, 23 (Spring): 19–24.

Trott, P. (2012) *Innovation Management and New Product Development* (5th edn). Harlow: Pearson Education.

Tuli, K.R., Kohli, A.K. and Bharadwaj, S.G. (2007) 'Rethinking customer solutions: from product bundles to relational processes', *Journal of Marketing*, 71 (July): 1–17.

Turnbull, P.W. (1990) 'Roles of personal contacts in industrial export marketing', in D. Ford (ed.), *Understanding Business Markets: Interactions, Relationships, Networks*. London: Academic Press, pp. 78–86.

Turnbull, P. and Valla, J.P. (eds) (1986) *Strategies for International Industrial Marketing*. London: Croom Helm.

Turnbull, P. and Zolkiewski, J. (1995) 'Profitability in customer portfolio planning'. *Proceedings of the 11th Annual IMP International Conference, Manchester, 7–9 September.*

Turner, A. (2003) *The Inaugural Carbon Trust Lecture* (public lecture). London: Carbon Trust.

Ueda, K. (1974) 'Sixteen ways to avoid saying "no" in Japan', in J.C. Condon and M. Saito (eds), *Intercultural Encounters in Japan*. Tokyo: Simul Press, pp. 185–92.

Ulaga, W. (2001) 'Customer value in business markets', *Industrial Marketing Management*, 30: 315–19.

Ulaga, W. and Reinartz, W.J. (2011) 'Hybrid offerings: how manufacturing firms combine goods and services successfully', *Journal of Marketing*, 75 (November): 5–23.

US Department of Justice (1996) 'Delaware explosives company agrees to plead guilty and pay $950,000 for rigging bids on commercial explosives contracts to Alaska customers', 6 March. Available at: www.usdoj.gov/atr/public/press_releases/1996/0559. htm (accessed 5 November 2013).

Usunier, J.C. and Lee, J.A. (2005) *Marketing Across Cultures* (4th edn). Harlow: Prentice Hall.

Van Raaij, E.M., Vernooij, M.J. and van Triest, S. (2003) 'The implementation of customer profitability analysis: a case study', *Industrial Marketing Management*, 32 (7): 573–83.

Vargo, S.L. and Lusch, R.F. (2004) 'Evolving to a new dominant logic for marketing', *Journal of Marketing*, 68 (1): 1–17.

Vargo, S.L. and Lusch, R.F. (2008) 'Service-dominant logic: continuing the evolution', *Journal of the Academy of Marketing Science*, 36 (1): 1–10.

Vargo, S.L. and Lusch, R.F. (2011) 'It's all B2B… and beyond: toward a systems perspective of the market', *Industrial Marketing Management*, 40 (2): 181–7.

Verhallen, T., Frambach, R. and Prabhu, J. (1998) 'Strategy-segmentation of industrial markets', *Industrial Marketing Management*, 27 (4): 305–13.

Voeth, M. and Herbst, U. (2005) 'Supply-chain pricing – a new perspective on pricing in industrial markets', *Industrial Marketing Management*, 35 (1): 83–90.

Walker, D. (2015) 'Does telemarketing have a home in the digital revolution?', *Digital Marketing Magazine*, 11 August. Available at: www.digitalmarketingmagazine.co.uk (accessed 26 July 2016).

Walter, A. and Gemünden, H.G. (2000) 'Bridging the gap between suppliers and customers through relationship promoters: theoretical considerations and empirical results', *Journal of Business and Industrial Marketing*, 15 (2/4): 86–105.

Walter, A., Ritter, T. and Gemunden, H.G. (2001) 'Value creation in buyer–seller relationships', *Industrial Marketing Management*, 30: 365–77.

WARC (2006) 'Intel launches new business brand', 26 April. Available at: www.warc.com (accessed 5 November 2013).

WCED (1987) *Report of the World Commission on Environment and Development: Our Common Future*, UN World Commission on Environment and Development. Available at: www.un-documents.net/wced-ocf.htm (accessed 1 June 2013).

Webster, F.E. (1991) *Industrial Marketing Strategy* (3rd edn). New York: Wiley.

Webster, F.E. and Wind, Y. (1972) 'A general model for understanding organizational buying behaviour', *Journal of Marketing*, 36 (2): 12–19.

Weilbaker, D.C. and Weeks, W.A. (1997) 'The evolution of national account management: a literature perspective', *Journal of Personal Selling and Sales Management*, 17 (4): 49–59.

Weinstein, A. (2006) 'A strategic framework for defining and segmenting markets', *Journal of Strategic Marketing*, 14 (2): 115–27.

Weitz, B.A. and Jap, S.D. (1995) 'Relationship marketing and distribution channels', *Journal of the Academy of Marketing Science*, Fall: 305–20.

West, D. and Ford, J. (2001) 'Advertising agency philosophies and employee risk taking', *Journal of Advertising*, 30 (1): 78–91.

Wiersema, F. (2013) 'The B2B agenda: the current state of B2B marketing and a look ahead', *Industrial Marketing Management*, 42 (4): 470–88.

Wighton, D. (2009) 'Cover price fines are a bargain for builders', *The Times*, 23 September. Available at: www.thetimes.co.uk/tto/business/columnists/article2621793.ece (accessed 5 November 2013).

Williamson, O.E. (1975) *Markets and Hierarchies: Analysis and Antitrust Implications*. New York: Free Press.

Williamson, O.E. (1979) 'Transaction-cost economics: the governance of contractual relations', *Journal of Law and Economics*, 22 (October): 233–61.

Wilson, A., Zeithaml, V.A., Bitner, M.J. and Gremler, D.D. (2012) *Services Marketing: Integrating Customer Focus Across the Firm* (2nd European edn). Maidenhead: McGraw-Hill.

Wilson, D. (1999) *Organizational Marketing*. London: International Thompson.

Wilson, D. (2000) 'Why divide consumer and organizational buyer behaviour?', *European Journal of Marketing*, 34 (7): 780–96.

Wilson, E. (1996) 'Theory transitions in organizational buying behaviour research', *Journal of Business & Industrial Marketing*, 11 (6): 7–19.

Wilson, E. and Woodside, A. (2001) 'Executive and consumer decision processes: increasing useful sensemaking by identifying similarities and departures', *Journal of Business & Industrial Marketing*, 16 (5): 401–14.

Wilson, S.G. and Abel, I. (2002) 'So you want to get involved in e-commerce', *Industrial Marketing Management*, 31: 85–94.

Winig, L. (2016) 'GE's bet on big data and analytics. Case study', *MIT Sloan Management Review*, 57 (3): 1–16.

Wise, R. and Baumgartner, P. (1999) 'Go downstream: the new profit imperative in manufacturing', *Harvard Business Review*, 77 (5): 133–41.

Woodward, J. (1965) *Industrial Organization: Theory and Practice*. Oxford: Oxford University Press.

Workman, J.P. Jr., Homburg, C. and Jensen, O. (2003) 'Intraorganizational determinants of key account management effectiveness', *Journal of the Academy of Marketing Science*, 31 (1): 3–21.

World Trade Organization (WTO) (1994) *Multilateral Agreements on Trade in Goods: Anti-dumping (Article VI of GATT 1994)*. Available at: www.wto.org/english/docs_e/legal_e/19-adp_01_e.htm (accessed 28 December 2005).

Yankelovich, D. (1964) 'New criteria for market segmentation', *Harvard Business Review*, 42 (2): 83–90.

Young, L. and Wilkinson, I. (1989) 'The role of trust and co-operation in marketing channels: a preliminary study', *European Journal of Marketing*, 23 (2): 109–22.

Zarkada-Fraser, A. (2000) 'A classification of factors influencing participating in collusive tendering arrangements', *Journal of Business Ethics*, 23: 269–82.

Zeithaml, V.A. (1988) 'Consumer perceptions of price, quality, and value: a means–end model and synthesis of evidence', *Journal of Marketing*, 52: 2–22.

Zelbst, P.J., Green, K.W., Sower, V.E. and Baker, G. (2010) 'RFID utilization and information sharing: the impact on supply chain performance', *Journal of Business and Industrial Marketing*, 25 (8): 582–9.

Zeng, F., Yang, Z., Li, Y. and Fam, K.-S. (2011) 'Small business industrial buyers' price sensitivity: do service quality dimensions matter in business markets?', *Industrial Marketing Management*, 40 (3): 395–404.

INDEX

NOTE: page numbers in *italic type* refer to figures and tables, page numbers in **bold type** refer to glossary entries.